Past and Present Publications

Lords and Peasants in a Changing Society

Past and Present Publications

General Editor: T. H. ASTON, *Corpus Christi College, Oxford*

Past and Present Publications will comprise books similar in character to the articles in the journal *Past and Present*. Whether the volumes in the series are collections of essays – some previously published, others new studies – or monographs, they will encompass a wide variety of scholarly and original works primarily concerned with social, economic and cultural changes, and their causes and consequences. They will appeal to both specialists and non-specialists and will endeavour to communicate the results of historical and allied research in readable and lively form. This new series continues and expands in its aims the volumes previously published elsewhere.

Volumes published by the Cambridge University Press are:
Family and Inheritance: Rural Society in Western Europe 1200–1800, edited by Jack Goody, Joan Thirsk and E. P. Thompson*
French Society and the Revolution, edited by Douglas Johnson
Peasants, Knights and Heretics: Studies in Medieval English Social History, edited by R. H. Hilton
Towns in Societies: Essays in Economic History and Historical Sociology, edited by Philip Abrams and E. A. Wrigley*
Desolation of a City: Coventry and the Urban Crisis of the Late Middle Ages, Charles Phythian-Adams
Puritanism and Theatre: Thomas Middleton and Opposition Drama under the Early Stuarts, Margot Heinemann
Lords and Peasants in a Changing Society: The Estates of the Bishopric of Worcester, 680–1540, Christopher Dyer
Life, Marriage and Death in a Medieval Parish: A Social, Economic and Demographic Study of Halesowen, 1270–1400, Zvi Razi

*Also issued as a paperback

Volumes previously published with Routledge and Kegan Paul are:
Crisis in Europe 1560–1660, edited by Trevor Aston
Studies in Ancient Society, edited by M. I. Finley
The Intellectual Revolution of the Seventeenth Century, edited by Charles Webster

Lords and Peasants in a Changing Society

The Estates of the Bishopric of Worcester, 680–1540

CHRISTOPHER DYER

Lecturer in Medieval History
University of Birmingham

CAMBRIDGE UNIVERSITY PRESS

Cambridge

London   New York   New Rochelle
Melbourne   Sydney

Published by the Press Syndicate of the University of Cambridge
The Pitt Building, Trumpington Street, Cambridge CB2 1RP
32 East 57th Street, New York, NY 10022, USA
296 Beaconsfield Parade, Middle Park, Melbourne 3206, Australia

First published 1980

Photoset and printed in Malta by Interprint Limited

Library of Congress Cataloguing in Publication Data
Dyer, Christopher, 1944–
Lords and peasants in a changing society.
(Past and present publications)
Bibliography: p.
Includes index.
1. Church lands – England – Worcester – History.
2. Landlord and peasant – England – Worcester – History.
3. Manors – England – Worcester – History.
4. Worcester, Eng. (Diocese) – History. I. Title.
HD610.W66D93   942.4'48   79-19090
ISBN 0 521 22618 X

Contents

Maps

Illustrations

Figures

Tables

Preface

My chief debt is to Professor R. H. Hilton, who first suggested the subject to me, has been a source of constant stimulus and encouragement, and has patiently read and criticized early drafts. I have gained a great deal from discussion with fellow students, colleagues, and my own students. Dr H. B. Clarke, Professor H. A. Cronne, Professor P. A. Rahtz, Dr W. E. Davies, and Mr P. Sims-Williams helped my understanding of the early medieval material, and Dr I. S. W. Blanchard gave me many insights into the later middle ages. Dr E. W. Ives helped me with legal and palaeographical problems. Dr Z. Razi helpfully criticized my work on demography, and Dr M. Walsh saved me from statistical blunders. Versions of some chapters have been read to seminars at the Universities of Birmingham, Cambridge, Edinburgh, Glasgow, and Sheffield, and to the Annual Conference of the British Agricultural History Society, and I have benefited from the ensuing comments. Mr K. Down, Mr M. J. Morgan, and Miss M. Jackson-Roberts put their knowledge of the episcopal and priory registers at my disposal. The staff of various libraries and record repositories have given me every assistance, particularly Miss M. Henderson and her colleagues at the Worcestershire County Record Office. The Trustees. of the Earl of Berkeley Will Trust allowed me to make use of the Berkeley Castle Muniment Room. I am grateful to Professor S. T. Bindoff for allowing me to see unpublished drafts of biographies written under his direction for the projected Early Tudor volumes of the *History of Parliament*. I received ready co-operation from the staff of the National Register of Archives, the Ordnance Survey, and Worcestershire County Museum. The authors of various unpublished theses listed in the bibliography allowed me to quote from their works. Illustrations have been made available by the courtesy of Mr C. J. Bond, University of Cambridge Committee for Aerial Photography, Mr E. G. Tasker, and Worcestershire County Record Office; Mr R. Swift helped with their preparation. I am indebted to Mr T. H. Aston for expediting the publication of this book. I am grateful for the assistance of William Davies, Nalini Chapman and the staff of Cambridge University Press. Mrs K. Coe coped gallantly with typing from my appalling handwriting, and tactfully saved me from spelling errors. My wife has supported my work in many ways. None of the people named here shares any responsibility for my errors.

CHRISTOPHER DYER

Birmingham, January 1979

Abbreviations

The titles of most periodicals and publishing societies have been abbreviated so that they should be readily intelligible, e.g. *Journ.* for *Journal, Rev.* for *Review, Trans.* for *Transactions.*

Annales ESC	*Annales, Économies, Sociétés, Civilisations*
AR	Account Roll(s)
CR	Court Roll(s)
CS	*Cartularium Saxonicum*, ed. W. de Gray Birch, 3 vols. (London, 1885–93)
DB	*Domesday Book* (Record Commission, 1783)
DNB	*Dictionary of National Biography*
GRO	Gloucestershire County Records Office
HC	*Hemingi Chartularium Ecclesiae Wigorniensis*, ed. T. Hearne, 2 vols. (Oxford, 1723)
Lib. Alb. Pri.	*Liber Albus of Worcester Priory*, ed. J.M. Wilson (Worcs. Hist. Soc., 1919)
Lib. Alb. Pri.	WCL, Dean and Chapter Register AIV
P and P	*Past and Present*
PRO	Public Record Office
RBW	*Red Book of Worcester*, ed. M. Hollings (Worcs. Hist. Soc., 1934–50)
Rec. AR	Receivers' Account Roll(s)
Reg. Giffard etc.	Printed episcopal registers of Worcester diocese. See Bibliography for full references
Reg. Maidstone etc.	Manuscript episcopal registers of Worcester diocese, now in Worcestershire County Record Office. See Bibliography for full references
SBT	Shakespeare Birthplace Trust Records Office, Stratford-upon-Avon
VCH Glos., Warks., Worcs.	*Victoria County Histories of Gloucestershire, Warwickshire, Worcestershire*
WCL	Worcester Cathedral Library
WCRO	Worcestershire County Record Office
White Book	*Liber Albus* of the bishopric, WCRO ref. 821 BA 3814

To avoid unnecessarily lengthy and numerous footnote references to the series of manorial documents, no reference is given if the source of the information is clear from the text. If the source is not readily apparent, the footnote will state the place, type of record and date, e.g. Hanbury AR, 1486–7. The archival reference can be found from the list of manuscript sources in the bibliography.

WEIGHTS AND MEASURES

qr =quarter
b =bushel
p =peck

NOTE ON LOCAL GOVERNMENT BOUNDARIES

In both text and maps the counties mentioned are those that existed between 1935 and 1974, the boundaries of which are substantially similar to those created in the late Anglo-Saxon period. However, it should be noted that the bishopric properties in the extreme north of Gloucestershire and the southern tip of Warwickshire, notably the demesne manors of Blockley and Tredington, lay in Worcestershire for the whole of the middle ages and until the boundary adjustments of 1931–5.

Since 1974 the bulk of the historic county of Worcestershire has been incorporated into the new county of Hereford and Worcester, and the south-west of Gloucestershire, including the bishopric property of Westbury, later known as Henbury and Stoke, has been transferred to the new county of Avon.

Introduction

This study of a large medieval ecclesiastical estate is written in the tradition of a series of English estate histories of the last fifty years. An estate is a useful unit for investigating medieval social and economic development because it encompassed a wide section of society, from its magnate owners, through the knights and gentry who held lands from it or acted as administrators, to the large numbers of peasants and townsmen who were its tenants. The documents are mainly gathered together conveniently in one archive and they are sufficiently limited in quantity to enable a long time-span to be covered. The manors of the bishops of Worcester lay in the west midlands, and the estates of this region have not been the subject of as many full studies as those in some other parts of England.[1] The bishopric estate was one of the largest in the region with lands scattered over three counties and can be regarded in some sense as representative, as the area was dominated by great ecclesiastics.

The estates of the bishops of Worcester have long been familiar to historians of the early middle ages as exemplifying elements of continuity in English society.[2] This study concentrates on change. Although the west midland region was in many ways a conservative one, it experienced much the same social and economic developments as the rest of England, indeed, of western Europe as a whole. In the early middle ages a feudal and seignorial régime was established; a period of expansion up to the early fourteenth century was succeeded by two centuries of contrary tendencies, combining decay and new growth. How do we explain these changes? Historians differ in stressing a variety of factors that determined the long-term trends in the economy – demography, developments in the market, social relationships and political and ideological

---

[1] The most notable recent estate study with a full account of west-midland manors is B. Harvey, *Westminster Abbey and its Estates in the Middle Ages* (Oxford, 1977), which appeared too late for its findings to influence this book. There are many parallels between developments on the Westminster Abbey and Worcester bishopric manors, for example in forms of tenure after 1350.

[2] See F. W. Maitland, *Domesday Book and Beyond* (Cambridge, 1897), where much of the second essay is based on Worcester material; H. P. R. Finberg, 'Roman and Saxon Withington', in *Lucerna* (London, 1964), pp. 21–65.

movements. This study is concerned with a long span of time, from the foundation of the see of Worcester in 680 to the Reformation, because its aim is to define the long-term changes and, if possible, to offer explanations. The survival of documents had led to some concentration on the later middle ages, when the principal problem is seen as one of the causes of the evolution of a traditional and restricted rural society towards the emergence of agrarian capitalism.

The focus on the problem of economic change means that this study will be different from other estate histories. The peasantry receive a good deal of attention, and the manorial documents are used to reveal as much as possible about their own lives, not just as dependents and rent-payers of the estate. This choice is determined by the belief that the peasantry, as the productive base of medieval society, must have made a major contribution to its development. The bishops appear in their social rôle, as nobles and landlords. This omits other, very important, aspects of their lives; the medieval bishops included among their number a few saints, many active ecclesiastics and numerous politicians and administrators. These activities are often irrelevant to our immediate theme so they will only be mentioned when they seem to have affected the running of the estate. The bishops' lordship extended over many feudal tenants, magnates, knights and gentry. Ideally, a complete estate history should consider their economic activities and social functions in detail but the need to limit the size of this study means that they have, regretfully, been treated in a cursory fashion. Nor has it been feasible to give the urban element of the estate the attention that it deserves.

The archives of the bishops have survived in considerable quantity, but their distribution over time is very uneven. The estate is one of the best documented in England for the Anglo-Saxon period. This is because of the survival of one volume, British Library, Cotton MS. Tiberius A xiii, commonly known as Hemming's Cartulary. This consists of two cartularies, one of the early eleventh century, the other compiled by the monk Hemming in c.1100.[3] Fragments of another, earlier, cartulary are known, and some individual charters.

---

[3] N. R. Ker, 'Hemming's Cartulary', in *Studies in Medieval History presented to F. M. Powicke* (Oxford, 1948), pp. 49–75.

Originally many more were kept at Worcester, but all that remains in some cases are the notes made by antiquarians in the seventeenth century. Many of the charters were of course altered or even fabricated in the eleventh and twelfth centuries, but the charters of the early eleventh-century cartulary are remarkably free from tampering. Invaluable help in assessing the authenticity of the texts is provided by the calendars of Finberg and Hart and in the handlist compiled by P. H. Sawyer.[4] Unfortunately Tiberius A xiii has lacked an editor since Hearne in the early eighteenth century and use has been made of the more reliable editions of Birch and Robertson. The charter evidence has been supplemented both by archaeological evidence and by reference to Domesday, whose survey of the Worcester estate is particularly informative. In spite of the relative abundance of materials, the results will be inevitably skeletal. We can only cast our eyes enviously across the Channel and regret that no ninth-century bishop compiled a *polyptique* which would reveal the social structure of the estate.

In comparison with other estates, the documents of the period from 1086 to the fourteenth century are patchily preserved. The main source must be the surveys of the twelfth and thirteenth centuries included in the *Red Book of Worcester*. The *Red Book* itself is lost, but an eighteenth-century transcription has been edited by Miss M. Hollings. A near-contemporary manuscript copy of a late thirteenth-century survey of the manor of Bredon suggests that not too much has been distorted by the three transcriptions to which the documents have been subjected.[5] It would be churlish to criticize the service that Miss Hollings performed for medieval history, but it must be pointed out that the edition has some imperfections. To take an important example, the printed texts carry the dates assigned to them by Dr Thomas, the eighteenth-century copyist, with some revision by Miss Hollings, but internal evidence shows that the twelfth-century surveys cannot be as late as 1182 but must have been compiled at least a decade earlier. They have been dated in this study to *c*.1170. Similarly there seems to be no sound basis for regarding the *Alia Extenta* as belonging to 1282 and *c*.1290 has

---

[4] H. P. R. Finberg, *The Early Charters of the West Midlands* (Leicester, 1961); C. R. Hart, *The Early Charters of Northern England and the North Midlands* (Leicester, 1975); P. H. Sawyer, *Anglo-Saxon Charters* (London, 1968).
[5] WCRO ref. 009:1 BA 2636/191 92625 1/12.

been preferred as a date.[6] The surveys contain a mass of information about demesnes, tenants, holdings, rents and services. Their chief drawback is that they provide a static picture and present a series of ideal types, somewhat removed from social reality. Their value would be greatly enhanced by a series of accounts and court rolls. All that survives is a stray membrane, containing two manorial accounts for 1246–7, revealing tantalizingly that the estates had an elaborate system of enrolled accounts, comparable with those of the bishopric of Winchester.

Changes in the twelfth and thirteenth centuries are indicated to some extent by the bishopric cartulary, the White Book. Like its predecessor, it contains two compilations, one of *c*.1300 and the other of the fifteenth century. The second book includes mostly charters granted before 1350. The cartularies consist mainly of grants made in favour of the bishops, but grants made by the bishops can be found in a variety of sources, such as marginal notes in the *Red Book*, the *Liber Albus* of the Cathedral Priory (because the prior and convent sometimes confirmed episcopal grants), and the chancery enrolments of the central government, after the land legislation of the late thirteenth century. Government documents are particularly useful also as they include accounts, in the pipe rolls and elsewhere, of the revenues collected from the bishopric during vacancies, as well as information of all kinds concerning the relationship between the bishopric and the crown, for example when enquiries were made into the judicial franchises. The series of bishops' registers, which begins with that of Godfrey Giffard (1268–1302), preserves the records of ecclesiastical administration, but a surprisingly large amount of material connected with the estates was also included.

---

[6] Dr Thomas thought that, as the twelfth-century surveys referred to Bishop Roger (1164–79), but not to Bishop Baldwin, they must belong to the time of Baldwin. However, there are relatively few references to Roger, and many to his predecessors, suggesting that the surveys were made in the early years of his episcopate. In the survey of Henbury there is a reference to Robert fitz Harding (*RBW*, iv, p. 406), who died in 1171 (see I. J. Sanders, *English Baronies* (Oxford, 1960), p. 13). It is possible that the surveys resulted from the enquiries into fees of 1166. They differ in character: notably the Blockley and Withington surveys depart from the format of those of the other manors, so that the twelfth-century surveys may not all have been made at the same time. The *Alia Extenta* must have been compiled after 1283, when Wast Hills was acquired. There are references in the *Alia Extenta* to Hugh de Poher and John in the Hale, who are mentioned as recently dead in the 1299 surveys (*RBW*, iii, pp. 244, 258; iv, pp. 348, 349).

A more human interest to supplement these administrative documents is provided by narrative sources, notably the 'Life of Wulfstan', a reworking by William of Malmesbury of an earlier text, and the 'Annals' of the Cathedral Priory.

From the late fourteenth century the evidence becomes abundant. For reasons which remain mysterious, the main series of estate documents begins in about 1370. Many of these were retained at Worcester until the nineteenth century, when they were taken over, with the estates themselves, by the Church Commissioners, only to be transferred to the Worcester County Records Office in 1959. Many documents were removed from the archive before the nineteenth century, sometimes because the manors themselves fell into lay hands, but often in unknown circumstances. Some of the dispersed documents are now available in record offices and muniment rooms, but others may still be in private hands. The documents consist of the usual types of manorial records, rentals, account rolls and court rolls. There are also quantities of central estate documents: receivers' accounts, valors and arrears rolls, mainly from the mid-fifteenth century. Unusual documents include the explanations offered by royal keepers for their inability to collect rents in the vacancy of 1433–5; a book of rentals, charters and estate accounts, including a complete set of accounts for 1419–20; a survey of rents, made with an eye to improvement in *c.* 1450; an early sixteenth-century lease book; 'census' material on servile families from 1476 to the 1530s; and court books containing the scrawled notes made in courts in the 1530s, including verbatim reports of suitors' comments.

These sources were designed to enable the contemporary administrators to assess developments in the lord's income, and we can use them with assurance in order to investigate the management of demesnes, leasing, developments in rent income, trends in manorial profits and the like. The main problem in their use is understanding the administrative processes that created them – otherwise they may be dismissed as mere fictions, recording out-of-date rents and optimistic valuations. They are also very incomplete, with runs of manorial accounts before 1500, for example, for only a half of the manors of the estate. The court rolls are also defective, in that they do not usually survive in unbroken series, which is necessary for the thorough investigation of the tenants.

In order to examine the peasantry, the use of manorial records, particularly court rolls, is essential but these were intended mainly to record those aspects of the peasants' activities that affected the lord or the village community. Many important aspects of peasant life, such as transfers of land or breaches of village by-laws, will appear in the court records, but others, such as the employment of servants or subletting of land, can be glimpsed only fleetingly. It is still necessary, in spite of the bulk of manorial material, to supplement it where possible with other sources. Some of these, such as the bishops' registers, vacancy documents or chancery enrolments, have already been mentioned. The main additional sources used here are the wills of tenants, taxation records, especially of the 1524 subsidy, an ecclesiastical court book relating to Hartlebury, Star Chamber documents and the archaeological evidence of deserted villages. These can often be linked with the manorial records so that a fuller picture emerges of individuals of all kinds, in particular the peasantry, who are the focus of the latter part of this study.

1. *Origins, 680—1086*

The episcopal see of Worcester was founded in 680 as part of the reorganization of the English church by Archbishop Theodore. The new bishopric was designed to serve the west-midland kingdom of the Hwicce. Who were the Hwicce? In the Tribal Hidage, a list of Anglo-Saxon peoples and kingdoms emanating from Mercia, perhaps in the late seventh century, they are assessed at 7,000 hides. This puts them in the middle rank of the groups included, comparable with the East or South Saxons, and exceeded only by such important kingdoms as Mercia, East Anglia, Kent and Wessex.[1] If the Hwicce formed a cultural or ethnic group, we might expect to see evidence for this in the grave goods from the pagan Anglo-Saxon cemeteries of the west midlands; however, they seem to be culturally diverse. Also the cemeteries are found in the east of the region, in the Avon valley and Cotswolds, so there is a lack of archaeological evidence for a Germanic population in the Severn valley and the western Cotswolds. It is possible that the Hwicce were a political entity created by the kings of Mercia, who installed a ruling dynasty over a mixed British and Anglo-Saxon population. The names of the ruling house of the Hwicce have been used to suggest that they came from a branch of a Northumbrian royal family.[2]

The bishops of the Hwicce became the bishops of Worcester, and it is assumed that the medieval boundaries of the diocese preserved those of the original Hwiccean territory. This consisted of the medieval counties of Gloucester and Worcester (omitting their western extremities) and southern and western Warwickshire (see Map 1).

The lands of the bishops mostly lay within the diocese. For much

[1] W. Davies and H. Vierck, 'The Contexts of the Tribal Hidage: Social Aggregates and Settlement Patterns', *Frühmittelalterliche Studien*, viii (1974), pp. 224–41.

[2] A. H. Smith, 'The Hwicce', in J. B. Bessinger and R. P. Creed (eds.), *Franciplegius: Medieval and Linguistic Studies in Honour of Francis Peabody Magoun Jr.* (London, 1965), pp. 56–65; M. Wilson, 'The Hwicce', *Trans. Worcs. Arch. Soc.*, 3rd ser., ii (1968–9), pp. 21–5; W. Stubbs, 'The Cathedral, Diocese, and Monasteries of Worcester in the Eighth Century', *Arch. Journ.*, xix (1862), pp. 236–41; H. P. R. Finberg, *The Early Charters of the West Midlands* (Leicester, 1961), pp. 167–80; A. Meaney, *A Gazetteer of Early Anglo-Saxon Burial Sites* (London, 1964), pp. 90–3, 257–63, 280–1.

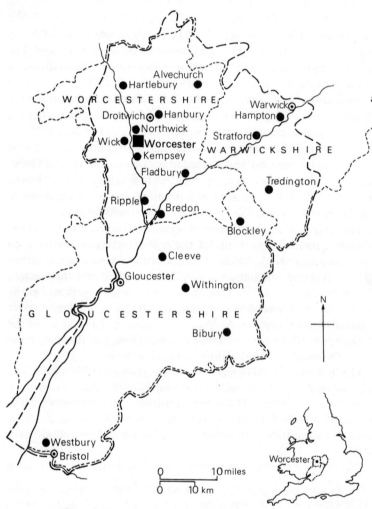

1   The diocese of Worcester, with the main bishopric manors

of the Anglo-Saxon period the estates should be regarded as belonging to the 'church of Worcester' (the cathedral monastery with its own endowment was created only at the end of the period). When the 'lands of the church of Worcester' were surveyed in Domesday Book in 1086 they were very extensive. The church was overlord of more than a quarter of the land in Worcestershire and substantial areas of Gloucestershire and Warwickshire. Corbett's calculations show that the Worcester estate was exceeded in value by only about thirty others recorded in Domesday, and it ranked sixth among the bishoprics. Because of its great wealth Worcester was held in plurality with the under-endowed archdiocese of York by a number of late Saxon bishops, notably the leading monastic reformer, Oswald, who was bishop of Worcester from 961 to 992 and held York from 972, and Wulfstan I, sermon writer and statesman, who simultaneously held York and Worcester in the years 1003–16.[3]

The estate was scattered over a variety of terrains within the diocese – the heavy soils of the north Worcestershire plateau, the limestone uplands of the Cotswolds, and the light soils of the valleys of the Severn, Avon and their tributaries. Most of the properties lay within thirty miles of Worcester; the most remote were at the confluence of the Bristol Avon and the Severn estuary, fifty miles from the cathedral city (see Map 2).

How and why were the lands of the estate acquired? How did its shape change during the four centuries after the foundation of the see? What was the nature of the estate's economy?

In attempting to answer these questions evidence from all of the lands associated with the pre-Conquest church of Worcester will be used, but attention will be concentrated on the seventeen demesne manors that formed the separate bishopric estate in the late eleventh century (see Map 1).

THE ACQUISITION OF LANDS, 680–900

It is impossible to compile a complete list of the various grants to the church in chronological order in spite of the survival of large numbers of charter texts. No records exist of the grants of some properties–

[3] *DB*, fos. 164–5, 172–4, 238; W. J. Corbett, 'England, 1087–1154', in *Cambridge Medieval History* (Cambridge, 1926), v, pp. 510–11; for Wulfstan, see D. Whitelock, 'Archbishop Wulfstan, Homilist and Statesman', in R. W. Southern (ed.), *Essays in Medieval History* (London, 1968), pp. 42–60.

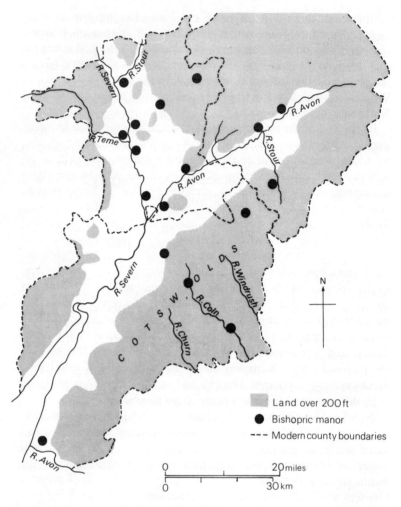

R.Stour

R.Severn

R.Avon

R.Teme

R.Stour

R.Avon

R.Severn

C O T S W O L D S

R.Windrush

R.Coln

R.Churn

N

R.Avon

Land over 200 ft
● Bishopric manor
--- Modern county boundaries

0   20 miles
0   30 km

2   Topography of the west midlands

for example, Blockley is not mentioned in a charter until 855 by
which time it was already in the hands of the church of Worcester.
Some charters are of doubtful authenticity, often reflecting the
desire of the eleventh-century monks to establish their title to
certain properties. Often charters do not record simple and
immediate grants of land; instead they promise eventual reversion to
the church which in some cases never happened or could take more
than a century to accomplish.

In spite of these difficulties we can gain an impression from the charters of the chronology of the estate's development. It seems reasonable to suppose, although documentary evidence is absent, that in the early years of its existence the church of Worcester gained lands around the cathedral, immediately to the north and east of Worcester, which were later centred on the demesne manor of Northwick or Whitstones.

By the end of the seventh century the new bishopric had probably gained rights over lands in the Avon valley at Fladbury and Stratford-on-Avon, and on the remote Severn estuary at Henbury-in-Salt-Marsh.[4] By the second quarter of the eighth century reliable documents are more numerous, and the church of Worcester can be shown to have acquired interests in Cotswold properties, at Bibury, Withington, Batsford and Woodchester, and in north Worcestershire, notably at Droitwich.[5] By the 750s the basic geographical framework of the estate had been established and the late eighth and early ninth centuries saw a considerable expansion of land-holding in the areas in which Worcester already had a foothold. Many of the properties that later became major episcopal manors are mentioned in association with the church of Worcester for the first time in the period 757–855: Bredon and Hampton in the Avon valley, and Tredington on its tributary, the Stour; Blockley on the Cotswold edge; Kempsey and Wick in the Severn valley; and Hanbury, and perhaps Alvechurch, on the northern plateau.[6]

In the course of the ninth century the number of grants made to Worcester declined. Some important new additions to the estate in the period 840–90 lay outside the diocese in Oxfordshire and London. It is possible that a major property in the Severn valley at Hartlebury was acquired in the third quarter of the ninth century but the evidence is Dugdale's list of Worcester charters which are now missing. The main developments in the mid- and late ninth century involved the consolidation of existing properties and the obtaining of privileges and immunities for them.[7]

[4] CS 76; CS 75.

[5] CS 166; CS 156; CS 163; CS 164; CS 137.

[6] CS 241; CS 239; CS 183; CS 488; Finberg, *Early Charters*, pp. 98, 102, 103; CS 219; CS 416; CS 234 does not name Alvechurch, but it concerns lands in the vicinity of the later manor of that name, and the eleventh-century cartulary has a marginal note identifying the lands as Alvechurch.

[7] Oxfordshire charters: CS 432; CS 509; CS 547. London charters: CS 492; CS 561. An example of a charter apparently consolidating an existing property by adding a small estate is that of Dunhampstead, see CS 349.

The charters of the ninth century suggest a change in relations between the church of Worcester and the laity. Disputes over land are known in the eighth century, but they became a more serious problem for the church in the ninth. An example is that involving Wulfheard who held land at Inkberrow and Bromsgrove, both properties having been bequeathed to Worcester by laymen, but Wulfheard was allowed to keep them for life. In the early 820s Ceolwulf, king of Mercia, requested that Bishop Heahberht should give him Bromsgrove. When the bishop asked Wulfheard to agree to this, Wulfheard attempted to use his influence with the king to allow him to gain possession of Inkberrow, presumably so as to prevent the church from regaining the land on his own death.[8]

Other documents also show laymen anxious to protect their property from acquisition by the church, and the ninth-century kings seem less generous than their predecessors in their dealings with the church. A number of disputes are recorded, and exchanges of land, rather than outright gifts, became more common.[9] A group of eleven charters of the period 840–75 record apparent sales of land and privileges. Nine of the purchases involved bishops or the abbots of minsters associated with Worcester paying precious metals, sometimes in the form of plate and jewellery, to the kings of Mercia. An example was the restoration to Worcester of properties associated with Bredon by Berhtwulf, king of Mercia, in 840 in return for plate weighing eleven pounds, a gold ring and six horses. The king had previously granted the lands to laymen, and this is one of a number of pieces of evidence that church lands were returning to lay hands at this period.[10]

The growth of the Worcester estate in the seventh to ninth centuries, followed by a period of stagnation or even decline, can be paralleled by other large church estates in England and by estates on the continent. The overall proportion of land held by the church in

---

[8] The original grants of Inkberrow and Bromsgrove are CS 256 and CS 313. For Wulfheard's scheming, see A. J. Robertson, *Anglo-Saxon Charters*, 2nd edn (Cambridge, 1956), pp. 6–7, 263–5.

[9] For disputes, see CS 309; CS 379; CS 575; Robertson, *Charters*, pp. 8–9; F. E. Harmer, *Select English Historical Documents of the Ninth and Tenth Centuries* (Cambridge, 1914), pp. 56–9. Exchanges are recorded in CS 351; CS 350; CS 368; CS 416; CS 540.

[10] CS 430; CS 432; CS 434; CS 436; CS 450; CS 455; CS 487; CS 488; CS 492; CS 509; CS 533.

Europe seems to have begun to fall in about 900 after a period of expansion.[11]

The explanation of this chronological pattern may lie in the political situation, which was similar in Mercia to that on the continent, with the development of a powerful monarchy in the eighth century which declined in the ninth.[12] The church of Worcester relied on the kings of Mercia to make grants: of the twenty-six most reliable documents of the period before 800, seventeen were primarily charters of Mercian kings. The other authorities involved, either independently or more commonly in conjunction with the Mercians, were the princes of the Hwicce, who appear as grantors or as those who gave their consent in eight of the twenty-six charters.

The size of the Worcester estate grew with the rise of the Mercian hegemony under Æthelbald (716–57) and Offa (757–96), and fewer grants were made in the ninth century as Mercia began to suffer from the rivalry of Wessex and from Danish incursions. Some of the sales of land and privileges may reflect the royal need for bullion to pay tribute to the Danes.[13]

The princes of the Hwicce declined as the bishopric estate grew. They were described as kings in the late seventh century, became 'sub-kings' in the eighth century, and disappeared completely by 800. As much of the land gained by Worcester had been in the hands of the rulers of the Hwicce, the bishops could be seen as replacing them as the main landowners of the region in a major transfer of property supervised by the kings of Mercia.[14]

The complex process by which lands were detached from lay

---

[11] e.g. Gloucester and Winchcomb Abbeys apparently acquired their estates early; see Finberg, *Early Charters*, pp. 153–66; W. Levison, *England and the Continent in the Eighth Century* (Oxford, 1946), pp. 249–59; for monasteries on the continent, see E. de Moreau, *Les Abbayes de Belgique* (Brussels, 1952), pp. 9–46; F. Lot. *Études Critiques sur l'Abbaye de Saint Wandrille* (Paris, 1913), pp. xiii–xxix; D. Herlihy, 'Church Property on the European Continent', *Speculum*, xxxvi (1961), pp. 81–105. There is an obvious contrast with the eastern English monasteries, which accumulated their estates in the tenth century.

[12] On similarities of political development, see J. M. Wallace-Hadrill, *Early Germanic Kingship in England and on the Continent* (Oxford, 1971), chapter v.

[13] On the rise of Mercia, see F. M. Stenton, 'The Supremacy of the Mercian Kings', *Eng. Hist. Rev.*, xxxiii (1918), pp. 433–52; for Mercians making peace with the Danes, see *Anglo-Saxon Chronicle*, ed. D. Whitelock, D. C. Douglas and S. Tucker (London, 1961), pp. 46–7 and CS 533.

[14] An apparently parallel situation can be seen in Sussex, a dependent kingdom of Mercia, whose kings declined as the bishopric of Selsey developed; see CS 132; CS 144; CS 237.

hands and gained by the church often had as an intermediate stage the creation of a number of well-endowed minster churches (*monasterii*) in the seventh and eighth centuries. At least thirteen of Worcester's major acquisitions began their association with the church as minsters founded by prominent families, often the Hwiccean princes. They may be equated with the false monasteries described by Bede in a letter of 734, though a genuine religious life could have been conducted in them.[15]

The charters show that these early minsters were family property and were inherited, sometimes through a number of generations. For example, Fladbury in the Avon valley had become a minster in the seventh century. In the 690s Æthelred, king of Mercia, granted its very large estate of forty-four hides to Oftfor, bishop of Worcester, so that monastic life could be restored. Oftfor's successor, Ecgwine, granted Fladbury to a layman, Æthilheard, in exchange for lands at Stratford-on-Avon, for life. Æthilheard was a prince of the Hwicce and he was succeeded in his control of Fladbury by others – Ælfred and then Ealdred, who granted the estate to Æthelburg, a female relative, who was also abbess of minsters at Withington and Twyning. Worcester did not gain control of Fladbury until after 814, when Coenwulf, king of Mercia, granted its reversion to the bishopric in exchange for Bishop Deneberht's surrender of his claim to the other proprietary minster at Twyning.[16]

Besides the Hwiccean family minsters of Fladbury, Stratford, Twyning and Withington, others came into the hands of the bishops of Worcester with which the Hwiccean princes had some connection, such as Bibury, Cleeve and Inkberrow.[17] Bredon minster also was eventually brought under Worcester's control, but this was founded and endowed by the family of Offa, king of Mercia.

---

[15] D. Whitelock, *English Historical Documents* (London, 1955), i, pp. 735–45; P. Sims-Williams, 'Cuthswith, Seventh-Century Abbess of Inkberrow, near Worcester, and the Würzburg manuscript of Jerome on Ecclesiastes', in P. Clemoes (ed.), *Anglo-Saxon England*, v (Cambridge, 1976), pp. 1–21, argues that Inkberrow was a proprietary minster of the Mercian royal house, and that the abbess owned a religious manuscript. On early minsters in general, see M. Deanesley, 'Early English and Gallic Minsters', *Trans. Roy. Hist. Soc.*, 4th ser., xxiii (1941), pp. 25–52.

[16] CS 76; CS 238; CS 217; Finberg, *Early Charters,* pp. 177–8; CS 350; CS 368; see also *Chronicon Abbatiae de Evesham,* ed. W. D. Macray (Rolls Series, 1863), p. 17.

[17] CS 166; CS 580; CS 246; CS 85 and Sims-Williams, 'Cuthswith, Seventh-Century Abbess', in Clemoes (ed.), *Anglo-Saxon England*, v, pp. 1–21.

Eanulf, Offa's grandfather, founded a minster at Bredon, and Offa endowed it in the 770s and 780s with lands in the Avon valley near the minster, on the Cotswolds at Cutsdean and Evenlode and places twenty miles to the north at Rednal, Cofton and *Woersetfelda.* In 781 Offa claimed that Bredon, together with four other Worcester properties, was part of his inheritance, but agreed to surrender them in return for lands at Bath belonging to Worcester.[18] He was no doubt using his family claims as a bargaining counter, but the case indicates the reality of the proprietary rights of lay families to the minsters, and the precariousness of the church's position. The main problem for successive bishops of Worcester in the eighth century was to detach estates from the control of lay families. They were not always successful; Twyning and Bath were both lost to Worcester's control, as we have seen. Those minsters that remained under Worcester's authority retained some independence in the mid-ninth century. Bredon, for example, had its own abbot as late as 841.[19] Little more is heard of the minsters after that and they were absorbed with their endowments into the Worcester estate. They provided a substantial proportion of the lands of the bishops and also left a permanent mark on the structure of the estate, as the lands attached to the minsters usually became demesne manors, so that at least ten of the seventeen demesne manors listed in Domesday had been associated with minsters in the seventh, eighth or ninth centuries.[20]

There were clearly some tension and rivalry between bishops and the proprietary minsters. The key to the ultimate success of the bishops of Worcester lay in the patronage that they received from the kings of Mercia. The long-term interests of the monarchy would have been best served by a strongly based episcopate. By contrast, in contemporary Ireland a plethora of family monasteries dominated the ecclesiastical organization and was associated with a very different political structure.[21]

[18] CS 236; CS 209; CS 234; CS 241; also P. Sims-Williams, 'Continental Influence at Bath Monastery in the Seventh Century', in P. Clemoes (ed.), *Anglo-Saxon England*, iv (Cambridge, 1975), pp. 1–10.

[19] CS 434.

[20] The ten were Bibury, Blockley, Bredon, Cleeve, Fladbury, Hanbury, Stratford, Tredington, Withington and Westbury. Ripple probably should be included, and possibly Hartlebury, which may have been connected with the minster at *Sture* in Ismere.

[21] K. Hughes, *The Church in Early Irish Society* (London, 1966).

The conditions of tenure must have been an important factor in determining the quantity of land that kings were willing to see granted to the church. It has been argued that the *trinoda necessitas*, the three burdens of military service, fortification building and bridge repairs, were not imposed on church land in Mercia until the mid-eighth century so that the early grants to Worcester would have been generous gifts indeed, involving a loss of much potential military service. However, it seems likely that military obligations existed at all times and that the only change in the eighth century was the addition of the more specialized constructional obligations.[22]

Little attention has been given to the other commitments of ecclesiastical landowners but it is likely that these were originally extensive and very valuable to the monarchy. Some late eighth- and early ninth-century charters show that it was normal for church estates to pay annual food-rents to the king. Westbury-on-Trym owed ale and corn and animals which included seven oxen and six wethers, and they alone would represent a heavier burden of taxation than was demanded by kings from church estates in the later middle ages. In the period 814–75 a series of charters exempted some of the Worcester estates from a number of burdens – food for the king, his ealdormen, retainers, horses, dogs, hawks and falcons, and the men accompanying these animals, huntsmen, those involved in Welsh expeditions and *foestingmen*, apparently royal messengers and servants.[23] The implication is that up to the mid-ninth century kings drew considerable benefits from church lands which must have made them less hesitant to make grants. They conceded immunities in the ninth century, perhaps under pressure to raise money, but also ceased to make further grants of land.

[22] W. H. Stevenson, in 'Trinoda Necessitas', *Eng. Hist. Rev.*, xxix (1914), pp. 689–703, thought that church land was not immune, but this was questioned in E. John, 'The Imposition of the Common Burdens on the Lands of the English Church', *Bull. Inst. Hist. Res.*, xxxi (1958), pp. 117–29. The most convincing view, adopted here, is that of N. Brooks, 'The Development of Military Obligations in Eighth- and Ninth-Century England', in P. Clemoes and K. Hughes, *England Before the Conquest, Studies in Primary Sources presented to Dorothy Whitelock* (Cambridge, 1971), pp. 69–84.

[23] Whitelock, *English Historical Documents*, pp. 467–8 (the Westbury renders); CS 241 shows that food-rents were due to the king from a number of Worcester estates; charters of immunity: CS 350; CS 357; CS 416; CS 434; CS 450; CS 489; CS 540. Compare F. W. Maitland, *Domesday Book and Beyond* (Cambridge, 1897), pp. 236–43.

THE LOSS OF LANDS, 900–1066

The records of more than a hundred leases from the tenth and eleventh centuries show that in the late Saxon period much of the Worcester estate was being held by laymen on dependent tenures. The surviving leases do not seem to mark the beginning of such arrangements. A few leases for life or lives are recorded in the eighth century, though often in the rather exceptional circumstances of the settlement of disputed claims. Evidently many leases were made by unwritten grants and it is sometimes possible to show that properties leased in the tenth century had been held by laymen as tenants of the church of Worcester in the ninth, as at Aston Magna, Inkberrow and Stoke Bishop.[24] It is possible that large-scale leasing began in the ninth century when church lands came under some pressure from the laity and the bishops' lands ceased to contribute to the support of prominent laymen through food-rents and the provision of hospitality.

Under the reforming Bishop Oswald (961–92) leases were regularly written down and preserved. They usually involved relatively small holdings of between one and six hides, often situated on the edge of the larger land units. They were granted to high-ranking laymen, mostly thegns, for terms of three lives. The land was supposed to revert to the bishopric at the end of the third life, but it seems to have been normal for the lease to be renewed or re-granted as most of the lands known to have been leased in the tenth century were still held by laymen in the late eleventh, and many continued as dependent tenures throughout the middle ages. In effect, leasing meant the permanent alienation of substantial amounts of land – about 45 per cent of the hidage of the estate recorded in Domesday was held by lay tenants.

The problems of church property in the eleventh century are reflected in the attitudes of the monk Hemming, who wrote a strongly worded and detailed account of the loss of lands 'taken away by wicked men' in the (not always reliable) cartulary that he compiled in the late eleventh century.[25] Hemming blamed the

---

[24] Robertson, *Charters*, pp. 34–5, 6–7; Harmer, *Select English Historical Documents*, pp. 53–4. On unwritten leases see E. John, *Land Tenure in Early England* (Leicester, 1960), pp. 129–30.

[25] *HC*, i, p. 248–88. On conflict between the church and laity over land, see F. Barlow, *The English Church, 1000–1066* (London, 1963), pp. 167–75.

Danes, the English and Norman nobility and the monks of Evesham Abbey for the losses. It is not always possible to show that the properties mentioned ever belonged to Worcester. Many of the lands were held on lease so that Hemming is often complaining that lessees had become too independent, sometimes as the result of mismanagement by bishops or the intervention of powerful local magnates like Edric Streona, who ruled *quasi subregulus* in the reign of Cnut, or Urse d'Abitot after the Conquest. Hemming's bitter tones seem to reflect a serious deterioration in relations between the church and the laity, in which churchmen were put on the defensive.

Hemming's interests were focused on the loss of Worcestershire lands in the eleventh century. However, some of the most serious erosions of the Worcester estate were in southern Gloucestershire, where the church had interest in such places as Sodbury, Tetbury and Woodchester in the eighth and ninth centuries, which were already under lay pressure in the late ninth century, and were totally lost to Worcester by the time of Domesday.[26]

In the late Anglo-Saxon period a further change was the division of the estate between the bishop and the cathedral priory. In the ninth century the cathedral clergy held properties apart from those of the bishop but a clear separation was not possible until the monastery of St Mary's was founded in the late tenth century.[27] Attempts have been made to date the foundation of the monastery to the year 964, but it seems more likely that the cathedral clergy was persuaded gradually to adopt a regular life.[28] The creation of a separate monastic estate could have been a gradual process also. An early stage could be marked by Oswald's securing of three hides at Spetchley for the cathedral clergy in 967 but in the late tenth century Oswald was leasing to laymen lands that were later to form part of the monastic endowment. The time of Bishop Ealdred (1046–62) is the most likely period for the division of the land

[26] Harmer, *Select English Historical Documents*, pp. 56–9; *VCH Glos.*, xi, pp. 264, 296.

[27] The cathedral clergy appear as owners of lands in CS 559 and CS 570.

[28] E. John, 'St. Oswald and the Church of Worcester', in *Orbis Britanniae* (Manchester, 1966), pp. 234–48, argues for a sudden, decisive change. For the gradualist interpretation, see J. Armitage Robinson, *St. Oswald and the Church of Worcester*, Brit. Acad. Supplemental Papers, v (1919), and P. H. Sawyer, 'Charters of the Reform Movement: the Worcester Archive', in D. Parsons (ed.), *Tenth-Century Studies* (Chichester, 1975), pp. 84–93.

between bishop and monks but transfers were still being made after the Conquest.[29]

The monastic endowment was created by splitting up some large land units, such as those of Bredon, Stratford and Tredington, and assigning small portions of them to the priory. The monks were in addition given geographically detached manors, often somewhat smaller than the bishop's demesne manors, such as Harvington and Sedgeberrow. The resulting estate was more compact than that of the bishops, lying mostly within twenty miles of Worcester, reflecting the special needs of monks, who were not able to travel round their estates as readily as a bishop could, or carry produce to the monastery from a distance.

SETTLEMENT AND THE EXPLOITATION OF LAND

Investigation of early medieval land units often reveals that they were very large, and the components of the Anglo-Saxon estate of the church of Worcester are no exception. The geographical extent of the lands granted in charters of the seventh to ninth centuries is not usually stated with any precision, but their approximate size can be estimated by working back from later evidence. It seems likely that the territories associated with such places as Fladbury, Stratford and Westbury-on-Trym at the time when they came under the control of the church of Worcester were each in the region of twenty square miles.

Did these large tracts of land come to Worcester as undeveloped wastes and forests or in a cultivated and settled form? There was once an assumption that much of early England, especially the midlands, was covered with impenetrable woods that were cleared in the Anglo-Saxon and medieval periods. This view is not supported by the available evidence.

Many of the lands granted to the church of Worcester had a history of settlement going back into Romano-British and prehistoric times. If we concentrate on the seventeen properties that were eventually to form the bishopric estate, we see that seven

[29] *HC*, i, pp. 183–5; F. E. Harmer, *Anglo-Saxon Writs* (Manchester, 1952), pp. 410–11; W. Davies, 'Saint Mary's Worcester and the *Liber Landavensis*', *Journ. of the Soc. of Archivists*, iv (1972), p. 477; the significance of the Alveston grant by Wulfstan II in 1089 is discussed in *The Cartulary of Worcester Cathedral Priory (Register I)*, ed. R. R. Darlington (Pipe Roll Soc., lxxvi, 1962–3), pp. xliii–xliv.

included or lay very near to the sites of important Roman settlements, small towns in most cases, at Worcester (Northwick and Wick), Dorn (Blockley), Droitwich (Hanbury), Sea Mills (Westbury), Tiddington (Stratford) and Wycomb in Andoversford (Withington). Two Cotswold estates, Bibury and Withington, contained the sites of Roman villas within their boundaries, and finds of Romano-British pottery and other objects implying the existence of settlements have been made on most of the others. On the river valley manors of Bredon, Fladbury, Hampton and Kempsey, aerial photographs have revealed the distinctive crop-marks of Iron Age and Romano-British farms and field boundaries under the arable fields used in the middle ages, showing that the lands chosen for occupation coincided in the period before the fifth century and in the later medieval period.[30]

Were the lands of the estate cultivated continuously from late Roman into Anglo-Saxon times? It seems likely that the settlements on the high quality valley land would have remained in spite of the upheavals of the fifth and sixth centuries. The end of Roman administration would not necessarily have led to the abandonment of good land and useful resources. Professor Finberg argued, on the basis of topographical evidence of estate boundaries at Blockley and Withington, that the organisation of Romano-British villa–estates survived to be taken over by Anglo-Saxons. It is difficult to see how this theory can be applied beyond the Cotswolds as there is little evidence of villas in the river valleys or

[30] For major Romano-British settlements: see P.A. Barker, 'The Roman Town' (of Worcester), *Trans. Worcs. Arch. Soc.*, 3rd ser., ii (1968–9), pp. 15–19; G. C. Boon, 'The Roman Site at Sea Mills, 1945–6', *Trans. Bristol and Glos. Arch. Soc.*, lxvi (1945), pp. 258–95; *Iron-Age and Romano-British Monuments in the Gloucestershire Cotswolds* (Royal Commission on Historical Monuments, 1976), pp. 12–13; W. J. Fieldhouse, T. May and F. C. Wellstood, *A Romano-British Industrial Settlement near Tiddington, Stratford-upon-Avon* (Birmingham 1931). For Roman villas: *Iron-Age and Romano-British Monuments*, pp. 13–14, 131–2. For other sites: *Iron-Age and Romano-British Monuments*, pp. 17, 106–7; C. N. S. Smith, 'A Catalogue of Prehistoric Finds from Worcestershire', *Trans. Worcs. Arch. Soc.*, xxxiv (1957), p. 26; *VCH Worcs.*, i, pp. 210–11, 219, 220; H. E. O'Neil, 'Court House Excavations, Kempsey, Worcestershire', *Trans. Worcs. Arch. Soc.*, xxxiii (1956), pp. 33–44; C. N. S. Smith, 'Two Romano-British Sites', *Trans. Worcs. Arch. Soc.*, xxx (1953), p. 81; *Medieval Arch.*, xii (1968), p. 162; G. Webster and B. Hobley, 'Aerial Reconnaissance over the Warwickshire Avon', *Arch. Journ.*, cxxi (1964), pp. 14, 15, 17–18, fig. 10; H. P. R. Finberg, 'Roman and Saxon Withington', *passim*; H. P. R. Finberg, 'Some Early Gloucestershire Estates', in *Gloucestershire Studies* (Leicester, 1957), pp. 1–16; information from Worcestershire County Museum and the Ordnance Survey.

north Worcestershire. The lack of material remains and written sources for the immediate post-Roman period prevents the conclusive demonstration of continuous occupation. The most convincing case is provided by the site of Worcester Cathedral itself, where there is archaeological evidence of late Roman artefacts and burials of the sixth century, and documentary evidence of the cathedral's foundation in the late seventh. For five of our seventeen manors – a high proportion for the region as a whole – pagan Anglo-Saxon cemeteries show the presence of at least a small population in the fifth, sixth and seventh centuries. [31]

The likelihood of a continuous occupation of places and land between the Roman and early medieval periods should not lead us to underrate some important discontinuities in settlement history. The cemeteries with their evidence of a distinctively Germanic material culture, and the almost universal adoption of Germanic place-names show that there was some immigration into the region. Also, at some time between late Roman times and the twelfth century, perhaps in the middle Saxon period, a dispersed settlement pattern in the river valleys was replaced by nucleated villages.

Besides the concrete evidence of Romano-British settlements and early Anglo-Saxon cemeteries, the earliest charters in themselves provide evidence that the lands were occupied. In each document the estate was said to consist of a number of hides, usually between ten and sixty, the Latin terms for them being *cassatae*, *cassati*, *manentes*, *mansae*, *mansiones* or *tributarii*. As is indicated by the round numbers of hides, often in tens, these were fiscal assessments, but the terminology used in both Latin and the vernacular shows that the fiscal arrangements derive ultimately from households and family holdings. The implication is that the estates were already inhabited and productive enough to yield some form of tax by the time that they first appeared in the Worcester charters. It is rare for charters to imply that the hidage figure represents the mere potential of the land. [32]

Occasional hints of topography are given in early charters. A

[31] P. A. Barker *et al.*, 'Two Burials under the Refectory of Worcester Cathedral', *Medieval Arch.*, xviii (1974), pp. 146–51; Meaney, *A Gazetteer of Early Anglo-Saxon Burial Sites*, pp. 91, 262–3, 280; *Annual Report of C.B.A. Groups 12 and 13*, iv (1969), p. 50 (I am indebted to Mr S. Bassett for this reference).

[32] T. M. Charles-Edwards, 'Kinship, Status, and the Origins of the Hide', *P and P*, lvi (1972), pp. 5–7; for a potential hidage see CS 76.

notable example is a grant of 'Stour' in the province of Ismere in 736, which contains a rare indication of boundaries, showing that the land, probably around Wolverley in Worcestershire, was bordered on two sides by the forests of Kinver and Morfe. This could be taken to imply that the land was a pioneer settlement, on the frontier between civilization and the forest.[33] However, although the forests of 736 have undoubtedly been eroded by medieval and modern clearance, there are still large areas of woodland to the west and north of Wolverley, so that eighth-century landscape may not have been so radically different from that of later periods.

Perhaps the use in a charter of a river-name, 'Stour', suggests an undeveloped countryside without settlements to provide a name for an estate. This is a characteristic of some eighth-century Worcester charters, and the other river Stour in south Warwickshire and the Coln in Gloucestershire initially gave their names to estates also. Examples from, or very near to, these three estates show that important place-names were being coined within the period of our documents, derived from the names of people known to have been estate owners in the eighth or ninth centuries. Bibury, the name adopted for the Coln estate, records a woman called Beaga, Tredington (on the Warwickshire Stour) is named after Tyrdda, and Wolverley derives from Wulferd.[34] An analogous case is that of Alvechurch, apparently originally included in a group of properties called *Woersetfelda*, Cofton, Rednal, *Weorsethylle*, Hopwood and *Witlafesfeld*, in charters of 780 and 849, which were not grouped under the name Alvechurch until some time after 850.[35] The absence of a dominant settlement after which properties could be named should not be taken to imply that there were no settlements at all; nor does late name-formation from eponymous landholders mean that settlements were being founded in the wastes. Rather the change in names suggests the development of administrative centres in the eighth and ninth centuries, no doubt through the initiative of lords. Perhaps the development was also

[33] F. M. Stenton, *Anglo-Saxon England*, 3rd edn (Oxford, 1972), p. 286.
    CS 166; CS 154; CS 241; CS 351; A. H. Smith, *The Place-Names of Gloucestershire* (Eng. Place-Name Soc., xxxviii–xli, 1964–5), p. 26; A. Mawer, F. M. Stenton and F. T. S. Houghton, *The Place-Names of Worcestershire* (Eng. Place-Name Soc., iv, 1927), pp. 172, 256–7.
[35] CS 234; CS 455.

associated with the tendency of dispersed settlements to come together to form larger nuclei.[36]

It should also be emphasized that some of the earliest Worcester charters mention places that have subsequently always been small, remote and on relatively poor land: for example, Bradley and Cofton in north Worcestershire. The existence of such settlements could be taken to mean that the countryside was extensively occupied even in the eighth century.

For many of the Worcester estates the evidence for early settlement reflects the high quality of the land that they occupied. Most of the estates lay in the river valleys of the Avon, Severn and Stour, where the gravel soils were light and fertile. The equivalent modern parishes contain substantial areas of land classified by the Ministry of Agriculture as grades one or two, that is, well suited to arable cultivation. Much of the land in the west midland region is classified as grade three: that is, of average quality, suitable for use as either arable or pasture. The Worcester bishopric manors which contained mainly grade three land were Alvechurch and Hanbury in the heavy soils of north Worcestershire and the Cotswold manors of Bibury, Blockley, Cleeve and Withington, with steep slopes and thin soils.[37] This land, though inferior for cultivation, still had its value for the estate. If the corn-growing capacity of the river valleys were used to the full, there would be little room there for large areas of pasture or woodland. A combination of different types of land within the whole estate ensured a balance of resources.

Woodlands are sometimes mentioned specifically in charters (as distinct from the references to woods in conventional formulaic lists of the assets being conveyed). When the places with charters that mention woodland are plotted on a map, they will be seen to occur most commonly in north and west Worcestershire, north Warwickshire and along the western scarp of the Cotswolds (see Map 3); these areas continued to be wooded in later medieval times. The inclusion of woodland properties within the estate was essential if important products were to be available, both for direct consumption by the estate owners and for use on the lands that lacked woods.

[36] On dispersal and nucleation of settlement, see B. Cunliffe, 'Saxon and Medieval Settlement-Pattern in the Region of Chalton, Hampshire', *Medieval Arch.*, xvi (1972), pp. 1–12.

[37] Ministry of Agriculture, Fisheries and Food, *Land Classification Maps*, sheets 130, 131, 143, 144, 156.

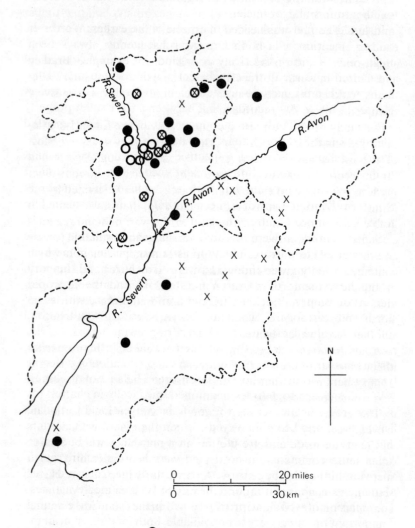

● References to woodland in charters
○ References to enclosures (*haga*, croft) in boundaries
X References to open field (headland, acre) in boundaries
⊗ References to both enclosures and open field

3   Land use: the evidence of pre-1066 charters

The charters and Domesday both show that woodlands provided swine-pastures and were sources of game, honey, building-timber and fuel. The fuel was needed in especially large quantities for the boiling of salt in the bishops' Droitwich salt-works.[38]

Throughout the Anglo-Saxon period there is evidence of specialized land-use in the attachment of woodland to larger land-units, which presumably consisted mainly of arable or pasture. A charter of 699 × 709 records a link between a river valley property and remote woodlands. In this document Offa of Essex granted Shottery (near Stratford), together with woodland at Nuthurst and *Hellerelege*, places situated respectively eleven and sixteen miles to the north. The connection was maintained in 872, when Nuthurst was leased to a layman, but with reversion to the minster at Stratford. Land at Lapworth, near Nuthurst, was still attached to Stratford in the late thirteenth century.[39]

Similar linkages were created during the formation of the Worcester estate. For example, Offa's family minster in the Avon valley at Bredon was endowed in the late eighth century with woodland to the north at Cofton and Rednal and Cotswold properties. At some point between the ninth and eleventh centuries the north Worcestershire woodland at Bradley was attached to another Avon valley estate, Fladbury.[40]

Apart from the close connections between specific properties, the whole structure of the Worcester estate should be seen as complementary, so that a variety of lands used as arable, pasture and wood, formed a federated whole.

The evidence of the more numerous and detailed tenth- and eleventh-century charters enables us to examine the topography of the estate more closely. We are aware of the existence of many small settlements, some of which escaped mention in other documents until the twelfth century. A particularly high density of such settlements is apparent around the city of Worcester in documents compiled before 1066, with twenty-five places named in an area

[38] Swine-pastures: see Robertson, *Charters*, pp. 8–9; CS 513; CS 1204. Fuel: see Robertson, *Charters*, pp. 64–7; CS 1087. Also *DB*, fos. 172–3.

[39] CS 123; CS 533; *RBW*, iii, pp. 254–5. For examples of similar linkages in the west midlands see W. J. Ford, 'Some Settlement Patterns in the Central Region of the Warwickshire Avon', in P. H. Sawyer (ed.), *Medieval Settlement* (London, 1976), pp. 274–94. Similar arrangements in the south-east of England are well known, see K. P. Witney, *The Jutish Forest* (London, 1976), *passim*.

[40] CS 236; CS 209; CS 234; CS 153; CS 256; CS 308.

nine miles long and five miles broad, so that there was one settlement for every two square miles.

The many boundary perambulations attached to tenth- and
eleventh-century charters describe the main topographical features
on the edge of estates. These are likely to be remote from settlements and often include natural boundary marks such as trees,
marshes and streams. However, many late Saxon boundaries seem
to move over a civilized and man-made landscape. For example,
the limits of a hide of land at Himbleton in 977 were marked by
hedges, crofts, headlands and a bridge. The only natural boundary
mark was a thorn bush, and that belonged to, or was associated with,
someone called Ecgbricht.[41]

Comparison between boundaries shows significant differences
between woodland and arable districts (see Map 3). References
to enclosures – croft and *haga* are the commonest terms – occur
most often in central, northern and western Worcestershire,
while apparently unenclosed lands, the significant terms being
headland, acre and *earth-land*, are mentioned frequently, again in
central Worcestershire and in the Avon valley and the Cotswolds.
The inference to be drawn from this is that in the northern and western parts of the estate a more wooded landscape was associated with
enclosed land, particularly on the edge of the properties surveyed,
while much of the land to the south and east of the region consisted
of unenclosed arable. A similar distinction was drawn by John
Leland, who gives a topographical description of the area in the
early sixteenth century. For example, as he travelled through
Hartlebury, in north Worcestershire, he 'rode ... by enclosed
ground, having meatly good grass and corn, and plenty of wood',
but south Warwickshire was champion country, 'somewhat barren
of wood, but very plentiful of corn'.[42]

Can the charters tell us anything of the field systems in use in the
late Saxon period? The terminology of acres and headlands, found
mainly in the south and east of the region, is similar to that employed
later to describe the elements of an open field of unenclosed strips.

[41] Robertson, *Charters*, pp. 116–17; G. B. Grundy, 'Saxon Charters of Worcestershire', *Trans. Birm. Arch. Soc.,* lii (1927), pp. 152–3.
[42] Grundy, 'Saxon Charters of Worcestershire', *Trans. Birm. Arch. Soc.,* lii (1927),
pp. 1–183; liii (1928), pp, 18–131; and G. B. Grundy, *Saxon Charters and Field Names
of Gloucestershire* (Gloucester, 1935–6); *Leland's Itinerary in England and
Wales,* ed. L. Toulmin Smith (London, 1964 reprint), ii, pp. 47, 52–3, 89–96.

Also the fact that such features appear in the boundary descriptions suggests that cultivation was so extensive that arable land reached out to the very edge of estates. The parcels of land were intermixed, implied by the use of the term 'dole-land' in charters of Clifford Chambers and Cudley. Details are given of the division of land, showing how the mingling and scattering of strips might arise. Land at Upthrop (in Bredon) was split between two brothers so that 'the eldest shall have three acres and the younger the fourth'. There are references to lands divided 'by every other acre' at Alveston and by 'every third acre' at Tiddington.[43] The term 'acre' is apparently being used here in the same sense as in the boundaries, as a physical division, a strip in the open field.

Can we go on from the evidence for open fields to establish that land was worked on regular rotations with common grazing? There is insufficient evidence for this, but if the cultivated area was very extensive, as some of the boundary descriptions signify, so that little permanent pasture remained, the evolution of a regular system of rotation with fallow grazing, all under communal control, would be a logical development. A hint of such an arrangement comes from a grant of land at Barbourne, north of Worcester city, in 904. This describes the property as 'sixty acres of arable land south of Barbourne and sixty acres to the north', which could be taken to mean a two-field system. Barbourne was later to form part of the bishopric demesne manor of Northwick/Whitstones and a two-course rotation was practised on its demesne in the thirteenth century.[44]

To sum up, the lands acquired by the church of Worcester in the two centuries after 680 were in the main settled and had been occupied for a long time. Much of the estate lay on high-quality and easily cultivated soils, but necessarily included woodlands and pastures to provide a balance of resources. From an early date land use was specialized, and by the tenth century, if not earlier, a predominantly arable and open-field landscape in the southern part of

[43] CS 1181; *HC*, i, p. 155; Robertson, *Charters*, pp. 88–9; 335; 130–3. See also H. P. R. Finberg (ed.), *Agrarian History of England* (Cambridge, 1972), i, part 2, pp. 487–96.

[44] For the argument that extensive cultivation would lead to communal control see J. Thirsk, 'The Common Fields', *P and P*, xxix (1964), p. 9. For the Barbourne charter, see Robertson, *Charters*, pp. 34–9; H. L. Gray, *English Field Systems* (Harvard, 1915), p. 60; Finberg, *Agrarian History*, pp. 495–6; *RBW*, i, pp. 1–3.

the estate contrasted with a mixture of arable, woodland and enclosed land in the northern and western properties.

THE ECONOMY OF THE ESTATE

How did the church of Worcester obtain revenues from its lands? By the late eleventh century the estate was organized in manors with land divided between demesnes and tenant holdings. The demesnes were worked by some slave labour, and by the labour services of the tenants. The bishop's income came from demesne produce and rents; at least some of his revenues were in form of money. Did such an organization for exploiting the resources of the estate exist for any length of time before the Norman Conquest?

The primary need of the landowner was the same throughout the Anglo-Saxon period – ample supplies of foodstuffs for the bishop, the cathedral clergy and their entourage of servants and guests. The people who could expect to live on the produce of the estate were no doubt numerous; witness lists, for example show that the cathedral clergy alone varied in number between nine and twenty-five.[45]

The scattered nature of the estate suited the needs of a bishop ideally. He could travel over his diocese, as his ecclesiastical and secular duties required, staying on his own lands and consuming the estate produce as he went. The allowance of food made for a bishop's household has not been recorded, but we do know of two food rents from the estate, one for the king from Westbury at the end of the eighth century, and another in 847 from Kempsey for the support of the cathedral clergy.[46]

These supplies may have been gathered from the inhabitants in the form of tribute but they could also represent the produce of a demesne. No Worcester charter mentions demesne land until the early tenth century but there is much earlier evidence from Wessex.[47]

The striking feature of the food rents, no matter how they were collected, is the discrepancy between the relatively small quantities

----

[45] CS 455; CS 533; *HC*, i, pp. 121–217, 232–40.
[46] Whitelock, *English Historical Documents*, i, pp. 467–8; Finberg, *Early Charters*, p. 103.
[47] Robertson, *Charters*, pp. 34–5; T. H. Aston, 'The Origins of the Manor in England', *Trans. Roy. Hist. Soc.*, 5th ser., viii (1958), pp. 59–83.

Table 1. *Food-rents*

	Westbury-on-Trym, 793 × 796	Kempsey, 847
ale	2 tuns 'pure' 1 coomb 'mild' 1 coomb 'Welsh'	3 barrels 3 casks 'Welsh'
corn/bread	30 ambers corn 4 ambers meal	600 loaves white bread
meat	7 oxen 6 wethers	3 cows 6 wethers hams
cheeses	40	60
other items	6 long *theru*	3 barrels mead 4 candles and oil

specified and the large size of the estates that owed them. If the 'amber' of the Westbury list contained four bushels and the standard loaf produced at Kempsey weighed two or three pounds, as recorded in the later middle ages, then the amount of bread corn rendered each year was about seventeen quarters at Westbury and no more than five quarters at Kempsey, representing the produce of about seventeen and five acres respectively, if yields were again anything like those of the later middle ages. Similarly the number of animals does not suggest very large flocks and herds. A flock of a hundred sheep would provide an annual consumable surplus of six wethers without difficulty. Yet the size of the estates of Westbury and Kempsey should be reckoned in terms of many square miles.

It is of course possible that yields of grain were very poor in the eighth and ninth centuries but these bread allowances, if calculated on the basis of the very lowest estimates of the productivity of continental estates of the period, would still represent a crop of less than fifty acres.[48]

Part of the answer to the problem lies in the number of consumers who shared the produce from the estates. The food rents quoted above represent only a fraction of the total needed from Westbury and Kempsey in order to supply the episcopal household and the

[48] Very low yields in the Carolingian period are postulated in G. Duby, *L'Économie Rurale et la Vie des Campagnes dans l'Occident Médiéval* (Paris, 1962), i, pp. 84–7, but this is disputed: see B. H. Slicher van Bath, 'Yield Ratios, 810–1820', *Afdeling Agrarische Geschiedenis Landbouwhogeschool, Bijdragen*, x (1963), p. 17.

clergy of the local minsters, as well as the kings, their servants and the cathedral clergy. It may also be that lords did not squeeze their tenants very thoroughly, or tackle the management of their estates with much vigour. After all, unless there was a market for surplus agricultural produce, there was not much point in accumulating large quantities of perishable foodstuffs beyond the immediate needs of the consuming households.

Important changes in the structure, and presumably in the economy, of the estate came in the ninth, tenth and eleventh centuries. The trend towards the fragmentation of the land units meant that instead of large tracts of land providing for the needs of many consumers, smaller units were created and assigned exclusively for the upkeep of a single household. So the leases from the ninth century onwards created new, small estates for laymen, whose predecessors may well have been supported as members of royal or other households, living partly off food rents owed by church estates. Also in the late Saxon period, perhaps in the late ninth century, the minster churches ceased to exist as separate monasteries and became no more than important local churches. Out of this change the church of Worcester obtained exclusive rights over much of the land which had originally formed the endowment of the monasteries but a substantial amount of glebe land was retained by the minsters. Such was the conservatism of medieval ecclesiastical life that even at the end of the middle ages the rectories which succeeded the minsters still stand out in comparison with other churches because of the great wealth of their livings.[49] A further division of lands came in the mid-eleventh century when the estate of the cathedral monastery was separated from that of the bishopric.

The bishops were faced with a long term reduction in the size of their estate. One reaction was to seek to secure the better land for themselves. When Bishop Oswald leased out land at Wolverton in 977 he reserved sixty acres of 'wheat land', presumably for his demesne at Kempsey.[50] On a number of estates such as Fladbury, the best quality arable land was retained in the episcopal demesne manor, while the lessees received the inferior clay lands at Ab Lench, Hill and Moor, and Throckmorton.

Smaller estates needed more careful management; they certainly

[49] *Valor Ecclesiasticus* (Record Commission, 1817), iii, pp. 256, 257, 265, 267.
[50] Robertson, *Charters*, pp. 114–15.

needed to be protected from any further reduction or fragmentation. Hence in the century before the Norman Conquest the concern of bishops and monks was to record the charters that established their title to lands, and the texts of leases, in three cartularies in succession. In this period also, detailed boundary perambulations were written down in order to prevent disputes and encroachment. At about the same time other landowners were recording details of the obligations of tenants and treatises on estate management.[51]

In the late Saxon period there was some development in the importance of money in the economy as a whole, which could have influenced the management of the estate. Charters of the period 840–72 record the purchase of land and privileges by the church from the kings of Mercia for horses, jewellery, plate and weights of precious metals. These should not be regarded as commercial transactions, but as mutual exchanges of gifts between kings and important subjects.[52] They show how wealth might be de-hoarded and put into circulation in a time of political troubles. Above all they indicate that the church of Worcester had accumulated a considerable store of gold and silver, doubtless partly from the gifts of the faithful but perhaps also from the payment of cash rents. As early as 803 a food rent on the estate had been commuted for cash (*'pecuniam daret pro pastu'*), and charters of 864 and 903 mention annual rents of thirty and fifteen shillings.[53]

The church of Worcester had commercial contacts from the eighth century. At that time English trading activity was con-

[51] D. C. Douglas and G. W. Greenaway, *English Historical Documents* (London, 1953), ii, pp. 813–18, for the *Rectitudines* and Tidenham survey, The *Gerefa* belongs to the same period, H. R. Loyn, *Anglo-Saxon England and the Norman Conquest* (London, 1962), pp. 193–4.

[52] The gold mentioned in these transactions was probably not in the form of coin, see P. Grierson, 'Carolingian Europe and the Arabs: the Myth of the Mancus', *Revue Belge de Philologie et d'Histoire*, xxxii (1954), pp. 1059–74; there seems to have been a large volume of silver coinage in circulation by the ninth century, see D. Metcalf, 'How Large was the Anglo-Saxon Currency?', *Econ. Hist. Rev.*, 2nd ser., xviii (1965), pp. 478–9 (in spite of subsequent criticisms). On gifts, see P. Grierson, 'Commerce in the Dark Ages: a critique of the evidence', *Trans. Roy. Hist. Soc.*, 5th ser., ix (1959), pp. 137–9.

[53] CS 309; CS 509; Harmer, *Select English Historical Documents*, p. 58. D. M. Metcalf, 'Sceattas from the Territory of the Hwicce', *Numismatic Chronicle*, cxxxvi (1976), pp. 64–74, argues for a monetary element in the economy of the region in the eighth century.

centrated in the south-east, and in 743 × 745 Bishop Mildred received a grant of toll exemption on two ships at London, perhaps implying that the bishop (together with other churchmen at the time who received similar privileges) was buying and selling in the port. By the mid-ninth century the bishops of Worcester had acquired property in London, again probably for trading purposes rather than for use as a residence. It was only when London developed as a capital at a much later date that provincial bishops needed London houses for social and political purposes. Within the diocese an early focus of exchange was at Droitwich, one of the few inland salt-making centres in England. Here the church of Worcester from the early eighth century had furnaces and salt houses, presumably at first to supply its own domestic needs but later producing salt for sale.[54]

The earliest urban development in the diocese can be recognized at Worcester itself at the end of the ninth century, when the city had a market, traders and streets – one source of trade being the salt-pans of Droitwich. The church, a focal point for travellers, doubt-less provided some stimulus to urban growth, and was a consumer of the products of trade and industry.[55] With the more widespread ex-pansion of towns in the tenth and eleventh centuries, a market for the produce of demesnes grew up. The need to gain access to the urban market would help to explain why by 1086 the bishops owned houses in a number of towns at Bristol, Gloucester and Warwick, as well as Worcester and Droitwich.

The relationship between landlords and towns was a complex one. A likely chain of interaction is that lords helped to encourage urban growth by their demand for the goods and services that towns could provide. The towns in turn fuelled the aristocratic appetite for more goods, especially luxuries, while themselves needing more produce from the land to feed their growing populations. The lords responded by seeking to extract more from their estates.[56]

[54] H. B. Clarke and C. C. Dyer, 'Anglo-Saxon and Early Norman Worcester: The Documentary Evidence', *Trans. Worcs. Arch. Soc.*, 3rd ser., ii (1968–9), pp. 27–30.
[55] Clarke and Dyer, *ibid*; the importance of royal and ecclesiastical establish-ments in early urban growth is stressed in M. Biddle, 'The Development of the Anglo-Saxon Town', in *Settimane di Studio del Centro Italiano di Studi sull'alto medioevo*, xxi (Spoleto, 1974), pp. 206–12.
[56] This argument has been fully developed with reference to the continental evidence in G. Duby, *The Early Growth of the European Economy* (London, 1974), pp. 157–270.

The crux of the discussion of the estate economy must be the nature of the relationship between the lords and their tenants and subjects. The ability to demand labour of slaves and peasants to cultivate demesnes, or to compel direct payment of goods or money by the peasantry, enabled the church of Worcester to obtain a surplus from the land.

The core of the labour supply for working the demesnes seems to have been provided in the late Saxon period by slaves. The stock belonging to land at Luddington at the time when it was leased to a layman by the cathedral clergy in the early eleventh century consisted of two teams of oxen, a hundred sheep, seed corn and twelve slaves. A marriage agreement for Archbishop Wulfstan's sister in 1014 × 1016 involved a grant of land in Worcestershire, together with gold, thirty horses and thirty men. Grants of land at Milcote in 922, and at Brightwell and Watlington in c.887, included 'men'.[57] Comparison with the Domesday evidence suggests that Anglo-Saxon manors had greater resources of slave labour than those of the post-Conquest period. For example, no slaves are mentioned in 1086 at Luddington.

Besides slave-labour, were the demesnes cultivated with the labour services of peasant tenants? This raises the vexed problem of the social status of the peasantry in the Anglo-Saxon period and the extent to which lords were able to exploit their services, especially in the shadowy seventh to ninth centuries. Professor Finberg, as part of his argument that the manor of Withington originated as a Roman villa estate, has suggested that Anglo-Saxon landowners inherited a subordinate tenantry from their Romano-British predecessors.[58] There is no direct evidence to support this, and any theory of continuity in social institutions must take into account the very varied conditions of rural society in Roman Britain, suggested in the west midlands by the large numbers of villa estates in the Cotswolds and their apparent absence in much of the rest of the region. Also, it is difficult to believe that the cessation of commodity production in the fifth and sixth centuries was not accompanied by a social upheaval affecting the relations between peasants and their superiors.

One shred of evidence for the social status of the early Anglo-

[57] Robertson, *Charters*, pp. 154–5, 148–9, 42–3; CS 547.
[58] Finberg, 'Withington', pp. 59–65.

Saxon inhabitants of the Worcester estate is the survival of the word *ceorl* in the place-name Charlton, at Cropthorne, Hartlebury and Westbury-on-Trym. Were these ceorls the free peasants, who, it is claimed, formed the basis of society as 'independent masters of peasant households'? Current revisions of Anglo-Saxon social history are casting doubt on the ceorl's independence. A Worcester charter suggests that in about 900 some ceorls were very much under the control of lords. The document records a grant of Elmstone Hardwicke by Bishop Werfrith to Cyneswith. In this grant he was able to include with the land the ceorls' wood (*ceorla graf*) and state that the ceorls 'shall belong to Prestbury'.[59]

By the late tenth and early eleventh centuries we are on safer ground in assuming that labour services played an important part in the estate's economy. Presumably the *geburs* who are mentioned in a boundary description of Laughern in 963 owed similar services, including week-work, to the *geburs* described in such late Saxon texts as the *Rectitudines Singularum Personarum* or the Tidenham survey, which both relate to conditions in the west midlands. When we find that some of the socially elevated recipients of Oswald's leased land in the late tenth century owed a few labour services, it increases the likelihood that a much heavier burden of work was exacted from the peasant tenants.[60]

The Anglo-Saxon documents mention few specific dues or services. Evidently many tenants owed churchscot, a rent in grain, probably once collected by the minster churches but then diverted to the church of Worcester. This is mentioned in Oswald's leases, and in Domesday and the later surveys. The twelfth-century surveys use apparently archaic vernacular terms for dues that probably date back to before the Conquest, such as 'tak', paid to enable peasants' pigs to feed in the lord's woods, the ploughing services known as 'benerth' and 'graserth'; and 'spenyngfee', a payment made in lieu of spinning yarn, a service presumably made obsolete by a growing division of labour.[61]

The scanty evidence allows us no more than speculation about

[59] H. P. R. Finberg, 'Charltons and Carltons', in *Lucerna* (London, 1964), pp. 144–60; Stenton, *Anglo-Saxon England*, p. 278; Aston, 'The Origins of the Manor', pp. 59–83; Robertson, *Charters*, pp. 28–31.

[60] See Grundy, 'Saxon Charters of Worcestershire', p. 125 for the *geburs* of Laughern; for leases involving labour services, see Robertson, *Charters*, pp. 66–7, 86–7.

[61] N. Neilson, *Customary Rents* (Oxford, 1910), pp. 69–74, 111, 193–7.

developments in peasant conditions in the Anglo-Saxon period. The break up of the great land units could have disrupted old arrangements to the peasants' advantage. More likely, the long-term consequence of changes in the structure of the estate and the growth of opportunities for exchange may well have intensified the demands made by the church on its peasant tenants.

A lord's ability to exercise jurisdiction over his tenants was an essential feature of manorial organization. By 1062 Bishop Wulfstan enjoyed 'sake and soke, and toll and team, over his land and over his men'. The history of the bishops' judicial rights can be taken back to the period 770–855, when immunity clauses in trust-worthy charters state that if anyone on some Worcester properties committed an offence against an outsider he should pay compensation, but no penalty was to be paid outside, showing that the church of Worcester enjoyed the profits of justice. That these profits derived from the bishops' own courts is indicated by the statement: 'if a criminal is caught in open felony three times he shall be delivered to the royal vill', implying that less persistent offenders would be judged by the landowner.[62]

By the late eleventh century the church of Worcester enjoyed a very high franchise in the triple hundred of Oswaldslow, 'by ancient custom, [the bishop] has all revenues of jurisdiction, and all customs therein, pertaining to his demesne, and the king's service and his own, so that no sheriff can have any claim there, neither in any plea, nor in any other cause'. The antiquity of these rights cannot be established, as the charter describing the liberty in 964 is a twelfth-century fabrication, but it seems reasonable to sup-pose that the bishops' judicial privileges date back to the early eleventh century when the triple hundred certainly existed, and could well have originated at a much earlier date.[63] An unusual fea-ture of the hundred of Oswaldslow was that the church of Worcester owned all of the land within its complex and fragmented boundaries – the hundred had been formed by grouping together many of the

[62] Harmer, *Writs*, p. 411; CS 202; CS 351; CS 357; CS 368; CS 487.

[63] *DB*, fo. 172; on the 964 charter, see John, *Land Tenure*, pp. 81–126, and Sawyer, 'Charters of the Reform Movement', pp. 84–93; the hundred presumably existed when Worcestershire was created as a 1200-hide shire, including some of the Worcester manors in Oswaldslow which became 'islands' of Worcestershire in Gloucestershire and Warwickshire; see C. S. Taylor, 'The Origin of the Mercian Shires', in H. P. R. Finberg (ed.), *Gloucestershire Studies* (Leicester, 1957), pp. 17–51.

church's estates (see Map 4). The right of holding the hundred court doubtless strengthened the church's control over its tenants.

THE ESTATE IN 1086

The end product of the evolution of the estate during the Anglo-Saxon period can be seen in the first survey that has survived, that which was included in Domesday Book in 1086. The sections devoted to the properties in the description of Worcestershire give an impression of a united estate because they are headed 'Lands of the church of Worcester'. In fact the separation of the episcopal and monastic manors is clearly indicated in the account of the church's lands in Oswaldslow hundred. In the other Worcestershire hundreds the distinction is not made and it has to be assumed that Alvechurch, Hanbury and Hartlebury belonged to the bishopric, as we know they did shortly afterwards. Alveston in Warwickshire was apparently in the bishop's hands in 1086, but this was a temporary arrangement. The form of the survey preserves the connection between the main demesne manors and the smaller estates split off from them and granted as dependent tenures to laymen in the late Saxon period. For example, at Kempsey we are told that the main demesne manor was assessed at 24 hides, of which 13 hides were retained in the bishop's hands as his demesne manor, and the other 11 hides, at Mucknell, Stoulton, Wolverton and Whittington were listed as being held by three lay tenants.

The total assessment of the whole estate amounted to 580½ hides, of which 241¾ were held in demesne by the bishop, 79½ by the monks, and 259¼ by named lay tenants. This rather underestimates the share of the laity, as at least a further 22½ hides included in the bishop's demesne manors were held by anonymous *radknights*. These figures underline the very large concessions of land made to laymen by successive bishops.

The resources of the bishopric were still substantial. The size of the seventeen demesne manors was much greater than the individual manors held by laymen, the bishop's manors varying from 3½ to 31½ hides each, with twelve being assessed at 10 hides or more, while the lay tenants' average manor was less than 4 hides.

One strength of the bishop's lordship lay in the inclusion of whole settlements within his demesne manors. When divisions had been made, the lay tenants tended to gain outlying hamlets leaving the bishops in control of the central villages. The demesne manors might contain a number of settlements, as indicated by the berewicks, four at Alvechurch and six at Hartlebury and the four 'members' of Westbury, all mentioned in Domesday.

The demesnes varied considerably in size, the main clue to the arable area being the numbers of demesne ploughs given in Domesday, from two to eleven. No geographical pattern emerges from the figures, small demesnes being found in the river valleys, and large ones on heavy soils, such as the seven-plough demesne at Blockley. The demesnes were manned by slaves, of whom 155 are mentioned, often at a rate of 2 per plough, showing that they worked as ploughmen. But the main human resources of the estate were the peasantry, of whom 705 are recorded. Their holdings contained the bulk of the arable land on the estate, judging from the fact that their ploughs outnumbered those of the demesnes in a ratio of 5 to 1 (380 to 71). Most of them, 424 in all, were *villani*, tenants of substantial holdings, with 261 *bordarii* or smallholders.[64] The large numbers of tenants would ensure that the demesnes were well supplied with labour services, the 'rustic work' as Domesday calls it at Wolverton in Kempsey. They also contributed to the bishopric's revenues in other ways. For example, thirty mills had been built on the estate by 1086, a total that had grown up over a long period as the first references to a mill on the estate occur at Stoke in Westbury in 883.[65] The mills might render substantial quantities in grain, ten loads at Hartlebury for example, but most often in cash, up to 50s. 0d at Northwick, deriving from the tolls taken on the peasants' corn.

At the top of the hierarchy of tenants on the demesne manors were twenty-one *radknights*, who held about a hide of land each (many of the *villani* presumably had a yardland, the fourth part of a hide, or less) and owed mainly riding services and duties of a fairly light and honourable nature. There were also three reeves, administrators who could also have large holdings.[66]

The penetration of exchange into the rural economy is indicated both by the numbers of urban properties, mentioned above, and the ability of the compilers of Domesday to put a cash value on each

[64] R. Lennard, *Rural England, 1086–1135* (Oxford, 1959), pp. 339–64.

[65] P. Rahtz and D. Bullough, 'The parts of an Anglo-Saxon mill', in P. Clemoes (ed.), *Anglo-Saxon England*, vi (Cambridge, 1977), p. 23.

[66] Lennard, *Rural England*, pp. 271–6.

manor. The values varied between £4 and £38, the estate total in 1086 being nearly £270. The values can be shown on other estates to represent the sums paid annually by farmers who took on the management of the demesnes. In reality they would have paid part of their farms in kind, but Domesday's assumption of a potential cash income is still significant.[67]

The Domesday description gives an impression of a large, populous and highly organized estate, yet there may have been room for growth. There were some hides described as 'waste'; thirteen of the seventeen manors had woodlands attached to them, some of them large by the standards of their region.[68] Even allowing for detached woods at some distance from the parent manor, like that at Ripple which lay in Malvern, there were evidently opportunities for clearance and the extension of the arable area, notably in the Severn valley.

Having traced the history of the gains, and then the losses and divisions of the church of Worcester's properties between 680 and 1086, and having used the fragmentary evidence to attempt an investigation of the topography, economy and social structure of the estate, we must pause to examine more closely the relationship between the bishops and their prominent lay tenants, before going on to follow the post-eleventh-century development of the land and its inhabitants.

[67] *Ibid.*, pp. 105–41.
[68] H. C. Darby and I. B. Terrett, *The Domesday Geography of Midland England*, 2nd edn (Cambridge, 1971), p. 245.

2. Feudalism and the bishopric

Is it possible to describe the organization of the estates of the church of Worcester as 'feudal' in the Anglo-Saxon period? The answer will depend on the definition of feudalism employed. If all that is required for a society to be regarded as feudal is that tenants of any kind should owe services in exchange for their lands, then the feudalism of the bishopric estate would be easily established, as by the tenth century both the peasants of the demesne manors and the lessees of the substantial pieces of land let by Bishop Oswald, had obligations to perform services for the bishop. However, a normal characteristic of medieval European feudalism was that in addition to the labour owed by the peasantry, which can be regarded as a necessary precondition for feudal development, the more substantial tenants owed military services for their lands and as vassals were in a dependent relationship with their lords, but that relationship had an honourable and reciprocal character.

The evidence from Worcester has been used as the corner-stone of the argument that Anglo-Saxon society in general was feudal. It is known from Worcester sources that late Saxon bishops had important secular responsibilities, such as the administration of the law.[1] Did they also have obligations to provide troops from their lands for the royal army? Just as Bishop Wulfstan II (1062–95) continued in office long after the Conquest, was there also a continuity in the military and tenurial arrangements of the see? These questions have caused controversy among historians for more than eighty years.

Both sides in the controversy recognize that in order to demonstrate the existence of feudal tenures it is necessary to find evidence for a contract between the king and his tenants, in this case the

[1] F. Liebermann (ed.), *Die Gesetze der Angelsachsen* (Halle, 1903), i, pp. 477–8 gives a list of episcopal duties, with much emphasis on secular responsibilities, apparently compiled at Worcester. On Wulfstan II's attendance at shire courts, see *Vita Wulfstani of William of Malmesbury*, ed. R. R. Darlington (Camden Soc., 3rd ser., xl, 1928), p. 21.

bishops, for the provision of troops and to show in turn that the bishops enfeoffed their dependents with lands in exchange for military service.

Evidence for both types of arrangement has been seen in the Worcester charters. The document known as *Altitonantis* is claimed as showing that the bishops were committed to provide a quota of troops for royal military service a century before the Norman Conquest. *Altitonantis* purports to be a charter of 964 by which Edgar created the triple hundred of Oswaldslow as a jurisdictional immunity and as a 'shipful', that is, a group of three hundreds providing sixty men at a rate of one man for each five hides for a ship in the royal fleet.[2] Its protagonists, F. W. Maitland and Eric John, recognized that *Altitonantis* is a post-Conquest fabrication, but assumed that it incorporates an earlier, now lost, text. The critics argue convincingly that the whole document was composed in the twelfth century, citing the absence of any trace of an original in the eleventh-century Worcester cartularies.[3]

The lands leased to laymen (*loenland*), discussed above, have been seen as fiefs granted for military service. The leases themselves sometimes refer to the three necessary services, including military service, and the Ditchford lease of 1051 × 1053 mentions service 'on the king's summons'. More explicit is Oswald's letter to Edgar which lays down the conditions on which leases were granted, mainly riding services and other miscellaneous duties owed to the bishop, and states that the lessees must 'fulfil the service due to him [the bishop] or that due to the king' and should be subject to the will of the bishop, who is referred to as *archiductor* (chief leader), in exchange for their benefice.[4] Services owed by the leaseholders are also mentioned in Domesday and in Hemming's narrative of the loss of lands. The critics emphasize that military service was owed as a public obligation on all land, but not as a specific duty by tenants of *loenland* rendered to their lord. Accordingly Oswald's letter contains no explicit reference to military service; it may refer to a specialized group of tenants, the *radmen* or *radknights*. In

---

[2] Maitland, *Domesday Book and Beyond*, pp. 267–318; John, *Land Tenure in Early England*, pp. 80–139.

[3] *The Cartulary of Worcester Cathedral Priory*, ed. Darlington, pp. xiii–xix; Sawyer, 'Charters of the Reform Movement', pp. 84–93.

[4] Robertson, *Charters*, pp. 208–9; R. Allen Brown, *Origins of English Feudalism* (London, 1973), p. 134.

any case, the letter may have been fabricated at the end of the eleventh century.[5]

The Maitland/John argument, besides seeing the essential characteristics of a feudal organization before 1066, goes on to propose that the arrangements continued after the Conquest, as the bishopric's feudal quota in the twelfth century was sixty, corresponding to the tenth-century shipful, and the twelfth-century knights' fees were assessed in five-hide units, so that one man served from five hides, as in the tenth century.[6] This is the weakest part of their case, as the sixty warriors of the pre-Conquest period came from the 300 hides of Oswaldslow hundred, whereas the *servitium debitum* of 60 (which the bishops claimed successfully should be only fifty) was raised from the 580 or so hides of the whole estate. The five-hide fees of the twelfth century were not universal among the episcopal knights, and the rule-of-thumb that 'five hides make one knight's fee' applied only to land held by tenants, while pre-Conquest calculations included in the hidation the lands held by the bishops in demesne.[7]

Does nothing remain, then, of the original Maitland hypothesis? Some elements are still valid. The critics, such as F. M. Stenton and R. Allen Brown, use such a specialized definition that any possibility of Anglo-Saxon feudalism is ruled out – they insist that feudalism must involve precise statements of services, the use of mounted knights in warfare and castles.[8] This is an unrealistic position. For example, the absence of detailed descriptions of a knight's services from Worcester documents of the twelfth century would lead us to deny, if these represented the only evidence for the period, the existence of feudal tenures even at that late date. It seems more appropriate to use as a model the developing feudalism of Carolingian Gaul, in which the main elements were the fusion of ties of clientage and grants of land conditional on service,

[5] F. M. Stenton, *The First Century of English Feudalism*, 2nd edn (Oxford, 1961), pp. 123–31; Allen Brown, *Origins of English Feudalism*, pp. 55–8; V. H. Galbraith, 'Notes on the Career of Samson, Bishop of Worcester (1096–1112)', *Eng. Hist. Rev.*, lxxxii (1967), pp. 100–1.

[6] M. Hollings, 'The Survival of the Five-Hide Unit in the Western Midlands', *Eng. Hist. Rev.*, lxiii (1948), pp. 453–87.

[7] C. Warren Hollister, *Anglo-Saxon Military Institutions* (Oxford, 1962), pp. 53–5; J. O. Prestwich, 'Anglo-Norman Feudalism and the Problem of Continuity', *P and P*, xxvi (1963), pp. 43–4; Allen Brown, *Origins of English Feudalism*, p. 62.

[8] Stenton, *The First Century of English Feudalism*, pp. 216–17; Allen Brown, *Origins of English Feudalism*, pp. 21–32.

together with the delegation and fragmentation of state power.

In spite of the discrediting of *Altitonantis*, it still seems likely that Oswaldslow formed a unit of military organization before the Conquest. The bishop's jurisdiction in Oswaldslow was regarded as ancient in 1086. The hundred could well have been in existence in the early eleventh century when the Mercian shires were created, and the provision of ships by groups of three hundreds ordered.[9] In the late eleventh century there are references to Oswaldslow landholders serving by land and sea, including a steersman who commanded the ship.[10]

The bishop's control over Oswaldslow in the eleventh century was such that the royal officials had no access to the hundred. The bishop 'has all revenues of jurisdiction... and the king's service and his own'. So as well as holding the hundred court, the bishop organized services, including the hundred's contribution to the king's army and navy.[11]

Who were the troops? If peasants served, there would have been hundreds of potential recruits in Oswaldslow hundred. It seems more likely that military service, at least in what C. Warren Hollister calls the 'select fyrd', would have been performed mainly by those with the wealth to acquire equipment and the leisure to train and fight.[12] These would have been substantial landowners, but as the church of Worcester owned all of the land in Oswaldslow there were no independent lay landowners to contribute their military service. Instead there were the thegns, *cnihts* and others who had been granted *loenland*. They can be identified with the 'freemen of another lord' mentioned in Worcestershire's Domesday entry, who, if they failed to do military service, paid a fine to their lord, who in turn paid it to the king. So it seems likely that the bishop's tenants performed service under the organization of the bishop. Some of these at least had ties of personal dependence with the bishop – the leases of the late tenth century refer to recipients of land as the bishop's 'man', 'faithful man' and 'client'.[13]

[9] Hollister, *Anglo-Saxon Military Institutions*, pp. 111–15.
[10] *DB*, fo. 173; J. H. Round, *Feudal England* (London, 1909), p. 309.
[11] This seems to be accepted by Stenton, *First Century of English Feudalism*, p. 128.
[12] Hollister, *Anglo-Saxon Military Institutions*, pp. 59–84.
[13] *DB*, fo. 172; *HC*, i, pp. 126–7, 158, 162–3, 167–8, 185–6, 192–3, 202–4, 207–10.

This still falls short of demonstrating that the tenants owed military service to the bishop in return for their lands. The opponents of the Maitland theory stress that the leases were held for miscellaneous services to the bishop, and the public obligation of fyrd service was something quite separate. It is true that Domesday's account of the services owed in 1066 suggests that there was no uniform system of tenure – this tenant 'served', that tenant 'served as he could bargain' (*serviebat sicut deprecari poterat*), some 'served as the bishop wills' and others paid farms. Most of the Domesday entries emphasize service to the bishop, though a few mention royal service: Edric, the steersman of the Oswaldslow ship, 'served with the other services belonging to the king and bishop'; Eadgyth 'rendered sake and soke in the manor [of Grimley] and all service to the king'.[14] Maitland's critics argue that these show that their obligations to the king and the bishop were different.[15] The services owed to the bishop were confined to escort duties, assistance with hunting, administrative work and so on. Had the bishops really given up hundreds of hides of land in the form of about seventy substantial holdings merely to obtain such relatively minor services? Surely some more important need lay behind the expensive and complex system of leased lands? The bishops must have granted leases on the understanding that their tenants would be available to serve in the king's fyrd. The principle lying behind their service may have been one of public obligation, but *de facto* the bishop had granted them their land, he was their lord, and in Oswaldslow he had been delegated with jurisdiction over them and administered the hundred's contingent to the fyrd. Brictric of Bushley, in 1066, 'rendered to the bishop's soke whatever he owed for the king's service', clearly stating the bishop's position as the intermediary between king and subject. The blurring of the distinction between obligations of different origins is suggested by Domesday's description of the terms of tenure of four free men who held Bishampton in 1066 – they owed 'sake and soke', churchscot, burial fees and military expeditions by land and sea. Jurisdictional obligations, ecclesiastical taxes and military duties had all been brought

[14] *DB*, fo. 173.
[15] Allen Brown, *Origins of English Feudalism*, pp. 55–9; M. Powicke, *Military Obligation in Medieval England* (Oxford, 1962), pp. 22–3, suggests that the riding services were public obligations, but still regards them as different from later military service.

together as dues and services under the bishop's control.[16] The juxtaposition of obligations could represent a stage in their seignorialization, by which the bishop would become the recipient of services in his capacity as lord.

The process by which the bishops became interposed in the social hierarchy between the king and his subjects was not necessarily confined to the rather peculiar case of Oswaldslow hundred. Many of the leases were granted outside Oswaldslow hundred. For example, five leases are known for lands associated with Bishop's Cleeve, and five tenants held land there in 1086. Cleeve was assessed at thirty hides, so presumably it was liable to provide six men for a Gloucestershire ship-soke. Surely the leasing of the Cleeve lands and the need to provide men for the fyrd are not unconnected? It is difficult to believe that a powerful lord like the bishop would not play some part in organizing the services from his estate regardless of whether he exercised hundredal jurisdiction.

We must conclude at least that all of the preconditions for feudalism were present on the Worcester estate before the Conquest. The main obstacle that prevents the general acceptance of this is the argument that the bishop's military functions were performed in his rôle as a substitute royal official rather than as a great lord. In view of the well-known tendencies of continental royal officials, notably the counts, to win relative independence in the period of emergent feudalism, it must be admitted that the same potential existed in late Saxon England. Perhaps the term 'proto-feudalism', despised by some historians, would be an appropriate term in the case of the Worcester estate.

The argument that the pre-Conquest bishopric exhibits proto-feudal characteristics can to some extent be separated from the notion of continuity of military organization.

There was undoubtedly a tendency for the same lands to be held as dependent tenures of the bishopric both before and after the Norman Conquest. One hundred and sixteen major pieces of land are mentioned in tenth and early eleventh-century leases. Fifty-two of these appear in Domesday as land held by tenants, and a further eighteen in twelfth-century texts. This leaves forty-six

---

[16] *DB*, fo. 173.

which were leased before the Conquest, but were not named as tenant lands later. Some appear in Domesday under different names: Battenhall was probably incorporated in the Domesday estate of Whittington, and Bentley in the land at Holt. Some were not mentioned as being held of the church in 1086 because they had been taken away from the church's control by the means which so worried Hemming (see Chapter 1); this applies in at least fifteen cases. So, with the exception of about six properties that had been taken back into the church's demesnes by the time of Domesday, the bulk of lands leased to the laity before 1066 subsequently remained in the hands of laymen.

Within this broad context of continuity, there were many changes both before and after 1066. This is indicated by the changes in hidage of leased estates; at Southam (in Cleeve) a two-hide property was leased in 991, a five-hide property in 1038 × 1046, and land there was assessed at six hides in 1086.[17] The hidages given in pre-Conquest leases coincide in only twenty cases out of seventy with those in later documents.

After 1066 changes continued. New tenancies were created, for example by letting out demesne land at Kempsey to Urse D'Abitot, and some lands held by tenants in 1066 or 1086 were taken into demesne in the late eleventh century, notably in the case of Alveston.[18]

There was a radical break in the personnel of the bishop's tenants. Although the Anglo-Saxon bishop survived the upheavals of the Conquest, an influx of Normans and other Frenchmen meant that by 1086 only eight out of the thirty-six tenants and subtenants had Anglo-Saxon or Danish names.[19]

There were also changes in the terms of tenure. If the leaseholds of 1066 were identical with the Norman knight's fees, we would expect a smooth transition from old to new arrangements. In fact Bishop Wulfstan II seems to have had problems in fulfilling the demands of the new system. He had to find a quota of knights numbering either fifty or sixty – the figures are not recorded until the twelfth century, though J. H. Round conjectured that a quota of fifty lay behind William II's demand for a relief of £250

[17] *HC*, i, pp. 232–3; Finberg, *Early Charters*, p. 69; *DB*, fo. 165.
[18] *The Cartulary of Worcester Cathedral Priory*, ed. Darlington, pp. xliii–xliv.
[19] O. von Feilitzen, *The Pre-Conquest Personal Names of Domesday Book* (Uppsala, 1937).

in 1095.[20] The bishops believed in 1166 that they had made enough enfeoffments by 1096 to secure the services of nearly fifty knights (forty-nine-and-four-fifths to be precise). If the idea that a five-hide estate would make a knight's fee is applied to the Domesday figures, we see that a total of about 260 hides held of the estate as dependent tenures in 1086, was just sufficient for fifty knights. The mathematics behind this arrangement in itself suggests a major change from the shipful system. But the new fiefs did not work as expected, because the tenants, according to the *carta* of 1166, admitted service of only thirty-seven-and-a-half knights. Wulfstan's *Vita* tells us that he kept knights in his household, perhaps because they had not been endowed with land.[21] New enfeoffments were still being made in the twelfth century to fill the gaps.

Now the discrepancy between the theoretical quota and the actual numbers owing service arose because of the behaviour of the 'powerful men', notably Urse D'Abitot, who obtained much land from the bishop but was not willing to do full service for it. This probably occurred, not just because of a change of personnel, but also because a transition to new tenures was involved. The version of Domesday included in Hemming's Cartulary states this clearly: 'he who holds that land on lease could not . . . retain it by usurping hereditary right, or claim it as his fee [*feudam*] except in accordance with the bishop's will and in accordance with the agreement'.[22] Leased lands were not fiefs and new contracts had to be negotiated after the Conquest. The circumstances under which this might happen are described by Hemming in the case of a hide at Greenhill, which had been held by an Anglo-Saxon tenant in 1066, but was subsequently seized by Urse D'Abitot who afterwards held it 'on condition that he would discharge all services due from it to the king'. In Domesday we learn that Croome had been held by Sirof in 1066 and on his death Wulfstan gave his daughter in marriage to a knight who held the land and served the bishop.[23]

We have seen that tenures varied considerably in 1066. They

[20] Round, *Feudal England*, p. 311.
[21] *RBW*, iv, pp. 412–13; *Red Book of the Exchequer*, ed. H. Hall (London, 1896), i, pp. 300–1; *Vita Wulfstani*, ed. Darlington, pp. 55–6 refers to knights billetted on Wulfstan in an invasion scare, but pp. 46–7 indicate that some knights normally lived in the household.
[22] *HC*, i, p. 287.
[23] *HC*, i, p. 257; *DB*, fo. 173.

continued to be mixed afterwards, creating complexities that continued to be contentious in the twelfth century.

The later history of Worcester's feudal organization has many similarities with other church estates. Worcester had been given a disproportionately heavy burden of knight service. Its quota of fifty or sixty knights was comparable with those of the much wealthier sees of Canterbury and Winchester.[24] The variations in the *servitia debita* often defy rational explanation, but perhaps Worcester's high figure was fixed in the knowledge of its large number of existing dependent tenures. Because of the difficulties in obtaining services from all of the tenants, new fees had to be created during the twelfth century in order to enable the bishops to meet their commitments to the crown. Four new fees were created in the period 1096–1112, and a further four in 1115–23. At least eight new grants for military service were made between 1125 and 1157, probably equivalent to two new fees. The arithmetic of the 1166 return of fees is confused, but the total seems to have been calculated at fifty-three-and-one-sixth fees. Some small holdings, not recorded until *c.*1182, show that a few new grants for knight service were made after 1166.[25]

The new fees were partly the result of changing the status of lands already held by tenants for non-military services. For example, *radmen*'s holdings at Darlingscott, Gotherington and Hallow were converted into tenures for knight service.[26] Some were carved out of the bishops' demesnes, as at Tidmington, Upton-on-Severn and some of the 'members' of Westbury-on-Trym.

Although the bishop's contingent served in the Welsh expedition of 1182 and on campaigns in the 1220s, they normally discharged their obligations by paying scutage.[27] Henry II demanded payment for sixty fees, but eventually allowed the bishop's claim of owing only fifty. In 1166 the bishop was found to have enfeoffed a surplus of three- and-one-sixth knights and the king claimed scutage

[24] H. M. Chew, *The English Ecclesiastical Tenants-in-Chief and Knight Service* (Oxford, 1932), pp. 4–7.
[25] *RBW*, iv, pp. 412–18, 430–49; *Red Book of the Exchequer*, pp. 41, 300–1.
[26] *RBW*, iv, pp. 441, 431, 440; *VCH Worcs.*, i, p. 325.
[27] *RBW*, iv, p. 441; Chew, *Tenants-in-Chief*, p. 52.

for these, but the agreed number by 1186 was forty-nine-and-a half.[28]

In the thirteenth century the size of the quota was drastically reduced to three, as was normal, and the bishops paid a fine in lieu of service. Early in the reign of Edward I the fine was assessed at £80, or £26 13s. 4d. per knight. This was increased to a total of £132 for the Scottish campaign of 1300.[29]

The bishops lost lands in order to make enfeoffments but derived some financial benefits. From the late twelfth century they were able to levy rather more in scutage than they paid to the king. In the late thirteenth century Bishop Giffard raised £99 from his tenants and paid a fine to the crown of £80. There were also the occasional profits of feudal incidents. Reliefs paid at the rate of £5 per fee in the thirteenth century were owed by incoming tenants; in the case of the large Beauchamp fee this amounted to £75. Wardships could also be lucrative. For example, the wardship of the half-fee held by the Russell family at Aust in Henbury was farmed for £11 6s. 8d. per annum in 1286.[30]

The 'centrifugal' tendencies of feudal society, by which tenants established closer control of their fiefs, limited the benefits available to the bishops as feudal lords. The late Saxon leases had been granted for three lives only and the lines of inheritance specified in some of Oswald's leases (those made in favour of members of his own family) were varied, not necessarily allowing the land to pass from father to son. The post-Conquest fiefs seem to have been heritable so that the lands became, in Bloch's phrase, 'the patrimony of the vassal'. Some of the tenants were powerful lords in their own right, such as Urse D'Abitot, whose large holding descended in the Beauchamp family in the twelfth and thirteenth centuries. These lands were always lightly burdened, so that in the late twelfth century it was believed that William Beauchamp should have owed twenty-two-and-a-half knights for his 109½ hides, but he provided only fifteen. Other magnates claimed similarly light services – the earls of Gloucester acknowledged one knight's fee and the Bohuns four, though the bishops thought they

---

[28] *Great Rolls of the Pipe* (Record Commission, 1844), p. 63; *Great Rolls of the Pipe, 5 Henry II* (Pipe Roll Soc., i, 1884), pp. 24 ff.; *Red Book of the Exchequer*, i, pp. 18, 41, 51, 59, 72, 85.

[29] Chew, *Tenants-in-Chief*, p. 32; *RBW*, iv, pp. 443–4.

[30] *Reg. Giffard*, pp. 73, 288.

were entitled to seven-and-a-half knights from each of them. By *c.*1182 these claims had been accepted by the bishops but a dozen lesser tenants were disputing the quantity of service owed.[31] In this respect, continuity with the late Saxon period is readily apparent; a very similar withdrawal of *loenland* from the bishop's control lies behind some of Hemming's complaints of lost land.

Sometimes the bishops were able to resist the erosion of their authority over their military tenants. Wulfstan recovered some lands lost before the Conquest and was able to win Alveston from lay control. Henry I supported the bishops when their feudal tenants were apparently questioning their rights of jurisdiction. In *c.*1186 the bishop of Hereford was made to recognize that he held Inkberrow of Worcester as a full knight's fee and not a half as he claimed, when the case was brought before a jury of twenty-four knights. In the 1230s and 1240s Bishop Cantilupe fought a number of lawsuits in order to reassert his rights over seven tenants by knight service.[32]

In the long term, in the fourteenth and fifteenth centuries, the holders of the Worcester fiefs established themselves as independent landowners. Their original military services ceased to be demanded, and the bishops received from them neither homage nor the incidents of feudal tenure (see Chapter 6).

The chief importance of the leases and enfeoffments for social history lies in the contribution they made to the landed resources of many laymen. In social terms there were some similarities between the pre-Conquest and post-Conquest distribution of lands among the tenants. In the tenth century, of sixty-eight lessees, fifty-two received one or two grants only, and the individual holdings of *loenland* do not seem usually to have exceeded six hides. The leaseholders may have had other lands, but most, described as thegns, were probably landholders on a small scale, and some could have lived exclusively on the lands granted to them by the bishops. It is possible that a few of the lessees held substantial amounts of land from the bishop, though the absence of surnames makes any certain identifications impossible. For example, eight separate

[31] *RBW*, iv, pp. 412–18, 431–44.
[32] *Vita Wulfstani*, ed. Darlington, pp. 24–5; *DB*, fo. 238; *Cartulary of Worcester Cathedral Priory*, ed. Darlington, pp. 17–18; White Book, fo. 40; *Annales Monastici*, iv, ed. H. R. Luard (Rolls Series, 1869), pp. 429–30, 432.

grants, totalling eighteen and a half hides, were made in the tenth century to 'Æthelweard'. The name could refer to two or more tenants but it has been suggested that at least some of the grants to Æthelweard were made to the Wessex ealdorman with that name.[33]

After the Conquest the Worcester lands were concentrated more into the hands of major landholders such as Urse D'Abitot. By c.1182 the Beauchamps, Bohuns and earls of Gloucester had very large holdings. But of the fifty mesne tenants recorded in the list of c.1182, only fifteen had more than five hides and much of this land was sublet. For example, William Beauchamp had fourteen subtenants, and some of these had yet more subtenants below them. So the main beneficiaries of the enfeoffments in terms of the actual occupation of the land were about eighty tenants and subtenants each holding five hides or less. The knight's fee or fraction of a fee held of the bishopric represented the main landed resources of some of these tenants and thus formed the basis of the fortunes of gentry and knightly families in later centuries. A notable example of continuous occupation of such land is provided by the Throckmorton family, who took their name from the village of Throckmorton in the bishopric manor of Fladbury where they held land from the late twelfth century onwards.[34]

[33] Hollings, 'The Survival of the Five-Hide Unit', p. 480.
[34] VCH Worcs., iii, pp. 356–7.

3. The seignorial economy, 1086–1350

The main lines of development of the large English estates in the twelfth and thirteenth centuries have been established from a number of well-documented examples. The twelfth century appears to have been a period of stability, in which landlords reduced their demesnes by letting out a part of them in order to fulfil feudal obligations or simply for rent payments from tenants. The remaining demesnes were generally farmed out for fixed renders.[1] All of this changed in the late twelfth and early thirteenth centuries; lords expanded their revenues from their estates.

This was partly achieved by acquiring new lands, by pious donations and purchase in the case of ecclesiastics and by marriage and politics, as well as purchase, by the laity. Not everyone gained in the redistribution of property, and we are aware of casualties among the small lay landowners who fell into debt and lost lands. Landlords could also benefit from the clearance of new lands, providing both additions to the demesnes and new tenant rents.[2]

Historians have often paid most attention to the managerial revolution of the decades around 1200, when demesnes were taken into direct management, allowing the lords to participate directly in the growing market for agricultural produce. On some estates this culminated in the phase of 'high farming' in the late thirteenth and early fourteenth centuries when demesne cultivation and administration reached a peak of efficiency.[3] However, an

[1] M. M. Postan, 'The Chronology of Labour Services', in *Essays on Medieval Agriculture and General Problems of the Medieval Economy* (Cambridge, 1973), pp. 89–106; E. Miller, 'England in the Twelfth and Thirteenth Centuries, an Economic Contrast?', *Econ. Hist. Rev.*, 2nd ser., xxiv (1971), pp. 1–14; R. Lennard, *Rural England* (Oxford, 1959), pp. 105–212.

[2] Good examples of estates expanding by purchase and marriage are those of Ramsey and the Clares, see J. A. Raftis, *The Estates of Ramsey Abbey* (Toronto, 1957), pp. 109–12; M. Altschul, *A Baronial Family in Medieval England: The Clares, 1217–1314* (Baltimore, 1965), pp. 28–39. On the contrast between large and small landowners, see M. M. Postan, *The Medieval Economy and Society* (London, 1972), pp. 159–69; E. King, *Peterborough Abbey, 1086–1310* (Cambridge, 1973), pp. 35–54; P. R. Coss, 'Sir Geoffrey de Langley and the Crisis of the Knightly Class in Thirteenth-Century England', *P and P*, lxviii (1975), pp. 1–37.

[3] R. A. L. Smith, *Canterbury Cathedral Priory* (Cambridge, 1943); I. Kershaw, *Bolton Priory* (Oxford, 1973), *passim*; D. Knowles, *The Religious Orders in England* (Cambridge, 1948), i, pp. 37–48.

essential feature of the thirteenth century was the maximization of income from rents. The tenants often provided much of the labour on the demesnes, and their cash payments could exceed in value the profits of selling corn and wool. Judicial profits and the dues arising from lordship were also exploited and could account for a substantial proportion of seignorial revenues.[4]

As a result of these changes, the incomes of individual landlords often more than doubled in the course of the thirteenth century, though expansion ceased during the early fourteenth.

Was this thirteenth century 'boom' a mere illusion? The change to direct management in the decades around 1200 was provoked by a sudden inflation which doubled prices between 1180 and 1210.[5] Prices tended to rise also in some decades of the thirteenth and early fourteenth centuries. As well as making high farming profitable, price movements also affected the lord's expenditure so that rising costs ate into real income. There were other areas of increased expenditure, notably in taxation. Also, critics of landlords' economic policies have noted a low level of capital investment, so that the thirteenth century 'boom' could be seen as a bubble, a short-term and short-sighted exploitation of land and people that was bound to lead to an eventual contraction.[6]

Because of the absence of a series of accounts, the bishops of Worcester's estates are much less well documented than others in this period, but it is still possible to sketch the major changes. Figures indicating the income of the bishops can be obtained from a variety of documents and they are summarized in Table 2.

The Domesday valuations probably correspond to the annual value at farm, so that the totals for the estate of £246 and £270 are a guide at least to the bishop's potential income. The figures are

---

[4] For an example of the prominence of rents see E. Miller, *The Abbey and Bishopric of Ely* (Cambridge, 1951), pp. 93–4. On the significance of profits of lordship see S. Painter, *Studies in the History of the English Feudal Barony* (Baltimore, 1943), pp. 121–3; R. H. Hilton, *A Medieval Society* (London, 1966), pp. 146–8.

[5] P. D. A. Harvey, 'The English Inflation of 1180–1220', *P and P*, lxi (1973), pp. 3–30.

[6] R. H. Hilton, 'Rent and Capital Formation in Feudal Society', in *The English Peasantry in the Later Middle Ages* (Oxford, 1975), pp. 177–90; E. Miller, 'The English Economy in the Thirteenth Century', *P and P*, xxviii (1964), pp. 21–40; R. H. Hilton, 'Y eût-il une crise générale de la Féodalité?', *Annales ESC*, vi (1951), pp. 23–30.

Table 2. *Annual income of the bishopric of Worcester, 1066–1313*

Date	Annual income	References and Notes
1066	£246	*DB*, fos. 164–5, 172–4, 238
1086	£269 14s. 6d.	*ibid.*
1161–2	*c.*£300	*Pipe Roll Soc.*, v (1885), p. 61.
1184–5	*c.*£250	*Pipe Roll Soc.*, xxxiv (1913), p. 126 (half-year only
		Gross income £131 15s. 6d.
		Net income £125 17s. 1d.)
1185–6	*c.*£330	*Pipe Roll Soc.*, xxxvi (1914), p. 42.
		(three-quarters of a year only
		Gross income £262 19s. 0d.
		Net income £245 11s. 6d.)
1211–12	£345 9s. 8½d.	*Pipe Roll Soc.*, new ser., xxx (1954), pp. 60–1.
1266	*c.*£580 +	M. Howell, *Regalian Right in Medieval England* (London, 1962), p. 231, quoting a pipe roll. (four–five months only – the date of the end of the vacancy is uncertain.
		Gross income £264 15s. 4½d.
		Net income £241 11s. 1d.)
*c.*1290	£1,170 1s. 8d.	*RBW passim*. Total of values in the *Alia Extenta*
1299	£1,191 10s. 6¾d.	*RBW*, iv. p. 401.
1302–3	£850 18s. 8d.	*RBW*, iv, pp. 546–7. Gross income £903 5s. 8d.
1311–12	£1,162 8s. 10d.	*Reg. Reynolds*, pp. 32, 33, 35, 44–6, 51–3.
1312–13	£1,307	*Reg. Reynolds*, pp. 58, 60, 68, 73.

something of an overstatement as those for some of the Gloucestershire manors include the sub-manors. The increase between 1066 and 1086 is mainly due to the increased valuations of the Warwickshire manors, and may not reflect any real growth in income, but may stem from variations in the Domesday survey from county to county.

The twelfth-century figures come from the royal pipe rolls, when the temporalities lay in the king's hands during vacancies. In 1161–2 the entry is partly illegible but shows that William Beauchamp was paying at least £300 for custody of the bishopric. The sums for the 1180s show the income from part of year only, but suggest that a full year's revenue was still in the region of £300.

A slight upward trend in income is apparent in the early thirteenth century. In 1211–12 gross receipts totalled £482 5s. 2½d., but £833s. 4d. of this came from arrears of the previous year, and expenses reduced the current income from the year to £345. The estates were probably worth more than this, as William de Cantilupe had proferred 500 marks and 5 palfreys to obtain custody of the bishopric; and he had been able to pay off £100 after two years, suggesting that he was making profits in excess of the sums paid into the exchequer.

A leap in income seems to have come between 1212 and the late 1260s. In the short vacancy of 1266, revenues to the exchequer imply an income of at least £580 per annum, and two years later an incomplete list of rents gives a total of £358 7s. 4¼d. per annum, a figure which excludes such items as perquisites of courts, as well as demesne profits.[7] No exact figure for total income can be given for the late 1260s, but it must have been near to double that of the late twelfth century.

More precise evidence is available at the end of the thirteenth century. The 'other extent' of c.1290 gives a 'total value' based on rents, farms, court profits and a valuation of demesne land, and also figures for the 'profit of wainage and stock'. The resulting total of £1,170 could well be an underestimate as it excludes some variable items such as pannage of pigs, tolls and feudal incidents. The valor total of 1299 of £1,192 is again likely to be a slight underassessment as the revenues from the borough of Stratford-on-Avon are omitted.

The keeper's accounts of the vacancy of 1302–3 record a meagre net income of £851 but in a normal year the estate would have yielded much more than this. The royal keeper sold the demesne grain while it was still green in the fields for about half of its current market price if harvested and pastoral husbandry yielded nothing because, according to custom, the demesne stock had been sold by the previous bishop's executors.

An annual income in the region of £1,200 suggested by the extents of the 1290s, seems to be confirmed by notes in the register of Bishop Reynolds. In the financial year 1311–12 the bishop's receiver sent £1, 035 to the bishop, who was absent in London because of his position as Chancellor. In addition £53 was paid to merchants in Worcester and London on the bishop's behalf and a further £74 allowed to the reeves of individual manors who had given money direct to the clerk of the bishop's household, making a total of

[7] *RBW*, iv, p. 465.

£1,162 of disposable income. In the following year the receiver sent £1,307 to Reynolds, but this sum may include income from the financial year 1313–14.

To sum up, it seems likely that the bishops' income in the period 1066–1212 was between £250 and £350 per annum. There may have been an upward movement, but it was small. By the late 1260s income had risen to at least £600, and in the years 1290–1313 the bishops could expect to receive about £1,200. This three- to four-fold increase, in about a century, represents a steeper rise than that recorded on other estates in the same period.

Income from spiritualities, that is, dues paid to the bishop in his episcopal capacity, are not as well recorded as the estate income. In the half-year vacancy of 1184–5 the archdeaconries rendered £26 6s. 8d. and in the vacancy of 1302–3 the cathedral priory received a total of £118 15s. 11d. from spiritualities.[8]

How did the bishops of Worcester increase their incomes so rapidly? The acquisition of new lands played a small part. The seventeen demesne manors surveyed in Domesday provided the bulk of the wealth of the bishops throughout the middle ages. As has been argued already, they provided the estate with a variety of resources and also formed a convenient network of residences for bishops moving round the diocese, as depicted in the *Vita* of Wulfstan and the registers of those late medieval bishops who were resident and active in their diocese.[9]

Subsequent additions were usually made in order to expand or consolidate existing properties so that the bulk of the transactions involved the bishops obtaining land from their own tenants. The main period of acquisitions covers the episcopates of Sylvester of Evesham (1216–18), William de Blois (1218–36), Walter Cantilupe (1236–66) and Godfrey Giffard (1268–1302). Most gains, about forty in all, were made by purchase and throw some light on the workings of the land-market.

The concentration of acquisitions in the thirteenth century contrasts with the grants of lands by the bishops for military service in the twelfth century. Indeed, some of the transactions show

[8] *Pipe Roll, 31 Henry II* (Pipe Roll Soc., xxxiv, 1913), p. 126; *Reg. Sede Vacante*, pp. xv–xxvii.
[9] *Vita Wulfstani*, ed. Darlington, pp. 21, 36, 37, 49, 51 (mentioning journeys); pp. 28–30, 30–1, 41–2 (mentioning him residing on bishopric manors).

bishops after 1200 recovering by purchase, grants made by their recent predecessors. A few gifts were made by thirteenth-century bishops to religious houses, notably the Cistercian nunnery of Whitstones and Little Malvern Priory, both receiving lands and other benefits on a very small scale.[10]

Land was bought for a variety of purposes. Tenant holdings were purchased for the sake of their rents. For example, at Bishop's Cleeve in the mid-thirteenth century Walter Cantilupe paid in three separate transactions sums of 28 marks, $3\frac{1}{2}$ marks and 40s. 0d. in order to gain some twenty-three holdings and various parcels of land held by a free tenant. The holdings were subtenancies from which the bishop could obtain income only by buying out the intermediate tenant. In 1299 these rents acquired by Cantilupe were valued at £4 6s. 1d. In some cases the purchased lands were bought to expand the demesne, like the enclosed pasture at Throckmorton bought by Bishop Blois for 5 marks. One of the most expensive deals was necessary to recover a lost asset – Blois spent 80 marks on Fladbury mill which his predecessor Sylvester had granted to his brother, Adam.[11]

Much land was bought in the woodland manors of north Worcestershire, Hanbury and Alvechurch. These were centres of assarting activity in the thirteenth century and the bishops seem to have taken advantage of the general expansion in cultivation by buying up recently cleared lands. These manors also had many free tenants, so there was a relatively fluid land-market.[12] At Hanbury Bishops Mauger (1200–12) and Blois bought properties on the eastern edge of the manor, in the area of Blickley, mainly from freeholders. The lands included an assart, a new purpresture and land 'in the field which is called *Stoking*', a name implying cleared land. The largest purchase was of property at Goosehill in the south of the manor; Walter Cantilupe bought this for 25 marks.

[10] For a similar policy of redeeming previous grants, see B. F. Harvey, *Westminster Abbey and its Estates in the Middle Ages* (Oxford, 1977), pp. 164–9; for grants to monasteries, see *VCH Worcs.*, iii, pp. 302, 559; B. S. Smith, *A History of Malvern* (Leicester, 1964), p. 95.

[11] Cleeve: White Book, fos. 54–5; *RBW*, iv, pp. 331–2, 346. Throckmorton: White Book, fo. 56; Fladbury mill: White Book, fo. 65.

[12] On the economic vitality of the north Worcestershire woodlands, see R. H. Hilton, 'Old Enclosure in the West Midlands', *Annales de l'Est* (1959), pp. 272–83.

The lands at Blickley and Goosehill were included in the Hanbury demesne by 1299.[13]

The Alvechurch charters record a continuous series of transactions, eighteen in all, throughout the thirteenth century. Assarting and enclosure of the waste in the north of the manor led to an angry reaction from the men of the adjoining village of King's Norton, who were losing their right to common pastures on West Heath and *Dodenhulleshaye*. In the 1270s and 1280s Godfrey Giffard was forced to make agreements with his free tenants to restrict their enclosures and in 1287 had to buy out the common rights of the King's Norton men for 10 marks.[14]

Bishop Cantilupe and Bishop Giffard pursued their own policy of enclosure in the south of Alvechurch and made agreements and exchanges with free tenants and the Cistercian abbey of Bordesley, whose park lay in the area, in order to define common rights and to extend the episcopal park.[15]

The largest gain at Alvechurch was the sub-manor of Wast Hills, held by William de Wasthull, who held land of the bishopric also in Fladbury and Tredington. He may have fallen on hard times in the 1280s, as he lost all of his lands then. Giffard acquired Wast Hills in 1283 and later added other properties in the area. It was valued in 1299 at £4 10s. 0d. per annum.[16]

Three other manors comparable in size with Wast Hills were added to the estate in the thirteenth century. (see Map 4) Aston (later called White Ladies' Aston) was held in 1086 by two tenants from the episcopal manor of Northwick. Bishops Sylvester and Blois in the early thirteenth century bought one manor from Ralph de Williton, together with the interest of Cecilia de Evercy. In 1258 and 1259 Walter Cantilupe acquired a lease (which later became permanent) of Richard de Bruly's manor in Aston for 16 marks and a quarter of wheat. Out of these acquisitions the Cistercian nuns of Whitstones received an endowment and the bishopric gained a small demesne manor valued at £10 13s. 3½d. in 1299.[17]

---

[13] White Book, fos. 59–62, 65; *RBW*, ii, pp. 172–3; *Reg. Giffard*, pp. 327, 443.
[14] White Book, fos. 71, 79.
[15] White Book, fos. 68, 83; *RBW*, ii, p. 208.
[16] *Reg. Giffard*, pp. 222, 329, 418–20; White Book, fos. 69, 96; *RBW*, ii, p. 236.
[17] White Book, fos. 57–8, 63–4; *RBW*, i, p. 89; *VCH Worcs.*, iii, pp. 558–9.

Knightwick was valued in 1299 at £6 13s. 4d. and had been granted by Great Malvern Priory to Godfrey Giffard in 1283. Giffard had been involved in an acrimonious dispute with the Malvern monks over his rights of visitation and was given Knightwick, which, like Aston, had been held as a dependent tenure of the bishopric, in exchange for concessions on the visitation issue. This rather dubious compromise still caused resentment among the monks of Worcester Cathedral Priory twenty years later.[18]

Bishop Giffard was an important landowner in his own right, and held two manors in the diocese, in north Gloucestershire. He did not always maintain a strict distinction between personal and episcopal properties, so that his own manors were mentioned in a list of bishopric rents compiled in 1268–9, and he claimed part of Wast Hills as his own, which his successor disputed.[19]

The temporary acquisition of the west Warwickshire manor of Coughton was probably another example of Giffard's personal affairs becoming entangled with those of the bishopric, so that the charters involved were copied into the episcopal cartulary. They show that two landowners in Coughton, John de Billesley and Randulph de Chastel, sold their lands to William de Spiney in the third quarter of the thirteenth century for a total of £133. Spiney also bought Hugh de Norfolk's demesne in Coughton for 40 marks. Both Billesley and Chastel referred to their 'great necessity' in their charters, showing that they were in financial trouble, a familiar problem in the thirteenth century among small landowners. By the 1280s Spiney in turn found himself in financial difficulties. In 1284 Bishop Giffard absolved Spiney from excommunication, and ordered the sheriff of Warwickshire to deliver him from prison; in the same year Roger de Spiney, William's son, agreed to pay Godfrey Giffard £46 owed to the deceased Walter Giffard, archbishop of York and Godfrey's brother. In 1289 Roger was granted Coughton by William and he sold it in the same year to Godfrey Giffard for £200. The bishop briefly enjoyed the profits from Coughton but in 1293 the land was granted back to William de Spiney, another son of the elder William.[20]

Giffard acquired Wast Hills, Knightwick and Coughton in

[18] White Book, fos. 44, 50; *Reg. Giffard*, pp. 218–20; *RBW*, iv, p. 401.

[19] *RBW*, iv, p. 465; *Calendar of Inquisitions Post Mortem*, iv, pp. 66–7; *Placitorum Abbreviatio* (Record Commission, 1811), p. 253.

[20] White Book, fos. 73–9; *Reg. Giffard*, pp. 231, 424, 437, 468; *VCH Warks.*, iii, p. 80.

the 1280s. This decade was one in which he seems to have pursued new sources of revenue, notably the appropriation of churches. He lobbied both Edward I and the pope for Bishop's Cleeve rectory (a well-endowed benefice, valued at £96 in the late fourteenth century), complaining that his estates were sterile, that his sheep flocks had suffered from disease, that he had incurred expenses because of Worcester's situation on the road into Wales used by armies involved in Edward I's wars. In 1286 Giffard sent a representative to the papal court, but was offered only an appropriation of Cleeve for life. Afterwards the bishop complained that the application had cost £200.[21]

Giffard had met with more success in obtaining the appropriation of Hillingdon church in Middlesex in 1281. This was justified on the grounds that the bishops needed somewhere to stay when visiting London. Hillingdon was valued at £26 13s. 4d. in 1299.[22]

The new lands gained in the thirteenth century, and especially in the 1280s, made a modest contribution to the rising value of the estate. A reasonable estimate would be that they represented an annual income of about £60 at the end of the century, or about 5 per cent of the value of the whole estate.

Expansion continued in the early fourteenth century. In 1335 Bishop Montacute secured the appropriation of Blockley church, a wealthy benefice of which the tithe corn alone was worth £42 10s. 0d. in the late fourteenth century, and Bishop Bransford purchased Hopwood, a sub-manor of Alvechurch, for 40 marks in 1344. An extent made at the time valued it at £5 per annum.[23]

The estate ceased to expand after 1344.

The urban element in the estate also grew in the period. In 1086 the bishops had forty-five houses in demesne in Worcester, and houses also in Droitwich, Warwick, Gloucester and Bristol. Although they were not mentioned in Domesday, the bishop presumably retained as well the London properties acquired in the ninth century. The holdings in Droitwich, Warwick and Bristol did not change significantly between 1086 and 1299. The Worcester properties may have expanded, as in *c.*1170 seventy-one tenants with ninety-nine holdings were said to lie 'in Worcester' from

---

[21] Corpus Christi College, Oxford, Bishop's Cleeve Rectory AR, 1389–90; *Reg. Giffard*, pp. 222–4, 257–8, 290, 301–3.
[22] White Book, fos. 43, 47–50, 100; *RBW*, iv, p. 401; *VCH Middlesex*, iv, p. 89.
[23] White Book, fo. 126; Blockley AR, 1383–4; *RBW*, ii, pp. 238–41.

the manors of Wick and Northwick, and a further twenty-six tenants held 'of the burgage of Worcester'. This could have resulted from suburban development of the city into the neighbouring manors.[24]

In the thirteenth century the London properties in the Strand grew with the purchase of a house from the brother of the bishop of Winchester by Bishop Mauger for 50 marks, and three further properties were bought by William de Blois. Other buildings and lands were added by purchase in 1281 and 1308 and grants were made by Henry III in 1265 and Thomas, earl of Lancaster, in 1316. The London property was valuable as a residence in the capital and as a source of rent income which increased from £1 8s. 3d. in 1211–12 to £4 8s. 0d. in 1302–3.[25]

Like other twelfth- and thirteenth-century magnates, the bishops created new towns on their estates. Their most successful venture was at Stratford-on-Avon, the early history of which is too well known to need detailed discussion here. In 1196 Bishop John of Coutances granted to the burgesses burgage tenure, holding their plots freely by hereditary right for 12d. per annum, being free from tolls, and having all the liberties of the Law of Breteuil. The size of the burgage plots was fixed at twelve perches by 3½ and presumably at the same time the regular gridiron pattern of the streets of the new town was laid out. To these basic facilities of a small town were added chartered markets and fairs, beginning with a market charter in 1196 and with others in 1214, 1239, 1269, 1270 and 1309. Conditions were favourable for growth as the town lay on good communication routes in a densely populated area with few rival markets. Immigrants were attracted, mainly from within a radius of sixteen miles, so that by 1251–2 the borough contained one hundred and twenty-four tenants holding 250 burgages, 14 shops, 10 stalls, 2 ovens and 2 dye-pans. The occupational surnames of the tenants suggest a wide variety of trades, including leather, cloth and metal working.[26]

[24] *RBW*, i, pp. 30–2, 37–8; ii, pp. 182–3; iii, p. 246; iv, p. 383.

[25] White Book, fos. 48–9, 52, 84, 103–5; WCRO ref. 829 BA 3332/4 no. 217; *Pipe Roll, 14 John* (Pipe Roll Soc., new ser., xxx, 1954), pp. 60–1; *RBW*, iv, p. 546.

[26] On new towns in general, see M. W. Beresford, *New Towns of the Middle Ages* (London, 1967); on Stratford in particular, see E. M. Carus-Wilson, 'The First Half-Century of the Borough of Stratford-upon-Avon', *Econ. Hist. Rev.*, 2nd ser., xviii (1965), pp. 46–63; the foundation charter, known hitherto only from Dugdale's description, survives in a cartulary copy, WCRO ref. 009:1 BA 2636/9 43696 fo. 93; for the market and fair charters, see White Book, fos. 42–3; *Cal. Charter Rolls*, i, p. 248; ii, pp. 115, 139; iii, p. 126; *Rotuli Chartarum* (Record Commission, 1837), p. 202; *VCH Warks.*, iii, pp. 236–7.

The bishops gained a substantial rent income from the borough: £16 0s. 6d in 1251–2, rising to £17 3s. 6¾d. by 1268–9, and then falling slightly to £16 19s. 6¾d. in *c.*1290. Court revenues were estimated at 30s. 0d. in *c.*1290 and there may have been other benefits to the lord; for example from mill tolls.[27] The land on which the borough was founded can only have been worth a few pounds at most when it belonged to the rural manor of Stratford.

The date of the foundation of Alvechurch borough is not known, but it may have been created at the same time as Henry III granted an annual fair and weekly market in 1239. A further charter in 1270 changed the market day. Perhaps the late date of foundation and the presence of nearby rival boroughs at Bromsgrove and Birmingham prevented a repeat of the Stratford success story. By 1299 there were only fifty-eight tenants in the borough holding 76½ burgages, with a few other plots, a shop and a workshop. In *c.*1290 the rents totalled a modest £4 2s. 0¼d., with £1 6s. 8d. from court perquisites.[28]

By obtaining fair charters in 1239, 1270 and 1286, the bishops promoted the development of Blockley as a commercial centre; the fair tolls were estimated at £4 in *c.*1290 and 1299, and in 1302–3 profits totalled £6 2s. 8d.[29]

So by encouraging urban and commercial growth and the purchase of urban property, the bishops gained about £30 in the thirteenth century in direct income from rents, tolls and perquisites. There could have been other benefits as the rural tenants may have been able to pay higher rents and dues through their access to the new markets.

The demesnes of the estate changed considerably in size in the course of the twelfth and thirteenth centuries. The long-term trend, indicated crudely by comparing the numbers of demesne ploughs listed in 1086 and *c.*1290, suggests an overall decline from 71 to 65, but to make the figures strictly comparable, the decline is from 71 to 60 as the manors of Aston and Wast Hills were not in the episcopal estate in 1086 and are therefore omitted from the thirteenth-century total (see Table 3).

The decline was in reality the result of a number of contradictory

[27] *RBW*, iv, pp. 497, 464, iii, p. 259.

[28] *Cal. Charter Rolls*, i, p. 248; ii, 139; *RBW*, ii, pp. 226–31.

[29] *Cal. Charter Rolls*, i, p. 248; ii, 139, 329; White Book, fos. 42–3; *RBW*, iii, pp. 296, 312; iv, p. 541.

tendencies. In the twelfth century, demesnes were considerably reduced in size by enfeoffments and the granting out of lands to tenants for cash rents. Sixty-six of the latter type of grant are recorded in the survey of *c.*1170 and mostly belonged to the years 1125–50. The creation of tenancies from demesnes was most marked in the twelfth century at Bibury, Fladbury, Hartlebury, Tredington and Westbury/Henbury, at all of which a reduction in the demesne ploughs is indicated in Table 3.

The growth of the arable demesnes was probably concentrated

Table 3. *Numbers of demesne ploughs, 1086–1303*

Manor	Number of ploughs 1086	Actual No. of ploughs *c.*1290	Recommended No. of ploughs *c.*1290	Actual No. of ploughs 1302–3
Alvechurch	2	2	2	2
Aston	(not comparable)	3	3	3
Bibury	4	2	2	2
Blockley	} 7 {	3	3	3
Paxford		3	2	3
Bredon	3	4	3	4
Cleeve	3	4	4	4
Fladbury	} 9 {	4	3	} 6
Throckmorton		2	2	
Hampton	2	3	2	2
Hanbury	2	5	5	?4
Hartlebury	4	2	2	2
Henbury (Westbury)	} 2 + 9 {	3	3	3
Stoke		2	2	2
Kempsey	2	4	3	4
Ripple	4	3	2	3
Stratford	3	2	2	2
Tredington	5	4	4	4
Wast Hills	—	2	2	—
Whitstones (Northwick)	4	5	5	?5
Wick	4	1	1	1
Withington	2	2	2	?2
Total	71	65	59	61
Total (excluding Aston & Wast Hills, which do not appear in 1086)	71	60	54	58

in the thirteenth century. By *c*.1290 increases are recorded at Bredon, Cleeve, Hampton, Hanbury, Kempsey and Northwick/ Whitstones. The largest increase, at Hanbury, can be connected with the purchase of land for the demesne by thirteenth-century bishops.

Some expansion was probably the result of seignorial assarting. The bishops were active in securing relaxations in forest law in the late twelfth and early thirteenth centuries. Richard I released from forest exactions 614 acres of assarts on bishopric and priory manors, notably at Ripple, Kempsey and Upton-on-Severn, and in 1218 Bishop Sylvester of Evesham paid 800 marks to secure the deafforestation of Ombersley and Horwell forests which included Hartlebury, Whitstones, Kempsey and parts of Fladbury and Ripple manors.[30] The bishops probably obtained these concessions in order to remove royal restrictions on their tenants, but they were also clearing land on their own account. In 1196 Bishop John of Coutances obtained permission from John, count of Mortain, and the countess of Gloucester, to assart 300 acres in Malvern forest at Welland. This can presumably be connected with the carucate of demesne arable held by the bishops at Welland in the early thirteenth century but subsequently rented out to tenants. Permission was obtained to assart 45 acres from Feckenham forest at *Sanden* (now Sandhills in Alvechurch) in 1269, and this appears in the demesne arable in 1299 as '*Newsondene*'. Bishop Cantilupe was said to have appropriated land at Hanbury in Feckenham forest and such clearing names as *Swynlande Stockinge* and *Ruding* are mentioned in 1299 in the Hanbury demesne. Other field names suggestive of assarting among the demesnes are *Bysshoprudying* at Kempsey and *Newland*, a large area of $267\frac{1}{2}$ acres of arable on the western edge of Northwick/Whitstones. There was also a *Wyghine-rudyinge* at Henbury.[31]

The developments in the demesne area underline the contrast that has been drawn between the economic history of the twelfth and thirteenth centuries. The twelfth century was a period of

[30] White Book, fos. 40–2, 44; *Annales Monastici*, iv, p. 410; *Cartulary of Worcester Cathedral Priory*, ed. Darlington, p. 173.

[31] Welland: see White Book, fo. 127; *RBW*, i, p. 103. Sandhills: see *Reg. Giffard*, p. 469; *RBW*, ii, p. 208. Hanbury; see *Rotuli Hundredorum* (Record Commission, 1812), ii, p. 284; J. West, 'The Administration and Economy of the Forest of Feckenham' (Univ. of Birmingham M.A. thesis, 1964), p. 218; *RBW*, ii, p. 172. Other field names, Kempsey AR, 1505–6; *RBW*, i, pp. 1–3; iv, p. 377.

pressure on landlords to create knights' fees, and a period when political upheaval in Stephen's reign may have affected the economy, but above all one when landlords contented themselves with a steady income from tenants. All of this changed under the pressure of inflation when lords had to take over their demesnes and, if possible, to increase their size in order to produce for the market.

For much of the twelfth century, and perhaps after 1200, the Worcester demesnes were leased to farmers. In the vacancy of 1184–5 most of the income of the estate came from 'the farms of manors'. At Kempsey a brief note shows that draught animals were included with the lease of the demesne. Only the vineyards, according to the survey of c.1170 and the vacancy account of 1184–5, can be shown to have been cultivated by the bishops.[32]

By 1246 most of the manors had been brought into direct management. Two surviving accounts for Fladbury and Tredington show that those two manors were run by reeves and bailiffs, and they exchanged grain and animals with the reeves who were in charge of fourteen other manors on the estate.[33] These and other documents reveal the administrative machinery created in order to cope with the new system of demesne management.

In order to make demesnes of convenient size, the three largest manors, Blockley, Fladbury and Westbury, were split up, creating new manors of Paxford, Throckmorton, Henbury-in-Salt-Marsh and Stoke Bishop. With the addition of Aston and Knightwick, the number of manors increased from seventeen in 1086 to twenty-two in the late thirteenth century (see Map 4).

Rent-collection and the organization of demesne cultivation on each manor were the responsibility of a reeve, assisted by such lesser officials as messors and beadles. They were recruited from the customary tenants, as was normal, and rewarded with release from rents and services.

Over the reeves, the bailiffs (sometimes called sergeants) supervised a manor or group of manors. Bailiffs of individual

---

[32] The pipe-roll evidence is often ambiguous; see P. D. A. Harvey, 'The Pipe Rolls and the Adoption of Demesne Farming in England', *Econ. Hist. Rev.*, 2nd ser., xxvii (1974), pp. 347–52; *Pipe Roll, 31 Henry II* (Pipe Roll Soc., xxxiv, 1913), p. 126; *Pipe Roll, 32 Henry II* (Pipe Roll Soc., xxxvi, 1914), p. 42; *Pipe Roll, 14 John* (Pipe Roll Soc., new ser., xxx, 1954), pp. 60–1; *RBW*, i, p. 85; ii, pp. 170–1. Some of the Worcester Priory demesnes were leased as late as the 1250s, *Annales Monastici*, iv, p. 442.

[33] Bodleian Library, Worcester Rolls no. 4.

manors are found most often in the early thirteenth century. By the early fourteenth century they looked after bailiwicks of between three and six manors. Bailiffs were also appointed to administer the judicial franchises of Oswaldslow, Henbury and Pathlow. They were sometimes recruited from the substantial free tenants of the estate, like Geoffrey de Hambury, bailiff between 1289 and 1303, who held a quarter of a knight's fee at Hanbury, or the late thirteenth-century bailiff of Henbury, Robert de Cesteneslode, who held a half-hide in Ripple and a yardland in Kempsey. They received a cash wage varying from 26s. 8d. to £10 per annum.[34]

Parallel with the bailiffs were local officials with specialized duties, such as the keeper of the Worcester palace, parkers, and wardens of woods, notably of Malvern Wood and the woods of Stock and Bradley.[35]

The central administrators for the whole estate consisted of financial officials and stewards. The receiver, who collected revenues and then paid them over to the bishop, or paid the bishop's creditors direct, was usually a prominent cleric (see Appendix 1). The bishops had the right to appoint the sacrist of the cathedral priory, and they took advantage of this patronage to promote men who could also act as receivers.[36] This happened in the case of Thomas the Sacrist in the 1240s and John de St Briavel in 1309–13. Other receivers were rectors of churches like Fladbury and Halford where the bishops were patrons. Specialist auditors are not recorded until the early fourteenth century but auditing accounts would have been an essential part of the financial administration earlier.[37]

The stewards had many functions within the central administration of the estate. They held courts, visited manors, made distraints,

[34] For bailiffs in charge of individual manors, see White Book, fo. 56; Bodleian Library, Worcester Rolls no. 4. For groups of manors: see *RBW*, iv, pp. 501, 512, 525, 536; *Reg. Gainsborough*, p. 32; R. M. Haines, *The Administration of the Diocese of Worcester in the first half of the Fourteenth Century* (London, 1965), p. 143; *Reg. Bransford*, p. 6. For bailiffs of franchises: see White Book, fo. 96; *Lib. Alb. Pri.*, p. 50; *Reg. Gainsborough*, p. 32; *Reg. Reynolds*, p. 34; *Reg. Cobham*, p. 121; Reg. Orleton, fos. 101, 163; *Reg. Bransford*, pp. 99, 333, 334. For bailiffs' holdings: *RBW*, iv, p. 174; i, p. 63; iii, p. 152. The unusually high fees of £10 were paid during the vacancy of 1302–3.

[35] White Book, fo. 62; *Reg. Reynolds*, p. 33; Reg. Montacute, fos. 11–12.

[36] Haines, *Administration of the Diocese*, p. 136.

[37] *Reg. Gainsborough*, p. 20; *Reg. Reynolds*, pp. 6, 18; Haines, *Administration of the Diocese*, p. 146.

audited accounts, leased lands and even sold grain.[38] Their importance can be judged from the fact that a record of their appointment
was sometimes entered in the bishops' registers, and their names
appear attesting charters (see Appendix 1). When Bishop Walter
Reynolds wished to change the running of the estate by leasing
demesnes and commuting labour services, he wrote to his steward
to implement the new policy. For most of our period only one
steward for the whole estate was appointed but in 1339 Bishop
Bransford split the office and appointed a separate steward for the
Gloucestershire manors. In line with their considerable responsibilities, stewards were of a higher social rank than other estate officials.
Those who were clergy had some of the richest benefices in the
diocese, such as Bishop's Cleeve, Bredon and Fladbury. The laymen, who tended to supersede the clergy in the early fourteenth
century, were drawn from the *buzones* who also occupied positions
in local government, on commissions and as sheriffs (see Appendix
1). The stewardship could be a stage in an administrative career.
For the clergy, service as steward often followed from holding
other positions in the episcopal administration, such as steward
of the household or sequestrator. For the more ambitious, whether
clergy or laity, experience as steward of the Worcester estate could
be followed by national office, as a baron of the exchequer in the
case of Peter de Leicester, or as royal escheator north of the
Trent for Robert de Cliderowe who was Walter Reynold's steward
both at Worcester and at Canterbury.[39]

Presumably the bishops made important decisions in the management of the estate, but only Reynolds can be shown to have ordered
changes in policy. Presumably they were advised by a council. However the records of Giffard's council show that it was mainly
concerned with ecclesiastical matters, though a request for
the return of Knightwick manor from its original owners, the monks
of Great Malvern, and a dispute over common pasture at Bredon,
were discussed. An early fourteenth-century *proforma* shows that
the council would normally consent to the leasing of a manor.[40] One
of the most important ways in which individual bishops could affect

[38] *Reg. Gainsborough*, p. 81 (auditing accounts); *RBW*, iv, pp. 383–4 (leasing
land); Hilton, *A Medieval Society*, p. 181 (selling grain).

[39] For similar careers see N. Denholm-Young, *Seignorial Administration in
England* (Oxford, 1937), pp. 68–85; King, *Peterborough Abbey*, p. 130.

[40] S. J. Davies, 'Studies in the Administration of the Diocese of Worcester in
the Thirteenth Century' (Univ. of Wales Ph.D. thesis, 1971), pp. 231–40, 788, 807–8.

the running of the manors was by their residence in, or absence from, their diocese. Walter Reynolds, an absentee, expected to receive a wholly cash income from the estate. Resident bishops, like Walter Cantilupe, would obtain produce from their demesnes for consumption in their households, as well as cash.

The main problem facing all medieval administration was the maintenance of control of the central authority over the local men, who might be inefficient, or might use their offices for their own benefit. The accounts of 1246–7 show that manors could be visited frequently by the lord himself or his officials. The main check lay in the efficiency of the accounting procedure. The documents themselves show that the Worcester estate had adopted the 'Common Form' of accounting, in which, unlike the Winchester system, unpaid rents were included with the expenses, but as on the bishopric of Winchester estates, enrolled accounts were made after the annual audit in imitation of the royal exchequer.[41] The annual audit for the whole estate was held in 1246 at Fladbury and the reeve there accounted for the expenditure of cash and food in entertaining a large gathering of officials. As the surviving accounts are fair copies, we cannot see how many alterations the auditors made, but the relatively small debts, of a pound or less, owed by the reeves at the end of the year point to a reasonable standard of efficiency.

The organization of demesne cultivation was one of the main functions of the administrative apparatus. What use did they make of the demesnes? The surveys of *c.*1290 and 1299 list the various types of demesne lands as follows, in acres:

	Arable	'Frisc'	Meadow	Pasture
*c.*1290	6,009½*	416¼	1,061½	835½
1299	6,968½	177	810¼	352½

* omits the Whitstones demesne arable of *c.*450 acres.

This suggests an overwhelming preponderance of arable, which, together with the 'frisc' (probably occasionally ploughed lands), accounts for 83 per cent or 86 per cent of the demesne acreage. Pasture was, however, often not assessed in acres, so its significance is under-represented in the table.

[41] Bodleian Library, Worcester Rolls no. 4; *Walter of Henley*, ed. D. Oschinsky (Oxford, 1971), pp. 215–18.

Arable cultivation was practised on a large scale throughout the estate, the smallest recorded demesne acreage being 161¾ acres in c.1290 at Wick, and the largest was 565 acres at Blockley in 1299. Large demesnes exceeding 400 acres were worked on Cotswold and woodland manors as well as those in the river valleys. The superiority of the lowland arable is reflected in the values given in the surveys, presumably estimating potential profits, which were often 3d. per acre or less in the Cotswold and north Worcestershire manors, rising to 6d. or 7d. on some river-valley and central-Worcestershire demesnes.[42]

The 1299 surveys imply that a two-course rotation was practised throughout the estate, as lands were valued on the basis of their use in alternate years: 'each acre is worth according to the common estimation in alternate years 6d., and so each year 3d.'. This is confirmed by the acreage of crops in 1302–3, which, at 3,413 acres, was almost exactly half of the arable area recorded in 1299. In eight cases, mainly in the Avon valley and Cotswolds, the arable lay in two fields. However, the surveys of nine Severn valley and north Worcestershire manors describe the arable as lying in between ten and twenty-seven divisions called fields (*campi*), furlongs (*culturae*), and crofts.[43] These complex field divisions, which were sometimes enclosed, were often found in areas with a more wooded landscape and they probably grew up as a result of piecemeal addition of new lands. Though we might expect to find variations from conventional rotations in such circumstances, the surveyors insisted on valuing these demesnes as if they were cultivated in alternate years. Although the two-course rotation may seem wasteful of land, it was predominant in the west midlands. As well as allowing land more time to recuperate, it provided more fallow pasture and greater freedom of choice in the proportions of winter- and spring-sown crops than the three-course system. In reality land use may not have been governed totally by any system. A departure from the rigidity of two-course husbandry is indicated by the large areas of 'frisc'. The term is ambiguous, meaning both lands newly

[42] There is some correlation between the values of the demesne arable and the ease of cultivation of the land implied by the acreage estimated in c.1290 as ploughable in one day.

[43] Two-field demesnes: Bibury, Hampton, Kempsey, Paxford, Stratford, Tredington, Withington and Blickley in Hanbury. Multiple-field divisions are recorded at Alvechurch, Aston, Hanbury, Hartlebury, Henbury, Stoke, Whitstones and Wick.

cultivated and lands allowed to revert from arable to grass, and both meanings could apply to the 'frisc' on the Worcester demesnes. It was prominent on some Severn valley, north Worcestershire and Cotswold manors, and suggests a flexible system of bringing marginal lands into occasional cultivation. The same flexibility may explain the puzzling changes in demesne acreage between the two surveys of *c.*1290 and 1299, but the discrepancies, sometimes exceeding 100 acres on individual manors, could be the result of variations in the methods of calculation used by the surveyors.[44]

The only detailed evidence for arable cultivation comes from Fladbury and Tredington in 1246–7. Four ploughs were employed on each demesne but the acreage cultivated was not recorded. The sowing figures show a high proportion of winter corn, wheat and rye, which were sown more thinly than the spring-sown crops, and so would have occupied a larger area:

	Wheat	Rye	Barley	Peas and Beans	Oats
Fladbury	17qr 6b	26qr 4b	26qr 5b	5qr	31qr 4b
Tredington	45qr 6b	—	16qr 1b	3qr	16qr 7b

The grain harvested in the autumn of 1246 amounted to 565 quarters at Fladbury and 558 quarters at Tredington. In each case about a fifth was reserved for seed, and another third was consumed by workers, bailiffs and animals on the manor, or sent to other manors on the estate. Only about a tenth was sold by the local manorial administration, leaving a third which was either consumed by the bishop and his servants on visits to the manors or sent to the bishop's household. At first sight, particularly in a year of high grain prices, the quantity sold – 56 quarters in each case — seems very small. However, it was rational for a resident bishop like Walter Cantilupe to live directly off his own produce and it is also possible that some of the grain sent to the bishop was marketed centrally, as happened on other thirteenth-century estates.[45]

Meadow and enclosed pasture occupied less than a fifth of the demesne acreage recorded in the late thirteenth century. The relative scarcity of both types of land is indicated by the values put on

[44] Some of the discrepancies defy rational explanation. For example, at Tredington, where there is no evidence of assarting or any other possible cause of change, the arable acreages were 355¾ in *c.*1290, and 506½ in 1299.

[45] Hilton, *A Medieval Society*, pp. 78–9.

them – in 1299 meadow normally varied from 1s. 0d. to 3s. 0d. per acre and pasture from 3d. to 2s. 0d. The largest areas of meadow lay usually on the river valley manors, but even there no manor in 1299 had as much as 100 acres. Most of the pasture resources of the estate consisted of common pastures shared with the tenants, which were most extensive on the Cotswold manors. An indication of the use of the pastures is provided by the potential animal population listed in the survey of c.1290. Many of these, 67 horses and 542 oxen, were the draught animals necessary for cultivation and their distribution varied with the size of the demesne arable. Of the 226 cows, the largest herds of 20 to 24 tended to be kept on the river-valley manors. The 5,650 sheep could be pastured, according to the c.1290 survey, on most of the manors of the estate in flocks varying in size from 120 to 800, with the largest flocks of 500 or more on the Cotswold manors. Flocks were transhumant, as the Tredington account of 1246–7 shows, between upland and lowland manors. In 1299 it was said that the Cleeve pastures could accommodate 1,000 sheep in the summer and 200 in the winter, showing that they left the hills in colder weather.

Wool must have been a major cash crop on the estate in the thirteenth century. As early as 1246 the sheep flocks were organized centrally on the manor of Blockley and the wool sold from there, probably *en bloc*, as happened in the fourteenth century.[46] The other animals might also have provided a source of cash income. At Fladbury in 1246–7 stock, butter and cheese worth £13 15s. 1d. were sold, but much meat and dairy produce was sent to the household of Bishop Cantilupe.

Woodlands are not fully described in the thirteenth-century surveys, and when they do appear they often seem to have been very small. A wood at Whitstones, for example, was assessed at 16 acres and was valued at 4s. 0d. Wood for use on Bibury manor was brought from Withington, seven miles away. This reflects the extent of clearance for cultivation and pasture. There were still larger areas of remaining woodland at Malvern Wood west of the Severn, Bradley and Bishop's Wood in Lapworth, which, as in the pre-Conquest period, were attached to the demesne manors of Bredon, Fladbury and Stratford, and were used as sources of fuel and as swine pastures (see Map 4). The bishops seem to have recognized

---

[46]   cf. Denholm-Young, *Seignorial Administration in England*, pp. 58–9.

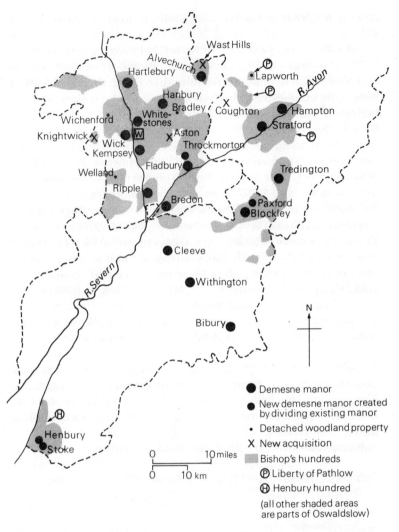

4   The estates and liberties of the bishopric of Worcester at the end of the thirteenth century

the value of preserving woodland and pasture by creating parks, not just as pleasure grounds but as profitable assets: 66 cattle could be pastured in the Alvechurch park, for example, and 100 bullocks at Henbury. In the vacancy of 1302–3 the royal keeper found plenty of timber to fell on some manors, 138 trees at Alvechurch alone, and the proceeds of timber sales from five manors totalled nearly £11.[47]

The labour needed to maintain demesne production was provided partly by wage labour, though the labour services of tenants also made an important contribution. In 1246–7 ten wage-earning *famuli* were employed at Fladbury and eight at Tredington, as carters, ploughmen, dairymaids and shepherds, but there was an almost equal number, nine at Fladbury, and six at Tredington, who were *enches*, that is customary tenants who were required to work full time on the demesne in exchange for release from rents and other services. Wage-earners contributed to the threshing and harvesting on both manors, and weeding and mowing at Fladbury, but much of the seasonal work was performed by the tenants. At Fladbury eighteen yardlanders and five cottars performed all of the heavy summer labour services that they owed between 24 June and 29 September. T. H. Lloyd has shown that at the end of the thirteenth century the demesne ploughs manned by the *famuli* could not have ploughed fully the demesne arable without the help of the labour of the customary tenants.[48] Even in the unusual circumstances of the vacancy of 1302–3, only a little more than a third of the labour services owed were commuted for cash.

In spite of the great productive capacity of the demesnes, their importance in the economy of the estate should not be exaggerated. The tenants supplied much of the labour needed to work the demesnes, but also provided, as on other estates, the bulk of the lord's cash income. This reflects the distribution of land on the manors, four-fifths of which was held by tenants.

Table 4. *Division of land between demesne and tenants, 1299*

Calculated for thirteen manors with fullest evidence of the size of tenants' holdings

Demesne	Customary tenants	Free tenants
21% (4,653½ acres)	61% (13,168 acres)	18% (3,989½ acres)

[47] *RBW*, i, p. 2; iv, p. 371; White Book, fos. 51–2. Timber felled in the vacancy, WCRO, ref. 009:1 BA 2636/192 92626 7/12.

[48] T. H. Lloyd, 'Ploughing Services of the Demesnes of the Bishop of Worcester in the late Thirteenth century', *Univ. of Birm. Hist. Journ.*, viii (1961), pp. 189–96.

The ratio between demesne and tenant land had very early origins; as we have seen, in 1086 tenant ploughs greatly outnumbered demesne ploughs. Similar proportions are found in the large manors of the east midlands surveyed in the Hundred Rolls of 1279, reflecting the ability of magnate landlords to provide their demesnes with ample reserves of customary labour.[49]

By the late thirteenth century the tenants, particularly those holding by villein or customary tenure, were paying great quantities of cash to the lord and these are listed in Table 5. The payments were of many different types – sums paid regularly for the tenants' holdings, the assize rents; customary rents paid in commutation of renders in kind or minor services, such as fishfee and spenyngfee; payments made in lump sums in recognition of lordship, the aids–or tallage; or in acknowledgement of the lord's right to hold the view of frankpledge – the common fines; church dues diverted into the hands of the lord, such as Peter's Pence and churchscot; and payments for the use of the lord's pastures, like pannage and herbage. The table includes perquisites of courts, which were not strictly rents, but consisted of payments made to the bishop through the courts as amercements, penalties, entry-fines and heriots, and also

Table 5. *Rents and dues in 1299*

to the nearest £	£
Assize rents	382
Works and customs	274
Rents in kind	10
Fishfee, spenyngfee, woodsilver etc.	4
Aid	41
Common fines	19
Peter's Pence	1
Churchscot	21
Pannage of pigs	4
Toll of ale	1
Perquisites of courts	61
Farm of mills	56
Miscellaneous	18
Total	£892

[49] E. A. Kosminsky, *Studies in the Agrarian History of England in the Thirteenth Century* (Oxford, 1956), pp. 99–106.

income from mills, included because they derived from the tolls paid at the lord's mill on the tenants' corn.

The totals reflect the potential value of the rents and dues – in practice some of the rents would have been relaxed, for example to reeves and *enches*, and some of the works, valued in all at £274, would have been used as labour services by the lord. In order to calculate the actual rent total of the estate, it seems reasonable to allow for the works commuted for cash rents a sum in the region of £96, which was the total commuted in 1302–3, and to assume that the rents allowed to reeves and others would be offset by the rents omitted from the 1299 survey – those of Stratford borough, Knightwick and London. This makes the likely total of rent income about £700 or 60 per cent of the total valuation of the estate.

The stages in the growth of these sums cannot be known. The survey of *c*.1170 gives the rents paid by the tenants who owed no service, the *censarii*, making rent totals of £4–£6 on some manors but it mentions only a few small cash rents owed by the *operarii*, those who did labour services. The customary dues of the tenants doing works, such as spenyngfee, are usually listed, and occasionally more substantial sums of aids are given. The general impression created is that the *operarii*, whose successors were villeins and customary tenants in the thirteenth century, contributed little in cash. Rent income is better documented in the thirteenth century. At Fladbury the assize rent total increased from £14 4s. 5½d. in 1246–7 to £19 10s. 3d. in 1268–9, and again to £26 13s. 3d. in 1299. The Tredington rents were much more stable and stayed in the region of £9–£10 in the same period. The general trend, judging from a comparison between rents on fifteen manors in 1268–9 and 1299, was for rent income to rise. Assize rents increased by £36 (13 per cent), mill revenues went up by £4 (21 per cent) and even aids, which might be expected to have been fixed by custom, increased by just over a pound (4 per cent).[50] These tendencies in the late thirteenth century presumably represent a continuation of a process that began earlier and played a major part in the general growth of the bishops' income. Increases in rent income were doubtless made possible by economic and social developments, such as rising tenant numbers or the upward movement in prices, which, for example, directly affected the value of mill tolls. The main factor must have been the lord's ability to extract more money from

[50] *RBW*, iv, pp. 459–65.

his tenants by adjustments in the ways in which they rendered services and by pushing up the customary dues.

In addition to the social controls exercised by the bishops as landlords, they also held extensive powers of franchisal jurisdiction over their own tenants and others. In the eleventh century, and perhaps earlier, the bishops had complete judicial powers in the triple hundred of Oswaldslow which contained most of the Worcestershire episcopal and monastic demesne manors, and the fiefs held of the church by laymen. The liberty was extended, probably in the early thirteenth century, to include the north Worcestershire episcopal manors of Alvechurch, Hanbury and Hartlebury[51] (see Map 4).

In *c.*1170 the liberty of Saltmarsh hundred, centred on the Gloucestershire manor of Westbury (later known as the hundred of Henbury), was said to include, besides the normal sake and soke, toll and team and *infangentheof*, the right to determine any plea arising within the hundred. Trials by combat and ordeals were to be carried out in the presence of royal officials from Winterbourne hundred, but if they failed to come, judgment could be made in their absence.[52]

By the late thirteenth century, but probably originating earlier, the bishops held the only private hundred in Warwickshire, the liberty of Pathlow, which included all of the episcopal lands in the county.[53]

This left only the Gloucestershire manors of Bibury, Cleeve and Withington outside the bishops' private hundreds. It is clear, however, that the bishops behaved as independently as possible in these manors, exercising hundredal jurisdiction. The tenants at Cleeve acknowledged the jurisdiction of Tibblestone hundred in the most perfunctory fashion, and in the early fourteenth century Cleeve was recognized as an independent hundred.[54]

[51] *VCH Worcs.*, iii, pp. 246–50; *Rolls of Justices in Eyre for Lincolnshire and Worcestershire, 1221*, ed. D. M. Stenton (Selden Soc., liii, 1934), no. 948; the transfer led to a dispute on the status of Cofton Hackett, *Rotuli Hundredorum*, ii, p. 284.

[52] *RBW, iv*, pp. 429–30.

[53] *Rotuli Hundredorum*, ii, p. 226.

[54] *Rolls of the Justices in Eyre for Gloucestershire, Warwickshire and Staffordshire, 1221, 1222*, ed. D. M. Stenton (Selden Soc., lix, 1940), no. 202, shows that the bishop was claiming hundredal jurisdiction at Withington; *RBW*, iv, p. 346 on Cleeve's performance of suit of court at Tibblestone Hundred; on Cleeve's independence, *Place-Names of Gloucestershire*, ii, p. 86.

Throughout their estates by the late thirteenth century the bishops held the view of frankpledge, assize of ale and waif and stray, and exercised the right of *infangentheof*, being able to hang thieves caught red-handed. In addition, they enjoyed two high franchises, return of writ (making their own bailiffs responsible for royal writs), and pleas of *vee de naam*, that is, cases involving pleas of replevin (distraint).[55]

Contemporaries invested the liberties with great importance, and they were constantly disputed. Bishop Giffard successfully defended his rights before the *Quo Warranto* enquiries of Edward I's reign, with the minor exception of the right to hold the assize of bread and ale over his London tenants. There were also frictions with the cathedral priory over the choice of the bailiff of Oswaldslow and his powers in the priory manors. The earls of Gloucester interfered with the bishop's jurisdiction in Bibury during the Barons' Wars of 1258–65 and in 1314–15 Cirencester Abbey objected to the bishop's bailiff exercising the return of writs at Bibury and Withington within the Seven Hundreds of Cirencester, the Abbey's own liberty.[56]

The principal threat to the episcopal franchises came from the Beauchamps, who were major landowners in Oswaldslow through their acquisition of the Abitot inheritance, and hereditary sheriffs of Worcestershire, and in 1268 became great magnates of national importance as earls of Warwick.

A major confrontation arose in the 1240s over the bishop's right to *vee de naam*. This was questioned in 1244, and the county court was asked to investigate. In 1249 there was an obscure incident on the river Severn, when the sinking of a ferry led to a large number of deaths by drowning. The 'bishop's household' at Kempsey were accused, and William Beauchamp, as sheriff, seized ploughs and animals in distraint. This led Bishop Cantilupe to object to the deprivation of his rights to *vee de naam*, excommunicating Beauchamp and taking the case to the papal court at Lyons in 1250. The pope wrote to Henry III asking him to forgive Cantilupe, Cantilupe

---

[55] The franchises are listed in a number of sources: *Rotuli Hundredorum*, i, pp. 167–8, 177, 179; ii, pp. 226, 228, 282, 283; *RBW*, iv, pp. 347–8, 401–2; *Reg. Giffard*, 253, 310, 323; *Placita de Quo Warranto, temp. Edward I, II and III* (Record Commission, 1818), pp. 264, 779, 783.

[56] *Quo Warranto*, p. 475; *Annales Monastici*, iv, pp. 439–40; *Lib. Alb. Pri.*, p. 34; *RBW*, iv, p. 376; *Rotuli Parliamentorum*, i, p. 322.

absolved Beauchamp from excommunication and Henry III granted a charter to the bishops giving them pleas of *vee de naam*. The dispute grumbled on, until in 1258 an agreement was made between the bishop and the sheriff in which Beauchamp acknowledged the bishop's franchise, but secured Cantilupe's assurances that various abuses and neglect of duties by his bailiffs should be remedied. A financial settlement was negotiated in 1258–9; the pleas of *vee de naam* were valued at £4 per annum, so the sheriff's farm which was paid to the king was reduced by £4, and Cantilupe took over responsibility for a payment of £4 previously made by the king to the nuns of Wroxall. This left no one better off; later, in 1280, William Beauchamp, the son of the earlier disputant, agreed to take over the payment to Wroxall but the bishopric was still paying in 1302–3.[57]

The case illustrates the tenacity with which franchise holders defended their rights, apparently showing more concern over principles than the financial benefits involved. The profits of the liberties can be shown to have been relatively small. In *c.*1290 the combined annual profits of Oswaldslow and Pathlow were estimated at £4, and in 1302–3 they brought in a little more than £5. In 1310 the bishops were granted the fines and amercements levied on their tenants in the king's courts but this seems to have been worth no more than a few shillings per annum. Even so, lords who held manors within the liberties were prepared to pay disproportionate sums in order to secure exemption from the bishop's jurisdiction. Simon Crombe agreed with Bishop Giffard to pay an annual rent of 20s. 0d. for exemption of his three small manors in Oswaldslow, and the Prior and Convent of Kenilworth paid a lump sum of £20 to remove their manor of Loxley from the liberty of Pathlow.[58]

There was always a possibility that the franchises would

---

[57] J. E. A. Jolliffe, 'Some Factors in the Beginnings of Parliament', in E. B. Fryde and E. Miller (eds.), *Historical Studies of the English Parliament* (Cambridge, 1970), i, p. 61; *Cal. Close Rolls*, 1242–7, p. 308; *Annales Monastici*, i, p. 139; *Cal. Pat. Rolls*, 1247–58, p. 45; *Annales Monastici*, iv, pp. 439–41; *Cal. Papal Reg.*, i, pp. 265, 270; White Book, fos. 39, 141; *Cal. Charter Rolls*, ii, pp. 6–7, 22; *VCH Worcs.*, iii, p. 533; *RBW*, iv, p. 546. The dispute between the bishops and the Beauchamps as sheriffs over the relationship between Oswaldslow and the shire continued, see *Reg. Giffard*, pp. 75, 77; White Book, fos. 142–3. On the whole quarrel see Davies, 'Administration of the Diocese of Worcester', pp. 50–3.

[58] Profits of the liberties: see *RBW*, i, p. 29; iii, p. 259. Profits of the grant of 1310: see *Reg. Reynolds*, pp. 19, 55; *Reg. Bransford*, pp. 301–2. Purchases of exemption: see *RBW*, iii, pp. 289–90; 257.

produce a lucrative windfall. In 1361 the bishopric officials claimed a cargo of wine that sank in a storm in the Bristol Avon under the franchise of wreck. It would have been worth £36 but the claim was disallowed.[59]

The chief importance of the liberties must have been as symbols of the bishops' ability to command men and exercise high authority without external restriction. The franchise of *infangentheof* gave the bishops the ultimate right of taking lives, and this was no mere theoretical privilege. When the bishops' right to hang thieves caught on the priory manors near Tredington was questioned, probably in the early fourteenth century, three cases were recalled with circumstantial details, presumably from the recent past. Sometimes the bishops' officials could be seen acting in defence of law and order in major cases, as when a 'chief of robbers', a lapsed monk of Much Wenlock, was hanged at Oswaldslow in 1285 and required a special escort to prevent his rescue by fellow criminals.[60] The liberties also gave the bishops' bailiffs the opportunity to act in an arbitrary and even dictatorial fashion, and cases of abuse emerged from royal enquiries in the 1270s. A particularly brutal case was recorded in 1303, when, according to reports made to the king's court, Geoffrey de Hambury, the bishop's bailiff, ordered the reeve of Kempsey and the men of Kempsey and Draycott to behead a clerk, John de Draycote, whose offence is unknown. The head was set up before the gate of the bishop's manor house at Kempsey.[61] Shortly afterwards Hambury was given a new post as bailiff of all of the manors in Worcestershire. Much of the bishops' income depended on their ability to command the respect and even fear of their subordinates. The possession of franchises gave their officials a speed and decisiveness of action which must have benefited the bishops in many ways.

In the thirteenth century most of the resources of the bishopric of Worcester expanded – property in both town and country, the size of demesnes (after shrinkage in the twelfth century) and rent income. Administrative developments enabled the direct exploitation of the demesnes, which were producing cereals and wool on a large scale.

[59] PRO E 136 14/13.
[60] *RBW*, iii, p. 294; *Annales Monastici*, iv, p. 487.
[61] *Rotuli Hundredorum*, i, pp. 168–9; ii, p. 283; *Reg. Sede Vacante*, pp. 50–1.

The first signs that expansion was slowing down are apparent in the 1280s, a troubled decade on other English estates.[62] In 1286 Bishop Giffard complained of the sterility of his lands and the mortality among his sheep, in a request to obtain the appropriation of a rectory. Such special pleading should be treated with caution, but sheep murraine is known elsewhere in England on a large scale in the 1270s and 1280s and the complaint of infertile demesnes was repeated by Giffard's successors. In 1306 the demesne manors of Alvechurch, Hanbury, Kempsey and Wick were said to lie in a 'barren district' (*de debili territorio*) and Bishop Reynolds commented in a letter to his steward on the barrenness of the demesnes 'so that it does not seem useful to till them'.[63]

Possible explanations for poor yields could lie in the imbalance between arable and pasture apparent on some demesnes. At Tredington, to take the most extreme example, the arable in 1299 amounted to 506½ acres. Few animals had been kept there in 1246–7 and in the 1290s there were no sheep and only a few pigs apart from the draught animals necessary for cultivation. M. M. Postan and J. Z. Titow have blamed a shortage of manure for deteriorating yields in the late thirteenth century, notably on the estates of the bishops of Winchester. Professor Postan's contention that assarting led to the cultivation of unsuitable marginal land seems to be supported by the example of *Newsondene* at Alvechurch, which was taken into cultivation in 1269 but was valued at only 2d. per acre thirty years later.[64]

Concern about the returns of demesne agriculture seems to lie behind the estate survey of *c.*1290. Like many contemporary calculations, this enquiry sought to assess 'the profit of wainage [cultivation] and stock'.[65] But the calculation was used, by giving the amount of ploughing that could be done by customary labour, and the amount of land that could be ploughed in a day, to arrive at a recommendation that the number of demesne

[62] I. S. W. Blanchard, 'Economic Change in Derbyshire in the Late Middle Ages, 1272–1540' (Univ. of London Ph.D. thesis, 1967), pp. 54–5.

[63] *Reg. Giffard*, 301–2; Denholm-Young, *Seignorial Administration in England*, pp. 60–1; *Rotuli Parliamentorum*, i, p. 198; *Reg. Reynolds*, p. 34.

[64] Postan, *Medieval Economy and Society*, pp. 57–66; J. Z. Titow, *Winchester Yields* (Cambridge, 1972), pp. 29–31.

[65] On calculations of wainage see Denholm-Young, *Seignorial Administration in England*, pp. 128–30; Oschinsky, *Walter of Henley*, pp. 219–21; E. Stone, 'Profit-and-Loss Accountancy at Norwich Cathedral Priory', *Trans. Roy. Hist. Soc.*, 5th ser., xii (1962), pp. 25–48.

ploughs should be reduced on six demesnes. Judging from the number of demesne ploughs maintained during the vacancy of 1302–3, the advised retrenchments were not carried out, except in the case of one plough at Hampton (see Table 3). Such a penny-pinching approach to estate management can be found in the administrative manuals of the period, such as 'Walter of Henley'.

The c.1290 survey also examined rent income and found that in most cases rents listed in the manorial accounts were less than those that should have been collected, the difference being about £15. The compilers of the survey also recommended an increase in the commutation of labour services.

The late thirteenth and early fourteenth centuries were also periods of high levels of taxation. Bishop Giffard complained in the 1280s of the burden of providing hospitality for the king and his servants *en route* to Wales, but the peak of fiscal demands came in the 1290s and early fourteenth century, when the payment of tenths (assessed at £48 11s. 3d. on the bishopric) to king and pope became virtually annual charges. From 1302 each new bishop had to pay services to the papacy which began at 300 marks but rose to 400 marks by 1313.[66]

Another factor that could have contributed to the problems of the estate was the rising expenditure on the bishops' entourage, buildings and luxuries. It has already been suggested that the rising cost of living stimulated changes in estate management in the early thirteenth century. During the thirteenth century the bishops would have needed to expand the number of their staff to meet the growing demands of ecclesiastical and estate administration. Bishop Giffard, according to the hostile Worcester monks, descended on the cathedral priory on one occasion with a household so large that it was provided with 140 horses.[67] The bishops had much in common with the secular aristocracy. Walter Cantilupe, for example, was associated intimately with the baronial reformers of 1258–65; both he and Godfrey Giffard were related to barons. They

---

[66] M. Prestwich, *War, Politics, and Finance under Edward I* (London, 1972), pp. 186–91; *Taxatio Ecclesiastica auctoritate P. Nicholai IV, ca. 1291* (Record Commission, 1802), pp. 225–6; W. E. Lunt, *Financial Relations of England with the Papacy to 1327* (Cambridge, Mass., 1939), i, pp. 311–418, 679, 681. On the effects of taxes on a church landlord on the continent see A. D'Haenens, 'La Crise des Abbayes Bénédictines au bas Moyen Age, St.-Martin de Tournai, 1290–1350', *Le Moyen Age*, lxv (1959), pp. 83–5.

[67] *Annales Monastici*, iv, pp. 503–4.

shared with their secular counterparts a taste for luxurious consumption. Giffard embarked on a major building programme in the early years of his episcopate, obtaining licenses to crenellate his manor-houses at Hartlebury and Withington, and the palace at Worcester.[68] Much of his work at Worcester still survives, showing that he built on a grand scale in stone. The ambitious complexes of moats and fish-ponds still visible at Alvechurch and Hartlebury probably date from this period and would have involved high labour costs for the moving of earth for dams and leats. Some insight into the episcopal lifestyle is provided by the purchase of wine worth about £36 by Bishop Reynolds in 1312 and the seemingly endless catalogue of jewellery, silver plate, silk vestments and armour bequeathed by Giffard in his will of 1301.[69] It is likely that the expenditure of the bishops, like that of their contemporaries, kept pace with or exceeded their income, so that they had limited reserves with which to face bad years or unexpected financial demands.[70]

The number of short episcopates in the early fourteenth century, when there were seven bishops in thirty-six years, would also have disrupted the economy of the estate. At the end of each episcopate the estate was denuded of many of its assets which by custom belonged to the outgoing bishop or his executors. In 1313, after his election to Canterbury, Walter Reynolds ordered his officials to sell all crops, animals and other goods as soon as possible. A later bishop, Thomas Cobham, complained that he took over a ruined estate: 'I had nothing, neither in money, nor in any other thing.' He bequeathed his successor the crops and 40 oxen, which he believed to be the ancient custom. This still left the new bishop with the task of restocking the manors with hundreds of cattle and thousands of sheep in order to re-establish demesne agriculture.[71]

Bishop Giffard's response to the troubles of the 1280s had been to expand the size of his estate by acquiring new manors and appropriating rectories. The enquiry of *c*.1290 suggested economies in the

[68] White Book, fos. 44–5.
[69] *Reg. Reynolds*, pp. 32, 53; J. Melland Hall, 'The Will of Godfrey Giffard, Bishop of Worcester, A.D. 1301', *Trans. Bristol and Glos. Arch. Soc.*, xx (1895–7), pp. 139–54.
[70] Kershaw, *Bolton Priory*, pp. 161–74.
[71] *Reg. Reynolds*, p. 77; *Reg. Cobham*, pp. 49–50.

costs of production. There is no strong evidence for a great expansion in demesne production as occurred elsewhere.

The long-term trend was towards the leasing of demesnes and the expansion of cash rents by commuting labour services. Leasing had hardly begun in 1299, only 57½ acres of demesne being recorded as at farm. The change of direction came under Walter Reynolds, who ordered his steward in 1312 to improve wastes and let them for rent, to lease out demesnes that were barren or inconveniently remote from buildings, as well as letting vacant holdings for money rents and commuting some labour services.[72]

Already in 1311 Reynolds had leased out one of the poorest pieces of demesne on the estate, Sandhills (*Sanden*) in Alvechurch, a field of 65½ acres, for £1 4s. 0d. per annum. In the next year 2 furlongs, containing 16 acres, were leased from the Blockley demesne. The first manors to be leased were the smaller ones: Knightwick in 1318, Aston in 1324 and Bibury in 1327. Stratford was the first large manor to go, in 1339 to John de Peyto for £60 per annum for both demesne and tenant rents. Parcels of other demesnes were also rented out: for example 78 acres at Bredon in 1344.[73]

Developments in rent income at the end of our period are less easily determined. Vacant holdings are recorded in 1299 at a number of manors, notably six at Tredington and thirteen at Alvechurch, and there are references to the problem in 1306 and 1312.[74]

A movement towards commutation of labour services is indicated by the letting of forty-eight holdings for cash rents in the period 1287–1342, which could reflect difficulties in persuading tenants to take on holdings on the normal terms (see Chapter 4).

The history of the seignorial economy between Domesday and the great plague can be divided into three periods: stability in the twelfth century, rapid expansion in the thirteenth and a slowing

[72] *Reg. Reynolds*, p. 34; on the improving of wastes, Bishop Gainsborough sought permission to do this in Feckenham forest in 1306, but it is not known if these schemes were carried out, see *Rotuli Parliamentorum* (Record Commission), i, p. 198. Only a single grant of a parcel of waste is recorded, see *Reg. Reynolds*, p. 35.

[73] *Lib. Alb. Pri.*, pp. 50, 83; *Reg. Reynolds*, p. 43; *Reg. Cobham*, pp. 75, 180–1; *Reg. Bransford*, p. 16; *Cal. Pat. Rolls, 1317–21*, p. 332; *ibid., 1324–7*, p. 59; *ibid., 1327–30*, p. 197; *ibid., 1338–40*, p. 320; Bredon AR, 1375–6. For a similar pattern of early demesne leasing see M. Morgan, *The English Lands of the Abbey of Bec* (Oxford, 1946), pp. 104, 113–15.

[74] *Rotuli Parliamentorum*, i, p. 198; *Reg. Reynolds*, p. 34.

down in the early fourteenth century. The changes in direction are difficult to explain in view of the relatively scanty evidence. The great inflation must have played an important part in the expansion around 1200, but the set-backs in the late thirteenth and early fourteenth centuries seem to have been the result of a combination of internal and external factors such as declining demesne productivity, a rising burden of taxation and the purely local circumstances of discontinuity of short episcopates. The unknown factor is the development of rent income, which played such an important part in the growth of the estate revenues in the thirteenth century but may well have ceased to expand as tenants experienced economic difficulties.

4. The peasantry, 1086–1350

In the previous chapter we have seen that after a period of stability in the twelfth century, the bishops of Worcester responded to economic stimuli in the thirteenth century and greatly increased their revenues. Various interpretations have been advanced as to how the peasantry fared in the same period. There is general agreement that the numbers of peasants expanded, but the significance of this change has been explained in quite different ways. Some regard population growth as a symptom of peasant prosperity, which is seen as the product of the technical advances of the period, such as those leading to an expansion of the cultivated area. Against this the influential school of thought led by M. M. Postan argues that technology was relatively static and that the later clearances of land were failures; the population rose and outstripped resources and this culminated in reduced yields and subsistence crises. The expansion of the market is seen by some as assisting the peasantry, leading to the development of commodity production and involvement in industry by the peasants. The Postan school regard the market as peripheral; the crucial factor in an essentially subsistence economy was the ratio between people and land, and the poor productivity of that land.[1] A different, but closely related, field of controversy lies between those who believe that the social conditions of the peasantry improved, so that they gained greater freedom, and the exponents of the view that, particularly from the late twelfth century, large numbers of villeins were brought under closer seignorial control and suffered serious economic disadvantages as a result.[2]

[1] Some arguments in favour of peasant prosperity in the period are to be found in L. White, *Medieval Technology and Social Change* (Oxford, 1962), pp. 57–76; J. C. Russell, 'Late Ancient and Medieval Population', *Trans. Amer. Phil. Soc.*, xlviii (1958), pp. 137–45; B. F. Harvey, 'The Population Trend in England between 1300 and 1348', *Trans. Roy. Hist. Soc.*, 5th ser., xvi (1966), pp. 23–42; the most authoritative general statements of the opposite view are in Postan, *Medieval Economy and Society*, pp. 121–34; J. Z. Titow, *English Rural Society, 1200–1350* (London, 1969), pp. 64–96.

[2] Some arguments for improvement are Titow, *English Rural Society*, pp. 55–61; H. G. Richardson and G. O. Sayles, *Law and Legislation from Aethelberht to Magna Carta* (Edinburgh, 1966), pp. 139–48; J. Scammell, 'Freedom and Marriage in Medieval England', *Econ. Hist. Rev.*, 2nd ser., xxvii (1974), pp. 523–37; for the contrary view, P. Vinogradoff, *Villainage in England* (Oxford, 1892), pp. 211–20; R. H. Hilton, 'Freedom and Villeinage in England', *P and P*, xxxi (1965), pp. 3–19.

In this chapter the peasant population, land clearance, lord–tenant relations, and the impact of the market on the bishopric tenants will be discussed in the context of these debates.

There is no direct evidence, as exists elsewhere, that the population of the villages on the estate increased in the twelfth and thirteenth centuries, but such an increase must lie behind the growth in the number of recorded tenants, from 950 in 1086, to 1,289 in *c.*1170, and again to 1,853 in 1299, a doubling in two centuries. The figures for individual manors are given in Table 6.

Problems over the nature of the documents prevent us accepting these statistics at face value. The Domesday survey in particular

Table 6. *Numbers of tenants recorded in 1086, c.1170 and 1299*

Manor	1086	*c.*1170	1299	Change, *c.*1170–1299
Alvechurch	29	42	150	+ 108 (257%)
Aston	—	—	14	—
Bibury	37	—	33	—
Blockley	111	79*	136	—
Bredon (including Welland)	56	77	110	+ 33 (43%)
Cleeve	50	83	102	+ 19 (23%)
Fladbury (including Bradley)	65	82	108*	—
Hampton	37	35	57	+ 22 (63%)
Hanbury	42	45	90	+ 45 (100%)
Hartlebury	43	69	113	+ 44 (64%)
Henbury (including Stoke)	120	134	151	+ 17 (13%)
Kempsey	52	102	154	+ 52 (51%)
Ripple	73	86	111	+ 25 (29%)
Stratford (including Lapworth)	30	66	92	+ 26 (39%)
Tredington	85	48	63	+ 15 (31%)
Whitstones	47	189	179	− 10 (−5%)
Wick	27	122	126	+ 4 (3%)
Withington	46	30*	64	—
Total	950	1,289	1,853	

* Figures from incomplete surveys.

NOTE: The 1086 figures cover all people mentioned in the survey, including priests and *servi*, who probably held no land of the bishopric. No attempt should be made to make direct comparisons between the Domesday and later figures, because the size of the manors changed between 1086 and *c.*1170, non-tenants are listed in Domesday, and some categories of tenants may be omitted.

tends to underenumerate. The *censarii*, rent-paying tenants, on the
Burton Abbey manors were apparently missed out of Domesday
and, as many similar tenants existed on the twelfth-century
Worcester estate, it is possible that they too were omitted from the
1086 figures.[3] In any case, the Domesday figures are not comparable
with those of the later surveys, as the size of the demesne manors
was often reduced by subinfeudation in the late eleventh and
twelfth centuries.

The tenant populations of *c.*1170 and 1299 can be compared, as
there was little subinfeudation in the intervening period, although
some of the surveys are incomplete. Table 6 shows that the largest
increases were registered on the north Worcestershire manors of
Alvechurch and Hanbury (the Alvechurch figure for 1299 is swollen
by the tenants of the new borough, but if these are excluded, the
increase was still very large – 143 per cent). The expansion on the
other manors varied between 13 and 64 per cent, with no strong
regional pattern apparent. The contraction or stagnation in
tenant numbers at Whitstones and Wick are the result of the
inclusion of various Worcester-city tenants in *c.*1170, but their
successors were only partly listed in 1299. The later survey also
excludes the tenants of Stratford borough, so concealing the
dramatic increase on that manor.

This could be seen as evidence of real economic growth. Some of
the new tenants migrated to the bishopric manors, presumably
attracted by the opportunities that they offered. Surnames formed
from place-names suggest that by 1299 people had moved mainly
from villages within a fifteen-mile radius, and sometimes from one
bishopric manor to another. Movements over longer distances
are indicated by surnames such as Clattercote (in Oxfordshire) and
Malmesbury (in Wiltshire), both recorded at Alvechurch.[4] The main
source of new tenants was probably natural increase. This could
cause the division of holdings between heirs, as there are some
indications in *c.*1170 of a limited amount of partible inheritance
among the tenants of holdings for works (the precursors of the
customary tenants), as in six cases brothers appear as joint-tenants,
presumably of their father's holding. The lord assisted the increase

---

[3] J. F. R. Walmsley, 'The *Censarii* of Burton Abbey and the Domesday Population', *North Staffs. Journ. of Field Studies*, viii (1968), pp. 73–80.

[4] *RBW*, ii, pp. 215–16, 227, 229.

by letting out parcels of waste and of demesne, and by allowing the old tenurial units to be split – in *c*.1170, and to some extent in 1299, two, three or four people were listed as the tenants of yardland or half-yardland holdings; in some cases they may have been joint-tenants, but often, we must assume that the tenements had been divided.

This picture of overall growth in numbers must be qualified, as set-backs seem to have interrupted the long-term trend. Particularly noticeable are the number of untenanted holdings in *c*.1170. More than twenty yardlands were reported as vacant, including five yardlands and a cotland at Throckmorton, and three or four yardlands each at Hanbury, Henbury, Ripple and Stratford. The problem had evidently been acute at Ripple, where fourteen holdings had been let for cash rents 'because the land was vacant'. We might be tempted to invoke the troubles of Stephen's reign in explanation, or some economic depression in the period, perhaps only in the short-term, for which there is evidence on other estates.[5] In 1299 less land was 'in the lord's hands', but the vacant holdings were concentrated on two manors – Alvechurch where there were thirteen, and Tredington where there were six – in greater numbers than could have been caused by a normal year's deaths or migration.

The main obstacle in regarding the growth in the tenant population as indicative of prosperity is that in both the twelfth and thirteenth centuries many holdings were of small size. Table 7 categorizes all tenants on the estate into those with large holdings (a yardland or more), middling holdings (a half-yardland up to a yardland) and smallholdings (less than a half-yardland). The exact size of the yardland is not known, but both internal deductions from the surveys in the *Red Book*, and later evidence can be used to show that this unit varied within a manor, and from one manor to another; the range of sizes was from twenty-four acres (in the river valleys) to fifty acres (on the Cotswolds). In order to achieve comparability between manors a median of thirty acres has been assumed and used

[5] For devastation in the region see John of Worcester, *Chronicle*, ed. J. R. H. Weaver (Oxford, 1908), pp. 50, 56–7, 60. For evidence elsewhere of a twelfth-century depression, see Du Boulay, *Lordship of Canterbury*, pp. 200–1; M. M. Postan, 'Glastonbury Estates in the Twelfth Century', in *Medieval Agriculture and General Problems of the Medieval Economy* (Cambridge, 1973), pp. 249–77; Raftis, *Ramsey Abbey*, p. 89.

Table 7. Analysis of size of tenant holdings recorded in c.1170 and 1299

c.1170	1 yardland, or 30 acres, and above	½–1 yardland, or 15–29 acres	Less than a ½ yardland, or 14 acres and below	Size of holding uncertain	Total (100%)
Tenants not owing specific rent or labour service (mainly by knight service)	132 (85%)	11 (7%)	5 (3%)	7 (5%)	155
Tenants paying cash-rents	97 (31%)	71 (22%)	92 (29%)	57 (18%)	317
Tenants owing labour services	138 (20%)	215 (31%)	328 (48%)	7 (1%)	688
Others (mainly urban tenants)			30 (23%)	99 (77%)	129
Total	367 (29%)	297 (23%)	455 (35%)	170 (13%)	1,289
1299					
Tenants by knight service	104 (88%)	2 (2%)	10 (8%)	2 (2%)	118
Free tenants	90 (21%)	38 (9%)	115 (27%)	179 (43%)	422
Customary tenants	268 (22%)	394 (32%)	515 (42%)	48 (4%)	1,225
Others (mainly urban)				88 (100%)	88
Total	462 (25%)	434 (23%)	640 (35%)	317 (17%)	1,853

on the few occasions when a holding was described in terms of acres rather than yardlands.[6]

Table 7 shows that smallholders represented the largest group of tenants, 35 per cent of the total in each survey. Table 8 attempts to isolate the peasantry from other tenants by omitting those holding by knight service, and the urban tenants, and also leaves out the holdings of uncertain size. In both surveys the smallholders formed nearly a half. In fact they were probably near to a majority, as many of the holdings of uncertain size consisted of a croft or an assart held at a low rent, and were almost certainly small. The tables show that there were substantial numbers of smallholders in *c.*1170, but it should not be assumed that there was no change between *c.*1170 and 1299. The incompleteness of some of the twelfth-century documents introduces complications into making direct comparisons between the two sets of surveys. More importantly, there was a good deal of subdivision of smaller holdings so that the numbers of very small holdings, those with 6 acres or less, grew from 143 (15 per cent of the total in Table 8) in *c.*1170, to 362 in 1299 (25 per cent of the total).

Table 8. *Size of tenant holdings in c. 1170 and 1299*

omitting tenants by knight service, urban tenants and holdings of unknown size

*c.*1170	1 yardland, or 30 acres, and above	½ yardland, or 15–29 acres	Less than a ½ yardland, or 14 acres and below	Total (100%)
Rent-paying tenants	97 (37%)	71 (27%)	92 (36%)	260
Operarii	138 (20%)	215 (32%)	328 (48%)	681
Total	235 (25%)	286 (30%)	420 (45%)	941
1299				
Free	90 (37%)	38 (16%)	115 (47%)	243
Customary	268 (23%)	394 (33%)	515 (44%)	1,177
Total	358 (25%)	432 (31%)	630 (44%)	1,420

[6] There are hints in *RBW* of a 30-acre yardland at Ripple (ii, p. 170) and a 48-acre yardland at Bibury (iv, p. 373). The fifteenth-century Kempsey CR's imply a 24-acre yardland. The problems of generalizing are indicated by the occurrence of wide variations on one manor according to later documents. For example yardlands at Blockley varied from 24 to 40 acres in 1647: see WCRO ref. 009:1 BA 2636/47 43955.

Realistic calculations of peasant budgets show that customary half-yardlanders would have been barely able, in the late thirteenth century, to feed their families and meet their obligations in rents and taxes from their landed resources alone.[7] So 44 per cent of the bishopric of Worcester's customary tenants in 1299, those with less than a half-yardland, lacked the resources from their holdings to fulfil their material needs. The free tenants paid less in rents, so the amount of land that they needed for their subsistence was rather less than that of the customary tenants, but a substantial minority of them also lacked adequate amounts of land. The category of those unable to provide all of their needs from their holdings thus included about 40 per cent of all tenants.

The surveys are deficient as statements of the landholding of individuals. They were compiled in order to record the tenants who were responsible for rendering rents and services to the lord, so that any subletting is concealed. The survey of Cleeve in 1299 mentions subtenants, cottars whose only obligation to the bishop was a day or two's service at harvest time. This submerged population would doubtless have increased still further the numbers of smallholders.[8]

The size of holdings recorded on the bishopric manors – and in the west-midland region as a whole – was larger than those found in other parts of England, notably in the east.[9] However, some manors contained more smallholders than others. For example, three manors near Worcester, Kempsey, Whitstones and Wick had 68 per cent, 91 per cent and 77 per cent of smallholders respectively in 1299. Holders of full yardlands occurred more commonly on the Cotswold and Avon valley manors, exceeding a half of all tenants at Blockley (63 per cent), Hampton (53 per cent) and Stratford (51 per cent), and also on the Severn valley manor of Hartlebury (52 per cent).

An optimistic view of developments in the twelfth and thirteenth centuries would see in the clearance of new land a safety valve that allowed the cultivated area to expand and so accommodate the growing population. As well as increasing total productive

---

[7] Kosminsky, *Studies in the Agrarian History of England*, pp. 230–40; Hilton, *A Medieval Society*, pp. 122–3.

[8] *RBW*, iv, p. 347.

[9] Kosminsky, *Agrarian History of England*, pp. 216–18.

capacity, the assarting of woodland and waste allowed scope for the initiative of the more independent elements in peasant society.

We have already seen that the bishops facilitated assarting by obtaining exemptions from the restrictions of forest law. Some assarts were added to the demesne, but the great majority, amounting to many hundreds of acres, were created and worked by the tenants. The new lands were let on relatively favourable terms, often as free tenures for cash rents, and at Alvechurch many were held on customary tenures for light rents and services, suggesting seignorial encouragement for clearance.

Maps 5 and 6 depict the areas of assarts and purprestures recorded in the twelfth and thirteenth centuries. They show that the main focus of assarting in the twelfth century lay in the Severn valley, notably 212 acres at Whitstones, and 210 acres at Kempsey. In the thirteenth century the emphasis shifted to the north and west of Worcestershire, so that the largest numbers of assarts in 1299 were at Alvechurch (69), Hanbury (34) and Welland (23). This helps to explain the doubling of tenant numbers on the north Worcestershire manors between *c.*1170 and 1299 (Table 6).[10]

Assarting enabled tenants of all kinds to expand the size of their holdings. Of eighteen tenants of assarts and new lands at Alvechurch in 1299 whose other holdings are recorded, eight had half-yardlands or yardlands, while the other ten had less than a half-yardland. Thirteen others held assarts only, and could include landless elements, or younger sons, obtaining land by clearance. Large-scale assarting required much labour and capital, and substantial tenants are usually found occupying big cleared areas. For example, two assarts of 20 acres at Kempsey were each held in *c.*1170 by yardlanders, while most individual assarts amounted to 5 acres or less.

As new lands were carved out of the waste, they tended to be held in severalty and enclosed, so that a distinctive landscape of hedged parcels developed in areas of assarting. This was already apparent in north Worcestershire in the tenth century. In the thirteenth century references to crofts, *placeae* and similar field names indicative of

[10] The sources of the maps are the surveys of *c.*1170 and 1299; the lists of assarts and purprestures of about the same date as the *c.*1170 surveys (*RBW*, iv, pp. 422–6); and the charter of Richard I granting exemption from forest law (White Book, fos. 41–2).

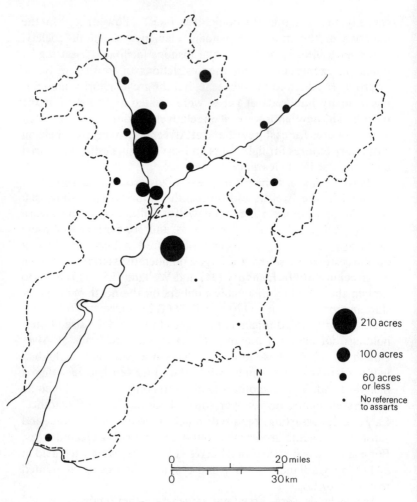

5   Assarts recorded, c.1170–89

enclosure are found most plentifully in north Worcestershire and
the Severn valley, at Alvechurch, Hanbury, Hartlebury, Henbury,
Ripple, Whitstones and Wick. Enclosure was also associated
with a dispersed pattern of settlement, where individual farmsteads
and small hamlets were established in the waste, indicating the
independence of those who had won their own land away from
the restricting environment of nucleated villages, with their com-

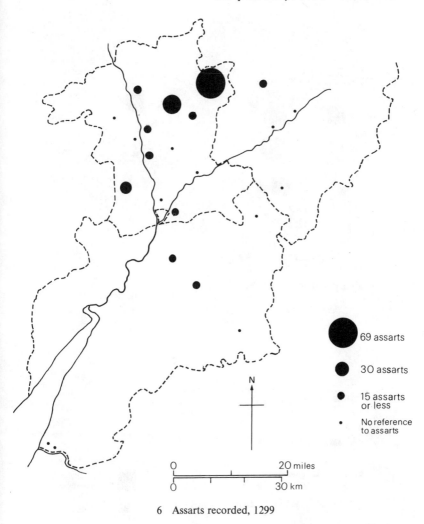

6   Assarts recorded, 1299

munal control of the open fields.[11] Maps 7, 8 and 9 contrast the
settlement patterns of three main types of manor. Fladbury
contained four substantial villages. The other Avon valley manors
also had a small number of large settlements. Ripple is typical of

[11] On dispersed settlement in a newly colonized west-midland parish, see
B. K. Roberts, 'A Study of Medieval Colonisation in the Forest of Arden,
Warwickshire', *Ag. Hist. Rev.*, xvi (1968), pp. 101–13.

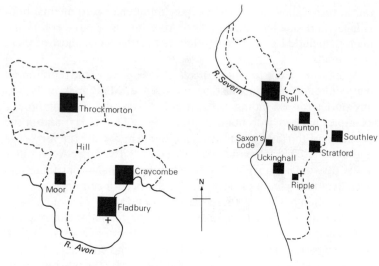

7   Fladbury settlements, c.1170

8   Ripple settlements, c.1170

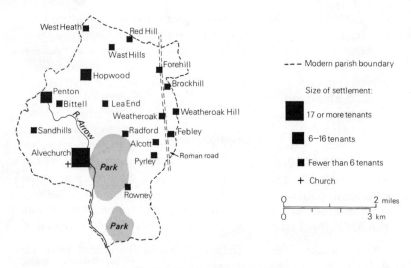

9   Alvechurch settlements, 1299

the Severn valley in having a larger number of settlements, both villages and smaller hamlets, and Alvechurch, a large colonizing manor, included a scatter of eighteen settlements, most of them very small.[12]

Again, the extent to which the clearance of new land represented real economic growth must be questioned. Many manors lacked any outlet for extending cultivation. Bibury and Tredington, for example, had no woodland at the time of Domesday, and in the twelfth and thirteenth centuries fuel and timber for the lord's use had to be fetched from outside the manor.[13] The other Avon valley and Cotswold manors had a little more woodland, but there had been extensive clearance long before the twelfth century, and, with the exception of Cleeve, there was little or no assarting in our period. The draining of the salt-marshes at Henbury, a major contribution to extending cultivation, seems to have been completed by the late twelfth century. The Severn valley manors had considerable room for new clearance in the twelfth century, but by the late thirteenth century assarts had to be concentrated in north and west Worcestershire, the only parts of the estate where extensive woodlands remained.

By the late thirteenth century assarting and the enclosure of waste were meeting with resistance. At some point shortly before 1273 the men of King's Norton threw down enclosures made on the heaths to the north of Alvechurch.[14] The bishops and neighbouring lords protected remaining woods and pastures by enclosing them in parks, and sometimes reversed the trends of the period by taking in cultivated lands and converting them to grass. The driving force behind opposition to further clearance was the shortage of pasture. This is indicated by the number of charters in the bishopric cartulary concerned with the regulation of pasture rights.[15] Pastures in the thirteenth century were already stinted; for example, a free holding of more than 20 acres at Cleeve had grazing rights for only 2 oxen and a cow and a calf.[16] In 1299 the tenants at Bibury were

---

[12] Source for the Alvechurch map: WCRO ref. f. 760/7 BA 1572 (tithe apportionment and map).

[13] *RBW*, iv, p. 371; iii, p. 281.

[14] White Book, fo. 71.

[15] The emparking of arable land in 1276 is shown by a Bredon charter: White Book, fo. 68; and *RBW*, iv, p. 377; other charters concerned with pasture rights include White Book, fos. 51–2 (agistment in Malvern Wood); 65 (common pasture at Fladbury and Bredon); 83 (common pasture at Alvechurch).

[16] White Book, fos. 55–6.

not allowed to use the bishop's demesnes as common pasture. In 1312 a heated dispute arose over pasture on Bredon Hill, in which Bishop Reynolds excommunicated the men of Kemerton for impounding 400 sheep and an ox belonging to his Bredon tenants. Even meadow land, in short supply at any time, was being ploughed up in c.1170 at Ripple. The ridge and furrow created by early ploughing, sometimes demonstrably belonging to the medieval period, can be shown at Blockley to have extended down to the edge of streams, encroaching on the natural meadow.[17]

Assarting did not always lead to economic individualism. At Cleeve in c.1170 a tenant called Girold held a total of 90 acres of assarts, but 'it is half in one field, and half in another', showing that the new land had been absorbed into the prevailing two-course rotation of the Cleeve open fields.[18] Presumably on other manors the tenant crofts and enclosures, like those in the demesne, were still subject to communal control of cropping, allowing common pasture on the fallow.

Internal colonization in the twelfth and thirteenth centuries should be put into the perspective of the settlement history of the whole estate. The total cultivated area in 1299 was probably in the region of 30,000 to 40,000 acres, of which perhaps 2,000 acres had been cleared in the previous century and a half. The new lands were inferior to those settled earlier; the assarts at Bradley, for example, occupied land classified by the Ministry of Agriculture today as of grade four, 'only suitable for low output enterprises'.[19] The great majority of the bishopric tenants – indeed, most of the rural population of medieval England – tilled old-cultivated lands, in open fields which were subject to communal regulation. On the Worcester estate the prevailing two-course rotation had presumably evolved to allow for the maximum of pasture on the fallow; there was little waste or woodland for permanent pasture, and any further encroachment by clearance would have damaged the interests of the villagers. Much of the increase in tenant numbers

[17] *RBW*, iv, p. 368; *Reg. Reynolds*, pp. 40–1; *RBW*, ii, p. 168; the observation on the ridge and furrow pattern is based on a survey of Blockley conducted by the author and Professor R. H. Hilton in 1966–7.

[18] *RBW*, iv, p. 351.

[19] Ministry of Agriculture, Fisheries and Food, Land Classification Map, sheet 131; assarting in the area is shown by a charter, White Book, fo. 62 and *RBW*, ii, pp. 139–40.

between *c.*1170 and 1299 resulted from the more intensive occupation of existing land, not from a large increase in the amount of
cultivated land.

Did changes in the relationship between the lord and his tenants in
the period in any way assist in the economic and social development
of the peasantry? The bishopric lands belonged to the type of
estate in which the lord was likely to be a pervading influence – the
manors included complete villages, often a number of settlements
on each manor, and the bishops had enjoyed continuous lordship
for many centuries.

The argument that the medieval peasantry progressed from
predominant subjection towards freedom in our period finds some
support from the decline of slavery in the eleventh century.
We have already seen that slaves were much more numerous in the
pre-Conquest period than at the time of Domesday. By 1086 there
were 155 slaves and bondwomen on the estate. The slaves seem
to have acted as ploughmen, and the bondwomen, who occur
mainly on the river-valley manors, could well have been dairymaids.
The existence of *coliberti* at Westbury at the time of Domesday
might suggest that slaves were already being freed. By the twelfth
century no slaves remained on the estate. It is well known that
Bishop Wulfstan preached against the slave trade at Bristol in
the late eleventh century, but the main reason for the disappearance
of the slavery was economic – lords found it more convenient to
grant a smallholding to their permanent labour force, rather than
to feed and house them directly.[20]

In the survey of *c.*1170 the successors of the eleventh-century
slaves appear as *avercmen* and *bovarii*, tenants of holdings smaller
than a half-yardland, owing very heavy labour services, up to five
days per week. Relics of the old arrangements can be seen in the
allowance of grain made to them, in the existence at Hampton of a
domus bovariorum (the house in which the *bovarii* lived), and perhaps
also in the concession made to them of the use of the lord's plough
on Saturdays for the cultivation of their own holdings. These
tenements with the potential obligation to 'hold the lord's plough'

[20] *Vita Wulfstani*, ed. Darlington, pp. 43–4; M. Bloch, 'Comment et pourquoi
finit l'esclavage antique', *Annales ESC*, ii (1947), pp. 161–70.

and do other full-time work survived as *enchelonds* in the thirteenth century.[21]

The survey of *c.*1170 lists 155 tenants whose services were not specified – they were mostly tenants by knight service; there were 317 tenants called *censarii* or *malmen*, who paid cash rents, though some owed services as well; 688 whose obligations were described primarily in terms of labour services, *operarii*, who included both tenants of yardlands or fractions of a yardland owing week-work, and smallholders who either owed light services like the *lundinarii* (mondaymen) or the heavily burdened *bovarii* and *avercmen* mentioned above. The survey records recent changes in tenures that clearly operated in favour of the tenants. The lord had let out about 66 holdings of demesne land; of the grants that are dated, most belong to the episcopate of Bishop Simon (1125–50). Also, often in the period 1125–60, some of the rent-paying holdings had been created from holdings owing labour services – a half-yardland at Cleeve, for example, 'which used to be worked', was now let 'for 4s. 0d. quit of all things'. A yardland and a half at Tredington 'which once worked', paid rents totalling 5s. 0d. per annum.[22] Particularly striking is the number of holdings of *bovarii, avercmen* and *lundinarii*, twenty in all, which paid rents. The tenants at Hartlebury were listed as paying cash rents, but these were clearly alternative to their performance of labour service, so that the survey states that the more substantial tenants 'ought to be *operarii*', and the *lundinarii* 'work each Monday if they do not pay rent'. A similar flexibility is implied by a note at Fladbury that 'if they [the *censarii*] have houses, they ought to work'.[23]

The letting out of demesne land and the conversion of holdings to rent payment, which were both happening in the mid-twelfth century, were presumably connected; labour services would not all be necessary if the demesne was shrinking. This could be seen as the result of the lord's initiative, in order to increase his income in cash, or it could have been a response to economic difficulties, as suggested also by the vacant holdings discussed already.[24]

[21] M. M. Postan, *The Famulus* (Econ. Hist. Rev. Supplement, no. 2, 1954), pp. 1–48.

[22] *RBW*, iv, p. 352; iii, p. 293.

[23] *RBW*, ii, pp. 206–7; iv, pp. 419–20.

[24] Miller, 'England in the Twelfth and Thirteenth Centuries', pp. 4–7, discusses and rejects the possibility of such a depression.

Whatever the cause of the twelfth-century tenurial changes, they were of long-term benefit to many peasants. The rents fixed by *c.*1170, usually at between 3s. 0d. and 6s. 0d. per yardland, were rapidly overtaken by inflation, and so seemed very cheap in the late thirteenth century. The Hartlebury tenants, who had secured a rent-paying alternative by *c.* 1170, made further advances by 1299, when they paid most of their rents in cash, and had lighter services than customary tenants elsewhere on the estate.

Cash payments continued to replace labour services in the thirteenth and early fourteenth centuries, both by individually negotiated agreements, like those of the twelfth century, and through more flexible commutations affecting all of the tenants from year to year.

Total conversions from labour services to rents are mentioned in thirty cases in the 1299 survey, some of them going back to the early and mid-thirteenth century. Forty-eight agreements are known from the period 1287–1342, so that it would appear that the movement gathered pace towards the end of our period, not in the mid-thirteenth century as recorded on other estates.[25] Nine of the recipients were servants of the bishops, receiving grants as rewards for service. More commonly the sitting tenants benefited, and in some cases they paid a premium for the grant. In 1316 Richard le Honte paid £2 to hold a cottage, 12 acres, 2 butts and a parcel of meadow at Bredon at a rent of 6s. 8d. per annum. Sometimes the remission of services was accompanied by manumission from serfdom, but the change to money-rent did not necessarily affect the personal status of the tenant. The tenants under the new arrangement sometimes held for life or lives only, but most tenures were apparently hereditary.

At some point between *c.*1170 and 1246 new arrangements were made for the rents and services of the *operarii*, which were not fully recorded until 1299. A cash 'rent of assize' was fixed for each holding, and all services were valued, so that tenants could be

---

[25] c.f. R. H. Hilton, 'Gloucester Abbey Leases of the Late Thirteenth Century', in *The English Peasantry in the Later Middle Ages* (Oxford, 1975), pp. 139–55. The grants are recorded as follows: *Reg. Giffard*, pp. 318–19, 369, 456, 463, 467, 496, 506, 508; *Reg. Reynolds*, pp. 2–3, 14, 18, 20, 35, 43, 44, 46, 74; *Reg. Cobham*, pp. 23, 106; *Reg. Bransford*, pp. 33, 100; *RBW*, i, 26–7, 55, 80; ii, 236–7; iii, 253; iv, 332, 348, 384, 401–2; *Lib. Alb. Pri.*, p. 39; Lib. Alb. Pri., fos. xxixa, xxx, xlviii, lviii, lxix, lxx, xcvii, xcviii, cxxxix, clv; *Cal. Pat. Rolls, 1317–21*, pp. 332, 499, 511, 523, 587; *1327–30*, pp. 175, 544; *1330–4*, p. 554; *1338–40*, p. 83.

required to fulfil their obligations to the lord in a combination of money and services. In theory they could have done all of their works, and so paid no cash rent, but in practice the demesnes were well supplied with potential labour services, and it was convenient for the lord to employ full-time *famuli* for regular jobs such as ploughing, carting and looking after stock. Casual wage-labour was also employed on such work as the harvest, perhaps because of its higher productivity.[26] So most tenants would have paid their assize rents, which varied from 3s. 0d. to 10s. 0d. per yardland, performed part of their services, and paid extra rents in lieu of the services that the lord did not need. In 1302–3 about a third of the potential services were commuted; this was an unusual year in a vacancy, but the proportion in a normal year may have been similar. The number of works 'sold' to the tenants probably increased in the early fourteenth century, in line with the recommendations in Bishop Reynold's letter to his steward.[27] Table 9 gives the rents of assize and valuations of works and customs owed by standard holdings in 1299. In theory, on most manors cash rents formed a third or more of the tenants' total obligations; in practice, they would have paid a higher proportion.

The flexible organisation of rents and services of the thirteenth century benefited the lord. He gained a considerable rent income, which was rising, as we have seen, in the last third of the thirteenth century, but retained the option of using the tenants' labour as necessary. However, the complete conversion of some holdings to rent-payment towards the end of our period suggests that the lord was under some pressure to make changes. Grants of holdings at rent reached a peak in the mid-1290s, when the bishop's burden of taxation was acute, and he needed money urgently. The tenants who presumably demanded the change tended to be those with larger holdings, who could afford to pay lump sums to secure greater certainty in their obligations. The lord may have experienced difficulties in persuading tenants to take on some holdings, and had to change the terms of tenure to make them more attractive; seven of the holdings concerned were at Alvechurch, where thirteen vacancies in 1299 suggest a slackening demand for land.

[26] Bodleian Library, Worcester Rolls no. 4.

[27] *Reg. Reynolds*, p. 34. There are many parallels for this process going on in the late thirteenth and early fourteenth centuries, e.g. Raftis, *Ramsey Abbey*, pp. 222–9; Miller, *Abbey and Bishopric of Ely*, pp. 103–4.

Table 9. *Assize rents and the valuations of labour services for standard customary holdings in 1299*

On manors where there was a good deal of uniformity of rents and services, the statistical mode of rents and services has been given. For those where there are many variations, the minimum and maximum have been noted

	Yardlands Rent	Services	Half-yardlands Rent	Services	Quarter-yardlands Rent	Services
Alvechurch			2s. 6d.	12s. 2¾d.		
Aston					3s. 0d.	8s. 1¾d.
Bibury	5s. 0d.	14s. 0d.	2s. 6d.	7s. 0d.		
Blockley	4s. 0d.	2s. 2½d.				
	4s. 0d.	15s. 4¾d.				
Bredon	6s. 0d.	18s. 9½d.	3s. 0d.	9s. 4¾d.		
Cleeve	8s. 0d.	14s. 1d.	3s. 10½d.	3d.		
			4s. 0d.	7s. 0½d.		
Fladbury	5s. 0d.	7s. 9d.	3s. 0d.	3s. 10½d.		
	6s. 0d.	7s. 9d.	4s. 0d.	3s. 10½d.		
Hampton	3s. 0d.	10s. 2d.				
	3s. 11d.	10s. 3d.				
Hanbury			4s. 0d.	7s. 0d.		
Hartlebury	3s. 0d.	8d.	1s. 6d.	1s. 3d.		
	10s. 0d.	4s. 11½d.	5s. 0d.	1s. 0½d.		
Henbury	8s. 0d.	20s. 0½d.	5s. 0d.	7s. 0d.		
	10s. 0d.	23s. 3½d.	5s. 0d.	11s. 7¾d.		
Kempsey			1s. 6d.	16s. 4½d.		
Ripple			5s. 0d.	7s. 3½d.		
Stratford	8s. 0d.	13s. 7½d.	4s. 0d.	6s. 9½d.		
Tredington	5s. 0d.	19s. 6d.	2s. 6d.	9s. 9d.		
Whitstones			5s. 0d.	19s. 1½d.		
Wick			7s. 0d.	12s. 11d.		

The movement towards rents was not a steady or uniform process. Indeed, probably in the late twelfth or early thirteenth century the trends were reversed. For example, many of the rent-paying tenants at Fladbury were expected to do labour services by 1246.

Conversion of holdings to cash rents was a significant trend, but comparatively small numbers achieved permanent commutation. In *c.*1170, 688 tenants were listed as *operarii*, and about a further 100 were liable to do services as an alternative to rent-payment, so that the *censarii* formed only about 22 per cent of the tenant population (excluding those owing military services). The proportion of rent-paying free tenants in 1299 was still only 26 per cent.

There is some evidence to suggest that the quantity of labour services demanded increased between c.1170 and 1299. In c.1170 the yardlanders usually owed four or five days of labour each week, and were also liable for carrying services on the other days. On some manors a day's work was defined as lasting until evening, except in the spring, when it ended at noon. Additional bedrips and boons – up to a maximum of eight in the year – were owed in the haymaking or harvest seasons. These often involved the services of more than one man, and sometimes the whole household. Extra work 'in the court' consisted of domestic tasks such as making malt, brewing and providing the brewing equipment. Some tasks were described in detail, like the ploughing, which involved a certain number of days – up to seven in the whole year – or a fixed area of the demesne to be cultivated, usually $\frac{1}{2}$ or $\frac{3}{4}$ acre. Some of the services were not strictly limited – carrying services were to be done as required, and domestic duties depended on the will of the lord. If the Fladbury haymaking had not been completed by 1 August, the tenants had to work for five days per week until it was finished.

The obligations of the smallholders were much more varied, with many involved only in light works, for example only one or two days per week in the case of the mondaymen, but the *bovarii* or *avercmen* on some manors were more heavily involved than the yardlanders in work on the demesne.

The lists of services in 1299 were more detailed than in the earlier surveys, and this might seem to have been to the advantage of the tenant. However, many of the changes had the effect of increasing the tenants' burdens.[28] The number of days of week-work did not usually change, but tenants might be expected to provide the labour of more than one man on certain days. Eight bedrips were owed at Bredon in c.1170 and in 1299, but at the later date the yardlander was expected to spend an additional two days stacking corn. Bedrips at Alvechurch in c.1170 had been done by the whole household, but by 1299 the tenant was supposed to bring three men – most households would probably not have contained three adult men, so this represents an increase. At Kempsey each yardland was liable to carrying services on Fridays and Saturdays in the twelfth century; by the thirteenth century Sundays had been added.

---

[28] As happened also on other estates: see Miller, *Bishopric of Ely*, pp. 101–2; Postan, 'Chronology of Labour Services', pp. 101–2.

In spite of the greater precision with which services were defined in the thirteenth century, an element of arbitrariness continued – haymaking and harvesting works had to be continued until finished, and domestic chores depended on the frequency of the lord's visits. A few details of the 1299 surveys favoured the tenants, such as the references to bedrips 'at the lord's cost', that is, with food provided, but the predominant tendency was to push up the tenants' obligations. This might at first seem inconsistent with the conversion of services into cash rents, but the primary purpose of the changes was probably to increase cash income by raising the value of the services, rather than to increase yet further the quantity of labour available for working the demesne.[29]

Some changes are apparent in the descriptions of the various dues and payments, often called 'customs', additional to the annual assize rents and labour services. These were the regular payments like aid, common fines, churchscot, Peter's Pence, fishfee, spenyngfee, woodsilver, and the compulsory ale drinkings (for which the tenants paid) called 'fustale'; or occasional charges, like tolls on the sale of oxen and horses, and on the brewing of ale for sale, pannage on the pasture of pigs, which depended on the numbers of animals kept, and the heriot paid when a tenant died. There were also restrictions on the movement of sons outside the manor, and on the marriage of daughters, giving rise to payments of *merchet*, the marriage fine, and *leyerwite*, the fine for incontinence.

The survey of *c.*1170 lists fairly thoroughly such dues as fishfee, spenyngfee, toll, pannage and churchscot, but is inconsistent in recording other dues. Aid, which represented a large sum of cash in 1299, is found on only five manors in *c.*1170.[30] Was it omitted from the other manors, or was it being imposed in the late twelfth century? It was certainly introduced on all manors before the 1250s, as Aston was acquired then, and the tenants of that manor escaped from any obligations to pay aid, as well as toll and pannage.

In 1299 the tenants' liability to aid, common fine and other customs, such as restrictions on marriage, was systematically recorded. This may be connected with the fact that since *c*1170 they had become tests of villein status. Domesday's description of the estate refers to 'each hide whether free or villein' owing churchscot, but

---

[29] Miller, *Bishopric of Ely*, p. 102.
[30] Hampton, Kempsey, Ripple, Stratford and Tredington.

this is probably making a distinction between land held by the major tenants on lease or as fees, and the lands held by the peasant tenants on the demesne manors. The many *villani* of 1086 were peasants with large holdings, as distinct from the smallholding bordars, and they clearly differed from the landless and unfree *servi*. In the late twelfth century the term 'in villeinage' was used to describe tenant land in general, not the land held by unfree tenants. At Welland a tenant held *de dominico et villenagio*, as if the alternative to land held in villeinage was land that had originally been in the lord's demesne. So villeinage seems to have been a neutral term as far as the personal status or obligations of the tenant were concerned. Tenants whose only obligation was to pay scutage held *de villenagio*.

Occasionally there are hints in the survey of *c.*1170 that the meaning of the word 'villein' was changing. In the survey of Withington (which differs markedly from the others, as if it were compiled at another date) those who held *de villenagio* were the tenants of substantial holdings owing labour services. Two Fladbury monday-lands were held by two brothers; one was *dismissus* – leased? – the other *villanus* – presumably owing labour services.[31] In *c.*1170 some of the tenants were undoubtedly subject to the personal control of the lord, and were regarded as having been born into servility – they were called *nativi*. A list of sixteen men living on manors other than the bishop's in Worcestershire is headed 'the names of *nativi* and fugitives' showing that they were not allowed to leave the manor. The payment of *leyerwite*, associated with the lord's control of marriage among his tenants, is mentioned on three manors. However, we do not know how many of the bishop's tenants were regarded as *nativi*; the statement in the Hartlebury survey, that only *nativi* were expected to bring their whole household to work at bedrips, suggests that not all tenants owing labour services were classed as serfs.[32] Perhaps only the descendants of earlier slaves were included in the category.

Elsewhere in England new and stricter definitions of serfdom can be shown to have been introduced in the decades around 1200, so that the performance of heavy labour services became

---

[31] Hilton, 'Freedom and Villeinage in England', pp. 6–13, discusses these changes of terminology.

[32] Fugitives: see *RBW*, iv, p. 418; *Leyerwite:* see *RBW*, iv, p. 409; i, p. 35; iv, p. 367; Hartlebury *nativi, RBW*, ii, p. 206.

equated with servile status. So 'villeinage' came to mean 'servility'. This is apparent from the categorization of tenants in the 1299 surveys; whereas the nomenclature applied to tenants in *c.*1170 had differentiated between types of service – *censarii* and *operarii* for example – by the late thirteenth century the emphasis had shifted to distinctions based on legal status. The rent-payers in 1299 were called *liberi tenentes* (free tenants), and the more substantial tenants who owed labour services appear under a variety of headings, including *bondi* (bondsmen), *consuetudinarii* and *custumarii* (customary tenants), *nativi* (born serfs) and *villenagium* (villeinage).

Now this process of definition, which meant that by the thirteenth century the majority of the peasant tenants of the bishopric estate were of unfree status, could be seen as an application of a mere legal theory, which had little effect on real life. It has been argued that strict demarcations of status were not possible, so that a large grey area lay between the free and the servile. Such shades of 'semi-freedom' have been recognized in East Anglia in particular, but the area of uncertainty was much narrower in the manorialized west midlands.[33] There are some tenants on the Worcester estate whose position seems anomalous. At Blockley a group of eighteen tenants were listed under the heading of 'customers' some of whom do not seem to have conformed with the normal villein, in that they paid cash rents or only light services, and all did not pay aid, toll or the other servile dues, though five did not have the freedom to marry off their daughters, a crucial test of villein status. Elsewhere some free tenants were expected to contribute to the payment of aid, which was normally confined to villeins.[34] These ambiguities were comparatively rare; nor did many tenants create potentially complex problems by acquiring both free and customary land: only twenty-seven are recorded with complete holdings of both kinds (as distinct from customary tenants with small assarts for which they paid cash rents) out of 1,853 tenants in 1299. There seems to have been a quite clear segregation between the free and servile peasantry of the estate.

In economic terms the unfree tenant was at a considerable disadvantage compared with his free neighbours. He was the tenant of

[33] Miller, *Bishopric of Ely*, pp. 126–9.
[34] *RBW*, iii, pp. 298–300; iv, pp. 329–31.

land burdened with heavy labour services, which made inroads into the amount of time available for work on his own holding, particularly at such crucial peaks of activity as haymaking and the harvest. If a customary holding was held only for money-rents, it paid much more than a free tenement of comparable size. In 1299 the rents of most free yardlands varied from 3s. 0d. to 8s. 0d. per annum. The annual rents negotiated when services were remitted on a customary yardland in the years around 1300 were between 10s. 0d. and £1 6s. 8d. In calculating the budget of a half-yardlander in the late thirteenth century, rents can be shown to have played a crucial role in tipping the balance against the peasant. In a normal year he could expect to harvest enough grain to provide food for his family and seed for the next year. Any saleable surplus, and any money deriving from wool, milk or meat, could be swallowed up in rents and taxes. The position was worsened by the uncertainties of the tenant's relationship with the lord. His quota of work might change from year to year. Any savings might be taken away by unexpected demands for amercements in the court, or payment of recognition to a new bishop. Restrictions on personal freedom could have inhibited the tenant's ability to accumulate property in his family through marriage, or to allow sons to move away to take advantage of opportunities on the labour market. The death of a tenant was a major set-back financially, as the successor not only lost a beast as heriot, a burden that affected free and unfree alike, but had to pay an entry-fine that would have been higher than the free tenant's relief. The only example known from the estate was £1 0s. 0d. for a yardland holding, paid at Hampton in c.1300, which was in itself a substantial sum, but fines could have been much more than this.[35]

Two compensatory factors only can be seen in the development of tenures on the estate. Firstly, the lord's anxiety to protect the integrity of holdings inhibited the fragmentation of customary tenements. The signs of some partible inheritance in c.1170 mentioned earlier had disappeared by 1299. The imposition of strict primogeniture may date from the same period as the closer definition of serfdom, and this probably lies behind the higher

[35] R. H. Hilton, 'Peasant Movements in England before 1381', in E. M. Carus-Wilson (ed.), *Essays in Economic History* (London, 1962), ii, pp. 74–8. The entry-fine comes from a fragment of a court roll for Hampton in *Reg. Reynolds*, p. 1. Much higher fines occur on the Glastonbury and Winchester estates, see Titow, *English Rural Society*, pp. 75–6.

proportion of holdings of middling size among customary tenants. Free tenants tended to split up their holdings by alienation and partible inheritance (see Table 8).[36]

Secondly, the assarting movement of the twelfth and thirteenth centuries shifted the balance slightly in favour of free tenure. This was statistically insignificant over the whole estate, but it created enclaves in which free tenants predominated, such as those at Alvechurch and Hanbury, and also on the detached woodland properties of Bradley, Lapworth and Welland.

In spite of the pressure of seignorial demands, surely all of the peasantry could have benefited from the expanding market of the thirteenth century?

The payment of cash rents by all tenants shows that they were able to acquire some money, either by selling produce or by their own labour. Those substantial customary tenants who received grants of their holdings for cash presumably calculated that they could make a success of marketing, and that it was worth paying a large sum of money each year rather than being exposed to the uncertainties of the lord's demands for labour. Access to the market became easier with the growth of new market towns, like Stratford-on-Avon and Alvechurch on the estate, or such towns as Campden, Fairford or Stow-on-the-Wold, which lay near to bishopric manors. The importance of small market towns is indicated by their appearance in the descriptions of tenant customs as possible venues for the sale of animals.[37]

The influence of the urban market on the peasant economy is indicated by Table 10, which shows that the level of rents, combined with the valuation of services, was considerably higher on the manors adjoining the large towns of Bristol and Worcester, at Aston, Henbury, Kempsey, Whitstones and Wick. This could be interpreted as a reflection of higher demand for land, but customary holdings were hardly open to free bidding, so the high rents are more

[36] J. Thirsk, 'The Common Fields', pp. 12–13, on early partible inheritance. On the tendency for customary holdings to be larger, see Kosminsky, *Studies in the Agrarian History of England*, pp. 220–4.

[37] On the growth of new towns, H. P. R. Finberg, 'The Genesis of the Gloucestershire Towns', in *Gloucestershire Studies* (Leicester, 1957), pp. 62–83. For references to tenants visiting local towns to sell animals: see *RBW*, i, p. 95 (Bredon tenants at Evesham and Pershore); ii, p. 158 (Ripple tenants at the same two towns); White Book fos. 51–2 show that Bibury tenants went to Fairford market.

Table 10. *Combined assize rents and valuations of services in 1299 for standard customary holdings, arranged by manor in ranking order*

Derived from Table 9, using either the statistical modes, or the maximum and minimum values in the case of manors with wide variations

	Yardlands	Half-yardlands	Quarter-yardlands
Whitstones		24s. 1½d.	
Aston			11s. 1¾d.
Wick		19s. 11d.	
Kempsey		17s. 10½d.	
Henbury	33s. 3½d.		
	28s. 0½d.		
Alvechurch		14s. 8¾d.	
Bredon	24s. 9½d.		
Ripple		12s. 3½d.	
Tredington	24s. 6d.		
Cleeve	22s. 1d.		
Hanbury		11s. 0d.	
Stratford	21s. 7½d.		
Blockley	19s. 4¾d.		
	6s. 2½d.		
Bibury	19s. 0d.		
Hartlebury	14s. 11½d.		
	3s. 8d.		
Hampton	14s. 2d.		
	13s. 2d.		
Fladbury	13s. 9d.		
	12s. 9d.		

likely to reflect the lord's ability to squeeze extra cash from tenants who enjoyed the advantages of a large urban market.[38]

The peculiarly small size of the holdings on the manors nearest to Worcester may also reflect urban influence – a similar phenomenon can be observed on the Gloucester Abbey manors on the outskirts of Gloucester. Tenants on such manors had a good chance of selling produce profitably, and could obtain employment in urban industries.[39]

Rural industries have been used to explain the ability of smallholders to survive in the later middle ages. We know of a cloth

[38] For a similar argument, I. S. W. Blanchard, 'The Miner and the Agricultural Community in Late Medieval England', *Ag. Hist. Rev.*, xx (1972), pp. 102–4.

[39] *Historia et Cartularium Monasterii Sancti Petri Gloucestriae*, ed. W. H. Hart (Rolls ser., 1863), iii, pp. 67–88, 110–19, 126–40, 149–76.

industry at Hartlebury, potting and tile-making at Welland and Whitstones, and, from surnames, a scatter of metal, cloth- and wood-workers over the estate. Peasants might also be able to exploit the natural products of rivers and woodland, or make salt (in the case of Henbury).[40]

The peasants of Upton in Blockley, some of whose houses have been excavated, had sufficient resources to enable them in the thir- teenth and early fourteenth centuries to build substantial dwellings and agricultural buildings with solidly constructed stone founda- tions. Their possessions included a wide variety of metal objects, even such luxuries as a gilded bronze ornamental fitting for a chest. However, it should be remembered that the most thoroughly excavated Upton holding almost certainly belonged to a yardlander, the predominant type among the tenants there, though they formed a minority among the tenants of the estate as a whole.[41]

The ability of peasants to pay heavy taxes in lay subsidies to the crown has been used as evidence for their prosperity. It is difficult to equate tax lists with manorial surveys because the former include the tenants of sub-manors who are not listed as tenants of the chief lord. If we take four places where these tenurial complications were minimal, we find that a total of 168 people, representing households, paid tax to the 1327 subsidy, amounting to 41 per cent of the 410 tenants listed in the same places in 1299 (it is unlikely that tenant number changed radically in the interven- ing years). This means that the majority of the tenants evaded the tax, or, in most cases, we may suspect that they had their goods assessed at less than 10s. 0d., and so were exempt. Those who contributed paid an average of 1s. 8d. each. These sums should be regarded as a difficult burden, exacerbating the peasantry's problems by adding yet more to their compulsory outgoings.[42]

---

[40] Cloth-working (implied by a fulling-mill), *RBW*, ii, p. 191; potting and tile- making, *RBW*, i, pp. 28, 107; salt-making, *RBW*, iv, p. 411. On non-agricultural employment in general, see J. R. Birrell, 'Peasant Craftsmen in the Medieval Forest', *Ag. Hist. Rev.*, xvii (1969), pp. 91–107.

[41] R. H. Hilton and P. A. Rahtz, 'Upton, Gloucestershire, 1959–64', *Trans. Bristol and Glos. Arch. Soc.*, lxxxv (1966), pp. 70–146, esp. pp. 111–13 and fig. 15, no. 18; P. A. Rahtz, 'Upton, Gloucestershire, 1964–8', *ibid.*, lxxxviii (1969), pp. 74– 126, especially p. 103.

[42] The four chosen are Alvechurch, Hampton, Hanbury and Hartlebury, *Lay Subsidy Roll for the County of Worcester I Edward III*, ed. F. J. Eld (Worcs. Hist. Soc., 1895), pp. 13, 25–6, 27–8; *The Lay Subsidy Roll for Warwickshire of 1327*, ed. W. B. Bickley (*Trans. Midland Rec. Soc.*, vi), p. 35. On the tax burden in the period, see J. R. Maddicott, *The English Peasantry and the Demands of the Crown, 1294–1341* (P. and P. supplement, 1, 1975).

For the many smallholders on the estate involvement in the market meant the purchase of foodstuffs from their earnings in agricultural employment. For them the market did not develop favourably in the thirteenth century, as the price of grain rose, and wages did not keep pace. A few could hope to become manorial *famuli*, earning about 5s. per annum and an allowance of grain, or find employment with richer neighbours: the surveys assumed that yardlanders and even half-yardlanders might have full-time servants.[43] It may be doubted whether there would always have been enough wage-work to keep the large numbers of smallholders on some manors, such as Kempsey, where 68 per cent of the tenants had less than a half-yardland.

It is generally assumed that a peasant land-market developed by the thirteenth century.[44] Although no court rolls survive on the Worcester estate to show this, charters indicate that some free tenants thrived and built up large holdings. At Cleeve Richard de Clyve accumulated a complex collection of lands by the mid-thirteenth century, amounting to a miniature manor, with more than 20 acres in his own hands, and twenty-one smallholdings let to subtenants. A group of Cleeve charters in the early fourteenth century records free tenants buying and granting many small parcels of land, from $\frac{1}{2}$ acre to $3\frac{1}{2}$ acres in each transaction. These show how a holding like Richard de Clyve's might be created. Thomas de Agmondesham, the son of a free tenant mentioned in the 1299 survey, obtained by sixteen deeds in the period 1327–43 parcels totalling $19\frac{3}{4}$ acres in the open fields of Cleeve and the adjoining villages of Gotherington, Southam and Woodmancote.[45]

Free tenants were more likely than customary tenants to hold large amounts of land. Thirty (12 per cent of those whose size of holding is known) are listed in 1299 as holding a yardland and a half, or more. Some retained large grants made to their predecessors, like those with pre-Conquest *radmen*'s lands. Others belong to the same

[43] For the remuneration of *famuli*, see Bodleian Library, Worcester Rolls no. 4; *RBW*, iv, pp. 498–547.

[44] The argument that peasant land-transfers were not new, see M. M. Postan, 'The Charters of the Villeins', in *Essays on Medieval Agriculture*, pp. 107–49; but this view has been modified by P. R. Hyams, 'The Origins of a Peasant Land Market in England', *Econ. Hist. Rev.*, 2nd ser., xxiii (1970), pp. 18–31; King, *Peterborough Abbey*, pp. 99–125.

[45] White Book, fos. 54–6; *RBW*, iv, pp. 331–2; GRO, D 1637 T6, 1–15; T14, 1–9.

type as Clyve and Agmondesham, having put together a number of small units. Customary tenants could create composite holdings, but only twenty-two are recorded as having done this in 1299, and only thirteen of these (1 per cent of the total) had a yardland and a half or two yardlands.

The land-market also led to the less able or less fortunate losing their land. In the late thirteenth century Richard de Clenefield of Alvechurch was selling land to his neighbours, and in seven deeds of *c.*1300–10 Thomas Bydoun of Kempsey granted, leased and sold various parcels to Peter Colle, a citizen of Worcester. Both Clenefield and Bydoun referred in their charters to their 'urgent business', suggesting that they were in debt.[46]

For most tenants, those with a half-yardland or less, the thirteenth century must have been a period of recurrent poverty. In 1246–7, when the price of wheat rose to 8s. 0d. per quarter (about double the normal) because of a bad harvest, Bishop Cantilupe authorized grants in alms of twenty quarters of grain from Fladbury and Tredington to the poor of his own and neighbouring villages. Such charity would have had little effect in relieving the more acute dearths of the period, or the famine of 1315–17, which we know to have had severe effects on the peasantry of some manors in the region, as elsewhere.[47]

The references to vacant holdings in 1299, particularly at Alvechurch and Tredington, suggest that tenants were unable to make their holdings pay, and on other estates there are many references in the early fourteenth century to the poverty of tenants that forced them to give up their holdings.[48]

Our conclusion, then, must be a pessimistic one. Against the gains of the minority who commuted their services for cash, especially on the favourable terms available in the twelfth century, or those

---

[46] Society of Antiquaries Lib., Pratinton coll., Worcestershire Parishes, ii, p. 12; Birmingham Reference Lib., Zachary Lloyd MSS., nos. 73–80.

[47] Bodleian Library, Worcester Rolls no. 4; R. K. Field, 'The Worcestershire Peasantry in the Later Middle Ages' (Univ. of Birmingham M. A. thesis), p. 164. On bad harvests, M. M. Postan and J. Z. Titow, 'Heriots and Prices on Winchester Manors', in *Essays on Medieval Agriculture*, pp. 150–85.

[48] e.g. 6 cases of surrender *pro paupertate* in a Worcester Priory court roll of 1346, WCL, E. 15. Also, A. May, 'An Index of Thirteenth-Century Peasant Impoverishment? Manor Court-Fines', *Econ. Hist. Rev.*, 2nd ser., xxvi (1973), pp. 389–402.

who won extensive assarts from the waste, and the very small numbers who built up large holdings on the land-market, must be set a seriously disadvantaged majority. Most tenants could not assart, or benefit from market opportunities, because their holdings were small, their land lay in old-cultivated and regulated fields, and they were subject to the burdens of the lord.

These problems may have paved the way for the catastrophe of the mid-fourteenth century, though we lack adequate evidence for the peasantry of the bishopric estate in the half-century before the great plague. Certainly, when the plague came in 1348–9, the bishopric tenants suffered a heavy mortality (see Chapter 10).

5. The lord's economy: the last phase of direct management, 1350−1400

Most of the great English landed estates were transformed in the fourteenth century by the leasing of demesnes. This was a response to declining and uncertain profits from cultivation. The chronology of this change was varied and long-drawn-out, with some demesnes, as on the Worcester bishopric estate, being leased in the early years of the fourteenth century, or even before 1300, but on most estates direct management, on at least some manors, continued until the 1390s or into the first two decades of the fifteenth century. The demographic collapse of 1348–9 was not followed immediately by leasing, nor is it possible to see the period as one of a steady erosion of the lords' position. It has been argued that the seignorial economy in the third quarter of the fourteenth century and into the 1380s experienced an 'Indian summer', with rent-income recovering from the effects of the plagues, or declining only slightly. In the same period demesne cultivation enjoyed some prosperity because of the buoyancy of grain prices. Landlords apparently experienced more problems at the end of the fourteenth century, though the indirect evidence of international trade and some branches of industrial production suggests a high level of consumption among the wealthier sections of society.[1]

The manorial accounts of the bishopric estate survive from the 1370s onwards, and enable us to see how the estate adapted to changing circumstances. They indicate movements in rent-income, and throw light on the management of demesne agriculture. In many ways the economic climate was unfavourable to the large estate, but the managers still had a range of options open to them,

[1] For the 'Indian summer' see G. A. Holmes, *The Estates of the Higher Nobility in Fourteenth-Century England* (Cambridge, 1957), pp. 114–15; Raftis, *The Estates of Ramsey Abbey*, pp. 259–66; J. Hatcher, *Rural Economy and Society in the Duchy of Cornwall, 1300–1500* (Cambridge, 1970), pp. 122–47; A. R. Bridbury, 'The Black Death', *Econ. Hist. Rev.*, 2nd ser., xxvi (1973), pp. 580–1; for evidence of relatively buoyant trade and industry see M. K. James, *Studies in the Medieval Wine Trade* (Oxford, 1971), pp. 27–30; J. Hatcher, *English Tin Production and Trade before 1550* (Oxford, 1973), pp. 155–63; I. S. W. Blanchard, 'Derbyshire Lead Production, 1195–1505', *Derbyshire Arch. Journ.*, xci (1971), pp. 127–9.

on the commutation of labour services, the agricultural use of the demesnes, and the extent to which demesnes should be partially or wholly rented out. This chapter is primarily concerned with the management of the estates, with the aim of explaining why direct cultivation continued during the period, and why the demesnes were eventually leased.

The bishops in the period for which our accounts survive presumably had an important influence over the administration of the estate, though the extent to which they were involved in detailed decision-making cannot be known. Between 1361 and 1375 there were three short episcopates of five years or less, with a total of almost four years of vacancies when the temporalities were in the hands of the crown. After this long period of discontinuity Henry Wakefield became bishop, and remained in office for nearly twenty years (1375–95). Wakefield had been a civil servant, with six years (1369–75) as Keeper of the Wardrobe, and he served briefly while bishop as Treasurer of the Exchequer in 1377, but after this he spent most of his time in his diocese and seems to have been active in its ecclesiastical administration.[2] His successor, Tideman of Winchcomb (1395–1401), owed his promotion to his position as physician at the court of Richard II, and we cannot be certain that he devoted as much time to the diocese as Wakefield.[3]

The estate's administrative machinery had much in common with that of the thirteenth century. Each manor was managed by a reeve, usually a customary tenant with a yardland or half-yardland holding, rewarded officially by remittance of rents and services. As became common elsewhere in the fourteenth century, reeves often served for a number of years consecutively, normally for between two and five years, but longer terms are recorded – at Bibury, Henry Man acted as reeve in the years 1371–84, and Robert Gyffard from 1384 to 1396.[4]

On the larger manors reeves were often assisted by beadles and rent-collectors; sometimes one man combined both offices. They accounted jointly with the reeve, but the rents and court dues for

    [2] *Reg. Wakefield*, pp. xxxiii–xliii.
    [3] H. Wharton, *Anglia Sacra* (London, 1691), p. 536.
    [4] H. S. Bennett, 'The Reeve and the Manor in the Fourteenth Century', *Eng. Hist. Rev.*, xli (1926), pp. 358–65.

which they were responsible were indicated separately on the accounts. These jobs seem to have been thankless and unpopular. Few served for more than a year, and at Whitstones, for example, tenants paid fines in order to avoid election.[5] Reeves, in charge of complex agricultural operations on the demesne, had many opportunities for making unofficial profits, but rent-collectors were charged with specific sums recorded on the rental, and would have had few chances for peculation.

In the late thirteenth and early fourteenth centuries the bailiffs provided a tier of management above the reeves, supervising groups of manors and receiving substantial wages. By the late fourteenth century bailiffs were confined to the supervision of such judicial franchises as the hundreds of Cleeve, Henbury and Oswaldslow, or might be put in temporary charge of a manor in exceptional circumstances, as at Hampton in 1377, when the reeve had fled. The minor importance of the work of the bailiffs is indicated by their modest remuneration of between 7s. 4d. and 13s. 4d. per annum and an allowance of grain. Their work was part-time, enabling the Henbury bailiff to act also as the bishop's parker.

Thus much of the work of supervising the local officials fell on the central administrators. The bishop's council, which met occasionally, consisted of the main estate officials, such as the steward, receiver and auditors, together with such prominent local landowners as Henry Haggeleye.[6] The council, by analogy with better-documented contemporary examples, dealt with major legal matters and made important policy decisions on the running of the estate.[7]

Stewards were recruited from the local gentry, such as John Brounyng (1375–87), who held lands in various Gloucestershire villages, and served as sheriff of Gloucestershire in 1398, and Richard Thurgrym (1381–96) who held the manor of Thorndon near Pershore. The receivers were recruited from prominent clergy, notably Robert Myle (1371–2), who held at least two rectories before becoming Warden of Stratford College in 1384, Robert Broun

---

[5] Whitstones CR, Dec. 1378; April 1379; Dec. 1392.

[6] Henbury AR, 1375–6; *VCH Worcs*, iii, p. 133, shows that Haggeleye held the north Worcestershire manor of Hagley and served as sheriff of Worcestershire in 1397.

[7] For example, see F. M. Page, *The Estates of Crowland Abbey* (Cambridge, 1934), pp. 45–9.

(1375–88), rector of Hampton Lucy, and John Newman (1392–1413) who held at least two livings successively in the diocese. Auditors were usually of lesser rank, being either minor gentry, like John Vampage (1392–6), or more obscure individuals of whom little is known. However, men who had served in more important positions, such as a former steward and former receiver, sometimes acted as auditors. Auditors often worked in pairs (see Appendix 1).

The manorial accounts contain ample evidence of the visits made by the stewards, receivers and auditors, and it is clear that they kept the estate under close supervision.

The steward had important legal responsibilities, attending on the lord's behalf the court of the Marches at Bristol, the sessions of the justices of the forest at Feckenham, and the sessions of the peace at Gloucester; on one occasion he also went to a 'love-day' to settle a dispute with the powerful Berkeley family in 1387.[8] The main duties of the steward were to tour the estate holding the bishop's courts, and to oversee the manors in general. He authorized major building projects and negotiated contracts with building workers. He took a detailed interest in stock husbandry, ordering the culling of sheep and the purchase of hay for feeding sheep. He concerned himself with the marketing of produce, as in delaying the sale of some hay at Henbury in 1375–6 in order to secure 'greater profit for the lord'. Naturally, the steward attended the most important single transaction on the estate, the sale of wool at Blockley. Any out-of-the-ordinary expenditure, no matter how small, required the steward's permission, even the tips of 6d. or so given to the manorial *famuli*. The steward played an important rôle in regulating relations with the tenants, and might, for example, be involved in negotiating the commutation of labour services.

The receivers and auditors, as well as collecting cash from the manors and auditing accounts, visited manors, compiled rentals, negotiated leases and commutation of services, and attended sheepshearings.

Much depended on the auditing of the accounts, which was carried out, as on other estates, in two stages, with a view of account during the year and a full audit for the final account after Michaelmas. The main audit was not conducted centrally, as in 1246–7, but locally, the eastern manors of Blockley, Hampton, Stratford and

    [8] Henbury AR, 1390–1; Hanbury AR, 1386–7; Bibury AR, 1384–5; Henbury AR, 1386–7.

Tredington being audited at Blockley, the south Worcester-shire manors at Bredon, and Henbury and Stoke at Henbury. The strict nature of the audit is indicated by the number of alterations on the accounts. An example is the Bibury account of 1387–8, in which twenty-four items, about a third of the total, were crossed out and altered. On the receipts side of the account the auditors disallowed most of the reeve's claims for grain sales and substituted higher prices. They questioned many items of expenditure, such as the cost of the iron-work of the ploughs, shoeing cart-horses, the purchase of tar and grease, and wage-payments for haymaking, winnowing and carting. In all £1 12s. 7½d. was disallowed on an account with a total charge of £24 18s. 3d. Such a critical attitude saved money for the lord, and doubtless reduced the reeve's private profit, though the same reeve continued to serve for another eight years, suggesting that he was still left with enough to make his labour worthwhile.

The auditors were strict about failures in the grain harvest, and deficiencies below a target yield were 'charged on the account' – the reeve had to make up the loss. Excuses offered by reeves were often disbelieved, such as the sheep at Bibury said to have been stolen 'by nocturnal robbers'.[9] Accounts were checked against other documents, such as the 1299 survey, or previous accounts, and local people were consulted about the price of goods, or the feasibility of levying a rent payment. Unusual payments were disallowed, unless authorized by the steward.

An important problem confronting estate officials, and auditors in particular, was how to deal with arrears, inevitable in a period when rents were tending to decline, and strict auditing could leave large sums, especially after a bad harvest, 'charged on account'. Arrears seem to have been kept within reasonable limits by a judicious policy of allowing or respiting items from year to year, but not too readily, so as to maintain pressure on manorial officials to pay up as much as possible. A group of documents attached to a Henbury account of 1383–4 illustrates the bargaining over arrears that went on between reeve and auditors. The reeve, Robert Chyld, submitted petitions for allowances on his debts incurred in the previous two years, 1382–3 and 1383–4. The items consisted mainly of grain and lost animals that had been 'charged on account', and also questionable wage-payments. The petition of 1383–4 totalled more than £8, but the auditors crossed out most of the items, and agreed to allow only £2 8s. 3½d. On the 1382–3 petition he was granted £2 9s. 4d. out of more than £6. This left Chyld with a total of £11 11s. 1¼d. still owed to the lord, and it might seem that the auditors were being unrealistic in expecting him to pay off such a large sum. However, in 1384–5 the ex-reeve paid £1 to a Bristol merchant for wine bought by the bishop, contributed 16s. 0d. to the expenses of estate officials staying at the manor, paid £4 to the bishop's receiver, and £5 to the clerk of the household. A further 10s. 0d. was pardoned, so nearly wiping out the debt. The lord had thus gained a good deal from the firm attitude adopted by the auditors.

The auditors were conscious of the out-of-date nature of the rentals that they used to check on rent collection, and often made a regular annual respite of sums that they acknowledged to have lapsed, but which had not been incorporated in the 'allowance of rent' section of the account. Regular respites could be substantial, £2 12s. 8d. at Stoke, for example, or £6 14s. 9½d. at Henbury.

The combination of firmness and realism ensured that arrears totals did not reach very high levels. An arrears roll of 1389 shows that the arrears of the whole estate amounted to £465. Much of this total, £261, stemmed from the arrears of a single manor, Blockley, where £134 was owed by the Chipping Campden wool-merchant, William Grevil, for the previous summer's wool clip, and this was likely to have been paid off during the year. On most manors the accumulated arrears total was less than £20.[10] The accounts of individual manors show that over the whole period arrears were kept within reasonable bounds. Bibury had an annual charge of between £20 and £30, and arrears never exceeded £10. Debts at Henbury and Stoke rarely exceeded £30, although their charges were usually four or five times those at Bibury. This contrasts with the huge totals of arrears in the mid-fifteenth century (see Appendix 2).

Rents, which had contributed so much to the estate's income in the thirteenth century, increased in importance in the fourteenth century. We have already seen that the demesnes of Aston, Bibury,

[10] WCRO ref. 009:1 BA 2636/193 92628 4/9.

Knightwick and Stratford were leased in the early fourteenth century. By the 1370s and 1380s Bibury and Stratford had been brought back into direct management, but demesnes of six other manors were leased, leaving fourteen manors out of twenty-two in hand.[11] For the manors which had been leased, rents, farms and court dues were the only source of revenue, but even on manors still under direct management, income from rents and court profits accounted for a half or more of the manorial income. The only exception, Bibury, had an unusually large demesne and small number of tenants (see Table 11).

A survey of rent income made in 1393–4 for the whole estate gives a total of rents and farms, with decays deducted, of £656. Allowing about £50 for the Alvechurch rents, which are omitted, we have a total of £700.[12] A further £100 for perquisites of courts would mean that rent, defined in the broadest sense, was bringing in well over three-quarters of the estate's income.

The receipts from the assize rents of tenants declined in the long term during the fourteenth century. At Bibury, for example, assize rents and works had been valued in 1299 at £11 4s. 6d., but in the last thirty years of the fourteenth century assize rents, including commuted works, amounted to between £7 and £8. Similarly the

Table 11. *Analysis of manorial income for manors under direct management, 1370–1400*

Given as a percentage of total income

Manor	Rents*	Court perquisites	Production income⁺
Bibury	21%	7%	72%
Bredon	50%	6%	44%
Hampton	46%	4%	50%
Henbury	42%	32%	26%
Stoke	65%	(Courts held at Henbury)	35%

*All rents, including farms, sales of pasture etc., with decays deducted.
⁺Includes valuation of demesne produce consumed directly in the bishop's household.

[11] This conclusion is based on the list of stock included in the 1389 arrears roll cited above (footnote 10) and references in accounts to grain and animals being sent to and from reeves or farmers. The six leased demesnes were at Hanbury, Hartlebury, Paxford, Throckmorton, Tredington and Wick.
[12] WCRO ref. 009:1 BA 2636/9 43696, fos. 33–8.

Hampton assize rents and works, worth £21 12s. 2d. in 1299, fell from £20 to £14 from 1371 to 1393. On the other manors the continued use of labour services prevents accurate comparison, but the fall in rents was less great than on these two manors.

The decline was partly because of holdings falling vacant, but mainly through tenants taking holdings at reduced rents on lease-hold, or by commuting labour services at less than their full valu-ation. So at Henbury between 1376 and 1391 the development of leasehold raised the revenue from 'farms' from £4 3s. 5½d. to £9 0s. 1¾d., but this was compensated by decays of rents, which rose from 7s. 3d. to £6 13s. 8d. in the same period, so that the combined total of assize rents and farms paid for tenant holdings declined from £41 19s. 11d. to £40 6s. 7½d.

Throughout the estate there was a long-term movement towards letting customary holdings for cash rents instead of a combination of rent and labour services. This was partly achieved by letting individual holdings 'at will' or on lease, a system which had begun before 1300 and had gathered pace in the late four-teenth century. By the 1380s five holdings at Henbury, and ten at Stoke, representing 13 per cent of the customary holdings, had been converted to the new type of tenure. Numbers of leasehold or 'at will' tenancies increased at Cleeve from nil in 1372–3 to thirty-one (46 per cent of the total) in 1393–4, and at Bredon from twenty-one (35 per cent) in 1384 to twenty-six (43 per cent) in 1394.

Wholesale commutation of services for large numbers of tenants had taken place at Bibury, Hampton and Hanbury by the early 1370s, and presumably also on the manors where demesnes had been leased. The needs of demesne cultivation were not the only consideration in deciding to commute services, as the Bibury and Hampton demesnes were still worked with wage-labour into the 1390s. On other manors where labour services were still used in the 1370s and 1380s mass commutation came around 1390. In 1389 services of twenty-one Bredon tenants were commuted at a rate of 13s. 4d. per yardland, the lord retaining only a few reaping and carrying services. The same type of agreement was made at Henbury in 1393, involving thirty-six customary holdings. As a result the money paid from the new commutation was headed in the manorial account 'rented villein lands' (*terra nativa arrentata*). The appear-ance of the same heading in the 1393–4 survey of rents suggests that

Kempsey, Ripple and Stoke tenants commuted their services at about the same time.[13]

These structural changes in the form in which rent payment was made, resulted in a substantial increase in the cash rent income recorded in the accounts, from £42 at Bredon in 1384–5 to £50 in 1392–3, for example.

Much of the lord's income from the tenants derived from dues associated with lordship and the exercise of jurisdiction. The customs paid by tenants declined during the fourteenth century: aid, for example, which had been valued for seventeen manors in 1299 at £38 was worth only £19 1s. 2d. by 1393–4. Court revenues, however, did not decline (see Table 12). On six of the eight manors for which we have figures court perquisites in the period 1371–96 were higher than in 1299 and 1302–3, and in the other two cases the decline was slight. These sums derived from such payments as amercements, entry-fines and marriage fines, which could be maintained at a high level through the vigorous exercise of the lord's authority, and can be paralleled on other estates where such sources of revenue were increasing at this time, in spite of any reduced population.[14]

In the 1370s and 1380s fourteen demesnes were still under direct

Table 12. *Perquisites of courts, comparison of annual totals of 1299, 1302–3 and in the late fourteenth century*

	1299*	1302–3	1371–96
Bibury	£1 10s. 0d.	£2 2s. 2d.	£2 9s. 9d. (average of 16 years)
Blockley	£3 0s. 0d.	£2 19s. 6d.	£6 7s. 1d. (one year)
Bredon	—	£5 9s. 1d.	£4 9s. 6d. (average of 5 years)
Cleeve	£3 0s. 0d.	£2 16s. 3d.	£14 4s. 6d. (average of 2 years)
Hampton	£1 0s. 0d.	£1 13s. 0d.	£2 13s. 11d. (average of 10 years)
Hanbury	£3 0s. 0d.	£1 19s. 7d.	£2 19s. 5d. (average of 9 years)
Henbury	£20 0s. 0d.	£18 8s. 9d.	£22 3s. 4d. (average of 14 years)
Whitstones	£3 0s. 0d.	£4 5s. 3d.	£5 15s. 5d. (average of 4 years)[+]

*contemporary estimates.
[+]calculations include figures deriving from court rolls, which may be incomplete in some years.

[13] *ibid.*, fos. 33–5.
[14] R. H. Hilton, *The Decline of Serfdom in Medieval England* (London, 1969), pp. 41–2.

Table 13. *Numbers of demesne ploughs in the fourteenth century*

Based on the numbers of ploughmen and draught animals

	1302–3	1389
Alvechurch	2	2
Aston	3	(at farm)
Bibury	2	1
Blockley	3	2
Bredon	4	2
Cleeve	4	2
Fladbury	4	2
Hampton	2	1
Hanbury	4	(at farm)
Hartlebury	2	(at farm)
Henbury	3	1
Paxford	3	(at farm)
Kempsey	4	2
Ripple	3	1
Stoke	2	1
Stratford	2	(at farm)
Throckmorton	2	(at farm)
Tredington	4	(at farm)
Whitstones	5	2
Wick	1	(at farm)
Withington	2	1
Total	61	20

management. The scale of demesne agriculture, particularly on the arable side, was much reduced during the fourteenth century. A comparison between the number of demesne ploughs employed in 1302–3 and 1389 gives an overall view of the decline, from sixty-one ploughs in 1302–3 to twenty at the later date. Half of the fall was the result of the total leasing of eight demesnes, but on the manors where direct management continued, except for Alve-church, the demesne ploughs had usually been halved in number (see Table 13).

The reduction in the cultivated area of the demesne did not occur in some cases until after 1375. At Hampton and Cleeve the area under crops in the early 1370s was greater than in 1299 (see Table 14). A larger area was cultivated at Bibury and Stoke before 1375 than in most subsequent years. A change of policy was apparently made after the accession of Henry Wakefield in 1375, and on most

Table 14. *Demesne acreage under cultivation per annum, 1299–1396*

Manor	Probable cultivated acreage, 1299	Cultivated acreage, 1369–73	Cultivated acreage, 1376–96
Bibury	223	96½–112	59¾–103
Blockley	282½	—	146
Bredon	195¾	—	113–139¾
Cleeve	195¼	215	125¾–132¾
Hampton	144¼	172	72¾–138
Henbury	141¾	—	55¾–91½
Stoke	123½	74–89½	48½–74½

manors only a third or a half of the potential demesne area was kept under the plough.

The reduction in demesne arable was achieved sometimes by conversion to pasture for the lord's stock, but mainly by letting parcels of demesne piece-meal to tenants. This had begun before 1350, and at Bredon 78 acres were still farmed out at the end of the fourteenth century as the result of a lease made in 1343–4. At Hampton, Henbury and Stoke parcels were sometimes rented out permanently, but more commonly 'sold' occasionally to tenants on an annual basis. At Henbury most of the parcels of demesne were recorded as having been in the hands of tenants at some time in the late fourteenth century. *Parkefeld*, for example, was rented out in four of nine recorded years. The amount let varied from year to year, depending on the production needs of the demesne – and the local demand for land. The rents asked were quite high, 8d. – 10d. per acre at Cleeve, or 6d. at Henbury, well above the valuations of the demesne arable in 1299 – and sometimes parcels could not be rented out, and were used by the lord.

It is not always possible to explain the reductions in the demesne area. The Bibury demesne was halved in its arable area between the 1290s and the 1370s, but there is no evidence that land was leased to tenants, or that the grazing area was increased. It is possible that the land became derelict, as is recorded in a number of south-east Gloucestershire villages in the fourteenth century.[15]

[15] *Inquisitiones Nonarum* (Record Commission, 1807), pp. 409–10.

Table 15. *Analysis of demesne crops, 1369–96*

Manor	Wheat	Rye	Barley/Drage	Legumes	Oats	Total acreage analysed (100%)
Bibury	13%	—	58%	11%	18%	(1,224¾)
Blockley	33%	—	38%	22%	7%	(146)
Bredon	36%	1%	30%	26%	7%	(601)
Cleeve	35%	—	29%	31%	5%	(473½)
Hampton	18%	22%	24%	27%	9%	(969)
Henbury	45%	—	15%	5%	35%	(931½)
Stoke	38%	—	15%	12%	35%	(604½)

The arable cultivation on the demesnes can be characterized as having been conducted with some flexibility, but it achieved neither a high level of productivity, nor much profit.

The choice of crops seems to have been determined by local soils and climatic conditions (see Table 15). The manors of Henbury and Stoke produced mainly wheat and oats, which was normal in the lower Severn valley. The Bibury demesne was largely given over to the traditional Cotswold crops of barley and drage. Blockley, Bredon, and Cleeve, all on the varied soils on the edge of the Cotswolds or their outlying hills, grew roughly equal proportions of wheat and barley/drage, with substantial amounts of peas and beans. Significant amounts of rye were grown only at Hampton, on light river-valley soils, as well as wheat, barley and drage, and legumes. Oats were grown on these last four manors in relatively small quantities. In common with other demesnes at this period spring-sown crops – barley, drage, legumes and oats – predominated on all of the manors.[16]. Only at Henbury was more than 40 per cent of the cultivated area given over to wheat, and the proportion at Bibury was only 13 per cent. The only evidence of innovation in the period was an attempt to increase the area under legumes at Bibury, from less than 10 per cent before 1382, to more than 30 per cent in 1389. In 1393 the pulse 'rotted in the fields', none was harvested, and in subsequent years none was planted again. The purpose of the experiment was presumably to increase the amount of animal foodstuffs.

[16] R. H. Hilton, *The Economic Development of some Leicestershire Estates in the Fourteenth and Fifteenth Centuries* (Oxford, 1947), pp. 63–5.

The reduction in the area under cultivation allowed much flexibility in crop rotations and land-use. Convertible husbandry, with land being used alternatively as pasture and arable, was practised. The Bredon pastures of *Bertonehull* and a plot 'behind the smith's house' were used as arable in 1375–6. Oats were sown on two pastures at Cleeve in 1394. At Stoke a field called *Catsbrayne* was rented out as a pasture in most years, but was planted with crops in 1386–7 and 1389–90. *Morelese*, another parcel of land on the same manor, was used as a pasture for the lord's oxen, except in 1388–9, when seven acres were sown with oats.[17]

When consecutive series of accounts are available, it is possible to reconstruct the method of rotation (see Table 16). The Bibury cropping units were the furlongs. Some seem to have been cultivated in alternate years (*Putforlong*, *Blakemanlond* and *Ruyforlong*), but the others were sown once in four years, suggesting a régime similar to the infield–outfield system in which part of the land was cropped occasionally after long periods of fallow. A similar arrangement prevailed at Henbury and Stoke, with parcels like *Ponebury*, *Garstone* or *Warborohull* being planted continuously for four- or five-year periods, while others, such as *Hawfeld*, were run for some of the time on a three-course rotation, but most of the units were planted intermittently.

The infield–outfield system is normally associated with poor soils and highland areas, but it could have been appropriate in any area where there was no great shortage of pasture. On our manors there was no real 'system' of rotation at all. Because the reeves did not need to cultivate as large an area as possible, they were freed from observing conventional husbandry practices, and made *ad hoc* decisions on the use of land from year to year.[18]

There is little else to suggest a spirit of enterprise or innovation in arable farming. The main concern of the estate administrators after 1375 was apparently to reduce costs by employing as few demesne ploughs as possible – one or two on each manor. The ploughs were of the traditional unwheeled type, drawn by

[17] Convertible husbandry was also practised on the Battle Abbey manor of Marley, see E. Searle, *Lordship and Community, Battle Abbey and its Banlieu, 1066–1538* (Toronto, 1974), pp. 272–87.

[18] Flexible use of fields has now been documented from many parts of the country, see A. R. H. Baker and R. A. Butlin (eds.), *Studies of Field Systems in the British Isles* (Cambridge, 1973), pp. 642–3.

oxen, eight on most manors, but as few as five or six at Bibury. The whole team, with repair costs, ploughmen's wages and grain liveries, fodder and replacements for the oxen, were expensive to maintain. In cash terms they cost £3 or £4 each per annum.

The reduction in the number of ploughs led to the skimping of ploughing. The agricultural treatises of the thirteenth century recommended that, in addition to ploughing land in preparation for sowing, the fallow should be ploughed twice, in the spring and summer.[19] These fallow ploughings are mentioned in a number of our estate accounts, but it is doubtful if they were carried out in full. At Bibury in 1387–8 the year's programme would have involved ploughing 74 acres for the winter- and spring-sowings, and the 103 acres that were to be cultivated in the following year should have been ploughed twice. The total of 280 acres, if ploughed at a rate of $\frac{3}{4}$ acre per day (as estimated for the Bibury demesne in *c.* 1290),

Table 16. *Cropping arrangements on the demesne arable, 1376–90*

BIBURY

Cropping unit	1382–3	1383–4	1384–5	1385–6
Putforlong	W*/S†	—	W/S	—
Blakemanlond	S	—	S	—
Brechforlong	S	—	S	W
Middleforlong	—	—	S	—
Ruyforlong	—	W	—	S
Burifeld	—	S	—	—
Weyforlong	—	—	—	S
Londoway	—	—	—	S
Ravethoreshull	—	—	—	S

STOKE

Cropping unit	1386–7	1387–8	1388–9	1389–90
Coddedoune	W	—	—	W
Ponebury	S	S	W/S	S
Wonacre	S	S	—	—
Morelese	—	—	S	—
Catsbrayne	?	—	—	S
Field near the park	S	S	—	—
Bourfeld	—	W	S	—

* Winter-sown crops
⁺ Spring-sown crops

[19] *Walter of Henley*, ed. Oschinsky, pp. 314–17.

Table 16 – *continued*

HENBURY

Cropping unit	1376–7	1377–8	1378–9	1379–80	
Parkefeld	W	W	—	—	
Garstone	W	W	S	S	
Wykeforlong	W	—	W	—	
Hawfeld	—	—	—	W	
Canford	—	S	—	—	
Warborohull	S	S	—	—	
Grundyesfeld	S	—	—	—	
Furlong near garden	—	S	—	—	
Under Shitshawe	—	S	—	S	
Estfeld	—	—	W	S	
Grenedich 'frisc'	—	—	—	—	
Canyngworth	—	—	—	W	
Chapmannescroft	—	—	—	—	
Furlong near mill	—	—	—	—	
	1382–3	1383–4	1384–5	1385–6	1386–7
Parkefeld	—	—	—	—	W
Garstone	—	W	S	—	—
Wykeforlong	S	—	W	—	—
Hawfeld	W	S	—	W	S
Canford	—	S	—	W	S
Warborohull	S	W	S	S	W
Grundyesfeld	—	—	—	—	—
Furlong near garden	—	—	—	—	—
Under Shitshawe	—	—	—	—	—
Estfeld	—	—	—	S	—
Grenedich 'frisc'	S	—	—	—	—
Canyngworth	—	—	—	—	—
Chapmannescroft	S	—	W	S	—
Furlong near mill	—	—	S	—	—

would have involved 373 days of work in the year. In reality, the plough would not have been able to cover the next year's planted area even once, as this would have made an impossible total of 236 days of work. On other manors labour services would have enabled more fallow ploughing, but even with their help the demesne ploughs would have been hard-pressed. The general conclusion must be that fallow ploughing was done hurriedly or even neglected altogether.

There is scanty evidence for practices designed to improve fertility. Seed-corn usually came from the harvest of the previous year. When new seed was brought in, it rarely amounted to more than a fraction of the total sown, like the five quarters of pulse purchased 'for better seed' at Bredon in 1392–3, when the total quantity sown was more than twelve quarters.

Manuring was sometimes done by the *famuli*, and so leaves no trace in the accounts. At Henbury and Stoke the customary tenants manured between 2½ and 20 acres of the demesne arable, only a small part of the whole area under cultivation. Sheep were folded on the demesne – at Henbury the sheep of a stranger (*bidentes alieni*) were kept in the lord's fold for twelve weeks in the summer when there was no demesne flock – but there is no evidence for such folding as a regular practice. Other measures, such as marling or intensive sowing, are not mentioned in the accounts. Legumes, which could add nitrogen to the soil, were grown in quantity on some manors, but not usually at Bibury, Henbury and Stoke.

The best guide to the effectiveness of arable farming techniques are the yield ratios, which can be calculated from consecutive accounts by dividing the grain harvested by the amount sown, or, using isolated accounts, from the yield calculations of the auditors (see Table 17). In general the yield ratios seem to be mediocre, rarely rising above five times the seed planted, and usually falling to between three and four for cereals, and to between two and four for legumes. Higher yields are recorded on other contemporary estates, such as those of Ramsey Abbey, but these figures are comparable with the 'meagre' results found on the manors of the bishopric of Winchester.[20]

The major factor in reducing the area under crops, and perhaps in discouraging much enthusiasm in developing agricultural techniques, was the downward trend in prices. Although information about prices is scanty for the 1360s and early 1370s, there are enough figures to show that in the west midlands, as elsewhere, high corn prices prevailed, with wheat fetching 6s. 0d. or more per quarter in all recorded years up to 1376 (see Table 18). At this period, as we have already seen, some demesnes had large areas under cultivation. From 1376 to 1396 on manors other than Henbury and Stoke wheat prices usually fell below 5s. 0d. per quarter, reaching a nadir of 3s. 0d. and 2s. 8d., except in 1379–84

[20] Raftis, *Ramsey Abbey*, pp. 174–8; D. L. Farmer, 'Grain Yields on the Winchester Manors in the Later Middle Ages', *Econ. Hist. Rev.*, 2nd ser., xxx (1977), pp. 555–66.

Table 17. Yield ratios of grain and legumes, 1371–95

HAMPTON

	W	R	B	Dr	L	O
1371–2	2.52	3.93	—	4.72	2.60	2.83
1376–7	—	—	—	4.00	4.46	4.30
1377–8	6.00	4.78	—	4.40	1.79	4.86
1380–1	3.33	4.25	—	3.92	3.25	3.07
1381–2	2.43	2.61	—	3.21	1.66	3.34
1385–6	2.28	1.73	—	2.40	2.78	2.52
1386–7	6.08	4.05	—	2.53	2.81	2.92
1388–9	—	—	3.35	—	3.19	—
1389–90	4.12	3.45	5.24	—	2.67	4.46
1392–3	4.95	4.54	6.56	—	3.18	4.38
Average	3.96	3.67	5.05	3.60	2.84	3.63

BIBURY

	W	B	Dr	L	O
1371–2	3.27	3.90	3.93	2.22	2.50
1372–3	2.38	4.34	3.28	4.47	2.84
1376–7	—	—	2.67	—	3.68
1379–80	2.95	4.45	3.89	—	2.37
1380–1	3.94	2.92	3.91	3.44	3.55
1381–2	3.56	4.60	2.90	2.44	3.40
1382–3	2.58	3.86	3.79	2.76	2.87
1383–3	4.28	4.14	3.43	2.46	4.43
1384–5	5.67	3.68	3.51	1.85	3.01
1385–6	2.45	4.18	3.39	0.99	2.78
1387–8	5.17	3.69	3.90	3.25	3.23
1388–9	2.75	3.19	3.45	3.44	2.74
1391–2	3.14	5.14	3.54	—	2.86
1393–4	3.11	3.12	3.35	0	2.85
1394–5	5.90	3.95	2.77	—	2.09
Average	3.65	3.94	3.45	2.48	3.01

STOKE

	W	B	B/Dr	L	O
1372–3	—	2.19	—	—	3.52
1377–8	—	4.70	—	4.15	4.00
1380–1	2.02	3.56	—	3.15	2.94
1381–2	2.58	3.35	—	2.73	2.48
1386–7	3.34	3.40	—	4.29	3.56
1387–8	2.88	—	4.11	3.30	2.19
1388–9	3.90	3.85	—	4.66	3.77
1389–90	4.13	3.93	—	4.00	2.55
Average	3.14	3.57	4.11	3.75	3.13

CLEEVE

	W	B	Dr	L	O
1372–3	—	—	2.99	—	—
1393–4	2.64	4.03	—	1.43	3.42
1394–5	6.21	4.03	—	2.75	1.61
Average	4.43	4.03	2.99	2.09	2.52

HENBURY

	W	B	Dr	L	O
1376–7	5.10	—	—	0.77	5.41
1377–8	4.00	4.58	—	—	3.14
1378–9	—	2.75	—	—	3.34
1379–80	3.39	4.49	—	3.89	3.84
1382–3	2.22	3.55	—	2.70	2.63
1383–4	3.12	3.00	—	1.80	3.59
1384–5	5.84	2.94	—	1.79	3.51
1385–6	3.22	4.05	—	1.13	4.42
1386–7	3.89	3.29	—	6.05	4.63
1389–90	2.69	3.47	—	3.13	4.14
1390–1	—	2.28	—	0.88	2.52
1393–4	3.00	2.79	3.00	0.30	3.43
Average	3.65	3.38	3.00	2.24	3.72

BREDON

	W	R	B	Dr	L	O
1384–5	3.12	2.63	—	4.03	3.14	4.10
1392–3	4.45	—	5.55	—	5.43	4.79
1393–4	4.43	—	5.14	—	5.61	4.66
Average	4.00	2.63	5.35	4.03	4.73	4.52

W = wheat
B = barley
L = legumes (peas or beans)
O = oats.
R = rye
Dr = drage

Table 18. *Grain prices (per quarter), 1362–97*

	All manors (except Henbury and Stoke)					Henbury and Stoke				
	Wheat	Barley	Drage	Legumes	Oats	Wheat	Barley	Drage	Legumes	Oats
1362–3	16s. 0d.					8s. 8d.	3s. 4d.		6s. 0d. 6s. 0d.	3s. 2d.
1368–9	13s. 4d.					10s. 8d.	8s. 0d. 7s. 0d.		6s. 8d. 5s. 0d.	
1369–70	4s. 4d.	3s. 4d.	4s. 0d.	2s. 0d.						
1370–1	5s. 4d.	3s. 8d.			1s. 8d.					
1371–2	6s. 0d. 6s. 8d.	4s. 0d.			2s. 0d.					
1372–3	6s. 0d.	3s. 4d.	3s. 4d. 4s. 0d.	2s. 0d.	2s. 0d.	6s. 0d.	4s. 8d.		3s. 4d.	2s. 8d.
1375–6	8s. 8d. 9s. 4d. 10s. 0d.	4s. 0d. 5s. 4d. 6s. 8d.	3s. 5d. 4s. 8d. 5s. 0d. 5s. 4d.	4s. 0d. 5s. 0d. 5s. 8d.	3s. 4d.	8s. 0d. 10s. 0d.	5s. 4d.		4s. 8d.	
1376–7	4s. 0d. 4s. 2d. 4s. 8d.	3s. 8d. 4s. 0d.	3s. 0d.	3s. 0d.	2s. 0d.	6s. 0d. 8s. 0d.	4s. 0d.		2s. 8d.	2s. 4d.
1377–8	3s. 4d.		2s. 8d. 3s. 0d.	2s. 0d.	1s. 8d.	3s. 4d. 4s. 0d. 3s. 4d. 3s. 8d. 4s. 0d.	2s. 8d. 3s. 0d. 2s. 8d.		2s. 0d.	2s. 0d.
1378–9									2s. 8d.	1s. 8d.
1379–80	5s. 8d.	3s. 4d.	2s. 8d.	2s. 0d.	2s. 0d.	8s. 0d. 8s. 4d. 8s. 8d.	4s. 0d.		2s. 4d.	1s. 8d.
1380–1	6s. 0d.	3s. 4d.	2s. 8d. 3s. 4d.	3s. 4d.	2s. 0d. 2s. 4d.	6s. 8d. 7s. 4d.	3s. 8d.		2s. 8d.	2s. 0d.
1381–2	5s. 4d. 6s. 0d. 6s. 8d.	3s. 4d.	3s. 0d.	3s. 0d.	2s. 0d.	6s. 8d.	4s. 0d.		2s. 8d.	2s. 0d.

Year								
1382–3	5s. 4d. / 6s. 0d.	3s. 4d.	3s. 0d.	2s. 0d.	6s. 8d.	4s. 0d.		3s. 4d.	2s. 8d.
1383–4	5s. 4d. / 6s. 0d.	3s. 5d. / 4s. 4d. / 3s. 0d.	3s. 0d. / 3s. 4d.	2s. 0d.	7s. 4d. / 8s. 0d.	4s. 0d.		3s. 4d.	2s. 0d.
1384–5	4s. 0d.	3s. 0d.	2s. 0d.	1s. 8d.	4s. 4d. / 4s. 8d. / 5s. 4d.	3s. 0d.		4s. 0d.	1s. 8d.
1385–6	4s. 0d.	3s. 0d.	3s. 4d.	2s. 0d.	5s. 4d. / 6s. 0d.	3s. 4d. / 3s. 8d. / 3s. 0d.		3s. 0d.	2s. 0d.
1386–7	3s. 4d.		2s. 0d.		4s. 8d. / 5s. 4d.			2s. 0d. / 2s. 8d.	1s. 4d.
1387–8	3s. 0d.	2s. 2d. / 2s. 4d.	2s. 0d.	1s. 8d.	4s. 0d.	2s. 0d.			1s. 8d.
1388–9	2s. 8d. / 3s. 0d. / 3s. 4d.	2s. 4d. / 2s. 8d.	2s. 4d.	1s. 8d.	4s. 0d.	2s. 8d.		2s. 0d.	2s. 0d.
1389–90 / 1390–1	5s. 8d.	2s. 8d.	2s. 0d.		6s. 0d. / [10s. 0d.]				
1391–2	[5s. 4d.]	3s. 4d.	2s. 4d. / 3s. 0d. / 3s. 4d.	1s. 8d.		3s. 4d. / 6s. 8d.		2s. 8d. / 4s. 0d.	2s. 0d. / 3s. 4d.
1392–3	[3s. 4d.]	2s. 8d. / 2s. 10d. / 3s. 0d.	3s. 0d.	2s. 0d.					
1393–4	3s. 4d. / 3s. 8d.	2s. 8d. / 3s. 0d. / 3s. 2d. / 3s. 4d.	2s. 2d. / 2s. 4d.	1s. 8d.	4s. 8d.		2s. 0d.	3s. 4d.	1s. 8d.
1394–5	2s. 8d. / 3s. 0d.	2s. 8d. / 3s. 0d.	2s. 8d. / 2s. 4d.	2s. 4d.	4s. 0d.				
1395–6	3s. 0d. / 3s. 4d.	3s. 0d.	3s. 0d.	2s. 0d.	4s. 0d.			3s. 0d.	
1396–7		6s. 8d. / 7s. 4d. / 8s. 0d.			6s. 8d. / 7s. 4d. / 8s. 0d.				

NOTE: [ ] indicates prices deriving from valuations rather than actual sales or purchases.

and 1389–92, but even then prices in excess of 6s. 0d. per quarter for wheat were unusual. These prices reflect those prevailing in the small market towns, such as Tewkesbury (where Bredon's grain was sold) or Cirencester (to which Bibury grain was taken). Henbury and Stoke produced grain for the much larger Bristol market, and their wheat prices were higher by 21 per cent, barley by 15 per cent and oats by 6 per cent than in the manors in more rural situations.[21]

Even in the period of relatively high prices prevailing before 1376, costs of production were very high, as wages and the price of manufactured goods (such as plough and cart parts) had risen since 1349. Table 19 attempts to assess the profit on grain cultivation at Bibury in 1371–2, an example chosen because all surplus grain was sold, and no labour services were used, so that a realistic balance sheet in cash can be calculated. There are various imponderables, notably the amount of hay fed to draught animals, but the estimate is based on a statement in a Stoke account that oxen and horses would consume the produce of 2 or 3 acres of meadow each, so the sum of

Table 19. *Balance sheet for grain production at Bibury, 1371–2*

Income	Sale of grain (9 qr 3 b wheat, 37 qr drage, 8 qr 4 b vetch, 15 qr 5½ b oats, 4 qr 3½ b barley)	£11	13s.	6d.
	Sale of straw and stubble		6s.	0d.
	Total	£11	19s.	6d.
Expenditure	Maintenance of ploughs		11s.	11d.
	Maintenance of carts, shoeing cart horses etc.		7s.	10d.
	Threshing		14s.	6d.
	Harvesting	£2	13s.	8d.
	Wages of ploughmen and carter	£1	10s.	0d.
	Grain livery of *famuli*	£3	2s.	3d.
	Famuli pottage		4s.	6d.
	Grain fed to oxen and horses		10s.	0d.
	Hay fed to oxen and horses		18s.	0d.
	Miscellaneous		7s.	5d.
	Total	£11	0s.	1d.
	Profit 19s. 5d.			

[21] These regional differences in corn prices are documented in N. S. B. Gras, *The Evolution of the English Corn-Market* (Cambridge, Mass., 1926), pp. 46–9.

18s. 0d. is an appropriate fraction of the costs of mowing and haymaking.[22] No allowance is made for the depreciation of agricultural buildings. The costs of carts and the carter's wages are included in full, but part of the carting work would not have been connected with arable cultivation. The year chosen should have been a favourable one, as grain prices were high (wheat was sold for 6s. 8d. per quarter), and the yields were not very different from normal. However, an expenditure of cash and goods worth £11 produced a profit of about £1. Ten years later wage costs were little changed, but far lower prices would have prevented much profit arising from grain production.

Calculations of profit are made more difficult after 1375 because of a change in the use of grain. Bishop Wakefield was permanently resident in the diocese after 1377, so that grain could be consumed in his household rather than sold. Whereas 75 quarters of Bibury grain were sold in 1371–2, and 60 quarters in 1372–3, after 1378 grain sales usually amounted to less than 40 quarters, and 30 quarters or more were sent either to the lord's household, or to other manors, for direct consumption. 60 quarters of Hampton grain were sold in 1371–2, and only 2 quarters sent to the household. After 1378 sales did not exceed 21 quarters in any one year, but up to 48 quarters went to the household. The importance of direct consumption is shown also in the Blockley, Bredon and Cleeve accounts.

A greater market orientation is found at Henbury and Stoke, which were too remote for grain to be carried to the household, and grain was consumed directly only when the bishop visited. Wakefield spent some time at Henbury in at least thirteen of his twenty years, often in the summer when he hunted in Pen and Sneyd parks. In these years Henbury grain was consumed by the household. At other times Henbury grain was sold in large quantities – up to 119 quarters in 1378–9. Stoke grain was invariably sold, regardless of the bishop's visits, again involving large amounts, up to 75 quarters. The high prices in the Bristol market made this advantageous, and a sensitivity towards marketing is more apparent in the Henbury and Stoke accounts than elsewhere on the estate. Grain was held back in the hope of obtaining better prices at a later date. 36 quarters of wheat from the 1377 harvest were kept in stack until the price rose from 3s. 4d. to 4s. 0d. per quarter. In 1385

---

[22] Stoke AR, 1377–8, 1381–2.

some wheat was sold in January for 4s. 4d. per quarter, but the bulk went to market in July, when the price had risen to 5s. 4d.

Arable cultivation, then, was conducted on a large scale, with most grain being sold, albeit for rather meagre profits, in the early 1370s. Under Wakefield low prices discouraged sales, and a resident bishop was able to make use of much grain in his household. Grain production was reduced, and costs were cut by cultivating a smaller area of the demesnes.

As the demesne area shrank because of leasing, the pastoral resources of the estate were inevitably diminished. The reduction was much less than for arable lands. The complete demesnes chosen for leasing were mainly those with small pastures. On the demesnes kept in direct management arable was converted into pasture, and some vacant tenant holdings were used as demesne pasture, such as the site of the deserted villages of Hatton and Upton, or on holdings at Cleeve in 1393–4. The bishop's rights to common pastures were not diminished.

So a comparison between lists of stock compiled in c.1290 and 1389 shows a drastic reduction in the numbers of oxen, because fewer plough-teams were employed, from 542 to 202, and numbers of cows also fell, from 226 to 96, but sheep declined by only 18 per cent, from 5,650 to 4,638.[23] So the relative importance of sheep-farming in the estate economy grew considerably in the fourteenth century.

The stock list of 1389 (see Table 20) shows that small numbers of cart-horses were kept on each manor, except at Alvechurch, where there was a small stud of 2 mares and 4 foals.

Oxen, because of their use in plough-teams, were the most numerous type of cattle, with 202 in 1389. The main herds of cows, consisting of some 24 to 31 animals, were kept on the river-valley manors of Bredon, Fladbury and Ripple in 1389, though in the 1370s and 1380s herds of cows of comparable size were also pastured at Hampton, Henbury and Stoke. These animals did not usually produce cheese and butter for sale by the bishop's officials, but instead the 'lactage' was rented out for between 3s. 4d. and 6s. 0d. per annum. Their calves helped to replace stock on the estate, and a herd of young animals was pastured normally at Hampton,

[23] WCRO ref. 009:1 BA 2636/193 92628 4/9.

Table 20. Stock numbers, 29 September 1389

	Horses	Oxen	Cows	Other cattle	Pigs	Sheep					
						Rams	Ewes	Lambs	2-year-olds	Wethers	All sheep
Alvechurch	10	22	6	1	—	—	—	—	—	—	—
Bibury	4	5	—	—	—	—	1	187	—	2	190
Blockley	6	20	1	—	78	—	—	47	—	863	910
Bredon	4	19	31	2	119	—	—	—	—	278	278
Cleeve	4	23	1	—	115	—	—	—	—	360	360
Fladbury	4	19	24	1	93	7	233	1	—	—	241
Hampton	5	11	3	42	55	6	241	381	20	—	648
Hartlebury*	1	1	—	—	—	—	—	—	—	—	—
Henbury	1	10	—	7	15	—	—	—	—	—	—
Kempsey	4	18	—	—	137	7	164	—	179	326	676
Ripple	5	9	24	1	92	6	241	—	—	—	247
Stoke	1	7	2	9	10	—	3	216	—	—	219
Stratford*	—	1	1	—	—	—	—	—	—	—	—
Whitstones	6	24	—	—	8	—	—	—	194	38	232
Wick*	—	2	—	—	9	—	—	—	—	—	—
Withington	3	11	3	—	9	3	281	3	58	292	637
Total of whole estate	58	202	96	63	740	29	1,164	835	451	2,159	4,638

* Manors at farm.

with up to 40 calves, yearlings, heifers, steers, bullocks and young bulls.

740 pigs were kept on the estate in 1389, mainly on the Cotswold edge and river-valley manors. They were involved in a certain amount of transhumance, with animals bred on the Cotswold manors being sent to lowland manors in the winter, and pigs from Cleeve and Bredon were pastured in the woods at Welland.

Sheep were kept on almost all of the demesnes, and, as in the mid-thirteenth century, flocks were organized centrally from a headquarters at Blockley. This manor had a very large flock of its own, and most of the other flocks were driven there in June for shearing. If animals on the more distant manors were sheared locally, the wool was often carried to Blockley for sale. Each manor had a specialist function in the pastoral system of the estate, as is shown by the list of Michaelmas 1389 (see Table 20). At that time, breeding flocks of ewes and rams, and flocks of younger animals, lambs and hoggasters (two-year-olds), were kept mainly on lowland pastures, while full-grown wethers, which made up nearly a half of the total, were concentrated on manors with upland pastures, Blockley, Bredon, Cleeve and Withington (though there was also a flock at Kempsey). The function of individual manors sometimes changed. Bibury normally had a flock of wethers in the winter, but lambs were kept there in the winters of 1389–92. The Hampton pastures were occupied only by a flock of ewes up to 1385, but when the demesne pastures expanded over the fields of Hatton, a flock of lambs joined them.

The distribution of sheep at Michaelmas indicates the pasturing arrangements for the winter. In the summer, flocks travelled up to forty miles from manor to manor. The normal pattern was for the Cotswold flocks to expand. In 1381–2, for example, 344 sheep, mainly wethers, wintered at Bibury, but by the following June the numbers had grown to 660, falling again to 327 in September. The additional summer flocks often consisted of ewes and lambs from the river valleys. In 1381–2, 214 ewes and lambs from Ripple stayed at Bibury from 1 May until 16 August. In the following year 323 sheep from Ripple arrived on 15 May and left on 6 July. In both cases the Ripple shepherd accompanied his charges, and received an allowance of grain from the Bibury reeve. Another Cotswold manor, Withington, had a similar rôle, receiving, for example, 224 sheep from Bredon and 127 from Kempsey in April 1394. Blockley took young animals from Fladbury, Hampton, Kempsey and Stratford in the summer of 1384. Numbers were also swollen at Blockley by sheep coming temporarily to the shearing, bringing the total to 4,000 animals assembled there.

Not all sheep movements fit into this pattern. There was a good deal of exchange of animals between one upland manor and another, or between valley manors. Also flocks of ewes and wethers often stayed on the same manor for the whole year. Henbury and Stoke were too remote to allow integration of their flocks into the main estate system, but in any case sheep-keeping was rather intermittent there, and for long periods there were none.

Flocks were partly maintained by breeding within the estate. The 1389 list shows that enough ewes were kept to maintain numbers, but the inroads of disease meant that purchases had to be made. In 1383–4, for example, the Blockley reeve bought 329 lambs. Care was evidently taken to ensure that stock of the right quality was purchased. It was apparently felt that Welsh sheep were best suited for the pastures at Henbury, and in 1379 the reeve and beadle went fruitlessly to St Briavels across the Severn estuary to buy sheep, but eventually bought a flock (presumably of Cotswold breed) at Chipping Sodbury. Welsh sheep were bought at Chepstow in 1380, and ferried across the estuary, and a large flock of 404 Welsh sheep were bought in 1385.

Acquisition of animals was not always so selective. In 1375–6, when all stock had to be replaced because of sales by the previous bishop's executors, any animals that came into the lord's hands were used to build up demesne flocks and herds. These included animals which came from tenants as rents and heriots, strays, and even from the chattels of an escaped felon.

The quality of stock was maintained by culling; according to the accounts animals were culled, 'because useless for the lord's stock', or 'because barren', or 'because of possible disease'.

Animal feeding was usually confined to hay, and cereals and legumes were used more sparingly. Pigs were fed in preparation for slaughter, 'for the lord's larder', and outdoor pigs were fed, usually with legumes, in the winter. At Hampton and Henbury 'draft', the malt dregs left after brewing, was bought as pig food. Cattle and horses were given grain only under special circumstances – when they were ill, or when draught animals were doing heavy work, or in the winter. Only the riding horses of estate officials were given oats regularly.[24] Full-grown sheep were fed with peas and beans in the winter, but probably only during spells of severe weather. The Bibury flock never received more than 6 quarters. The younger animals kept at Hampton in the late 1380s were fed more systematically with up to 20 quarters of pulse in a year. Milk was also bought to feed lambs in the winter.

The main evidence of care being taken in animal husbandry is the building of sheepcotes, large buildings in which fodder could be stored and at least part of the flock sheltered in bad weather.[25] A second sheepcote built at Blockley in 1383–4 was eight bays long (c.120 feet) with an expensive roof of stone tiles, the whole structure costing at least £11 7s. 7d. The Hampton sheepcote was a four-bay structure in 1386–7, when it was repaired and another two bays added, making a building about 90 feet long. Between 1392 and 1394 a new sheepcote, of at least four bays, was built at Bibury, again with a stone-tiled roof, for which the roof alone cost about £6.[26]

An indication of the quality of animal husbandry is the extent to which animals succumbed to disease. Young pigs were particularly susceptible to death from 'murrain', and the death rate often exceeded 10 per cent. Efforts were made to protect sheep from disease by the traditional applications of grease and tar, and by culling sick animals. The sheep at Hampton were provided in 1385–6 with 'foot stalls' (leather boots) to protect them from foot-rot. Death-rates among sheep were much the same as on other estates, exceeding 10 per cent in about one year in five. Two of the most severe outbreaks of disease were at Henbury and Stoke. In 1376–7 at Henbury 12 per cent of a flock of wethers died of 'le pokkes', and a flock of 216 lambs at Stoke in 1389–90 suffered losses of 127 (59 per cent) from 'le squyrt'. After both episodes sheep-keeping was temporarily abandoned on these manors. Otherwise the worst incidence of disease was among the lambs at Hampton, where mortality rose above 40 per cent in 1377–8, 1380–1 and 1381–2.[27]

[24] In this respect the animal husbandry on the Worcester manors was inferior to that recorded on other estates, see R. Trow-Smith, *A History of British Livestock Husbandry to 1700* (London, 1957), pp. 115–18.

[25] On the functions of sheepcotes see *The Duchy of Lancaster's Estates in Derbyshire, 1485–1540*, ed. I. S. W. Blanchard (Derbyshire Archaeological Soc. Record Series, iii, 1967), p. 11.

[26] Bibury AR, 1393–4.

[27] Trow-Smith, *Livestock Husbandry*, pp. 153–7, shows that the Worcester estate's experience of disease was not untypical.

Pastoral farming, and particularly the keeping of sheep, was maintained at a higher level than cereal production because it enjoyed the two-fold advantages of a favourable market and lower costs. Grain prices declined in the late 1370s. Wool prices moved in the same direction as those of wheat, but wool was still a more profitable product than grain. The Worcester estate enjoyed an added advantage in its high-quality wool. Whereas the annual mean of English wool prices in the 1380s has been calculated as varying between 2.98 and 4.61 shillings per stone, the 1384 wool clip was sold to William Grevil, the Chipping Campden wool merchant for £133, at £9 6s. 8d. per sack or 7.18 shillings per stone. In 1389 Grevil owed the bishop £134 6s. 8d. for a clip that probably contained about 3,400 fleeces, making a price of about £8 10s. 0d. per sack or 6.54 shillings per stone. The importance of the breed of sheep in determining the price of wool is indicated by wool sales at Henbury, which were conducted separately. In 1380 wool from sheep bought at Chipping Sodbury, presumably Cotswold animals, was sold for 6.34 shillings per stone, but in 1385 and 1386 the wool of Welsh sheep fetched only 3.00 shillings per stone.[28]

There can be no doubt about the profitability of sheep farming. Labour costs were much lower than for grain cultivation, as one shepherd could manage a normal manorial flock of 200–300 animals, while a full-time staff of three was required for the cultivation of even the smallest demesne. There were no major seasonal tasks comparable with the grain harvest, washing and shearing being accomplished in a few days. The calculation of profit for Bibury in 1383–4 (Table 21) contains elements of uncertainty. The amount of hay fed to the sheep has been estimated on the basis of slender evidence. Specific allowances for capital depreciation have not been made, but expenditure on the sheepcote and the value of sheep that died during the year have been included. The calculation suggests that the profit on a flock of 350 wethers was about £8. A breeding flock would have been worth less, because of higher expenditure on foodstuffs, and lambs in their first year required expenditure without providing any wool.[29]

[28] T. H. Lloyd, *The Movement of Wool Prices in Medieval England* (Econ. Hist. Rev. Supplement no. 6, 1973), pp. 38–44, for regional variations in wool-prices.
[29] The profits on the mixed Hampton flock in 1377–8 have been estimated at £5 on an expenditure of £6 0s. 0d.; see C. Dyer, 'Population and Agriculture on a Warwickshire Manor in the Later Middle Ages', *Univ. of Birm. Hist. Journ.*, xi (1968), p. 121.

Table 21. *Balance sheet for sheep-farming at Bibury, 1383–4*

Income	Sale of wool (314 fleeces @ 10.4d.)	£13 12s. 2d.
	Sale of wool-pells	5s. 11d.
	Sale of locks	6d.
		£13 18s. 7d.
Expenditure	Tar, grease, hurdles, red stone, driving sheep	17s. 9½d.
	Shearing, packing and carriage of wool	6s. 6d.
	Maintenance of sheepcote	2s. 10d.
	Shepherd's wages, liveries, and pottage	£1 6s. 11½d.
	Hay (estimate only)	10s. 0d.
	Dead sheep	£1 4s. 0d.
	Tithe and shepherd's fleece (36 @ 10.4d.)	£1 11s. 2½d.
		£5 19s. 3½d.
	Profit £7 19s. 3½d.	

Sheep were reared almost entirely for the sake of their wool. Animals were not usually sold until they had reached the end of their useful lives, when they were old or diseased. Some sheep were consumed in the lord's household, but wool production took priority over the needs of the bishop's table, and consequently elderly wethers were sent to provide tough mutton for the bishop's servants.

Other animals yielded some cash income, notably from the lactage of cows, but most were kept for their contribution to arable cultivation, or, in the case of pigs, their meat was often used in the bishop's household. Pigs were fattened on cereals and sent to fill the lord's larder in large numbers from Bredon and Cleeve, up to 52 animals in one year from the former manor, for example. Again, Henbury and Stoke were unusual in that calves and pigs were regularly sold.

The profitability of demesne production depended on the level of costs, in which the payment of wages played a major part.

The use of labour services for the cultivation of the demesnes varied to some extent with the level of demesne production. When the cultivated area at Cleeve was very high in 1372–3, 67 per cent of the potential services were used in labour on the demesne, and very few were sold. Twenty years later a much smaller scale of demesne cultivation was associated with a reduction of labour demands to only 31 per cent of services. At Stoke 35 per cent of services were used in 1372–3, but less then 30 per cent in later years, when the cultivated area was reduced by a fifth or more. Some demesnes could, however, function with virtually no labour services at all, as happened as Bibury and Hampton for more than twenty years, and on other manors for at least a few years after large scale commutations around 1390.

The estate management clearly had to make a finely balanced decision as to whether cash rents or labour services would be most advantageous to them, and doubtless had to take into account pressure from tenants for commutation. Much use of labour services was made at Henbury and Stoke, the manors with the strongest commercial orientation on the estate, indicating the well-known link between the influence of the market and labour services.[30] On these two manors between 22 per cent and 31 per cent of services were utilized, so that on relatively small demesnes a high proportion of the tasks were performed by customary labour – all harvesting and haymaking, much ploughing, as well as such miscellaneous tasks as carting, ditching and work around the manorial buildings. Also, at Henbury one of the demesne ploughmen was the tenant of an *enchelond*, who worked full-time in exchange for remission of all his rents.

On the Bredon demesne in the same period *enches* were employed as ploughmen, and major tasks such as mowing, harvesting and some ploughing were done by labour services. In 1375–6, 33 per cent of potential services were used. A more modest use of customary services was made at Blockley and Cleeve; no *enches* were required to act as ploughmen, and much of the harvesting was done with hired labour.

By the early 1390s tenants' services had become a minor source of labour on most manors. The reason for this can be seen by comparing the cash income derived from rents with the profits of agriculture. Commutation of services at Henbury in 1393 increased rent income by about £16. The bulk of the tenants' works had been used in the previous twenty years to produce grain, which only

[30] M. M. Postan, 'The Chronology of Labour Services', *Essays on Medieval Agriculture and General Problems of the Medieval Economy* (Cambridge, 1973), p. 90.

occasionally was sold for more than £16. Rents were also a more stable source of income than grain sales.

In the absence of services, wage labour was hired. The costs of labour showed no consistent trend in the last quarter of the century, and seemed to mark a plateau in the secular rise in wages of the late medieval period.[31] Piece-work rates tended to fall slightly, admittedly from some very high levels in the 1370s. Harvest workers at Hampton received 1s. 1d. per acre in 1377, but from 7½d. to 10½d. in the 1380s, and harvesting at Bibury cost from 8½d. to 10d. between 1376 and 1381, but 7½d to 9½d. thereafter. The rate for threshing grains other than wheat at Bibury fell from 2½d. per quarter in 1380–6 to 2d. per quarter in 1386–95.

The daily wage-rates of building workers show no clearly marked trend, with such skilled workers as carpenters and thatchers receiving 4d. per day from 1372 to 1396, with only slight upward or downward movements.

The category of workers whose wages did increase in our period were the *famuli*, the full-time employees who performed the basic tasks on the demesnes of manning the ploughs, carting and looking after animals. They were employed on an annual contract, and received both a cash wage and an allowance of grain, usually at a rate of 4½ quarters per annum. The contemporary records of the enforcement of the labour laws show a persistent reluctance of wage-earners to enter into annual contracts, preferring the uncertainties, but also the freedom, of employment by the day.[32] Consequently employers had to improve substantially the remuneration of *famuli* in order to attract recruits. The *tenator* (ploughholder) at Bibury received a cash wage of 8s. 0d. per annum up to 1385, when it rose to 10s. 0d. A *fugator* (driver of the plough-team) at Henbury and Stoke, who received 6s. 0d. in the 1370s, was given 7s. 0d. in 1380 and 8s. 0d. from 1384. The Hampton ploughmen received 7s. 0d. and 8s. 0d. in the 1370s, 9s. 0d. and 13s. 4d. by 1377, and from 1381 the differential between them was removed and both were paid 13s. 0d. The quality of the grain liveries of the *famuli* was

[31] E. H. Phelps Brown and Sheila V. Hopkins, 'Seven Centuries of Building Wages', in E. M. Carus-Wilson (ed.), *Essays in Economic History* (London, 1962), ii, p. 177; W. Beveridge, 'Wages in the Winchester Manors', *Econ. Hist. Rev.*, vii (1936), pp. 22–43.

[32] N. Kenyon, 'Labour Conditions in Essex in the reign of Richard II', in E. M. Carus-Wilson (ed.), *Essays in Economic History*, ii, pp. 92–4.

improved at Hampton in 1388 and Bibury in 1385 with the introduction of a small quantity of wheat, and the wheat content of the
Stoke liveries increased in the 1380s.[33]

Wage costs of the *famuli* increased substantially in our period,
but other wages were either static or falling slightly. However, wages
had risen before the 1370s, cutting into the profits of arable cultivation, as we have seen. The decision to reduce the amount of customary labour used in demesne cultivation greatly expanded the wage-
bills of such manors as Henbury and Bredon, and made the eventual
leasing of those demesnes more certain.

In view of the low profits of arable cultivation on those manors
where labour services were commuted before the 1370s, it is difficult to see why direct management continued for so long. It is also
doubtful if there was any advantage in using labour services in order
to produce low-priced grain on other manors.

Higher wages, and the increased cost of manufactured goods, such
as building-materials, in the late fourteenth century, raised the cost
of renewing and maintaining the lord's capital assets, notably
agricultural buildings and equipment. On most estates before 1350
capital spending was low – about 5 per cent of receipts. The Hampton accounts have been used to show that a higher level of capital
investment can be found after 1350, as expenditure on capital goods
cost 10 per cent of receipts.[34] This is not noticed to such a marked
extent on the other manors of the estate. Expenditure on buildings
and equipment amounted to 8.8 per cent of manorial profits at
Bibury, 6.3 per cent at Bredon, 4.5 per cent at Henbury and 6.7 per
cent at Stoke. These figures give a misleadingly high impression of
the level of capital formation, as for three manors they include
figures for 1375–6, the first year of Wakefield's episcopate, when
profits were small and the reeves had to replace the carts, ploughs
and other equipment taken by the previous bishop's executors.

The rate of capital spending was therefore not much higher than
that prevailing before 1350. It has already been suggested that the
estate managers attempted to economize by reducing the number
of demesne ploughs, and some of the expensive projects, such as the

---

[33] The improvements in the remuneration of *famuli* are paralleled at Battle:
see Searle, *Lordship and Community*, p. 307.

[34] R. H. Hilton, 'Rent and Capital Formation in Feudal Society', in *The
English Peasantry in the Later Middle Ages* (Oxford, 1975), p. 191.

building of sheepcotes, were in the most profitable sector of demesne agriculture.

Some of the capital assets of the estate decayed, notably mills,
which were in ruins at Bibury, Bredon, Cleeve and Hanbury. The
Stoke mill was repaired in 1377–8, but was ruinous and empty by
1386. The reason for this neglect is apparent from the decline of the
Brentry windmill at Henbury. This was repaired in 1369, but was
again in need of maintenance in 1375. Medieval windmills were
relatively light and inexpensive to build, unlike watermills with their
dams, sluices and substantial structures, but constant expenditure
was still needed, especially on sailcloths and the replacement and
recutting of millstones.

Over a five-year period when the mill was under the lord's management, profits averaged about 10s. 0d. per annum. In the 1380s a
miller was persuaded to take over and pay a farm of £1. It is difficult
to see how this could have been forthcoming, and by 1395 the mill
had fallen into disrepair, and was not used again. This was the result
of high costs and low grain prices, to which might be added the low
volume of grain ground, which could reflect a reluctance among
the tenants to use their lord's mill (see Table 22).

The calculation of manorial profit is notoriously difficult. The cash
liveries to the receiver or direct to the lord, representing the cash
taken out of the manor each year, provide a basic figure. However, much grain and other produce came to the household for
direct consumption. This can be valued with some accuracy by using
sale prices recorded in most accounts. The profits of the sheep flocks

Table 22. *Henbury windmill, 1375–80*

Expenditure, income and profits				
Year	Expenditure	Toll corn (quantity)	Value of corn	Profit or loss
1375–6	19s. 1d.	7qr 0b 1p	£2 5s. 2½d.	+£1 6s. 1½d.
1376–7	12s. 2½d.	8qr 3b 1p	£1 13s. 2d.	+£1 0s. 11½d.
1377–8	6s. 8d.	6qr 3b 0p	£1 0s. 2d.	+ 13s. 6d.
1378–9	£2 0s. 11d.	6qr 7b 0p	£1 2s. 8d.	− 18s. 3d.
1379–80	£1 4s. 1d.	6qr 5b 0p	£1 12s. 8d.	+ 8s. 7d.
Totals	£5 2s. 11½d.	35qr 2b 2p	£7 13s. 10½d.	+£2 10s. 11d.

of individual manors are more hazardous to estimate, as wool was weighed and sold centrally. Fleece weights on the estate varied from 1.36 to 2.50 lbs, depending on the breed and type of sheep, the weather and other factors. A median fleece weight of 1.69 lb has been calculated from those recorded, and prices have been taken from the estate accounts (where they exist), Cotswold prices quoted by Lloyd, or if both are lacking, the Cotswold price in the nearest year. The resulting figures are bound to lack precision, but the likely margins of error are small. The graphs indicate the figures deriving from cash liveries and payments in kind separately (see Appendix 2).

No conclusions can be drawn about levels of profit in the early 1370s as some of the few figures are distorted by unusual circumstances (230 sheep were sold from the Bibury flock in 1371–2, for example). A more coherent pattern emerges after 1375. The profits of 1375–6 were generally very low. This was Wakefield's first year, when animals and equipment had to be purchased in order to begin demesne cultivation again after the vacancy. Hanbury was the exception because it was on lease, so the farmer paid his rent, and the king in addition granted Wakefield part of the previous year's farm. On the manors with directly managed demesnes recovery was rapid, so that manorial profits reached a peak in the late 1370s and 1380s, followed by a decline in the late 1380s. At Henbury the best year was 1382–3, with profits of £88, but between 1384 and 1390 they varied from £50 to £69. The peak at Hampton was £36 in 1380–1, and afterwards profits varied between £24 and £27. Bibury profits fell from £36 in 1383–4 to between £10 and £29 in subsequent years. The causes of this cycle of rising and falling income are not easily discerned, but the most likely explanation lies in fluctuations in grain prices. An inexplicable exception was Stoke, with good years in 1387–9. In the 1390s profits recovered somewhat, but still lay below the earlier peak (except at Hampton, but the 1392–3 profits were a freak, caused by the sale of produce when the demesne was leased). Profits in cash were higher on some manors in the 1390s because of the increased rent income resulting from the commutation of services.

The figures show that manorial income was volatile in the last quarter of the fourteenth century, with sudden changes from year to year, which was an inevitable hazard of direct involvement in the market. Leasing provided greater stability, as suggested by the relatively steady profits from Hanbury. They also show that actual cash income was very small from some manors. For much of the 1380s both Bibury and Hampton were producing cash liveries of less than £10. Demesne farmers would have provided a cash income, which would have been essential for a non-resident bishop.

A comparison between the late fourteenth-century manorial profits and those obtained after 1400, when the demesnes were leased, shows no great change, or that there was even, at Henbury and Stoke, a tendency for profits to increase slightly after leasing. The apparent decline at Bibury is misleading because sheep pastures were kept in hand there in the early fifteenth century, and the profits of these are not recorded. Thus it is apparent that manorial profits had reached a point by the late 1380s and 1390s where the differences between the returns from direct management and leasing were negligible, and leasing offered advantages of stability and convenience.

To sum up the history of the estate in the late fourteenth century, it is convenient to divide the period between the successive bishops.

Under William Lenn (1369–73) it is probable that about eight demesnes had been leased out, though one, at Stratford, was brought back into direct management in 1373.[35] The manors still in hand had a rather archaic appearance, resembling the 'grain factories' of some thirteenth-century estates. Large areas of arable were cultivated in order to produce grain for the market. On some manors, notably Cleeve, much use was made of labour services on the demesne, but already wage-labour was mainly employed at Bibury and Hampton.

After the vacancy of 1373–5, Henry Wakefield took over an estate stripped of its moveable assets by the executors of Bishop Lenn; grain production had virtually ceased. Animals, seed-corn and equipment had to be purchased out of the rent income of 1375–6, and Wakefield's revenues in that year must have been negligible. The aim of the estate administration was to restore the estate as an agricultural enterprise, but only on a modest scale. The arable area was reduced, and expenditure on ploughs and other capital assets kept at a low level. The emphasis in grain and meat production shifted from large-scale marketing to self-sufficiency and direct consumption by the lord's household, which was convenient as he

[35] *VCH Warks.*, iii, p. 259.

lived within the diocese. A high level of commodity production was maintained in the sheep-farming of the estate, and wool sales brought in more than £130 in two recorded years in the 1380s.

Rent income seems to have also had mixed fortunes under Wakefield. Assize rents tended to decline, partly because of vacancies but also because of the need to attract tenants by leasing holdings. There was a trickle of individual commutation agreements in the 1370s and 1380s and a series of large-scale commutations from 1389. Yet concessions to tenants were not made over the profits of lordship, as is indicated by the high level of court perquisites.

The compromises adopted in Wakefield's episcopate paid off at first, judging from the high profits in the late 1370s and early 1380s, but after that profits declined partly because of low grain prices. The extent of the depression should not be exaggerated. Arrears were not particularly high, in spite of the vigilance shown by the auditors.

The estate officials recognized that there were problems in the running of the estate towards the end of Wakefield's episcopate. From 1391 calculations of value were made on each manorial account, not just for the whole manor, but also for each sector of demesne agriculture. For example, the Bibury account of 1393–4 contains valors of 11s. 4½d. for grain, 4s. 6d. for stock, £11 13s. 9d. for wool and £18 1s. 10d. for the manor, including rents. The method of calculation used is obscure, but the purpose of the valors was clearly designed to assess profitability. The low value invariably placed on grain must have helped to convince the officials of the futility of continuing arable cultivation under direct management.

In 1393–4 a survey of rents over the whole estate was compiled, including realistic calculations of net rents made by deducting decays and allowances from each item. This followed a number of major commutations of services that increased the proportion of rent income considerably, and shows that the estate management's interest in rents was increasing.

These administrative measures were accompanied by the beginnings of a new phase of demesne leasing. Stratford was leased in about 1389, and Hampton in 1392, but the main break came with Wakefield's death in 1395.[36] In the usual way the estate lost much of its stock, which was sold by the executors of a will which cont-

[36] Hampton AR, 1389–90, 1392–3.

ained cash bequests of at least £575. (They included £100 'to be distributed among my poor tenants, and particularly those who were injured by me', tempting us to infer that Wakefield was aware of the social consequences of the high profits of jurisdiction exacted during his period as landlord.)[37]

The new bishop, Tideman of Winchcomb, was confronted with the same problem of rebuilding the estate's assets as his predecessor was. He was able to transfer some stock from his former see of Llandaff, notably some oxen that were sent to Withington.[38] Demesne cultivation was resumed on at least one manor, Bredon, in Tideman's first year, but this expensive process was avoided at Bibury and Henbury in 1395 by leasing the demesnes. This probably occurred at the same time on other manors. Bredon was leased by 1401, and it is likely that all demesnes had been farmed out by the first decade of the fifteenth century.[39]

There is no difficulty in explaining the move towards demesne leasing in the late fourteenth century. All of the economic and social trends of the period converged to make it the most advantageous method of managing demesnes. The main problem lay with arable cultivation; some sheep pastures were kept in hand long after the main demesnes had been put into the hands of farmers.

Why were the demesnes not leased much earlier? The problems were all present by the 1370s. The estate managers' understanding of grain price movements must be taken into account. High prices in the period up to 1376 probably encouraged the continuation of demesne cultivation under Lenn and its resumption in the first year of Wakefield's episcopate, and the high profits in the early 1380s seemed to justify the decision. Falling grain prices were probably seen as a temporary aberration, and it was not until the 1390s that the estate officials would have been convinced that prices were following a long-term downward trend. In any case, the investments involved in setting up demesne agriculture again in 1375 would have made them loath to change policies too rapidly. There were also some advantages in direct consumption of demesne produce as the lord was resident in the diocese. The conservatism of the manage-

---

[37] *Reg. Wakefield*, pp. xliv–xlvi.

[38] Henbury AR, July–Sept. 1395.

[39] Bredon CR, March 1401; the demesnes seem to have been leased by the time of the 1408 survey, see White Book, fos. 30–7.

ment may also have influenced them – the directly managed demesne represented an element of the old order.

So it was with some reluctance, doubtless with an awareness of the difficulties of any subsequent restoration of directly cultivated demesnes, that decisions were made from 1389 onwards to farm out the remaining arable demesnes. The bishops of Worcester, in company with other magnates, had been forced by economic circumstances to become *rentiers*.

Postscript to Chapter 5. The end of direct management

By the opening years of the fifteenth century the demesnes of the bishopric estate had been leased out, but, as on many other estates in the period, some sheep pastures were retained under direct management.[1] The largest flocks were kept on the Cotswold manors of Blockley and Withington, but smaller numbers of sheep were also pastured at Bibury, Hampton and Kempsey. In 1412 sales of wool totalling 10 sacks, 3 todds and $1\frac{1}{2}$ stones were recorded, representing the clip of about 2,200 sheep.[2] In 1448–50 the master shepherd was in charge of flocks varying between 2,215 and 2,927.[3] This was a remarkable number for four or five manors to support, about 60 per cent of the flocks in the 1380s, when pastures on eleven manors were available for sheep-grazing. The pastures were being used intensively, particularly at Blockley, where between 1,400 and 1,760 sheep were kept, compared with fewer than 1,000 in the 1380s. The area of pasture had been extended over former demesne arable, such as the land at Stapenhill in Blockley.[4] Also, pastures were rented from other landowners in the Blockley neighbourhood, at Combe Baskerville and Lemington. There are references to sheep being kept at Ragley and Studley in south Warwickshire, but these may have been temporary arrangements for flocks *en route* for sale at Warwick. By the 1440s sheep were not kept in any number at Hampton and Kempsey, so that the old transhumance pattern could not be practised. The flocks consisted entirely of wethers, which were hardy enough to survive on upland pastures through the winter. Numbers were maintained by purchase: in 1449–50 new wethers were bought for 1s. 9d., and old animals sold at 1s. 0d. each.

Wethers needed less care than breeding animals and lambs, so that labour could be kept to a minimum. In 1449–50 only five shepherds were employed, each looking after 400–500 sheep,

---

[1] Postan, *The Medieval Economy and Society*, pp. 106–7.
[2] Kempsey CR, April 1411; Hampton AR, 1454–5; Arrears Roll, 1412.
[3] WCRO ref. 009:1 BA 2636/193 92627 9/12; /192 92626 8/12.
[4] Blockley AR, 1458–9.

compared to a normal flock of 250–300 per shepherd in the late fourteenth century.

The income from the flocks came partly from selling old animals for meat. In 1449–50, 145 sheep were bought by William Shoteswell, a Warwick butcher, who probably disposed of them on the urban markets of north Warwickshire.[5] Wool sales were the main source of profit: 10 sacks were sold in 1412, more than 12 in 1449 and 10 in 1450. The purchasers included John de Leona, a 'Lombard' merchant, and local wool-merchants from Worcester and Tetbury. The critical factor in justifying continued direct management was the selling price of wool. In line with national trends, this was declining. In 1412 the prices were lower than those of the 1380s, at 5.25s.–5.38s. per stone, but in 1450 only 3.33s.–4.62s. was obtained.[6] This can hardly have made direct management worthwhile, and it has been suggested that other mid-fifteenth-century demesne sheep flocks, particularly when wethers only were kept, actually made a loss.[7] The master shepherd's accounts do not allow a full calculation of profit, but in 1449–50 we can reasonably estimate that sales of old sheep, wool and skins brought in about £80, and £35 was spent on the purchase of sheep. Other costs, such as wages, repair of buildings and rents for extra pasture, must have reduced the profit margin to less than £30.

The uneconomic character of demesne sheep flocks was recognized in a survey of about 1450, which suggested that leasing lands at Withington would make 'greater profit'. By 1454 the sheep, reckoned as a flock of 2,500, were farmed out to Thomas Bleke, the lessee of the Bibury and Withington demesnes, for £26 13s. 4d. or about 2½d. per sheep. This arrangement continued until 1458, when the sheep were sold outright to Bleke, the pastures were leased, and the bishop of Worcester's major agricultural activities came to an end.[8]

Other examples of continued direct management in the fifteenth century were on a much smaller scale. A horse stud was recorded in Pen park at Henbury in the period 1411–32. In 1411–12 it consisted

[5] On Shoteswell, and the north Warwickshire butchers in general, see C. Dyer, 'A Small Landowner in the Fifteenth Century', *Midland History*, i (1972), p. 7.

[6] Lloyd, *Wool Prices*, pp. 42–4, shows a decline in 1412–50 in Cotswold prices from 6.32s. to 3.33s., and in the national mean from 4.17s. to 2.73s.

[7] Lloyd, *ibid.*, pp. 25–6.

[8] WCRO ref. 009:1 BA 2636/193 92627 10/12; Valor, 1454, 1457; Blockley AR, 1458–9.

of a stallion and 7 mares, with 17 foals at the beginning of the year and 13 at the end (the drop in numbers was the result of disease). The purpose of the stud seems to have been to provide the bishop's household with draught or riding animals, though in one year, 1427–8, 6 horses were sold. The prices that they fetched – the mares went for about 7s. 0d. each – do not suggest that they were thoroughbreds. The stud involved a good deal of trouble and expense, and deprived the bishops of pasture rents from the park, and the whole operation was abandoned by the 1450s. At about the same time a small herd of cattle, 15 in 1412 for example, was kept at the neighbouring manor of Stoke, but its function is not clear.[9]

After 1458 the only vestige of direct management was the continued use of meadows to supply the household with hay. These were at Alvechurch, Bredon, Hartlebury, Kempsey, Henbury and Stoke in the 1450s and 1460s, and they usually provided fewer than a hundred waggon loads of hay. Demesne meadows were still kept in hand at Kempsey and Hartlebury in the early sixteenth century.[10] Woods also were not leased out, and provided fuel for the household, timber for the buildings of lord and tenants, and a cash income of varying size throughout our period.

The long-drawn-out decline of demesne exploitation in the fifteenth century re-emphasizes the superior profitability of pastoral over arable husbandry, and also indicates the reluctance of the estate management to abandon direct participation in agriculture, after even sheep had ceased to give much return.

[9] Henbury AR, 1411–12, 1426–7, 1427–8, 1431–2; Stoke AR, 1411–12.
[10] Valors, *passim*; Kempsey AR, 1505–6, 1508–9, 1514–15, 1520–1, 1525–6; WCRO ref. 009:1 BA 2636/37 (iii) 43806, fo. 83.

6. The lord's economy: administration and income, 1400−1540

*

The changing fortunes of the great landowners in the fifteenth century are still subject to dispute. The most convincing argument advanced so far is that the main economic trends of the early and mid-fifteenth century were against the magnates, as rents, which formed the bulk of their revenues, declined. However, it has been alleged that some tendencies counteracted any effects of falling rents. Some of these, such as the concentration of property in fewer hands through marriage or the profits of war, are applicable only to the laity, but in the case of both lay and church landowners, such as the Greys of Ruthin or the archbishops of Canterbury, it has been maintained that skilful management could stabilize or even increase estate revenues.[1]

Similar problems are presented by the changing circumstances of the early sixteenth century. Economic developments, notably rising prices, should have enabled landlords to increase their incomes, yet there are doubts about the extent to which lords took advantage of these opportunities, particularly in the case of ecclesiastics.[2]

In order to deal with these problems, it is necessary to examine the administration of the bishopric estates, to define developments in their revenue, and then to see if there is any connection between them.

Many of the bishops between 1400 and 1540 were absentees. Richard Clifford (1401−7) spent only seventeen months of his six

---

[1] Postan, *The Medieval Economy and Society*, pp. 175−8; A. J. Pollard, 'Estate Management in the Later Middle Ages: the Talbots and Whitchurch, 1383−1525', *Econ. Hist. Rev.*, 2nd ser., xxv (1972), pp. 553−66; both argue for overall decline in magnate incomes. Contrary views are K. B. McFarlane, *The Nobility of Later Medieval England* (Oxford, 1973), pp. 10−16; Du Boulay, *Lordship of Canterbury*, pp. 219−20, 243−5; *The Grey of Ruthin Valor*, ed. R. I. Jack (Sydney, 1965), pp. 3−7, 27−57.

[2] J. Thirsk (ed.), *The Agrarian History of England and Wales* (Cambridge, 1967), iv, pp. 306−32.

years in the diocese. Philip Morgan (1419–26) was involved in diplomatic missions in the first two years of his episcopate, and from 1422 he was in constant attendance at the council that ruled during Henry VI's minority. Thomas Bourgchier (1435–43), promoted as a young man because of his high birth, also had duties away from the diocese as Chancellor of Oxford University and on the king's council. John Alcock (1476–86) held such positions as President of the Council of the Marches, tutor to Edward V and royal councillor, which must have taken him from the diocese a good deal. The Italian bishops, notably Silvestro de' Gigli (1499–1521) and Geronimo de' Ghinucci (1523–35), spent their time in London or on diplomatic work in Italy, and hardly visited their see at all.[3]

The most notable exception was John Carpenter (1444–76). It has been suggested that he was born at Westbury-on-Trym on the manor of Stoke, and this is supported by the appearance of two tenants called Carpenter at Westbury in a rental of *c.*1410. If the identification is correct, he was the only medieval bishop of Worcester whose family were tenants on the estate. After a distinguished career at Oxford, and service as a royal clerk, Carpenter became bishop in 1444, when he was probably in his late forties. Although he visited London often, he was usually resident in the diocese and active in its ecclesiastical administration. He conducted ordinations personally, and carried out two visitations of the diocese. He founded two libraries at Worcester and Bristol, but his main achievement was the refoundation of the college of Westbury-on-Trym.

A most unusual action of his was to issue a set of Injunctions in 1451, resembling the episcopal legislation of earlier periods, which dealt with such matters as wandering clergy, poor-relief and sexual morality. It is significant that a thorough investigation of the temporalities was made at about the same time, as if all aspects of the bishop's responsibilities were being put in order. Carpenter lived to a great age, but in his last decade as bishop, when he was

[3] For Clifford, see *Reg. Clifford*, p. 23; on Morgan, see *DNB*, xiii, pp. 921–2; on Bourgchier, see *DNB*, ii, pp. 923–6; on Alcock, see *DNB*, i, pp. 236–7 (and supplement), and J. R. Lander, *Crown and Nobility, 1450–1509* (London, 1976), p. 311; on the Italian bishops, see M. Creighton, 'The Italian Bishops of Worcester', in *Historical Essays and Reviews* (London, 1902), pp. 202–34, and D. S. Chambers, *Cardinal Bainbridge in the Court of Rome, 1509 to 1514* (Oxford, 1965), pp. 9–10, 42–3, 143–40, 145–50.

in his seventies, there is less evidence of activity in ecclesiastical matters.[4]

Hugh Latimer (1535–9), the first protestant bishop, was the only other bishop of Worcester in our period who is known to have devoted much time to his diocese, but his episcopate was brief.[5]

The basic administrative structure established in the thirteenth and fourteenth centuries remained in use, and a council, a steward (or stewards after *c.*1460, when a separate stewardship was created for the Gloucestershire manors), a receiver and an auditor carried out much the same functions as before (for details of the officials, see Appendix 1).

One of the main changes in the fifteenth century was the appearance of a new type of official, the *supervisor* or surveyor. This was a later development than on some lay estates, and the post was a subordinate one, or sometimes combined with other offices.[6] In the early fifteenth century the office was independent, but by the 1460s the receiver was also acting as surveyor. In the early sixteenth century the procurator who collected revenues from the receiver for Silvestro de' Gigli also had the title of surveyor, but as he lived in London the duties were performed by a deputy who was also understeward. The receiver doubled as surveyor in 1509–10 and 1522–3, but between 1523 and 1525 William More, prior of Worcester, acted as surveyor, and in the 1530s the office was held by Sir John Russell. The duties of the surveyors included (in the early fifteenth century) the sale of wool and timber; in the early sixteenth century they travelled over the estate with the steward and negotiated the letting of lands with tenants.[7]

An important move towards administrative centralization is indicated by frequent references in estate documents to the council,

[4] *DNB*, iii, p. 1065; WCRO ref. 009:1 BA 2636/9 43696, fo. 163; R. M. Haines, 'Aspects of the Episcopate of John Carpenter, Bishop of Worcester, 1444–76', *Journ. Eccl. Hist.*, xix (1968), pp. 11–40; R. M. Haines, 'Bishop Carpenter's Injunctions to the Diocese of Worcester in 1451', *Bull. Inst. Hist. Res.*, xl (1967), pp. 203–7.

[5] *VCH Worcs.*, ii, pp. 44–5; M. L. Loane, *Masters of the English Reformation* (London, 1954), pp. 108–9.

[6] A surveyor was established on the Beauchamp estates by 1395, see *Ministers' Accounts of the Warwickshire Estates of the Duke of Clarence 1479–80*, ed. R. H. Hilton (Dugdale Soc., xxi, 1952), p. xxiv.

[7] Arrears roll, 1412 (wool-sales); Hanbury AR, 1448–9 (timber sales); PRO St. Ch. 2 21/136 (letting lands).

which tend to support A. E. Levett's contention that councils expanded their functions in the fifteenth century.[8] Membership of the council, besides the chief officials of the estate, included powerful and well-connected local figures, like Sir Humphrey Stafford and John Throckmorton in the early fifteenth century. At the end of the century the councillors were lawyers, such as Humphrey Conyngesby, William Grevile, William Hunteley and Thomas Lygon. The council met to discuss major disputes affecting the bishopric, such as a problem over Bredon church in 1453–4, and 'the business between the lord and William Jenetts' in 1465–6, but the details of these cases are not known.[9] The council also presided over the routine administration of the estate. From the 1420s the annual audit of accounts was held centrally for the whole estate in the bishop's palace at Worcester, sometimes before the council.[10] Decisions which had previously been taken by individual officials, notably the steward or auditor, were made by the council. These included such matters as the amount paid in wages to local officials, allowances of arrears to indebted officials, building operations or the enclosure of parks. Apparently the most mundane subjects were discussed in council, such as an order to make new beds at Henbury, at a cost of 8s. 4d., when Bishop Polton visited the manor.[11]

Towards the end of our period there were significant changes in the social position and political importance of the estate officials, particularly the stewards. In the first half of the fifteenth century, their standing was similar to that of their fourteenth-century predecessors. They were important gentry in Worcestershire or Gloucestershire, but their interests and influence did not extend much beyond those counties. They tended to hold such positions as sheriffs, members of parliament, justices of the peace and escheators. Thomas Throckmorton, William Woollashill and John Wode were all attached to the powerful Beauchamp family, who may well have influenced successive bishops in appointing their followers

---

[8] A. E. Levett, 'Baronial Councils and their relation to Manorial Courts', in *Studies in Manorial History* (Oxford, 1938), pp. 21–40; this interpretation is criticised in McFarlane, *Nobility*, pp. 214–15.

[9] Rec. AR, 1453–4, 1465–6. William Jenetts was a tenant of the manor of Hanbury, see Hanbury CR, April 1466.

[10] Henbury AR, 1411–12, and Bibury AR, 1417–18, show that an audit for the Gloucestershire manors was held at Henbury. By 1426–7 (Henbury AR) the Henbury reeve was travelling to the Worcester audit. Rec. AR, 1464–5 refers to auditing before the council.

[11] Henbury AR, 1426–7.

as stewards. Later on, especially under the Italian bishops, stewards were often men of national importance, with a record of royal service, such as Sir Richard Croft, long an official in the royal household; Sir Gilbert Talbot, also a courtier, privy councillor, ambassador and Captain of Calais; Sir William Compton, courtier and soldier; and Sir George Throckmorton, courtier and later a leader of opposition to the Reformation legislation of the 1530s. Unlike their predecessors, all were knights, and Talbot was the son of an earl. Their landed wealth much exceeded that of earlier stewards, and extended beyond the diocese. They probably obtained their offices through patronage at the highest level. Sir George Throckmorton, for example, was recommended by Wolsey.[12]

The main change among the receivers was that the clergy, who had monopolized the position since the thirteenth century, tended to be replaced by laymen from 1448. The lay receivers were of lower status than the stewards, being gentlemen rather than esquires or knights, and often without much property. They did not hold important positions in local government. Little is known about some of them, such as Thomas Arnold of Cirencester, the first lay receiver, who was apparently involved in the wool and cloth trades, judging from the list of aliases given when he was pardoned for offences against statutes regulating the wool trade: 'gentleman, alias clothman, alias woolman, alias chapman'.[13] Auditors had similar social backgrounds to the receivers.

Changes are also apparent in the recruitment of lesser officials. Before 1400, and in the early fifteenth century, reeves were quite distinct from bailiffs, being customary tenants, with the remission of rent as their reward. In the mid- and late fifteenth century the difference between reeves and bailiffs disappeared, and the two terms were used interchangeably. Both usually received a cash wage, and came from the top rank of village society. They were yeomen, like Thomas Yardington of Cleeve or Richard Kynne of Hampton, who both farmed the bishop's demesne, or, like Robert Weston of Fladbury and John Barnesley of Hartlebury, who were assessed above their neighbours in the 1524 subsidy.[14] The pro-

[12] History of Parliament, unpublished biographies.
[13] M. M. Postan and E. Power (eds.), *Studies in English Trade in the Fifteenth Century* (London, 1933), p. 53.
[14] PRO E 179 200/128.

fessionalization of their offices is indicated by the long terms served: Richard Kynne from 1454 to 1479, the Thomas Yardingtons, father and son, from 1488 to 1526, and John Williams, bailiff of Kempsey and Whitstones in the period 1506–26.[15]

The position of woodward, sometimes a rather humble one in the fourteenth century, attracted gentry families, like the Gowers who acted as Welland woodwards, or William Wybbe and William Wode, successively in charge of the woods of Hanbury and Stock and Bradley.[16]

The rise in the social status of the officials could have benefited the bishopric by increasing the authority of the administration, and bringing in expertise, such as knowledge of the law. Any advantages must have been outweighed by the employment of men whose activities in other spheres meant that they could have spared little time for the bishopric's affairs. An example is William More, the prior of Worcester, who also acted as surveyor in 1523–5. His position as prior meant that he spent most of his time in the vicinity of Worcester, as is recorded in his *Journal*. In the spring of 1524 he was able to spare three weeks for travel round the bishop's courts, but only one week in 1525.[17]

Much of the work was in fact done by deputies, particularly in the late fifteenth and early sixteenth centuries. Understewards were appointed locally, notably at Henbury and Stratford, but understewards also acted over the whole estate, such as Roger Mores between 1479 and 1489, and Richard Bukke in 1498–1511.[18] Receivers might also have deputies, like Thomas Sybley, who acted for Thomas Arnold and John Salwey, before himself becoming receiver in 1471. Even manorial officials, such as reeves and woodwards, had deputies.[19]

The deputies came from a lower social position than the chief officials. Richard Bukke, for example, seems to have been no more

---

[15] Hampton, Cleeve, Kempsey, Whitstones AR, *passim*.

[16] Bredon AR, 1463–4, 1477–8; Hanbury AR, 1436–7, 1448–9; Reg. Carpenter, i, fo. 42.

[17] *Journal of Prior William More*, ed. E. S. Fegan (Worcs. Hist. Soc., 1914), pp. 189–90, 207.

[18] Misc. AR, *passim*, for payment of Mores' fee; Rec. AR, 1497–8, 1510–11, for Bukke.

[19] Three cases of reeves' and woodwards' deputies occur in the accounts of the estate of 1518–19, WCRO ref. 009: 1 BA 2636/ 177 92503.

than a substantial tenant of free and customary holdings in the episcopal manor of Kempsey.[20]

These developments affected the relationship between the bishop and his officials. In the early and mid-fifteenth century some officials were embarking on an administrative career when they served the bishops. Mr Richard Ewen, who was receiver in the 1440s, went on to become surveyor on the estates of the bishops of Winchester. William Nottingham was only thirty-five years old when he was appointed steward in about 1450, and subsequently rose in royal service as king's attorney, baron of the exchequer and privy councillor. The stewards in the early sixteenth century were older: Croft was fifty-nine and Talbot fifty-eight when they were appointed.[21] They had reached the end of their careers in national affairs, and may well have treated their position as a sinecure, to support them in their retirement.

The practice of appointing officials for life must have reduced the bishops' ability to control their activities. Such life appointments were made in the case of Thomas Arnold, as auditor, Humphrey Stafford, as steward and many of the woodwards. From 1488 the post of steward of the Gloucestershire manors was held by three members of the Poyntz family in succession, suggesting that, at least by custom, the post had become hereditary. The dangers of such an arrangement were indicated by the last of the three, Sir Nicholas Poyntz, who has been described as 'irresponsible and spendthrift', and who served the interests of the estate badly, as will be seen later.[22]

Some officials used their position to secure financial advantages. The fees did not change very much, with stewards and receivers customarily obtaining £10 per annum, though in the early sixteenth century receivers' fees increased to £13 6s. 8d. and £16. Auditors and surveyors were usually given £5 or £5 10s. 0d., understewards £2 13s. 4d. to £5, councillors between 13s. 4d. and £3 6s. 8d., and manorial officials 10s. 0d. to £3. These sums represented a substantial income for the recipients, when many beneficed clergy and gentry had incomes of £10 and £20 per

[20] Kempsey CR, April 1497, July 1497, Oct. 1497, April 1512.

[21] J. C. Wedgwood, *History of Parliament, Biographies* (London, 1936), pp. 642, 237, 838.

[22] History of Parliament, unpublished biographies.

annum, and £5 per annum was 'a good living for a yeoman'.[23]

Estate officials had other opportunities for profit. They took on more than one post, such as Roger Russell, steward of the bishop's household, who was made woodward of Welland in 1452, at £2 per annum, and John Salwey, who succeeded him as woodward in 1460, in the year that he became receiver.[24] They also obtained grants of assets on preferential terms, like Sir Gilbert Talbot, who, while steward, was granted the Droitwich salt works, previously farmed for £2 per annum, for no payment at all.[25]

John Wode, steward to Bishop Polton, received in the period 1426–32 a grant of fees of £13 6s. 8d. and £20 per annum for life, and a generous eighty-year lease of the Whitstones demesne.[26] When Thomas Arnold was receiver in 1458, he was given a sixty-year lease of Bibury for £4 per annum (the previous tenant paid £7 6s. 8d.). In 1460 he was made auditor for life at a fee of £5 per annum; in 1473 the lease was renewed for a further sixty years, and the fee increased to £6 13s. 4d.[27]

The prime example of apparent opportunism at the estate's expense is provided by the receiver of 1505–35, John Hornyhold. His fee from 1522 was £16. He also engrossed minor offices: Withington woodward at £2 per annum, keeper of Hartlebury park for £3 0s. 8d. and a robe worth 13s. 4d., and even reeve of Hampton for £1 per annum. He took on a number of demesne leases: of Bredon for ninety-nine years at a farm of £14 (his predecessor paid £20), Upton in Blockley, again for ninety-nine years, and Withington. He also acquired smaller holdings of land in Alvechurch, Hartlebury and Wick. There is no evidence that he had any lands of his own, so he gained a considerable income entirely from the exploitation of his official position.[28]

K. B. McFarlane has discussed the tendency of fifteenth-century

[23] Sir John Fortescue, *The Governance of England*, ed. C. Plummer (Oxford, 1885), p. 151.

[24] Bredon AR, 1452–3; Rec. AR, 1453–4; Reg. Carpenter, i, fo. 141.

[25] Misc. AR, 1506–7.

[26] WCRO ref. 009:1 BA 2636/174 92465; Misc. AR, 1436–7.

[27] Bibury AR, 1458–9, 1460–1, 1473–4.

[28] Rec. AR, 1505–6, 1522–3; Withington AR, 1518–19; Hartlebury AR, 1518–19; Hampton AR, 1518–19; WCRO ref. 009:1 BA 2636/37 (iii) 43806, fos. 23, 49; Hartlebury CR, Oct. 1537; Wick CR, Oct. 1537; WCRO ref. 009:1 BA 2636/18 43765.

officials to act independently of their employers, but has shown that on lay estates measures were taken to prevent this going too far.[29] Clearly on the bishopric estate, particularly in the early sixteenth century, these activities were not curbed, and the estate suffered from the loss of assets and the payment of unnecessary fees. More important is that the behaviour of some officials suggests a self-interested attitude towards their work which could have damaged the interests of the bishops. Two episodes at Henbury illustrate the problems that could arise. In 1525 Robert Pers acquired two messuages and a half-yardland and five acres, both customary holdings, on payment of a fine of 30s. 0d. This provoked a protest from the tenants, and led Pers to take a case to the Council of the Marches and to the Star Chamber complaining that he had been deprived of the holding by two Henbury tenants. The petition of the tenants to the bishop and the proceedings before Star Chamber show that Pers was the brother of the surveyor, William More (*né* Pers), prior of Worcester, and that William had shown preferential treatment by granting the holdings at a low fine, and ignoring claims to the land by members of the previous tenant's family. The steward, Anthony Poyntz, seems to have opposed More, so that two of the bishop's most important officials were seen to be at logger-heads over a nepotistic deal that caused ill-feeling among the tenants.[30] In 1533 Nicholas Poyntz, Anthony's son and successor as steward of the Gloucestershire manors, was said to be keeping 'the courts ... without the assent of my lord or his officers', and that at Henbury he had 'given orders that none of the tenants there should appear at any time before my lord's officers', thus provoking a rent strike among the tenants.[31]

This degeneration in the quality of administration seems to belong especially to the early sixteenth century. There were earlier periods when the officials acted with vigour and effectiveness. In particular the 1450s saw a combination of a resident and conscientious bishop, John Carpenter, and William Nottingham, an able and professionally successful lawyer as steward, with Thomas Arnold, the first lay receiver, a man with commercial interests. The style of administration in their time was very different from that prevailing

[29] McFarlane, *Nobility*, pp. 213–27.
[30] PRO St. Ch. 2 21/136; GRO D 1799 M28.
[31] *Letters and Papers of Henry VIII*, vi, no. 533.

under absentee bishops, sinecurist stewards, and a self-seeking receiver in the early sixteenth century.

Reading fifteenth-century manorial accounts is an exercise in distinguishing between theory and reality. They begin with a statement of arrears carried over from the previous year, and then give figures for the supposed income from rents, farms, court perquisites and sales of wood. The total of arrears and income is then calculated. A section of allowed and decayed rents follows, which shows that many of the rents listed earlier were not paid. These decays were added to the expenses and cash liveries made to the receiver or the lord, giving a total of 'losses, expenses, and liveries' that can be deducted from the total of receipts. The difference is the debt, the sum owed by the accounting official and his predecessors. This debt is often modified by respites and allowances that show that yet more rents could not be collected. The debt is then itemized to show the liabilities of individuals, and finally a valor, an assessment of the value of the whole manor, is given.[32]

The estate administrators were fully aware of the fictitious nature of the lists of rents that made up the charge side of the account, but retained them, presumably because they represented the potential income from the estate. The valor derives from the same approach: although we cannot establish the exact calculation, the sum arrived at seems to be based on the total of receipts on the account, and so indicates how much money ought to have been forthcoming. Another type of fifteenth-century valor, not employed on the Worcester estate, used the cash liveries as the basis of the calculation, and was designed to show real income.[33]

After the auditing of the manorial accounts, a receiver's account was compiled, showing how much money had been delivered by the manorial officials, and how the receiver had disposed of it. An arrears roll was drawn up from the itemized debt section of each account, and a valor for the whole estate, again using information from the manorial accounts. The estate valor also contains a

[32] On the problems of fifteenth-century accounting, see *Ministers' Accounts ... of the Duke of Clarence*, pp. xi–xxiii; E. M. Carus-Wilson, 'Evidences of Industrial Growth on some Fifteenth-Century Manors', *Econ. Hist. Rev.*, 2nd ser., xii (1959), pp. 196–7.

[33] R. R. Davies, 'Baronial Accounts, Incomes, and Arrears in the Later Middle Ages', *Econ. Hist. Rev.*, 2nd ser., xxi (1968), pp. 214–18, on types of *valor*.

mixture of the ideal and the real. One part tells us how much cash came to the lord from the estate, and how much was spent on administration, building and other local expenses, but its first calculation is 'The sum of values of all manors this year', which adds together the valors entered on the manorial accounts. The resulting total represents the hoped-for value of the estate – it did not change very much in the fifteenth century, being £1,121 in c.1410, and between £1,098 and £1,175 in the years between 1454 and 1466.[34]

A detailed breakdown of the sources of potential income can be worked out from two nearly complete groups of manorial accounts for 1419–20 and 1506–7, given in Table 23.[35] The two sets of figures should not be compared too closely, as the earlier accounts are not as complete as those for 1506–7, and some items of income were recategorized, from farms to assize rents, for example. They show that well over half of the potential income of the bishopric came from the rents of free and customary tenants' holdings, which can be broadly classified as assize rents. Almost a third in each case came from farms of the lord's assets, mainly demesnes, and the remainder derived from other rents (such as customs) and farms. Most of the sums were fixed by custom or contract; only the court revenues and wood sales were variable from year to year.

Table 23. *Potential income of the estate, 1419–20 and 1506–7*

	1419–20	1506–7
Assize rents (with related items: works sold, rent of holdings in the lord's hands, increased rent, 'discovered' rent)	£607	£708
Other tenant payments: customs, rents in kind, chevage etc.	£38	£35
Perquisites of courts	£64	£46
Farms (mostly of demesnes, pastures, mills, fisheries etc.)	£332	£353
Sales of wood	£11	£23
Miscellaneous (markets and fairs, tithe-corn, salt-works etc.)	£71	£62
Total	£1,123	£1,227

[34] WCRO ref. 009:1 BA 2636/9 43696, fos. 30–32; /175 92477; /175 92479; /175 92481; /174 92472; /174 92470 1/6; /191 92625 4/12; /176 92486.

[35] WCRO ref. 009:1 BA 2636/9 43696, fos. 116–57; /176 92498.

The task facing a conscientious estate administration was two-fold. The first was to maximize the potential value of the estate by keeping the rents and farms as high as possible; the second was to collect as much of the money due as was feasible. We will begin our examination of the estate in the fifteenth and early sixteenth centuries by looking at the first of those aims, and seeing how the lord's demands for different types of income developed.

'Assize rents' is a term used here to encompass the assize rents total of each account, with the additions made to that total by means of separately listed increases of rent and commuted labour services, and with deductions of decays, allowances and respites. When these complicated calculations have been made, it is found that the annual totals for each manor did not change greatly during the period. At Bredon, for example, the total varied from a minimum of £42 7s. 10d. to a maximum of £45 6s. 5d. in the years 1407–1519. There was generally a downward trend in the early fifteenth century, for example, from £8 1s. 2d. at Bibury in 1407–8 to £6 15s. 6d. in 1436–7, or at Stoke from £42 5s. 7¼d. in 1411–12 to £39 16s. 11¾d. in 1435–6. Then in mid-century the assize rent totals often increased slightly, as at Bredon from £42 9s. 10d. to £43 13s. 10d. in about 1450. After this they usually remained stable or fell back very slightly in the rest of the fifteenth and early sixteenth centuries.

The main trends in the assize rents can be related to the general level of administrative activity. Rentals were an essential means of checking on tenants and ensuring that disputed matters were settled. They were troublesome to produce, involving the traditional procedure of the inquest, with a jury of tenants responding to the enquiries of an estate official. The expenses of rental-making were 7s. 10d. at Whitstones in 1456, and 4s. 4d. at Cleeve in 1474–5.[36] They could help to reveal and prevent the loss of income. A Kempsey rental of 1411–12 ends with the statement that a holding paid no rent 'because no-one knows who answers for the issue'. Such lapses of memory would be less likely if rentals were frequently renewed. The careful making of a rental might also disclose obligations beyond those charged in the manorial account, and lead to the addition of a sum of *redditus repertus*, literally, 'rent discovered'. Sums of *redditus repertus* of 9s. 11¾d. resulted from the Kempsey

---

[36]   Valor, 1465; Cleeve AR, 1474–5.

rental just quoted, and 7s. 2d. from a Bibury rental made in the following year.[37]

Few rentals were made in the early fifteenth century. A survey of rents for the whole estate was compiled in 1408, and four rentals of individual manors of the period 1410–13 are known, either because they have survived, or through references to them in other documents. Only four rentals are recorded between 1419 and 1442.[38]

In about 1450 there was an orgy of administrative activity. A general enquiry was made into the state of the bishopric's finances, probably by the newly appointed steward, William Nottingham. The investigation apparently began with a search through the estate archives, notably the *Red Book* extents of 1299. These were compared with more recent documents, and the discrepancies put for explanation to juries around the estate. The juries were able to bring up other problems. The resulting document reveals much about the deterioration of the bishops' revenues over the previous century and a half. Physical decline was reported: at Ripple thirteen holdings were 'in decay', and in the lord's hands for lack of tenants. At Wick there were complaints of a 'great decay and falling down of the buildings of tenants for lack of repair, and various tenants are not resident... within the lordship to the annoyance of the tenants.' Rents had fallen, and somewhat unrealistic comparisons were made with the situation in 1299. The Hanbury customary half-yardlands had once paid 11s. 0d. each: now they paid only 7s. 0d., 8s. 0d., 9s. 0d. and 10s. 0d. Free tenants at Cleeve formerly paid £6 10s. 9d., but the total was now £6 0s. 1½d., and it could not be said where the reduction had occurred. Individual holdings had been rented too cheaply; one at Stoke was let for 30s. 0d., but 'it could be let at a greater rent, or at a good fine, for the lord's profit'.[39]

These changes were perhaps acknowledged as inevitable, and little could be done about them. Others were the result of previous failures in management, or perhaps the duplicity of tenants. Some holdings had been lost. At Shottery in Stratford there had been twenty-three yardlands, but now there were only fifteen. In the case

[37] Kempsey AR, 1508–9; Bibury AR, 1417–18.
[38] White Book, fos. 30–7; WCRO ref. 009:1 BA 2636/9 43696 fos. 26–30, 162–3; Bibury AR, 1417–18; WCRO ref. 009:1 BA 2636/185 92574b and / 165 92226 4/7; Fladbury AR, 1506–7; Bibury AR, 1430–1; Hanbury AR, 1443–4.
[39] WCRO ref. 009:1 BA 2636/193 92627 10/12.

of six holdings at Kempsey the jury did not know what had become of them. The site of a sheepcote at Hanbury had once been rented for 12d., but the jury 'do not know where the land lay'. When holdings and tenants could be identified, there were disputes about the amount of rent to be paid. Some denied either part or all of the rent, claiming that it had been reduced by a previous bishop.

The whole investigation was clearly intended to produce results. If a jury failed to give a satisfactory answer, as in the case of the missing eight yardlands at Shottery, they were sent away 'to enquire better'. If they revealed the present tenant of a 'lost' holding, as happened at Stratford, he was distrained to pay the old rent. If tenants claimed to have had their rents reduced in the past, they were ordered to produce their charter or copy of court roll. Unsatisfactory responses produced the drastic order that the holding should be seized.

Further evidence of the vigour, even the aggression, of the estate administration is provided by the compilation of rentals in the early 1450s, of which twelve are known.[40] Only one of these new rentals failed to produce *redditus repertus*, varying from 6s. 5½d. (at Hampton) to £2 4s. 3¾d. (at Blockley). There was a new phase of rental making in the years 1466–75 on at least eight manors. A few more are recorded subsequently in the 1480s, and one in 1507–8.[41] Although there is little evidence of new rentals in the early sixteenth century, new totals of *redditus repertus* were added to accounts of some manors in the years 1507–15. Increases of rent, to both leasehold and copyhold tenures, were occasionally made in the second half of the fifteenth century. By 1506–7, largely as a result of changes made after 1450, the total of *redditus repertus* for the whole estate had reached £27 12s. 2d., and new and increased rents amounted to £17 3s. 11½d.[42] To some extent these increases were offset by allowances and decays, but they helped to prevent further decline – the rot

[40] Bibury AR, 1450–1; Blockley AR, 1458–9; Cleeve AR, 1474–5; Hampton AR, 1450–1; Hanbury AR, 1450–1; Hartlebury AR, 1506–7; Henbury AR, 1455–6; Kempsey AR, 1508–9; Ripple AR, 1456–7; Stratford AR, 1464–5; Tredington AR, 1523–4; Valor, 1465 (referring to Whitstones); all mention rentals made 1450–6.

[41] Alvechurch AR, 1524–5; Blockley AR, 1506–7; Cleeve AR, 1474–5; Hampton AR, 1506–7; Hanbury: WCRO ref. 009:1 BA 2636/168 92332; Kempsey AR, 1508–9; Stratford AR, 1506–7; Withington AR, 1506–7 refer to rentals made in 1466–75. Later rentals: Whitstones, Society of Antiquaries Lib., Pratinton Collection, Worcestershire Parishes, vii, pp. 39–46; Stoke AR, 1518–19; Hartlebury: WCRO ref. 009:1 BA 2636/37 (iii) 43806, fos. 78–83; Wichenford AR, 1507–8.

[42] WCRO ref. 009:1 BA 2636 176/92498.

that had set in during the first half of the fifteenth century had been stopped.

Not all of the measures taken in the mid-fifteenth century to prevent decline in rents were of the rather punitive type depicted in the enquiry of *c*.1450. There was a certain amount of investment in the buildings of peasant holdings, particularly in the period 1454–71. This could take the form of direct payments of cash, or allowances of arrears of rent. Both types are listed in the valors, which show that the total spent or allowed varied between £5 9s. 10d. and £10 9s. 7d. per annum.[43] Individual tenants usually received sums of between 3s. 4d. and £1 0s. 0d. The sums were relatively small, and the number of tenants so helped a fraction of the total, but nonetheless the payments suggest a forward-looking attitude on the part of the administrators, who clearly hoped to make holdings more attractive for future tenants and so maintain income from rents.

Almost all of the estate's assets were leased out by the early fifteenth century – franchises, dovecots, fishing and hunting rights – as well as mills and demesnes, though the latter produced most money and so will receive more attention here. Unlike assize rents, leasehold rents or farms could be changed radically at the beginning of a new term. Fig. 1 shows that in the early fifteenth century leasehold rents fell sharply. In addition to the examples shown in the graphs, the annual farm of the Cleeve demesne fell from £18 6s. 8d. in the 1410s, to £16 13s. 4d. in the 1420s, and at Stratford the demesne was leased in 1419–20 for £10, but this had declined to £8 in 1430.[44] In the period 1440–85 leasehold rents were often increased. The Kempsey demesne was leased in 1455 for £10, having paid £7 6s. 8d. in the early fifteenth century.[45] The main exception was at Bibury, where although the leasehold rent increased in 1451 from £4 to £7 6s. 8d., it fell back again to £4 in 1461, but this was probably a favour to the lessee, Thomas Arnold, who was also an estate official.

Increased rents in the mid-fifteenth century were often associated

---

[43] Expenditure on tenants' buildings on a greater scale is found on other estates, see Hilton, 'Rent and Capital Formation', p. 192; N. W. Alcock, 'The Medieval Cottages of Bishop's Clyst, Devon', *Med. Arch.*, ix (1965), pp. 146–53.

[44] WCRO ref. 009:1 BA 2636/9 43696, fos. 134, 155–6; Cleeve AR, 1426–7; WCL, Lib. Alb. Pri., fo. cccclxxxxiiii.

[45] WCRO ref. 009:1 BA 2636/9 43696, fo. 127; Reg. Carpenter, i, fo. 134.

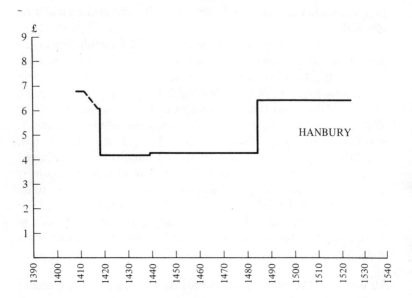

1 Leasehold rents of demesne lands, 1390–1540

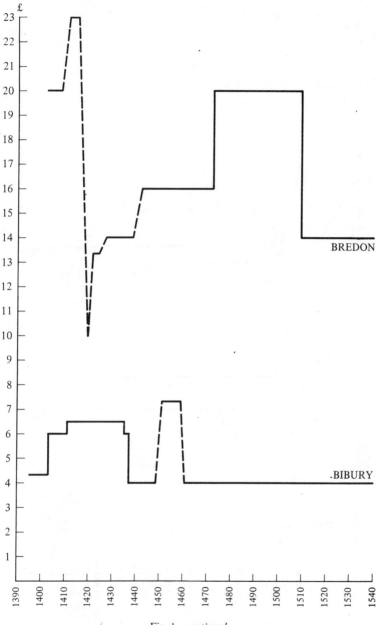

Fig. 1 – *continued*

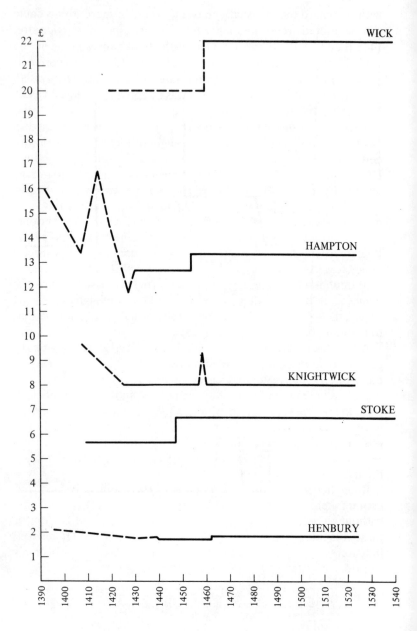

Fig. 1 – *continued*

with increased terms, usually to twenty years or more. Rents could still be altered when the longer terms ended, but in practice after 1485 they became fossilized. One of the few changes in the period 1485–1540 was a reduction in the farm of Bredon, again representing preferential treatment for an estate official, John Hornyhold. A firmer attitude towards leases was adopted from around 1450. Unsatisfactory tenants were sometimes removed, like Nicholas Poyntz, farmer of the Bibury demesne, whose lease was 'resumed' in 1449, probably because of his bad payment record. The Stratford demesne had been leased at the low rent of £8 for forty years to John Huggeford in 1430; he was bought out in 1457, and the demesne leased at the increased rent of £11 6s. 8d. James Wyke, the lessee of the Hampton mill, was also bought out in 1465–6 after a few years of a sixty-year term, at a cost to the bishop of £13 6s. 8d. The only case of this type after the mid-fifteenth century concerned the Blockley demesne in 1502–3. Some indentures indicate a stricter policy towards leases in the decades after 1450. The Bibury lease of 1451 contained a husbandry clause requiring the lessee to leave the demesne arable with thirty acres manured and ploughed. Specific requirements to rebuild, instead of the normal general injunctions to maintain buildings, appear in leases of 1464 and 1474.[46]

All of these changes in leaseholds can be associated with the general tightening-up of the administration of the estate. The enquiry of *c.*1450 investigated leases – demesne lands had been 'lost', rents had fallen (from £5 6s. 8d. to £3 0s. 0d. in the case of Blickley Field at Hanbury, for example), and some minor assets, like fisheries, were producing no rents at all. Some demesne farmers were not observing the terms of their leases, like John Wode, lessee of Whitstones, who failed to pay the expenses of the steward holding the manorial courts.[47]

Remedies were proposed for some of the problems raised, and action taken. It was found that lands had been leased on five manors without an indenture having been drawn up. In the case of three of these, Blockley park and the demesnes of Kempsey and Tredington, indentures were made in 1454 and 1455 and entered in the bishop's or priory registers.[48] A rent of only 20s. 0d. was being paid for the

[46] Bibury AR, 1449–50; Lib. Alb. Pri., fo. cccclxxxxiiii; Rec. AR, 1465–6, 1502–3; Reg. Carpenter, ii, fos. 34–5; WCRO ref. 009:1 BA 2636/37 (iii) 43806, fo. 86.
[47] WCRO ref. 009:1 BA 2636/193 92627 10/12.
[48] Reg. Carpenter, i, fos. 133–4; WCL Lib. Alb. Pri., fos. cccclxxxxi–cccclxxxxiii.

agistment of Pen park at Henbury, although it had recently been enlarged by the addition of a furlong of demesne land; the rent was raised to 30s. 0d. in 1460. The Blickley Field rent mentioned above was eventually increased to £5 0s. 0d. in 1484.[49]

The resources of the estate had decayed a good deal. There had been thirty-one mills in the 1290s, but at least twelve of these had decayed by the early fifteenth century. Yet of those that survived, the Fladbury, Kempsey and Whitstones mills could still pay as much as or even more in rent than in the thirteenth century.[50] The buildings of the leased demesnes were also dilapidated: they were sometimes presented as in need of repair at the manorial courts.[51]

The enquiry of c.1450 noted the ruinous state of mills and buildings, and recommended that the lord should pay for repairs on the mills of Fladbury, Hampton and Withington, and on barns and other buildings at Cleeve and Fladbury. The enclosing activities of some demesne farmers and neighbouring landowners were noted;[52] it was suggested that the bishop should pay for enclosures on the Hampton demesne, as the farmer was threatening to abandon his lease unless an enclosure was made, and increased rents might be forthcoming.

Most of the evidence for capital investment in the early fifteenth century relates to the maintenance of fences round demesne woods and parks, but more expensive projects include the rebuilding of Hampton mill in c.1415 for £10, and in 1435–6 £48 was paid, and a further £46 13s. 4d. promised, for the construction of a row of eight houses on the bishop's London property in the Strand.[53]

From c.1450 to c.1480 capital expenditure is recorded in some quantity, sometimes in line with the recommendations of c.1450, and often resulting in an increase in rent. In 1454–5 part of the Hampton demesne, *Polefurlong*, was enclosed at a cost of £3, and an extra 13s. 4d. added to the annual farm of £13. Stapenhill in Blockley was 'newly enclosed' in 1458, and brought in a new rent of £3 6s. 8d. The pasture of Wontley in Cleeve (the site of a deserted village)

[49] Henbury AR, 1460–1; Hanbury AR, 1488–9.

[50] *RBW*, ii, p. 125; i, p. 61; i, p. 26; WCRO ref. 009:1 BA 2636/9 43696, fos. 116, 126; WCRO ref. 009:1 BA 2636/37 (iii) 43806, fo. 68.

[51] Bredon CR, March 1401; Cleeve CR, Oct. 1412.

[52] Enclosures at Stratford, Wick and Withington are recorded in the survey of c. 1450.

[53] Hampton AR, c. 1415; Rec. AR, 1435–6.

had been rented for 13s. 4d. for much of the fifteenth century, but in about 1480 it was enclosed and leased for £6 13s. 4d.[54] Mills were rebuilt, in line with the advice given in the c.1450 enquiry, at Hampton in 1461–2 and at Fladbury at some time between 1476 and 1486. The Hampton mills cost £11 to build, with a further £1 16s. 10d. spent on the sluice gates in 1467–8, and this led eventually to an increase in the annual farm from 8s. 8d. to £4. Work on the Fladbury mills raised the rent from £6 to £7 6s. 8d. The Stratford mills were always profitable, bringing in £10 per annum, and presumably to maintain this income £18 was spent on repairs to the floodgates in 1460–1.[55] The estate also invested in repairs and new buildings on the demesnes, again as proposed in c.1450. A new barn at Fladbury cost £7 6s. 8d. in 1458–9 and £4 17s. 8d. two years later. £6 4s. 0d. was spent on barns at Henbury in 1462–3 and £11 14s. 9d. at Northwick in 1465–6. Also farmers might be allowed part of their arrears in order to spend the money on manorial buildings – £6 13s. 4d. at Ripple in 1456–7, for example. Such expenditure could produce benefits from more ready payments by the lessees. The farmer of the bishop's salt works at Droitwich paid nothing in the early 1460s, but in 1465–6 £3 5s. 6d. was spent on repairing the seal-house (the building in which the brine was boiled), and for a few years the payment of rent improved considerably.[56]

The level of capital spending was never very high. In the middle years of the fifteenth century the total was only about 3 per cent of net income, including all projects that could possibly be regarded as adding to the capital assets of the estate, and counting allowances on arrears as expenditure. Of course the bishop's contributions to such expenditure represented only part of the total, as tenants, particularly the demesne farmers, must also have spent on buildings and enclosures. The bishop's investments were often delayed, taking between four and twenty-five years to undertake the projects proposed in the c.1450 enquiry. The scale of investment that was possible, and that may well have been needed ideally on some of the bishopric demesnes, is indicated by the expenditure on the manor of Dowdeswell, purchased in 1463–4 by Bishop Carpenter from

[54] Hampton AR, 1454–5; Blockley AR, 1458–9; Cleeve AR, 1486–7.
[55] Hampton AR, 1461–2, 1467–8; Fladbury AR, 1506–7; Rec. AR, 1460–1.
[56] Valor, 1459; Rec. AR, 1460–1; Henbury AR, 1462–3; Rec. AR, 1465–6; Valor, 1457; Misc. AR, 1465–6.

Richard Beauchamp as part of the endowment of his new college of Westbury. The purchase price of the property was £73 6s. 8d.; as its annual value was assessed at £8 in the early sixteenth century, the price was evidently equivalent to nine years' value, which was less than normal in the period.[57] Presumably the low price reflects the poor state of the buildings and land. Certainly Carpenter proceeded to spend large sums on Dowdeswell: £40 15s. 6d. on building a sheepcote and ridding the pastures of bushes, and a further £13. 9s. 6d. on stocking it with a flock of 164 sheep. If capital spending on this scale was needed on the bishop's own demesnes, the lessees themselves would have had to provide the money.

In spite of these reservations about the scale of investment, it must be acknowledged that the expenditure on capital assets shows that the administration was concerned with more than an artificial maintenance of outdated rents. The modest programme of investment presumably contributed to the long-term future of income from leasehold rents. However, the efforts of the period 1450–80 did not seem to have been followed up. The Hampton mills, for example, rebuilt at considerable expense in the 1460s, were in ruins again by 1506.[58] All capital investment in the early sixteenth century was left to the initiative of the tenants.

The profits of jurisdiction represented a small proportion of the estate's potential income, amounting to about 6 per cent in 1419–20 and 4 per cent in 1506–7. They were a flexible source of income, as much of the total of court perquisites consisted of entry-fines, paid when a new tenant entered a holding, and variable according to the demand for land. In the early fifteenth century court perquisites seem to have been relatively high, continuing the buoyancy already noted at the end of the fourteenth century. For example, court perquisites at Cleeve in three recorded years between 1412 and 1420 varied from £4 16s. 6d. to £8 9s. 3d., compared with £3 in 1299. At Hampton also the early fifteenth-century totals exceeded those of a century earlier. The court revenues of the whole estate in 1419–20 amounted to £63 16s. 1d., comparable with the total for 1299 (see Table 24). After 1420 a decline set in, so that by the mid-fifteenth century the estate total could sink as low as £38; on some individual manors perquisites were down to a half of those of

[57] Rec. AR, 1463–4, 1464–5, 1465–6.
[58] Hampton AR, 1506–7.

Table 24. *Perquisites of courts totals*
for the whole estate, 1419–1519

1419–20	£63 16s. 1d.
1453–4	£57 17s. 3½d.
1456–7	£37 19s. 6½d.
1458–9	£43 16s. 9½d.
1464–5	£63 14s. 6¼d.
1465–6	£38 16s. 11d.
1506–7	£46 5s. 9d.
1518–19	£49 10s. 4d.

the late fourteenth and early fifteenth centuries. Court profits recovered somewhat in the early sixteenth century with an increase in entry-fines. In the 1520s Cleeve perquisities exceeded £3 per annum, and at Kempsey were in the region of £7, in both cases double the normal figures of half a century earlier.[59] Some very high totals are recorded at Henbury, in excess of £35 in some years at the end of the fifteenth century. Tenants there were apparently liable to pay substantial fines at the beginning of an episcopate, judging from the high perquisites in those years.

Profits of franchisal jurisdiction were drastically reduced. The hundred courts of Pathlow and Oswaldslow were both farmed out, presumably in an attempt to stabilize revenues. The annual farm of Pathlow increased in the early fifteenth century from £2 to £3, but then fell steadily to £2 in 1458, £1 6s. 8d. by 1478, 15s 0d. in 1488, and 13s. 4d. in 1510. Eventually it was granted out for nothing. The liberty of Oswaldslow also yielded nothing for most of the period, and an attempt to farm it in the 1450s to 1470s for £2 was unsuccessful.[60]

The only way after the 1450s in which the estate could participate directly in the market was through selling timber and underwood from the bishops' parks and woods. The enquiry of *c.*1450 was critical of the management of timber resources, showing that damage had been done, more fencing was needed, and, at Stoke, trees had been sold for the private profit of the parker and demesne farmer. In the 1450s and 1460s wood sales brought in between £10 and £14 per annum, and rather larger sums, up to £30, in the early sixteenth

[59] The absence of a more marked increase in early sixteenth-century perquisites is at first puzzling, in view of the rise in entry-fines in the period. To some extent they were offset by a decline in the number of amercements and heriots, see Chapter 13.
[60] Misc. AR, *passim.*

century, but there is little evidence of the systematic cropping found on other estates. Instead woods were left uncut for a number of years, and then sold off in large quantities, usually in the first years of a new bishop, when he needed extra cash. So wood sales rose to at least £41 in 1427–8, at least £40 in 1497–8, and up to £156 when Bishop Latimer found himself in a financial crisis in 1537–8.[61]

A further minor contribution to the income of the bishopric were the profits of feudal incidents from tenants by knight service, particularly rights of wardship. These were potentially lucrative. In 1382–3 Bishop Wakefield acquired rights of wardship over two manors in Gloucestershire belonging to Joan Lech, valued at £13 13s. 4d. per annum, and obtained a substantial part of that sum. In the fifteenth century similar opportunities arose. In the 1420s the lands of a potential ward, John Trye, were valued at £8, and William Knyght's holding in Hanbury, which came into the lord's hands in 1445, was supposed to be rented for £3 13s. 10d. Any profits from these wardships were frustrated because other tenants gained control of the lands, presumably through such devices as enfeoffment to uses.[62] The enquiry of c.1450 attempted to investigate tenants by knight service, but it was clear that the links between the bishops and their most powerful tenants were becoming very weak. Homage, for example, was often not done. By 1460 attempts to obtain revenues from wardships seem to have been abandoned.

If the potential income of the bishopric could have been fully realized, the bishops would have received £1,100–£1,200 per annum throughout our period, and their revenues would have increased in the mid-fifteenth century. The problem facing the estate managers was the gap between money owed and money actually collected, so that actual income fell short of the projected sum.

The total income of the bishopric can be calculated from the valors of 1454–66. These tell us how much cash was delivered to the

[61] Henbury AR, 1427–8; Bredon AR, 1427–8; Hampton AR, 1427–8; Stoke AR, 1427–8; Rec. AR, 1497–8; WCL Dean and Chapter Reg. A VI (3) fos. 15–16. For contrasting policies of systematic management, see O. Rackham, *Trees and Woodland in the British Landscape* (London, 1976), pp. 69–73.
[62] Henbury AR, 1382–3, 1427–8; Hanbury AR, 1448–9; McFarlane, *Nobility*, pp. 217–19 gives similar examples.

receiver, to the lord himself, or to his household, and also the value of liveries in kind, such as hay and stray animals. Contemporary receivers' accounts give the administrative costs, such as the fees of officials, that can be deducted to give net income.

From 1497 to 1535, under the Italian bishops, almost all money passed through the hands of the receiver. Provided an allowance is made for the London and Hillingdon rents, which were collected by the bishop's *procurator*, an Italian resident in London, net income at this period can be calculated from the receivers' accounts alone.

The resulting figures are listed in Table 25, together with a sum derived from the *Valor Ecclesiasticus* of 1535.[63] The figures show that net income fluctuated rather wildly in the 1450s and 1460s, from £820 to £1,044. From 1497 to 1540 income was much more consistent, remaining between £945 and £994 in ten of the thirteen recorded years. Some of the exceptional years in the early sixteenth century can be explained in terms of strong variations in profits from the manor of Henbury, which were low in 1510–11, but very high in 1539–40, the latter year being the first year of Bishop Bell, when some tenants at Henbury probably paid fines to their new lord.

Table 25. *Annual net income of the bishopric of Worcester, 1453–1540*

1453–4	£949	From estate valors
1456–7	£1,044	
1458–9	£820	
1464–5	£884	
1465–6	£951	
1497–8	£994	From receivers' accounts
1498–9	£961	
1500–1	£945	
1501–2	£986	
1502–3	£983	
1503–4	£959	
1504–5	£983	
1509–10	£989	
1510–11	£900	
1522–3	£927	
1523–4	£965	
1535	£986	*Valor Ecclesiasticus*
1539–40	£1,074	Receiver's account

[63] *Valor Ecclesiasticus* (Record Commission, 1817), iii, pp. 217–20.

Besides gaining in stability, the bishops' income rose between the mid-fifteenth and early sixteenth centuries. Comparison between the average of net income in 1453–66 and 1497–1540 suggests an increase in the order of 5 per cent. However, the mid-fifteenth century figures may be distorted by an exceptionally high total for 1456–7, so the true increase over the late fifteenth century was probably nearer to 10 per cent.

A longer and fuller picture of trends in income can be obtained from the income from individual manors, the accounts of which give the total amount of cash delivered by the reeve or bailiff to the receiver, the lord or the household. The graphs of manorial profits (Appendix 2) also include some figures taken from receivers' accounts, for the manors and periods of time when all cash was normally delivered to the receiver.

Figures are not very plentiful in the early fifteenth century. Strong local variations are indicated up to the 1440s. Profits at Bredon, Cleeve, Henbury and Stoke seem to have been quite high, comparable with those of the late fourteenth century, with a decline in the 1430s and 1440s. Low profits are found at Aston, Hanbury and Hampton, and also at Bibury, but this last case can be explained by the continued direct management of its sheep pastures, the income from which is not recorded. We can be certain about the tendency for profits to rise towards the end of the fifteenth century. For example, Hampton profits fell below £35 in twelve years between 1435 and 1470, but remained above that figure in the years 1470–1500. Profits at Cleeve often fell below £50 in the period 1445–70, but were frequently in the region of £60 after that date.

As is suggested by the figures for the net income of the whole estate, a period of instability in the mid-fifteenth century gave way to a much greater consistency of income in the late fifteenth and early sixteenth centuries. Whereas profits at Stoke, for example, had fluctuated between £40 and £67 in the period 1443–65, the variation was between £45 and £57 after 1465. Exceptions to this are Hampton, Hanbury and Henbury, where fluctuating court perquisites and occasional sales of wood make some years' profits unusually high.

Against the background of these long-term trends in the level of manorial profits it is tempting to identify a number of short-term movements. Income from some manors seems to have been high in the 1430s, followed by a decline in the 1440s, which continued on some manors in the 1450s. The early 1460s saw an increase on all manors except Cleeve, Hanbury and Stoke, followed by a decline in the late 1460s, with some evidence of a further recovery in the 1470s, with a pronounced rising trend in the late 1480s (except at Stoke). After 1500 the generally stable pattern seems to have been interrupted by slight depressions in 1505–10 and in the early 1520s.

The levels of net income fall well below the potential income assessed by the estate officials. This, and the fluctuations in income, can be partly explained by examining arrears.

Arrears were calculated at the end of each account, and later totalled in an arrears roll and in the valors. At the end of each episcopate all arrears disappeared from the accounts, as they were regarded as belonging to the individual bishop, and so were in theory to be collected by him if he had been translated to another see, or by his executors if he had died. The arrears totals given in Table 26 show that the peak was reached in 1460, with the enormous sum of £1,499, which had built up steadily in the 1450s. After 1460 the

Table 26. *Totals of arrears, 1389–1519.*

Year	Amount	Source
1389	£465	From arrears rolls
1412	£252	
1453	£1,112	
1454	£1,194	
1456	£1,382	From valors
1457	£1,282	
1458	£1,414	
1459	£1,463	
1460	£1,499	From arrears rolls
1462	£1,134	
1464	£1,157	
1465	£1,109	From valors
1466	£1,005	
1473	£896	From arrears rolls
1482	£378	
1498	£109	From arrears rolls appended to receivers' accounts
1499	£131	
1501	c.£200*	
1507	£129⁺	From manorial accounts
1519	£95‡	

*The manuscript is partly illegible.
⁺The figures from Alvechurch and Stoke are not available for this year.
‡The accounts for 4 manors are lacking in 1518–19, but figures have been taken from accounts of 1516–17, which are unlikely to be very different from those of two years later.

total diminished to £896 in 1473. This episode of exceptionally high arrears falls in the time of Bishop John Carpenter, and it might be thought to be the result of a long episcopate in which arrears had many years to accumulate. The record of individual manors shows that arrears even in Carpenter's early years were greater than at a comparable stage in the time of other bishops. At Bibury, for example, the arrears in Carpenter's sixth year had reached £26, compared with 3s. 5d. in the fifth year of Bishop Peverel (1411–12) and £12 in the fifth year of Polton (1430–1) (see Appendix 2). The accumulation of arrears under Bishop Alcock (1476–86) tended to be greater than under the early fifteenth century bishops, but less than in Carpenter's time. After 1486 arrears totals were comparatively small.

What caused arrears to accumulate? Analysis in some detail is possible, as debts were itemized, sometimes with an explanation.

Corruption and slackness among officials could have contributed to the problem. Our suspicions are aroused by bailiffs with substantial debts who left the area and could not be traced, but it does not seem likely that this was a major cause.

Evidence already published shows that many of the arrears can be attributed to a deliberate refusal on the part of tenants to pay rents and exactions, mainly from the 1430s. These included collective dues like recognitions and common fines, and also individual assize rents and some commuted labour services. Many court dues, such as amercements and fines, were not paid. Bad debtors included some demesne farmers, like Richard Bayly of Stoke, and gentry, like the Throckmortons, whose attempts to substitute tenant rents for their fee-farm for the manor of Throckmorton led to decades of refusals to pay rents and a heavy accumulation of arrears.[64]

Were some rents unpaid because tenants were short of cash, particularly in a period of declining agricultural prices? This would explain the delayed payment of rent, so that in the mid-fifteenth century about a third of the bishop's income came from arrears of payments that should have been made a year or two before. The problem can be investigated by looking at the payments of demesne farmers, who were commodity producers and therefore most vulnerable to depressions in the market.

An example is Nicholas Poyntz, the farmer of the Bibury demesne.

His payment record (Table 27) begins with the full amount in 1435–6, but in 1436–7 he gave nothing. In that year Bishop Bourgchier reduced his farm by £2, and in 1437–40 Poyntz settled his debts and paid his rent. From 1443 he began by paying the full amount for the demesne (£4), but nothing of the 16s. 0d. rent of a holding called Dagelettes that he also leased. From 1445 the main farm payment dwindled, until he paid nothing in two successive years, and the lease was taken back by the lord. There is some correlation between Poyntz's payments and the price of grain that he presumably sold to pay his rent. He paid most during the years of bad harvests in the late 1430s, when, as a large-scale cultivator, he could have produced enough grain to do well from inflated prices; he slipped behind when grain prices were low in the 1440s. However, his payment record was at its worst when grain prices picked up slightly in the late 1440s, so the correlation between rent-payment and market opportunities is by no means exact.

A likely explanation of Poyntz's behaviour is that he used his rent as a means of securing concessions from the lord. He paid nothing in 1436–7, and immediately obtained a substantial reduction in his farm. He then gratefully paid up, helped no doubt by the high grain prices of 1437–40. Encouraged by this success, he then

Table 27. *Payment record of Nicholas Poyntz,*
demesne farmer of Bibury

Year	Amount due	Amount paid	Price of wheat (valuation of churchscot)
1435–6	£6 16s. 0d.	£6 16s. 0d.	4s. 0d.
1436–7	£6 16s. 0d.	0	4s. 0d.
1437–8	£4 16s. 0d.	£8 16s. 0d.	8s. 0d.
1438–9	£4 16s. 0d.	£3 4s. 0d.	13s. 4d.
1439–40	£4 16s. 0d.	£7 4s. 0d.	8s. 0d.
1443–4	£4 16s. 0d.	£4 0s. 0d.	—*
1444–5	£4 16s. 0d.	£4 0s. 0d.	3s. 4d.
1445–6	£4 16s. 0d.	£2 0s. 0d.	3s. 4d.
1446–7	£4 16s. 0d.	£1 13s. 4d.	—*
1447–8	£4 16s. 0d.	0	5s. 4d.
1448–9	£4 16s. 0d.	0	4s. 8d.
1449–50	Lease resumed into lord's hands	£2 0s. 0d.	4s. 8d.

*no records.

attempted to have the Dagelettes rent reduced or removed, and refused to pay it from 1443. When this did not work, he paid less and less of his farm. The administration was less benign this time, and its response was to cancel the lease and find another farmer.

A similar problem arises with the payments made by successive farmers of the Droitwich salt-works.[65] Their capacity to pay should have been related directly to the price of salt[66] (see Table 28). In-

Table 28. *Payment record of the farmers of the Droitwich salt-works*

Salt prices are taken from Thorold Rogers' Cambridge series, with the annual average in parentheses if no Cambridge prices are available

Year	Amount due	Amount paid	Salt price (Thorold Rogers) per quarter
1430–1	£2 6s. 8d.	0	2s. 10d.
1435–6	£2 6s. 8d.	£2 6s. 8d.	3s. 8d.
1436–7	£2 6s. 8d.	£2 6s. 8d.	3s. 8d.
1437–8	£2 6s. 8d.	£2 6s. 8d.	5s. 4d.–10s. 8d.
1439–40	£2 13s. 4d.	£2 6s. 8d.	3s. 4½d.
1445–6	£2 13s. 4d.	£2 6s. 8d.	3s. 4d.
1447–8	£2 13s. 4d.	£2 6s. 8d.	2s. 8d.
1453–4	£2 13s. 4d.	£1 6s. 8d.	3s. 4d.
1456–7	£2 13s. 4d.	£3 6s. 8d.	3s. 0d.
1458–9	£2 13s. 4d.	£2 0s. 0d.	2s. 5d.
1460–1	£2 13s. 4d.	£2 12s. 2d.	5s. 4d.
1461–2	£2 13s. 4d.	£1 6s. 8d.	3s. 8d.
1462–3	£2 13s. 4d.	0	(3s. 0d.)
1463–4	£2 13s. 4d.	0	2s. 8d.
1464–5	£2 6s. 8d.	0	(2s. 8d.)
1465–6	£2 6s. 8d.	0	2s. 8d.
1466–7	£2 6s. 8d.	£1 0s. 0d.	3s. 5d.
1470–1	£2 13s. 4d.	£2 0s. 0d.	—
1471–2	£2 13s. 4d.	0	—
1478–9	£2 0s. 0d.	£2 0s. 0d.	3s. 5d.
1479–80	£2 0s. 0d.	0	5s. 4d.
1481–2	£2 0s. 0d.	£2 0s. 0d.	4s. 0d.
1487–8	£2 0s. 0d.	£2 0s. 0d.	4s. 4d.–4s. 8d.
1488–9	£2 0s. 0d.	£2 0s. 0d.	4s. 4d.

[65] Misc. AR, *passim*.

[66] In the absence of a west-midland price series for salt, the Cambridge series has been used: see J. E. Thorold Rogers, *A History of Agriculture and Prices in England* (Oxford, 1882), iii, pp. 337–40. Rogers' annual averages are particularly unreliable for salt prices, see A. R. Bridbury, *England and the Salt Trade in the Later Middle Ages* (Oxford, 1955), pp. 161–3.

deed, the farmer had a good payment record in the 1430s, when salt prices were relatively high, and fell behind in his rent in the 1440s and 1450s, when prices declined. Salt prices reached their lowest point in the early 1460s, and for four years the farmer paid nothing at all. He paid his farm in full during an upward price trend in the 1480s. But prices cannot provide the only explanation. It is difficult to see, even in a year of low prices, why nothing at all was paid in rent. It is perhaps significant that in the period 1439–48 the old farm of £2 6s. 8d. was paid after an increase to £2 13s. 4d. Was this a protest against the increase by the farmer? Similarly the failure to pay in 1462–6 could have been designed to put pressure on the lord to repair buildings, as this work was carried out in 1465–6. Payment lapsed again in the early 1470s, and by 1478 the rent had been reduced. Again an economic explanation of the tenant's behaviour must be combined with an appreciation of the use of rent-payment as the tenant's weapon to secure advantages.

Support for the argument that the economic climate had some effect on the ability of demesne farmers to pay their rents comes from their practice of paying off debts in the 1450s and 1460s in kind. Grain and hay worth between £8 and £15 per annum were delivered to the household in lieu of cash payments between 1454 and 1466, suggesting that the farmers were willing to pay, but had difficulty in raising the cash to do so.[67]

Also there was some relationship between the level of arrears and the general economic state of different manors. Judged by the level of demand for land among tenants, or the amount paid in entry fines, the most economically depressed manor was Bibury. Here the arrears total in 1460 was £78, six times the valor of the manor assessed at about the same time. The ratio between arrears and valor of other manors was much less, down to between 1:1 and 2:1 at Henbury and Stoke, the manors which seem to have had the healthiest economic environment.

So economic trends, and particularly the reduced prices of agricultural produce, may have helped to increase the amount of arrears in the 1440s and 1450s, particularly affecting those tenants involved in large-scale commodity production. But a growth in assertiveness by tenants was a major factor – how else can we explain the not infrequent occurrence of a farmer paying nothing at all?

[67] Valors, 1454–66.

Tenants were not the only people who could be assertive, and an examination of official attitudes to arrears shows that problems were partly created by the intractable position adopted by the estate managers. A realistic auditor, recognizing problems of rent-collection, would make concessions. So in the early fifteenth century small sums of arrears were occasionally pardoned, and allowances made at the end of the accounts. Reductions were also made in assize rents and farms, but in the late 1440s and 1450s such adjustments stopped. As we have seen, rents and farms were often increased. Auditing procedures became particularly severe, so that pardons were rare, and allowances on debts virtually unknown on some manors. Small sums among the perquisites of courts were admitted as being impossible to collect and were deducted as 'unlevyable amercements'. However, this was a narrow category. For example, at Bibury in 1445 the abbots of Gloucester, Osney and Cirencester were each amerced 18d. for failing to attend the bishop's courts. Everyone involved must have known that these sums would never be collected, yet for the next fifteen years these amercements were listed on each Bibury account, and copied on to the estate's arrears roll.[68]

The high total of debts that accumulated in the 1450s was the result of the irresistible force of tenant truculence, meeting the immovable object of a determined administration. Movement began with 'allowances' on arrears being made to tenants of all kinds, ostensibly to enable them to repair buildings, in 1457. Then in 1458 and the next few years, larger sums were allowed and pardoned, so reducing the arrears total of the whole estate by about £400 between 1460 and 1465. This created a new atmosphere, in which tenants seem to have been willing to pay part of their arrears if substantial pardons were made. Richard Bayly of Stoke, who had paid nothing of his farm since 1451, agreed in 1458 to pay £10, in exchange for a pardon of £34 of his old debts. The Bibury demesne farmer, who owed £22 in 1459, paid up £13 6s. 8d. in 1461–2, after a number of pardons had been made.[69] Evidently sums had been held back because of the obstinacy of the auditing process, and manorial profits often show a considerable increase in payments to the lord in the year or two after pardons had been granted.

A new build-up of arrears was prevented in the 1460s by a series

[68] Bibury AR, 1445–6, et seq.
[69] Stoke AR, 1457–8; Bibury AR, 1461–2.

of concessions. Small sums were regularly pardoned and allowed. The farmer of Hatton pasture in Hampton evidently had problems in paying the full rent of £8 negotiated in 1450. By 1458 he owed £9 6s. 0d., part of which was pardoned. In almost every year in the 1460s, between 13s. 4d. and £1 0s. 0d. was allowed on the farm. Eventually, in the 1470s, the farmer was able to pay the full amount.

Arrears problems are evident again in the later years of Bishop Alcock, notably at Henbury, where arrears rose to £44 in 1483 and £73 by 1485 (see Appendix 2). No explanation is given in the accounts, but it is possible that frictions were developing over the payment of court revenues, as exceptionally high court perquisites of £37 were recorded in 1482–3. High totals of debt were also recorded at this time for Bredon and Cleeve.

1486 seems to mark a turning point in the history of arrears on the estate. In that year Bishop Alcock left the diocese, and the debts to him disappear from the estate records. Under his successors arrears did not build up, and remained at a relatively low level, less even than in the late fourteenth and early fifteenth centuries. There was a slight, but short-lived, upward movement in arrears in the early 1520s.[70] Why were the arrears totals so much reduced? Money was paid over much more promptly. In the mid-fifteenth century about a third of the money received each year came from arrears, the remainder from the current income of the year. By the early sixteenth century less than a tenth of money collected by the receiver came from arrears, so that most rents were being paid in the year that were due. This could reflect less reluctance on the tenants' part to pay rents, and greater ease for them in obtaining cash. A comparison between the outstanding debts of 1473 and 1519 indicates the main areas of change (see Table 29).

By 1519 only £14 was owed by manorial officials.[71] Much of the arrears total was made up of rents, reliefs and heriots that individual tenants had refused to pay, but these tended to be gentry tenants: among the list of debtors appear such names as Robert Cassy, Sir John Darrell, Sir Anthony Pimpe, Robert Vampage and John Washbourne, esquire. The only lessees to owe money were the farmers of the Blockley tithe-corn, always prominent among fifteenth-century debtors, and the townsmen of Stratford-on-Avon, who were

[70] This was most pronounced at Cleeve, where arrears were nil in 1515, 1517 and 1521, but rose to £6 4s. 11d. in 1522–3.
[71] Arrears roll, 1473; WCRO ref. 009:1 BA 2636/177 92503.

Table 29. *Analysis of arrears in 1473 and 1519*

	1473	1519
Debts of beadles, bailiffs and reeves	£290 (32%)	£14 (15%)
Throckmorton rents	£261 (29%)	—
Unpaid rents	£71 (8%)	£26 (27%)
Unpaid farms	£179 (20%)	£15 (16%)
Unpaid farms of Blockley tithes	£32 (4%)	£19 (20%)
Collective dues	£45 (5%)	—
Debts from franchisal jurisdiction	£8 (1%)	—
Reliefs, heriots, fines, court revenues	£11 (1%)	£20 (21%)
Miscellaneous	—	£1 (1%)
Total	£897 (100%)	£95 (100%)

in dispute with the bishop over the payment of a farm of £1 for fair tolls, which had not been paid for fourteen years.

The refusal to pay rents and dues, widespread in the mid-fifteenth century, was mainly confined in the early sixteenth century to the upper classes. Some tenants had relented over rent payments. The long-standing quarrel over the Throckmorton rents was settled in the 1470s. By 1470 successive members of the Throckmorton family had paid nothing of their £10 fee-farm for thirty years, but in 1470–1 Thomas Throckmorton, then the estate steward, paid £10 of his accumulated debt of £240. This was evidently no more than a gesture, as nothing more was contributed in the next two years. Thomas died in 1472, and responsibility for payment passed to his widow, Margaret. By 1478 she seems to have accepted an obligation to pay a farm of £12, which she and her successors did regularly thereafter.[72]

Some unpaid dues do not appear among the 1519 arrears because the estate administrators had been forced to concede defeat. Unpopular collective dues had been given up; recognitions were not demanded in 1476 or at any later date, and common fines on some manors were forgotten soon after 1507.

In some respects the estate administration had won too. Their failure to reduce rents in the mid-fifteenth century, or their references in the survey of c.1450 to the good old days of the thirteenth century, may seem unrealistic and even foolish; yet their intransigence prevented rent reductions which would have been difficult to restore later in the century. Their policy was ultimately vindicated by the ability of the estate to collect many of the old rents by 1486.

[72] Misc. AR, *passim.*

Tenants who had been reluctant to pay, whether because of the new social climate or through real economic difficulties, paid up most of their rents on time, and thus created a greater stability (and an increase) in income. The administration seems to have been content with this state of affairs, and in the early sixteenth century gathered in most of what was due, but did not notably step up the pressure on tenants in order to further increase the bishops' income.

Having examined the different elements that went into determining the income of the bishopric estate, it is possible to bring these together in a chronological survey of the period between 1400 and 1540, in order to see the relative importance of underlying economic trends and social pressures, as compared with administrative action, in causing changes in the bishops' income.

1400–35

The evidence is rather thin in the first third of the fifteenth century. From some larger manors the bishops' income was relatively high. Accumulations of arrears were not particularly great, suggesting that a high proportion of rents were being paid. Court revenues were maintained on some manors at the buoyant level of the period immediately before 1400. But the trend in court perquisites and rents, both customary and leasehold, was downwards.

This picture of some quite high manorial profits, but with a tendency towards decline, has been noted on other estates, in Derbyshire, Kent and Cornwall. Factors in the economy that could have helped to provide a temporarily favourable climate for seignorial revenues include a slight recovery in grain and wool prices from their low level in the late fourteenth century. Such indices of economic activity as cloth exports show vitality in some decades of the period.[73]

At this time the tenants do not seem to have exploited their bargaining position, as the first references to the non-payment of rents and dues appear in the mid-1430s.

---

[73] I. S. W. Blanchard, 'Economic Change in Derbyshire in the Late Middle Ages, 1272–1540' (Univ. of London Ph.D. thesis, 1967), p. 88; Smith, *Canterbury Cathedral Priory*, p. 194; J. M. W. Bean, *The Estates of the Percy Family, 1416–1537* (Oxford, 1958), pp. 12–42; Hatcher, *Rural Economy and Society in the Duchy of Cornwall, 1300–1500*, pp. 149–59; Lloyd, *Wool Prices*, pp. 46–7, 67; E. Carus-Wilson and O. Coleman, *England's Export Trade, 1275–1547* (Oxford, 1962), pp. 138–9.

In this period the administration does not seem to have been particularly active, apart from an episode in 1408–13, when a survey of the estate's income and a number of rentals were drawn up under Bishop Peverel. Officials seem to have been willing to concede lower rents, and to make allowances for shortfalls in expected income. The first evidence of a major estate official receiving advantages on an apparently irresponsible scale comes from the episcopate of Thomas Polton (1426–33), who heaped rewards on his steward, John Wode.

1435–76

In the mid-fifteenth century, income from the estate reached its lowest point. After a brief period of prosperity in the late 1430s, manorial profits were unstable, and tended to move downwards, rising only briefly in the early 1460s, and not showing signs of real growth until the 1470s and 1480s. At the same time arrears mounted, reaching a peak in about 1460, and remained a recurrent problem until the late 1480s.

This troubled period coincides with the major economic depression of the later middle ages. The late 1430s was a period of famine and hardship for much of the population, but manorial profits were sometimes high, presumably because large-scale producers, like the demesne farmers, did well from high prices and paid their farms in full. Between c.1440 and c.1475 grain and wool prices reached their all-time low, and the volume of both industrial production and international trade slumped in the same period.[74] The decline in market opportunities made it difficult for commodity producers, such as the demesne farmers, to pay their rents in full, and rent-payments were delayed or even paid in kind.

Economic problems connected with the market cannot explain all of the shortfall in income in the mid-fifteenth century. Tenants became more assertive, and refused to pay some of their rents and dues.

The estate officials could do little about the prevailing economic and social climate. However, this was a period of vigorous admin-

[74] Lloyd, *Wool Prices*, pp. 46–7; Carus-Wilson and Coleman, *Export Trade*, pp. 122–3, 138–9; Hatcher, *Tin Production*, pp. 152–63; H. A. Miskimin, *The Economy of Early Renaissance Europe, 1300–1460* (Englewood Cliffs, New Jersey, 1969), pp. 129–31.

istrative activity. A zealous and resident bishop, John Carpenter, came to the see in 1444. He appointed as steward the youthful and ambitious William Nottingham, to replace the much-rewarded John Wode, and at about the same time a gentleman with trading interests, Thomas Arnold, became the receiver. They enquired into the bishopric's resources in *c.*1450, compiled new rentals that pushed up the theoretical income of the estate, raised some leasehold rents, tightened up the terms of leases, refused to make the smallest concession on unpaid rents and embarked on a modest programme of capital investment. They recognized the futility of continuing with direct management and sold off the sheep flock in 1458.

In the short term this aggressive administration caused serious difficulties, with arrears piling up in the 1450s to unheard-of levels. Unrealistic demands may have exacerbated the problem by making tenants all the more determined not to pay their rents in full.

In 1459–60 Nottingham and Arnold moved to less important posts. Nottingham became steward of the Gloucestershire manors, Arnold gave up the receivership to become auditor. Perhaps there is some connection with the softening of attitudes towards arrears at about the same time. Debts were pardoned, and tenants paid off some of their old arrears, perhaps helped in the early 1460s by a temporary upturn in grain prices. For the next twenty years the administrators continued to make concessions on arrears, while still clinging to the old rent demands; leasehold rents were sometimes raised, new rentals compiled, and investment continued.

1476–1500

The last quarter of the fifteenth century saw a general recovery in estate revenues. Manorial profits showed an upward trend, particularly marked in the late 1480s, and were not liable to violent fluctuations from year to year. Arrears lessened, and remained at a low level after 1486. There are signs of recovery in other parts of England, such as Derbyshire and Kent.[75]

Some general expansion can be seen in the same period. Agricultural prices picked up only slightly and temporarily in the late 1470s and 1480s, but there was a marked revival in exports and

[75] *The Duchy of Lancaster's Estates in Derbyshire*, ed. Blanchard, pp. 11–13; Du Boulay, *Lordship of Canterbury*, p. 220.

industry.[76] Tenants, while still holding back payment of some un-popular dues, were willing and able to pay rents promptly.

The administrators now reaped the benefits of the policies of their predecessors, and were able to collect the 'unrealistic' rents fixed in the middle years of the century. No great administrative efforts accompanied this improvement; new rentals were rarely compiled after 1475, and some officials were acting through deputies.

1500–40

After 1500 manorial profits continued at the higher level established at the end of the fifteenth century, but there was no further increase. Occasionally extra money was raised by selling timber, or levying fines on the tenants of Henbury. There were slight depressions in profits in 1505–10 and 1522–3. Arrears were always low, though they increased somewhat in the early 1520s.

The underlying economic trends of the early sixteenth century were generally expansionary, with marked increases in prices from the 1510s. The slight reductions in manorial profits in the first decade and in 1522–3 coincide with trade slumps. The trends in the bishops' income do not reflect the long-term economic revival, associated with rising prices and seignorial profits elsewhere in the 1520s and 1530s.[77]

The failure of large church estates to benefit from the economic upswing in the early sixteenth century was a general phenomenon. Stagnant or falling revenues have been found on the episcopal estates of Bath and Wells, Canterbury, Coventry and Lichfield, and Ely.[78] An important reason for this was the leasing of demesnes for

---

[76] Lloyd, *Wool Prices*, pp. 46–7; Carus-Wilson and Coleman, *Export Trade*, pp. 138–9, though the revival in Bristol cloth exports was short-lived, see Carus-Wilson and Coleman, *Export Trade*, pp. 142–3.

[77] Thirsk (ed.), *Agrarian History*, iv, pp. 817–18, 835–6, for prices; I. S. W. Blanchard, 'Commercial Crisis and Change: Trade and the Industrial Economy of the North-East, 1509–32', *Northern History*, viii (1973), pp. 64–85 on 1522–3; E. Kerridge, 'The Movement of Rent', in E. M. Carus-Wilson (ed.), *Essays in Economic History* (London, 1962), ii, pp. 216–17, 221.

[78] P. M. Hembry, *The Bishops of Bath and Wells* (London, 1967), pp. 52–78; Du Boulay, *Canterbury*, pp. 230–1, 317–29; R. O'Day, 'Cumulative Debt: the Bishops of Coventry and Lichfield and their Economic Problems, c.1540–1640', *Midland History*, iii (1975), pp. 77–93; F. Heal, 'The Tudors and Church Lands, Economic Problems of the Bishopric of Ely during the Sixteenth Century', *Econ. Hist. Rev.*, 2nd ser., xxvi (1973), pp. 198–217.

long terms (often ninety-nine years) without any increase in rents. Leasehold rents, although changeable in legal theory, were regarded as fixed. In his indentures of leases granted in the late 1530s Bishop Latimer referred to 'the old accustomed rent'.[79]

It has been suggested that lords were compensated for fixed lease-hold rents by fines on new leases, but the Worcester fines, occasionally recorded in the receivers' accounts, seem quite small: for example, £8 for an £18 farm of the Fladbury demesne, or £6 13s. 4d. for a fifty-year lease of the Stratford mills at a farm of £10 per annum.[80]

The static bishopric revenues in the early sixteenth century must be seen as the result of administrative failure. Were the administrators conservative, or lacking in awareness of economic developments? Such officials as Sir George Throckmorton or John Hornyhold exhibited much acquisitiveness in increasing their own properties, particularly by taking on leases of church property at fixed rents and for long terms. The self-interested attitudes of the bishopric officials could sometimes lead to disruptive disputes, as happened at Henbury in the 1520s and 1530s.

Were the officials out of sympathy with the bishopric on religious grounds? Their positions varied, from Throckmorton's conservatism to the reforming views of Nicholas Poyntz, the Gloucestershire steward. Their opinions probably took second place to a desire to gain lands and profits at the church's expense. Sir George Throckmorton, in spite of his opposition to Reformation legislation, acquired monastic properties as early as 1525, after Wolsey's first essay in dissolving religious houses. Both he and Poyntz gained monastic lands at the main Dissolution.[81] No sharp distinction was drawn by predatory laymen between episcopal and monastic temporalities as the Reformation progressed, and Ralph Morice, secretary to Archbishop Cranmer, singled out estate officials as leading the attack on the Canterbury estates; 'our new officers', he called them, 'brought up and practised in subverting of monasterial possessions'.[82] It is possible that in the anti-clerical atmosphere in the years preceding the Reformation that lay administra-

[79] WCL, Dean and Chapter Reg. A VI (3), fo. 26.
[80] Rec. AR 1497–8, 1498–9.
[81] The biographical material here is derived from History of Parliament, unpublished biographies.
[82] Du Boulay, *Lordship of Canterbury*, p. 320.

tors felt no impetus to strive to expand the revenues of rich ecclesiastics.

Our general conclusion must be that no matter how much vigorous action an administration took in the difficult days of the early and mid-fifteenth century, the landlord's income was bound to decline in the face of economic and social change. In the long term, administrative activity could bring benefits by preventing permanent rent-reductions, but only when the economic situation ameliorated. The stagnation in income of the early sixteenth century shows that if his administration lacked drive, a landlord could miss economic opportunities, even in a period of expansion.

Postscript to Chapter 6. Additional sources of income

Although the estate provided the bulk of the bishops' income, they had other resources. The most important of these, available to all bishops, was the income from spiritualities which was derived from the bishop's ecclesiastical functions. Strictly, these included the profits of the appropriated rectories of Blockley and Hillingdon, but the bishops' estate officials accounted for these, so they have been treated as part of the temporalities in previous chapters. Here we are concerned with the payments received by the bishops' ecclesiastical officials, notably the commissary-general, from the clergy, such as the customary dues of pensions, synodals and pentecostals, or, from the laity, Peter's Pence and fines associated with the probate of wills. The evidence is too scanty to suggest more than minimum figures. Firstly, the almost static customary payments (Peter's Pence, pensions, synodals etc.) amounted to about £90 per annum, rising somewhat between 1380 and 1534 because more pensions were paid with the increase in the number of appropriated churches (see Table 30). Not all of these sums were actually paid. In 1452, for example, the commissary-general petitioned for allowances of more than £10 for Peter's Pence and pensions that were not collectable. Variable amounts came from proving wills and 'corrections' of laymen, from £10 in a seven-month period in 1474–5 to £53 11s. 0d. for a full year in 1419–20. The 1419–20 account provides the fullest record of spiritualities as it includes the revenues collected by officers other than the commissary-general, including £15 for the perquisites of the archdeacons, and £88 from the 'office of the vicar [-general]', which were described as the issues of the seal, presumably fees paid for documents drawn up in connection with the business of the consistory court. In 1419–20 Philip Morgan, the bishop, was absent for much of the time, and a vicar-general would have acted as the head of ecclesiastical administration.[1]

[1] R. L. Storey, *Diocesan Administration in the Fifteenth Century* (St Anthony's Hall Publications, 16, York, 1959), p. 7.

Table 30. Income from spiritualities, 1380–1535*

Date	Peter's Pence	Pensions	Pentecostals	Synodals	Wills and corrections	Others	Total
1380 (one year)	£30 9s. 1d.	£31 14s. 0d.	£5 0s. 6d.	£18 10s. 4d.	—	—	£85 13s. 11d.
1419–20 (one year)	£32 0s. 11d.	£35 19s. 0d.	£5 10s. 8d.	£18 13s. 0d.	£53 11s. 0d.	Vacant churches (9s. 0d.) Perquisites of deacons (£15 6s. 8d.) Issues of seal of vicar-general (£88 2s. 8d.)	£249 12s. 11d.
26 March 1435– 29 Sept. 1436 (1½ years)	—	—	—	—	—	—	£124 3s. 8d.
1 Aug. 1452– 22 Dec. 1452 (5 months)	£30 16s. 0½d.	£16 17s. 0d.	—	£6 9s. 2d.	£16 11s. 0d.	—	Gross £70 13s. 2¼d. Net £50 5s. 5d.
21 Dec. 1474– 1 Aug. 1475 (7 months)	—	£20 7s. 4d.	£5 10s. 8d.	£12 4s. 4d.	£10 2s. 8d.	—	Gross £48 5s. 0d. Net £40 18s. 0d.
1480 (one year)	£30 14s. 11½d.	—	{ £24 4s 10d	(brace)	—	—	Gross —
1535 (one year)	0	£44 5s. 11½d.			—	—	Gross £68 10s. 9¼d. Net £61 17s. 5¼d.

* Reg. Wakefield, pp. 166–9; WCRO ref. 009:1 BA 2636/9 43696, fos. 158–61; Rec. AR, 1435–6; WCRO ref. 009:1 BA 2636/190 92614/10 43699; Lunt, *Financial Relations of England with the Papacy, 1327–1534*, p. 719; *Valor Ecclesiasticus*, iii, p. 219.

These figures show, then, that the minimum income from spiritualities in the fifteenth century would have been in the region of £100 per annum from the payments due to the commissary-general (allowing £10 for unpaid dues, and assuming a revenue of at least £20 from wills and corrections). If the items recorded in 1419–20 are regarded as typical, this would raise the possible yield of spiritualities to more than £200. Net income cannot be properly calculated, as there is little evidence of administrative costs. From 1534, as the *Valor Ecclesiasticus* shows, there was a reduction in income because of the abolition of Peter's Pence by the Reformation parliament.[2]

Individual bishops would have been able to supplement their income with fees and salaries from other posts. For example, Philip Morgan would have been entitled to an annual salary of £133 6s. 8d. as a regular member of the royal council in the early 1420s.[3]

[2] *Statutes of the Realm* (London, 1817), iii, pp. 464–71.
[3] J. F. Baldwin, *The King's Council in England during the Middle Ages* (Oxford, 1913), pp. 174–5.

7. Real income and expenditure, 1375–1540

Previous chapters have shown that, in common with many other late medieval landowners, the income of the bishops of Worcester declined, from about £1,200 around 1300, to between £820 and £1,044 in the mid-fifteenth century, and then rose slightly to between £900 and £1,074 in the period 1497–1540. Did the long-term decline in money income affect significantly the spending power of the bishops? Did they suffer any financial hardship?

The changes in the real income of the bishops can be related to the fluctuating costs of goods and services by using the index of the price of a 'composite unit of consumables' compiled by Phelps Brown and Hopkins.[1] For our period the choice of goods included in the index was based on the account book of a household of Bridport chantry priests in the mid-fifteenth century. This was intended to reflect the consumption patterns of building workers, whose real income was the object of Phelps Brown and Hopkins' study, but the chantry priests would have had a better standard of living than most building workers, so the index was not perfectly suited to its original purpose. It was not entirely satisfactory for calculating a bishop's real income either, as bishops enjoyed a much better standard of living than chantry priests. Some allowance for this can be made by using another index compiled by the same authors to represent changes in the price of a unit of industrial products, such as cloth and building-materials, which bishops would have purchased in large quantities.[2] In Figures 2 and 3 the estate income of the bishopric between 1453 and 1540 has been expressed in terms of both indices. Fig. 2, using the index of consumables (mainly basic foodstuffs), suggests that real income rose between the mid-fifteenth century and the late 1490s, but fell drastically in the

---

[1] E. H. Phelps Brown and Sheila V. Hopkins, 'Seven Centuries of the Prices of Consumables, compared with Builders' Wage Rates', in E. M. Carus-Wilson (ed.), *Essays in Economic History* (London, 1962), ii, pp. 193–4.

[2] E. H. Phelps Brown and Sheila V. Hopkins, 'Wage-rates and Prices: Evidence for Population Pressure in the Sixteenth Century', *Economica*, xxiv (1957), p. 306.

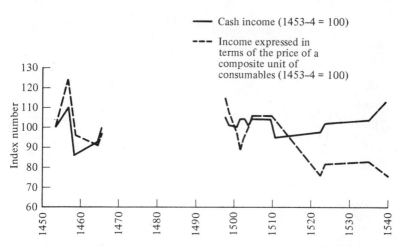

2   Real income, in terms of consumables, 1453–1540

1520s and 1530s. Fig. 3, based on the price of industrial products, indicates a similar trend, but on a less extreme scale, with a recovery in the 1530s. The fall in real income between 1510 and the 1520s was about 15 per cent in terms of manufactured goods, compared with 25 per cent or more in terms of consumables. Real income, therefore, was stable or increasing in the second half of the fifteenth century, and declining in the early sixteenth.

The changes in real income in the last century of our period should be seen in the context of the secular decline in real income. A calculation using the index of the unit of consumables for 1311–12 suggests that between that date and 1453 real income fell by 20 per cent. Although no index of industrial products has been calculated for the fourteenth century, their prices rose so much that income expressed in terms of such goods would have fallen by more than 20 per cent.[3]

The falling incomes of the great landlords in the later middle ages is a familiar concept, but, as K. B. McFarlane has pointed out, there is little evidence that the aristocracy suffered any privations. Con-

[3] M. M. Postan, 'The Trade of Medieval Europe: the North', in *Medieval Trade and Finance* (Cambridge, 1973), p. 177.

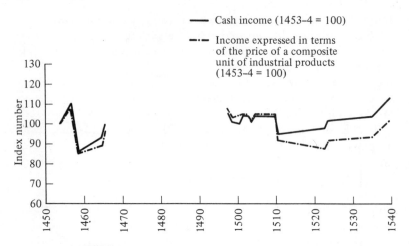

3   Real income, in terms of industrial products, 1453–1540

spicuous consumption in diet, clothing and buildings continued, and the nobility were able to live within their means.[4]

Although their income was reduced, the bishops of Worcester seem to have maintained a relatively high standard of living, and had cash to spare for expensive projects. But in spite of their declining income, some changes favoured them. After the leasing of the demesnes, they did not have the problem of restocking the manors after animals and equipment had been sold by the previous bishop or his executors;[5] also there was some reduction in taxation. The services paid by each new bishop to the papacy since the early fourteenth century continued in the fifteenth century, and by the end of the fifteenth century they amounted to £632.[6] This represented about two-thirds of annual temporal income, so that each bishop began his episcopate in debt. However, the payment of tenths and subsidies to the popes declined in frequency in the period. The assessment for tax purposes was based on Pope Nicholas' valuation of 1291, so that the early fourteenth-century bishops owed £48 11s. 3d. when a tenth was paid. Papal demands for tenths were

---

[4] McFarlane, *Nobility*, pp. 83–101.

[5] The lay nobility also benefited from the legal devices that prevented estates falling into the hands of royal escheators, see J. M. W. Bean, *The Decline of English Feudalism* (Manchester, 1968), pp. 231–4.

[6] W. E. Lunt, *Financial Relations of England with the Papacy, 1327–1534* (Cambridge, Mass., 1962), ii, p. 304.

frequent in the early fourteenth century, but diminished after 1336 and virtually disappeared in the fifteenth century.[7] Royal taxation on the clergy, which also took the form of tenths based on the 1291 valuations, was levied in almost every year for much of the fourteenth and early fifteenth centuries. After 1422 payments became less frequent, and there were long gaps between grants after the mid-1450s.[8]

Smaller and more irregular payments to pope and king, such as papal procurations, and fees paid to both papal and royal courts, are difficult to quantify, but there is no reason to believe that they increased greatly in the fifteenth century.

After paying his compulsory share of taxes, the main call on a bishop's income was the need to maintain his household. A bishop was equated by contemporaries with an earl in lay society.[9] To supply his needs in administration and domestic service, he had to keep a large staff, and a liveried entourage would be necessary to maintain his social standing. He would also be expected to extend hospitality to a constant stream of guests.[10] The lifestyle and social tone of an episcopal household are indicated by the critical comments of two contemporaries. Hugh Latimer, preaching a decade after his resignation of the Worcester see, saw the lordliness of bishops as a bar to their effectiveness as leaders of religion:

> ever since the prelates were made lords and nobles the plough
> [a metaphor for preaching] standeth; there is no work done, the
> people starve. They hawk, they hunt, they card, they dice; they
> pastime in their prelacies with gallant gentlemen, with their
> dancing minions, and with their fresh companions... They are so

[7] *ibid.*, pp. 75–168; *Taxatio Ecclesiastica auctoritate P. Nicholai IV, ca.1291* (Record Commission, 1802), pp. 225–6,

[8] Lunt, *Financial Relations*, p. 88; E. F. Jacob, *The Fifteenth Century* (Oxford, 1961), pp. 118–20, 203–4; W. Stubbs, *The Constitutional History of England*, 6th edn (Oxford, 1903), iii, pp. 106–225. In the receivers' accounts of 1435–6, 1467–8 and 1469–70 payments of tenths and half-tenths are recorded, based on an assessment of £56. The increase over the 1291 figure was presumably caused by the appropriation of Blockley rectory.

[9] e.g. R. B. Dobson, *The Peasants' Revolt of 1381* (London, 1970), pp. 107, 109; *The Boke of Nurture by John Russell*, ed. F. J. Furnivall (Early Engl. Text Soc., 1868), pp. 186, 188.

[10] The size and character of a late medieval episcopal household is indicated by the household accounts of Ralph Shrewsbury, bishop of Bath and Wells, *Household Roll of Bishop Ralph of Shrewsbury*, ed. J. A. Robinson (Somerset Record Soc., *Collectanea*, 59, 1924), pp. 72–165.

troubled with lordly living, they be so placed in palaces, couched in courts, ruffling in their rents, dancing in their dominions, ... pampering of their paunches ...[11]

In 1417 another caustic commentator, Margery Kempe, visited the then bishop of Worcester, Thomas Peverel, at his Henbury manor-house. She was delayed in seeing him because he was still in bed:

When she came into the hall, she saw many of the bishop's men, all slashed and pointed in their clothes. She, lifting up her hand, blessed herself. And then they said: 'What devil aileth thee?' She said to them: 'Whose men be ye?' They answered back: 'The bishop's men'. And then she said: 'Nay, forsooth; ye are more like the devil's men.'[12]

Some insight into the costs of setting up an episcopal household is provided by the sums paid by Bishop Thomas Bourgchier's receiver in 1435–6.[13] The items bought included practical necessities such as horses (nine in all) and their saddles and harness, totalling £15 4s. 4d., and kitchen equipment, pots, pans, chests and baskets, costing £23 1s. 7d. The most lavish expenditure was on clothes for the bishop and his household, amounting to £181 17s. 8d., including Bourgchier's parliament robe, of scarlet with an ermine lining, which cost £16 10s. 0d. For the bishop's table a set of silver dishes, saucers and chargers cost £50, and other items like basins, candelabra, gold rings and seals brought the total bill for silver and gold items to £131 1s. 8d.

The initial expenditure on household goods and clothing (£350), together with papal services (£600), fees in chancery (£13), and the expenses of travelling to Gloucester to do homage to the king (£17), absorbed a year's income from the bishopric.

The everyday running costs of Bourgchier's household were much more modest: £439 for a year and a half, or about £300 per annum. The expenditure was organized in eight departments, an elaborate household administration comparable with other magnates of the time.[14] Spending was as follows:

[11] G. R. Elton, *The Tudor Constitution* (Cambridge, 1962), p. 327.

[12] *The Book of Margery Kempe, 1436*, ed. W. Butler-Bowden (London, 1936), pp. 160–1.

[13] Rec. AR, 1435–6.

[14] For example, the archbishops of Canterbury had a household with ten departments, see Du Boulay, *Canterbury*, p. 260.

Pantry (bread)	£38 10s. 0d.	(9%)
Buttery (ale)	£49 10s. 3d.	(12%)
Cellar (wine)	£53 13s. 4d.	(13%)
Spices	£12 6s. 8d.	(3%)
Kitchen (meat and fish)	£132 0s. 0d.	(33%)
Chaundlery (candles)	£17 13s. 4d.	(4%)
Hall (fuel)	£14 10s. 0d.	(4%)
Stable (fodder)	£87 8s. 0d.	(22%)

In addition, servants' wages came to £32 2s. 6d., and the laundry bill was £1 15s. 0d. The size of Bourgchier's household seems to have been relatively small; judging from the quantity of ale consumed, it contained about twenty people.[15] Some contemporary lay households with lower incomes were as large as or larger than Bourgchier's.[16] The figures for 1435–6 are likely to have fallen rather below the cost of maintaining the bishop's household in a normal year, and so have led to an underestimate of the numbers of servants, officials and guests maintained, as he spent part of the time covered by the account staying with his mother in Suffolk and in the royal household, presumably receiving hospitality during these visits.

Bourgchier's household lived well, spending, for example, £36 per annum on wine: this was enough to buy about 1,600 gallons, and represented as a high a proportion of expenditure as found in the households of the great magnates of the period, such as that of Elizabeth Berkeley, countess of Warwick.[17] Henry Wakefield's household seems to have consumed wine on a similar scale, judging from his expenditure of £33 on wine at Bristol in 1386–7, when prices were comparable with those of the 1430s.[18]

A luxurious standard of diet at the bishop's table can be glimpsed from references in estate documents to the consumption of venison from the parks, a barrel of sturgeon and metheglin (spiced mead).[19]

[15] The calculation is based on the assumption that each person drank a gallon of ale per day. £33 spent on ale at 1d. or 1½d. per gallon would buy 6,000–8,000 gallons.

[16] McFarlane, *Nobility*, p. 110 shows that Sir John Fastolf had a household of twenty-nine when his income was only £600 *per annum*. The Bryene household maintained about 20 on expenditure of rather less than £300, see *Household Book of Dame Alice de Bryene*, ed. V. B. Redstone (Suffolk Institute of Archaeology and Natural History, Ipswich, 1931).

[17] C. D. Ross, 'The Household Accounts of Elizabeth Berkeley, Countess of Warwick, 1420–1', *Trans. Bristol and Glos. Arch. Soc.*, lxx (1951), p. 97.

[18] Henbury AR, 1386–7.

[19] Henbury AR, July-Sept. 1395; Blockley AR, 1383–4; Rec. AR, 1464–5.

The household had to be provided with liveries as well as food and drink. Bishop Carpenter paid £10 to £15 for cloth for this purpose in a number of years, and Silvestro de' Gigli, on his only recorded visit to the diocese in 1504–5, spent £12. In spite of the existence of cloth industries within the diocese, notably at Worcester itself, Carpenter bought cloth at Frome in Somerset and Coventry.[20]

As they moved from one residence to another, like all medieval magnates, the bishops had to pay for the upkeep of a number of domestic buildings. Here there is some evidence that expenditure was restricted, perhaps because of declining income, as the number of manor-houses in use seems to have been reduced. Bishop Bransford (1339–49) issued letters and documents from fifteen of his manors, indicating that he lived in all of them.[21] Henry Wakefield is known to have stayed at eleven or twelve[22] but by the mid-fif-teenth century money seems to have been spent on maintaining only nine: the Worcester palace, the London house in the Strand, Hartlebury castle and six manor-houses. In most years repairs to these buildings did not exceed £30, but there is sometimes evidence of more extensive building works. Bishop Carpenter spent £28 on the Worcester palace in 1460–1, and was also involved in major projects at Hartlebury. The existing great hall at Hartlebury castle was built in the fifteenth century, and the now-demolished gate-house has been attributed to Carpenter. Expenditure on residences continued in the early sixteenth century, notably in 1504–5, when work on the Worcester palace, Northwick manor and Hartlebury castle cost £73.[23]

Hunting provided one of the principal pastimes of successive bishops, and parks were maintained at Alvechurch, Blockley, Hartlebury, Henbury and Stoke. Henry Wakefield usually spent a period of up to three months each year at Henbury and hunted in his two parks at Pen and Sneyd. Expenditure, normally on fences and gates, but occasionally on lodges, rarely exceeded £5 per annum in

[20] Rec. AR, 1453–4, 1465–6, 1469–70, 1504–5.
[21] *Reg. Bransford, passim.*
[22] *Reg. Wakefield, passim.*
[23] Bredon AR, 1395–6 records the carriage of 22 'great oaks' from Welland to Hartlebury, presumably for a major building project in the time of Bishop Tideman; Henbury AR, 1427–8 shows that £22 was spent on buildings; Rec. AR, 1460–1, 1467–8, 1469–70 show expenditure on Worcester and Hartlebury; Rec. AR, 1504–5. On Hartlebury see *VCH Worcs.*, iii, p. 382.

the mid-fifteenth century. Such spending was only partly for pleasure, as parks provided an income from pasture rents.[24] Bishops needed to travel a good deal both inside and outside their diocese. When they went further afield, journeys involved considerable expenditure on accommodation and horses. Bishop Bourgchier, who moved between Worcester, Oxford, Gloucester, London and Suffolk in his first year and a half as bishop, spent £118 on travelling, but this was probably exceptional.[25]

The available documents contain only occasional references to the money spent on the bishop's ecclesiastical functions, like the pension of £2 10s. 0d. granted by Carpenter to his suffragan. The only item to appear regularly in the receivers' accounts was expenditure on the episcopal prison in the Worcester palace. Here criminous clergy and lay offenders, including those accused of heresy, were kept, sometimes in chains, at a cost that varied between ¼d. and 1d. per day. The total came to between £3 and £7 per annum.[26]

Although expenditure would far exceed income in the first year of an episcopate, afterwards the fifteenth-century bishops of Worcester would have had a substantial surplus of disposable income. The figures given above suggest that regular annual commitments would amount to no more than £50 on taxes, £300 on feeding the household, £15 on liveries, and probably no more than £100 on building, parks and travel, making a total of less than £500. It is possible that our estimate of household costs, deriving from the peculiar first year and a half of Bourgchier's episcopate, falls below the normal expenditure of a fifteenth-century bishop. Even if we allowed a further hundred or even two hundred pounds per annum for household expenses, this would still leave our fifteenth-century bishops living well within their means. Such a comfortable situation could well have been achieved in the context of the long-term decline in income from the estate by prudent economizing, for example by reductions in the numbers of buildings maintained, or in the size of the household.

---

[24] This is based on valors and manorial accounts of the appropriate manors.
[25] Rec. AR, 1435–6.
[26] Rec. AR, 1467–8; 1505–40. Some of the Lollard prisoners are named. In 1510–11 Margery Bryan was imprisoned for 13 weeks 1 day, and William Peynter for 3 weeks and 2 days. Peynter was apparently an eccentric rather than a heretic, see J. A. F. Thomson, *The Later Lollards, 1414–1520* (Oxford, 1965), p. 49.

Bishop Carpenter was able, even at the nadir of estate revenues in the mid-fifteenth century, to dispose of an annual surplus of several hundreds of pounds. Like many other members of the lay and ecclesiastical nobility in the later middle ages, Carpenter devoted his money to a collegiate church, that of Westbury-on-Trym.[27] The ambitious nature of his scheme can be judged from the surviving gatehouse of the college building, and the substantial amount of Carpenter's work still visible in Westbury church. The sums spent on the buildings, the purchase of property as endowments, and gifts to the dean and clergy of the college, are shown in Table 31.

The figures are far from complete, and so represent only a fraction of the total cost. Late medieval building costs were usually spread equally over a number of years, so that it is likely that between £250 and £300 per annum was spent on the college buildings between 1453 and 1457.[28] The sums spent on the endowment involve only seven properties, but the college had thirty by the early sixteenth century, some of which also had probably been bought by Carpenter.[29]

Table 31. *Expenditure on Westbury College, 1453–70*

Year	Building expenses	Purchase of property	Other expenses
1453–4	£290 14s. 3½d.	—	—
1456–7	£256 6s. 7½d.	£100 0s. 0d.	—
1460–1	10s. 0d.	—	8s. 8d. (expenses of drawing up a charter)
1463–4	—	£73 6s. 8d.	—
1464–5	—	£13 9s. 6d.	—
1465–6	—	£40 15s. 6d.	£11 6s. 8d. (gift and loan)
1467–8	—	£120 13s. 4d.	£14 0s. 8d. (gifts)
1469–70	£17 2s. 8d.	£207 13s. 6d.	£40 0s. 0d. (gift)

[27] A. Hamilton Thompson, *The English Clergy and their Organization in the Later Middle Ages* (Oxford, 1947), pp. 146–60 et seq.

[28] On paying for buildings in equal instalments, L. F. Salzman, *Building in England* (Oxford, 1967), pp. 448–50, and many other examples.

[29] *Valor Ecclesiasticus* (Record Commission, 1817), iii, pp. 432–4. Some of the endowment went back to Bishop Giffard's patronage of Westbury in the thirteenth century.

The purchases shed some light on the fifteenth-century land market. Carpenter had to range over the whole diocese to find suitable properties, which suggests that not a great deal of land was being put on the market. He bought land at Westbury itself, at Dowdeswell and Wormington in Gloucestershire, Barford in mid-Warwickshire, a holding in Worcester city, and in north Worcestershire at Gannow in Stock and Bradley, and Henwick in Hallow. The rural properties were mainly small manors belonging to gentry families. The sellers may belong to the type identified by McFarlane, those who lacked male heirs and therefore were not as concerned as others with the maintenance of their inheritance. This could apply to Richard Beauchamp, who sold Dowdeswell in 1463–4, and Thomas Wybbe, the vendor of Gannow four years later. Wybbe may have had financial problems, as he is known to have been in debt for substantial sums in the course of his life.[30] The prices paid by Carpenter for land can be compared with the clear value recorded in 1535, a valid comparison because land values did not change greatly in the intervening period (see Table 32). The prices seem to have been in accord with the fifteenth-century assumption that land should be sold at about twenty times its annual value, but in the case of Dowdeswell the price was much lower, perhaps reflecting the run-down state of the land.[31]

Even after spending so much on Westbury College, Carpenter still had money to spare for other religious purposes. He founded

Table 32. *Prices at which land was purchased for the endowment of Westbury College, 1456–70*

Date	Property	Purchase price	Clear value in 1535	Ratio of price to value
1456–7	Holding in Worcester city	£100	£4 13s. 0d.	22:1
1463–4	Dowdeswell (Glos.)	£73 6s. 8d.	£7 19s. 4d.	9:1
1467–8	Gannow (Worcs.)	£53 6s. 8d.	£3 5s. 6d.	16:1
1469–70	Barford (Warks.)	£183 12s. 6d.	£10 9s. 2d.	18:1

[30] On the short supply of land, see McFarlane, *Nobility*, pp. 53–6; on Richard Beauchamp, see Wedgwood, *History of Parliament*, p. 54; on Thomas Wybbe, see *VCH Worcs.*, iii, p. 378; *Cal. Pat. Rolls, 1429–36*, p. 167; *1441–6*, p. 384; *1452–61*, p. 233.

[31] On prices of land, see McFarlane, *Nobility*, pp. 56–7.

two libraries for public use at Worcester and Bristol, spending £18 on the building of the Bristol library in 1463–4, and £12 6s. 8d. on books, probably for the Worcester library, in 1460–1.[32] Carpenter contributed regularly to the fabric funds of parish churches in the diocese. The sums for individual churches varied from 6s. 8d. to £6 13s. 4d., the peak year being 1456–7, when he paid out £25 to six churches.[33]

In his Injunctions of 1451 Carpenter urged adequate parochial fund-raising for the poor, and he made personal contributions, albeit on a modest scale, to individual tenants on the estate or to a whole village, as when he gave £1 to help the Hartlebury tenants with their subsidy payment in 1463–4. He also made grants to public works, like bridges and ferries. The individual donations were usually of less than a pound, and the recorded total in any one year did not exceed £5. Part of the income of Westbury College was used for charitable purposes.[34]

John Carpenter may have been unusual among late medieval bishops in his devotion to the religious life of his diocese, but other bishops of Worcester also spent a good deal on church buildings. John Alcock, Carpenter's successor, was responsible for a substantial rebuilding of Little Malvern Priory, of which an impressive fragment still survives. Henry Wakefield is credited with contributions to the construction of the porch and western end of the nave of Worcester Cathedral.[35]

Thomas Bourgchier spent his money on less worthy projects. A few months after he had been appointed to Worcester in 1435, the bishopric of Ely became vacant. This was a desirable see, with estates worth twice as much as those of Worcester. Bourgchier persuaded the prior and convent of Ely to elect him, against the wishes of the king, who was seeking to promote the bishop of St David's. Bourgchier secured papal support, but eventually a compromise candidate was found, and he had to wait until 1443 for his translation to the richer see.[36] The cost of sending messengers to Ely,

[32] Haines, 'Aspects of the Episcopate of John Carpenter', pp. 32–4; Rec. AR, 1463–4, 1460–1.
[33] Rec. AR, 1456–70; Valor, 1457; Cleeve AR, 1474–5. The grants suggest dates for some perpendicular church buildings; for example contributions were made to Winchcomb in 1469–75, and to Stratford-on-Avon in 1456–61.
[34] Haines, 'Injunctions', p. 36; Rec. AR, 1460–1, 1463–4, 1465–6; Valor, 1465.
[35] VCH Worcs., iv, p. 400.
[36] Hamilton Thompson, The English Clergy, pp. 21–2.

London and Rome, and the employment of lawyers at the papal curia in connection with these negotiations, came to £1,131 16s. 0d. This should perhaps be seen as a speculative investment, which, if successful, would have been recovered in a short time from the revenues of Ely.[37]

Their resources of surplus cash meant that the bishops of Worcester could lend money to kings and lay nobles who needed to finance wars and retinues. Henry Wakefield lent £200 to Thomas of Woodstock, one of the most impecunious of late medieval magnates; Bishop Peverel made loans of £400 to Henry IV and £300 to Henry V; Richard, duke of Gloucester, borrowed £40 from John Carpenter in 1469–70, probably in connection with the military expenses of the 'readeption' crisis.[38] There is little evidence of indebtedness among the bishops. Richard Clifford was slow in repaying the bankers who forwarded his services to the papacy in 1401, and he was threatened with excommunication, but finding these large sums at the beginning of an episcopate was always a problem. Bishop Carpenter borrowed £40 from two Worcester merchants, which he repaid in 1460–1. Presumably the money was needed for the Westbury College project.[39]

The evident wealth of the bishops, in spite of their falling income, puts into perspective the lack of investment in the estate in the fifteenth century. Carpenter and Alcock spent modestly on rebuilding barns and mills, and enclosure, but otherwise mills were left in ruins and pastures unenclosed for decades. Clearly there was no shortage of finance if there had been a will to invest. Successive bishops had higher priorities, in terms of expenditure on personal luxuries, collegiate churches or schemes for promotion. Like many late medieval landlords, they were content to raise as much revenue as possible from existing assets, rather than plan for the future by improving their resources.[40]

The first direct evidence that the bishopric was affected by serious financial problems appears, not at the low point of cash income in the fifteenth century, but in the 1530s. A combination of circumstances reduced the fortunes of the see in the time of Hugh

[37] Rec. AR, 1435–6.
[38] *Reg. Wakefield*, p. xlv; A. E. Goodman, *The Loyal Conspiracy* (London, 1971), pp. 90–4; *DNB*, xv, pp. 1019–20; Rec. AR, 1469–70.
[39] Lunt, *Financial Relations*, ii, p. 215; *Reg. Clifford*, pp. 28–9; Rec. AR, 1460–1.
[40] Hilton, 'Rent and Capital Formation', pp. 177–80.

Latimer (1535–9). The income from the estate was stable, but rising prices were cutting into the real value of his revenues (see figures 2 and 3). The Reformation legislation of 1534 had led to the replacement of the old papal services of £632 by annates of £1,050, paid, like the services, in the first year of the episcopate, and tenths, raised to £105, were demanded each year at Christmas.[41] Also the abolition of Peter's Pence reduced the income from spiritualities by about £20.

Late in 1538 Latimer wrote to Thomas Cromwell about the state of his finances.[42] He had received more than £4,000 since becoming bishop (three years and a term of income from both temporalities and spiritualities would have yielded rather less than £4,000, but Latimer had raised extra cash by selling large quantities of timber). From this, he had spent £1,700 on royal taxes, repairs and payments of debt. He had spent very little on plate and hangings. He now hoped to obtain £180 from rents at Christmas, of which £105 would go to the king in tenths, and £20 as the new year gift, leaving £60 for the Christmas festivities. Latimer, expressing characteristically radical views of the social functions of a bishop, preferred to 'feed many grossly and necessarily than a few deliciously and voluptuously'.

Latimer's financial predicament was partly caused by the rising cost of living and the unenterprising management of the estate under his immediate predecessors. A further contribution to his problems were the high levels of taxation imposed in the 1530s, the result of changes in church–state relations and a shift in lay attitudes to the church's wealth. Some laymen had for a long time questioned the necessity for the higher clergy to lead such a lordly style of life; now the bishops were beginning to feel the force of that argument.

[41] Lunt, *Financial Relations*, ii, p. 304.
[42] *Letters and Papers of Henry VIII*, xiii (1538) part ii, no. 1133.

8. Demesne leases and lessees, 1370–1540

Demesne leases have been mentioned already as sources of rent income, but as we shift our attention from the lord to the tenants, the farmers of the demesnes deserve examination in their own right. The problem of the demesne lessees epitomizes that of late medieval social and economic history in general. We suspect that the rise of the farmer is typical of a number of significant changes: small men taking over the economic initiative from magnates, increasing opportunities for social mobility and the development of a commercially oriented agriculture organized along capitalist lines. Two recent studies have emphasized leasing as indicative of the economic vitality of the gentry.[1] Yet these suppositions are difficult to investigate because our evidence tells us much about the leasehold contracts or the rent paid by the lessee, but very little about the internal management of the demesne.

Despite these problems, the basic questions must be posed, even if definite answers cannot be provided: what was leased, and how? Who took on the leases? What use was made of the demesnes by the lessees?

Demesne leasing often began in the fourteenth century by detaching small parcels of land and renting them out temporarily. With the cessation of direct cultivation by the lord at the end of the century some demesnes were let piecemeal, while the majority were leased *en bloc* to a single tenant.

Demesnes were leased in parcels for at least part of our period at Alvechurch, Blockley, Hanbury, Hartlebury, Henbury, Kempsey and Paxford.[2] The reasons for this varied. Some demesnes were divided geographically: for example, an area of demesne in Hanbury lay at Blickley on the eastern side of the manor, so that it was logical

---

[1] F. R. H. Du Boulay, 'Who were Farming the English Demesnes at the end of the Middle Ages?', *Econ. Hist. Rev.*, 2nd ser., xvii (1965), pp. 443–55; B. Harvey, 'The Leasing of the Abbot of Westminster's Demesnes in the Later Middle Ages', *Econ. Hist. Rev.*, 2nd ser., xxii (1969), pp. 17–27.

[2] WCRO ref. 009:1 BA 2636/37 (iii) 43806, fos. 6–12, 82–3, 115–19; Blockley AR, 1458–9; Hanbury AR, 1430–1; Kempsey AR, 1505–6.

to let it separately. In the case of Blockley the continuation of sheep-farming by the bishops until 1458 meant that the whole demesne could not have been leased initially. Perhaps some of the divided demesnes fitted well into the landholding structure of the local peasantry. Often areas of enclosed pasture, not just on the seven manors listed above, were leased separately because of a specialized demand for that type of land from graziers.

Most of the demesnes were leased as large, complete units, con-sisting of land of all kinds, and buildings. Occasionally the buildings were described in detail, indicating the considerable assets being conveyed. At Wick Episcopi, a small demesne, the lease of 1460 mentions a hall of three bays, a kitchen of two bays, a granary of five bays and another of three, a cow-house of three bays, all with thatched roofs, and a building called the Old Hall, 40 feet long, with a tiled roof.[3]

Farmers received no stock with their leases, the only exception being a temporary arrangement by which Thomas Bleke took on the bishop's sheep flock, as well as the pastures, in the 1450s.[4]

The farmers were not required to cultivate the land in any parti-cular way, except in a Bibury lease of 1451 which stated that 30 acres should be manured and fallow-ploughed.[5] The most common obligation was for the lessee to agree to repair buildings and fences, and, in early leases, to pay the expenses of the steward, but these conditions were often not observed.

The tenures by which the demesnes were held evolved during our period. The earliest 'sales' of parcels were very informal agreements lasting for a year at a time. The first grants of complete demesnes, and the piecemeal lettings over a longer period, were often tenancies at will. In the mid- and late fifteenth century lease-hold for terms of years developed, often conveyed by means of an indenture.

The length of the leases gradually increased. In the early fifteenth century leases were rarely granted for more than twenty years, and often for less than ten. In the mid-fifteenth century terms lengthened, to twenty, forty or more years. By the early sixteenth century, although fifty- or sixty-year terms do occasionally occur, by far

---

[3] Reg. Carpenter, i, fo. 183.
[4] Blockley AR, 1458–9.
[5] Bibury AR, 1450–1.

the commonest were leases of seventy, eighty and ninety-nine years; leases for lives appear occasionally only.[6]

These developments helped to increase the attractiveness of the lands for the tenants. The precariousness of tenure at will was replaced by the more certain leasehold; the term came to exceed the normal lifespan of a tenant, until it covered a number of generations. It should be added (see Figure 1) that leasehold rents declined in the early fifteenth century, recovered slightly in mid-century, and then remained stable.

The lessees were a socially mixed group. The great majority were peasantry and gentry, but there was also a smattering of clergy and merchants. Of course, the peasantry predominated as lessees on those manors, such as Henbury and Kempsey, where the demesnes were parcelled out in small quantities. Among the farmers of complete demesnes, the peasantry were initially the most numerous group; the ten identifiable lessees of 1420 consisted of seven peasants, a carpenter, a cleric and a single representative of the gentry, John Wode, who leased Whitstones. By 1540 the situation had been reversed. Of thirteen lessees whose social position is known, ten were gentry with titles of gentleman, esquire, and knight, one was a cleric, one a citizen of London, with only one demonstrable peasant, Thomas Yardington of Cleeve. The changeover from peasantry to gentry was a gradual movement of the late fifteenth and early sixteenth centuries, coinciding with the lengthening of the leasehold terms. A few of these gentry tenants were also estate administrators, notably John Wode, Thomas Arnold and John Hornyhold, and it should be emphasized that their acquisition of demesnes, often on favourable terms, represented a form of patronage from the bishops.[7]

How did the farmers run the demesnes? Were they innovators in their management, and did their position as lessees change their lives significantly?

A distinction must be drawn between the peasant lessees of the early fifteenth century and their socially superior successors.

[6] The Ripple demesne was leased for three lives in 1468, Reg. Carpenter, i, fo. 220.

[7] On leases as patronage, see Du Boulay, *Lordship of Canterbury*, pp. 232–3.

The period of peasant demesne farmers represents a transitional phase between direct management under a tenant reeve and later leasing. Often the peasant farmers seemed to be the natural choice, as they had served as reeves and in other official positions. They were also subordinate to the lord, as customary tenants and sometimes as serfs (*nativi*). An example is John Hale of Bredon, who farmed the demesne there at various times between 1401 and 1440; he held a customary yardland holding, and was described as a *nativus*. He served in various offices on the manor, as beadle, reeve and affeeror. He held the demesne at will, for brief terms of four and seven years, and his tenure was supervised through the manorial court, which sometimes ordered him to repair the buildings of the manor. He paid a great deal in rent for the Bredon demesnes: for example, £20 and £23 per annum in the first two decades of the fifteenth century, as compared with as little as £14 and £16 later in the century. Demesne leasing clearly presented Hale with economic opportunities, but the restrictions on him inhibited his ability to take full advantage.[8]

The experience of taking on a large demesne required a considerable adjustment on the part of the peasant, who encountered commodity production and the need to employ labour on a scale that he would not have known before. The need to sell large quantities of produce sometimes led peasant farmers to develop their links with market towns. William Mondy and Robert Otehull, lessees of the Blockley demesne from 1446, joined the Guild of the Holy Cross at Stratford-on-Avon at about the same time. Thomas Russhemere farmed the Kempsey demesne from 1408 to 1438. He was often involved in pleas of debt and trespass with other tenants while he was farmer. From 1438, when his lease finished, Russhemere appears regularly in the court records as miller, brewer and a victualler (*vitillarius*), selling bread and ale in a tavern. Perhaps this peasant farmer was encouraged by his period of commodity production to take up other commercial activities in his retirement. Russhemere died in 1450 with a substantial customary holding of two messuages, a yardland and 3 acres.[9]

[8] Bredon AR, 1407–8, 1411–12, 1421–2, 1427–8; Bredon CR's July 1398–Dec. 1409.
[9] Blockley AR, 1458–9; *The Register of the Gild of the Holy Cross...of Stratford-upon-Avon*, ed. J. H. Bloom (London, 1907), pp. 98–9; Kempsey CR's, Oct. 1408–April 1450; WCRO ref. 009:1 BA 2636/9 43696, fo. 127.

The most successful peasant lessee was Thomas Yardington, who held the Cleeve demesne from 1471 to 1525. A rental of 1474–5 shows that he held a customary tenement of only 6 acres. Between 1488 and his death Yardington occupied various positions of responsibility, as reeve, bailiff and juror in the manor court. When the demesne was granted in 1541 to Yardington's son, another Thomas, he was described in the indenture as a yeoman, which suggests that demesne farming had led to the promotion of the family from smallholding to a high status within their community.[10] Another kind of social mobility is illustrated by the history of the Boys family of Wick. John Boys leased the Wick demesne in the 1420s and William Boys followed him in the 1430s. Both were described as *nativi*. By c.1450 William was claiming to be free and in 1452 he was living off the manor at nearby Kenswick. Five years later he was described as farmer of the Kenswick demesne, which suggests that his activities as a lessee had provided him with an escape route from servility.[11]

When the demesne was leased in small parcels to a number of tenants there was a tendency (at Kempsey, for example) for the distribution of leasehold land to reflect the existing structure of landholding within the village community. Thirty-seven tenants became lessees of the Kempsey demesne in 1471; we know something of the customary landholding of eighteen of them, and they seem to represent a cross-section of the tenant population, weighted somewhat towards the wealthier peasants, with four smallholders, nine half-yardlanders and five with a yardland or more. At Henbury the smallholders were more prominent. Ten of the thirty-three lessees of the early sixteenth century held less than a half-yardland, usually a five-acre tenement. Of the others, fourteen held half-yardlands, and nine had a yardland or more. The acquisition of parcels of demesne could make a great difference to the position of individuals. Among the Henbury tenants John Washborough held only 5 acres by customary tenure, but in about 1530 he was the lessee of 44½ acres on an eighty-year term, so surpassing in landed resources the most substantial villagers of previous generations. Leasing of this type could greatly modify the

---

[10] Cleeve AR and CR, *passim*; WCRO ref. 009:1 BA. 2636/37 (iii) 43806, fos. 58–9.
[11] WCRO ref. 009:1 BA 2636/9 43696, fo. 125; Rec. AR, 1433–5; WCRO ref. 009:1 BA 2636/193 92627 10/12; Wick CR, Oct. 1452, Oct. 1457.

landholding structure of a peasant community. The farmers could also change the use of the lands that they gained. The demesnes at Henbury and Stoke, which had contained large arable acreages under the lord's management up to the 1390s, consisted mainly of enclosed pastures by the early sixteenth century.[12]

In the long run the non-peasant lessees gained most from the tenure of the demesnes. They tended to take on the leases from the mid-fifteenth century onwards, when the terms were becoming more favourable. Their resources were greater than those of the peasantry, so they were more easily able to make technical innovations, particularly enclosures. In c.1450 we find three separate references to these activities. John Wode, the Whitstones farmer, had exchanged lands with other tenants and enclosed a furlong. At Stratford, 'the tenants of Shottery claim to have common... within the demesne lands of the lord, newly enclosed by John Huggeford [the lessee], and occupied by him in severalty'. There were also complaints at Wick: 'Enquire if William Pullesdon, the farmer of the demesne land, or his deputy, has occupied or usurped any land of the lord's tenants, except those which were occupied of old by the farmer. And if William has made any enclosures or ditches to the annoyance of the tenants or the prejudice of the lord.'[13]

Some of the lessees, those with mercantile backgrounds, could have brought capital acquired through trade into agriculture: these were Richard Baylly, a Bristol merchant who took a lease of the Stoke demesne in 1447; Thomas Busshe of Northleach, who leased Withington in 1510; Walter Knight, citizen of London, who leased Wick in 1526; Thomas Davys of Stow-on-the-Wold, to whom Stapenhill pasture in Blockley was leased in 1508; Walter Hykks and Robert Arche, both of Winchcomb, who leased Wontley pasture in Cleeve in about 1480; and probably also Thomas Arnold of Cirencester, the lessee of Bibury who was also an estate official.[14] Presumably these merchants applied their expertise to the marketing of the produce, and it is possible that the Cotswold sheep pastures

[12] Kempsey AR, 1505–6; WCRO ref. 009:1 BA 2636/37 (iii), fos. 115–19.
[13] St. Johns view, April 1450; WCRO ref. 009:1 BA 2636/193 92627 10/12.
[14] For Baylly, see Dyer, 'A Redistribution of Incomes', p. 29; for Busshe, Knight and Davys, see WCRO ref. 009:1 BA 2636/37 (iii), 43806, fos. 287, 254, 26; Hykks and Arche, Cleeve AR, 1486–7; Arnold see chapter 6. There are many European parallels for a combination of mercantile and grazing activities, e.g. D. Herlihy, *Pisa in the Early Renaissance* (New Haven, 1958), pp. 177–9.

were acquired by wool merchants so that they were able to produce their own commodities. Certainly Busshe was a Merchant of the Staple with land in four (wool-producing) counties, and Thomas Arnold was a 'woolman'.[15]

When the demesnes were taken by a gentleman lessee, they became part of an economic organization quite different from the bishopric estate. Sometimes the new arrangement can be seen to have a potential for efficient management; for example, William Harewell esquire leased the Stratford demesne between 1464 and 1500. This fitted well into the group of lands already held by Harewell in the Stratford district, notably at Shottery and Wootton Wawen. One of the advantages enjoyed by a landowner like Harewell was the personal supervision that he could give his lands, without the cumbersome bureaucracy found on a great estate.[16]

The new grouping of lands might be more specialized in its productive capacity than the old estate. For example, Thomas Bleke was a Cotswold grazier who occupied demesnes with extensive pastures at Bibury, Blockley and Withington in the mid-fifteenth century.[17]

For many gentry lessees the demesnes were probably not run as agricultural enterprises under direct management, but were simply sublet. This seems inevitable when we find that the leasehold lands were remote from the other lands of the tenant, like the Solihull estate of John Boteler, for example, fifteen miles from the Hampton demesne which he leased in 1507. Nor could a busy lawyer like William Grevile have devoted much time to the management of his pasture of Upper Ditchford in Blockley, also acquired in 1507.[18]

The name of the subtenant or deputy farmer is sometimes revealed in court rolls, or in accounts when he paid money direct to the bishop's receiver. In the 1460s the Bredon demesne was leased to Thomas Haukyns, Master of St Oswald's Hospital at Worcester, but cash liveries were made on his behalf by John Tasker, described

[15] Postan and Power (eds.), *Studies in English Trade in the Fifteenth Century,* pp. 53–4.

[16] Stratford AR, 1464–5; WCRO ref. 009:1 BA 2636/37 (iii) 43806, fo. 206; W. Cooper, *Wootton Wawen, its History and Records* (Leeds, 1936), pp. 16–18.

[17] Bibury AR, 1450–1; Blockley AR, 1458–9; Rec. AR, 1433–5.

[18] WCRO ref. 009:1 BA 2636/37 (iii) 43806, fos. 136 (Boteler), 23 (Grevile); *VCH Warks.*, iv, pp. 68, 257.

as the farmer. He was a customary yardlander on the manor, and presumably the actual cultivator of the demesne.[19]

In spite of the changes introduced by some farmers, they were still confronted by the same basic problems as had caused the bishops to lease the demesnes in the first place. Stagnant agricultural prices continued throughout the fifteenth century and into the first two decades of the sixteenth; wage labour continued to be expensive. The complete demesnes were too large to be cultivated with family labour, though some lessees who lived near the leased manor could have consumed produce directly, such as the Dean of Westbury College, who leased the Stoke demesne in 1523.[20] The problems of large-scale production for the market in the period have already been mentioned; the supply of grain by farmers to the bishop's household in lieu of cash payments being one piece of evidence for the difficulties of selling produce.

One explanation of the lessee's economic position was that his profits may have been no greater than the bishop's when the manor had been under direct management, but that the lessee would have been content with a relatively small margin. For example, when the demesne at Stoke was managed by a reeve in the 1380s its profits were about £10 per annum. The demesne was leased in the early fifteenth century to Walter Filly, a carpenter, for £5 13s. 4d. If the demesne continued to produce profits of £10, Filly would have retained about £4 after paying his rent. For a carpenter, who could not normally have earned more than £4 or £5 in a year, the profits of the demesne, though meagre by the bishop's standards, represented a small fortune, a doubling of his income.[21]

It is also likely that some lessees made the demesnes more profitable through investment, technical innovation and concentration on the most marketable products. Some could exercise a flexible, personal management over the land, and change land-use and crops with much more ease than the old estate bureaucracy.

There can be no doubt that the leased demesnes became very desirable assets in the mid-sixteenth century. Most had been granted out in the early years of the century on very long terms for the same rents as in the late fifteenth century. As inflation

[19]   Bredon AR, 1463–4, 1468–9.
[20]   WCRO ref. 009:1 BA 2636/37 (iii) 43806, fo. 186.
[21]   Stoke AR, 1411–12.

developed, the gentry who held many of the large demesnes or enclosed pastures, and the peasantry of such manors as Henbury and Kempsey, enjoyed the advantages of selling highly priced agricultural produce while paying a fixed rent. This must have contributed to the wealth of yeoman farmers, and to some prominent gentry families, like the Greviles, Russells, Cloptons and Blounts.

Demesne leasing represents one way in which the social changes of the later middle ages led to the creation of agricultural units of middling to large size, from John Washborough's 50 acres, to the 500-acre demesnes held by some of the gentry lessees. It is possible to see these as embryonic capitalist farms of modern type, with tenants enjoying long term control of extensive lands, investing in buildings, enclosures, equipment and stock, relying for their labour supply on wage-earners, and pursuing profits by production for the market on a considerable scale.

Leasing provides an example of an institutional change that could have far-reaching social and economic consequences. Its impact was limited by the relatively few individuals and small amount of land involved. In order to investigate developments among the majority of the estate's tenants, we must examine the range of factors that led to more general social change – population, lord–tenant relationships, landholding, land-management and the market.

9. Population change, 1348–1540

Recent interpretations of medieval social and economic history have been dominated by the idea that population change lies at the root of other developments. Before this hypothesis can be accepted, we need to know much more about the demographic history of the period.

The date of the beginning of the late medieval population decline is a matter for controversy, with opinions ranging between c.1300 and the first plague outbreak of 1348–9. There is general agreement that population had reached a low level by the end of the fourteenth century, but when did expansion begin? Both J. C. Russell and J. M. W. Bean, using different evidence, believe that recovery was in progress in England by the 1450s, and this finds some support from continental experience.[1] M. M. Postan, arguing from such indirect evidence as rents and wages, regards the 1470s as a turning point. I. S. W. Blanchard finds that the upswing that began in the 1470s was not continuous, but was checked soon after 1500, and decisive expansion did not resume until the 1520s.[2]

The problem is therefore one of explaining, not just a sharp reduction in population, but a long period, probably approaching two centuries, of demographic decline and stagnation. This is particularly puzzling in view of the well-known capacity of populations to make good the losses of even catastrophic mortality. Most medievalists invoke continued high mortality from disease as the main factor. Both J. M. W. Bean and T. H. Hollingsworth believe that periodic outbursts of bubonic plague kept the population down until the third quarter of the fifteenth century. J. Hatcher sees the effects of plague and other diseases continuing to have a depressing effect on the population until the 1520s. S. Thrupp describes the period as the 'golden age of the bacteria', and hints at the unknown

---

[1] J. C. Russell, *British Medieval Population* (Albuquerque, 1948), p. 280; J. M. W. Bean, 'Plague, Population, and Economic Decline in England in the Later Middle Ages', *Econ. Hist. Rev.*, 2nd ser., xv (1963), pp. 423–37; M.-T. Lorcin, *Les Campagnes de la Région Lyonnaise aux XIVe et XVe siècles* (Lyons, 1974), pp. 209–32.

[2] M. M. Postan, 'Some Agrarian Evidence of Declining Population in the Later Middle Ages', in *Essays on Medieval Agriculture and General Problems*, pp. 186–213; I. S. W. Blanchard, 'Population Change, Enclosure, and the Early Tudor Economy', *Econ. Hist. Rev.*, 2nd ser., xxiii (1970), pp. 427–45.

biological effects of the fourteenth-century plagues on subsequent generations. Fisher stresses the importance of influenza epidemics as a check on population growth in the mid-sixteenth century.[3] A dissenting voice is provided by an epidemiologist, J. F. D. Shrewsbury, who was sceptical of the high levels of mortality claimed for the fourteenth-century epidemics, and in particular denied the major rôle ascribed to bubonic plague in the later middle ages, substituting as possible causes of high mortality a catalogue of other infectious diseases.[4] Demographers with experience of later, better-documented pre-industrial populations, such as Helleiner and Wrigley, doubt that fluctuations in the death-rate can have been the sole cause of population change in the late medieval period.[5] Bean's work could well be used to support their view. He argues that as there is little evidence for plague outbreaks in the late fifteenth century, the population must have expanded. It could be suggested that, as much evidence suggests continued demographic stagnation long after 1450, some other factor must have been affecting the population, such as the birth-rate.

Blaming disease for demographic change is perhaps too easy an escape from the problems of the later middle ages. If biological factors are seen as the driving force behind change, social and economic developments become mere side-effects of natural phenomena. If epidemics are found not to have determined the level of population, the historian is left with the difficult task of investigating the ways in which social change could have influenced demography.[6]

Much of the data used hitherto for demographic analysis tends to relate to social groups that may not be representative of the popula-

---

[3] Bean, 'Plague, Population, and Economic Decline in England', pp. 423–37; T. H. Hollingsworth, *Historical Demography* (London, 1969), pp. 380–8; J. Hatcher, *Plague, Population and the English Economy, 1348–1530* (London, 1977), pp. 63–7; S. Thrupp, 'The Problem of Replacement Rates in Late Medieval English Population', *Econ. Hist. Rev.*, 2nd ser., xviii (1965), pp. 101–19; F. J. Fisher, 'Influenza and Inflation in Tudor England', *Econ. Hist. Rev.*, 2nd ser., xviii (1965), pp. 120–9.
[4] J. F. D. Shrewsbury, *A History of the Bubonic Plague in the British Isles* (Cambridge, 1970), pp. 1–156.
[5] K. F. Helleiner, 'The Population of Europe', in *Camb. Econ. Hist. of Europe*, iv, pp. 68–79; E. A. Wrigley, *Population and History* (London, 1969), pp. 79–80.
[6] For a criticism of the demographic hypothesis, see R. Brenner, 'Agrarian Class Structure and Economic Development in Pre-Industrial Europe', *P and P*, lxx (1976), pp. 30–75.

tion as a whole, such as tenants-in-chief of the crown, the wealthier inhabitants of towns, the parish clergy, or even monks. Most of our evidence for epidemics comes from the vague and probably inaccurate reports of chroniclers.

Direct demographic evidence occurs most frequently in manorial records in the form of statements in court rolls to the effect that tenants have died. Deaths were promptly reported in the Worcester bishopric court rolls. Before 1490 the month in which the tenant died is given; after 1490 the formula used is that 'John Smyth died since the last court.' As the court roll provided customary tenants with evidence of title, it was in the interests of the heir or new tenant to have the transfer of property following a death properly registered.

Records of tenant deaths must be handled with great care, as not all tenants died while holding land. The sick or aged might surrender their land and retire, and their deaths would not be mentioned. So the number of deaths appearing in court rolls is no more than the number of tenants who died while still in possession of a holding; however the effects of epidemics should be reflected, and the deaths recorded will be the most demographically significant. The demise of a retired, elderly tenant, whose reproductive career had ended, would not affect subsequent generations, but deaths of young and middle-aged tenants would disrupt the procreation of the next generation. Thus the deaths of sitting tenants cannot be regarded as *the* death-rate in the same way as the burial entries in a parish register, but they ought to reflect the extremes of epidemic years, and should indicate the extent to which adults were dying prematurely.

Fortunately we have some indication of the size of the population group within which the deaths occurred, in the form of rentals, and the lists of tenants compiled to check on court attendance in 1544. Tenant numbers did not change greatly from year to year, or even over longer periods, so that it is possible to estimate with reasonable accuracy the tenant population, and thus roughly calculate the proportion of those tenants who died in a particular year.

The numbers of deaths come from court rolls recording the proceedings in more than 1,300 courts and views of frankpledge. The best series relates to Kempsey, with only a few breaks between 1432 and 1539. There is information from three other manors, Bredon, Hanbury, and Whitstones, between 1375 and 1400, some material from nine manors in the fifteenth century, and for all manors in some years in the early sixteenth. The period 1430–1520 is most fully documented, and some gaps can be filled by the lists of heriots in early sixteenth-century accounts.

The validity of the method can be tested by comparing the mortality evidence from court rolls with other sources. The Hartlebury court rolls can be used in conjunction with the probates of wills recorded in the court of peculiar jurisdiction for the parish.[7] The probates cover a wide section of the community, as all inhabitants, including women, might make wills. In forty-five documented years between 1403 and 1528 the number of probates in most years varied from one to five. They exceeded six in only five years, with the highest numbers in 1465, when there were nine, and 1473, when there were fifteen. The court rolls of Hartlebury record about two tenant deaths per annum, and the largest number appears in 1473–4, when seven tenants died. So both sources agree in identifying 1473 as a year of exceptionally high mortality, with at least three times the normal number of deaths.

It is also possible to compare court-roll evidence with parish registers in the 1540s. Parish registers and narrative sources record an epidemic in the years 1543–6 in many parts of England. J. F. D. Shrewsbury accepts that this was an outbreak of bubonic plague, as it caused high mortality in the late summer. The epidemic reached the west midlands in 1545, when nearly 220 burials, compared with a normal annual figure of fewer than a hundred, are recorded in the parish registers of six Worcester parishes.[8]

A complete set of court rolls survives for the bishopric estate from the autumn of 1544 to the spring of 1546, and these can be compared with similar records for the 1520s and 1530s. At this time courts were held twice each year, so that each group of court rolls lists the deaths that had taken place in the previous six months. Usually between eleven and fifteen deaths occurred in each six-month period, but forty-seven tenants died in the summer of 1545, and fifty-four in the following winter. So the mortality of 1545–6 caused an increase of between three and four times in the number of deaths. The percentage of tenants who died can be calculated by using the lists of tenants of 1544. There were about nine hundred and fifteen

[7] WCRO ref. 009:1 BA 2636/11 43700.
[8] Shrewsbury, *A History of Bubonic Plague*, pp. 178–82; A. D. Dyer, *The City of Worcester in the Sixteenth Century* (Leicester, 1973), p. 21.

individual tenants, so that the normal death rate in the court rolls
of the 1520s and 1530s of twenty or thirty per annum (eleven to fifteen in each six-month period) represents a 2 per cent to 3 per cent
mortality. In 1545–6 one hundred and one tenants, 11 per cent of the
total, died. There was much variation between manors, from as
little as 5 per cent at Alvechurch to 20 per cent at Blockley and
25 per cent at Cleeve. As well as showing a close correlation between
the evidence of court rolls and parish registers, the 1545–6 plague
provides a yardstick by which the effects of other epidemics can
be judged.

The evidence of death-rates in court rolls and other sources will
not correspond exactly, as the tenants are imperfectly representative of the whole population. They were mainly men between the
ages of twenty and sixty; women are under-represented, and children omitted. Nonetheless, the tenants cover a wide range of landholding groups in society, from gentry to cottagers, and are more
characteristic of the population as a whole than some of the groups
hitherto studied in medieval demographic research. Of course, the
main disadvantage in using tenant deaths for demographic history
is the small size of the tenant population. On a manor with fifty
tenants – that is, a manor of above average size in the fifteenth
century – the occurrence of five deaths represents a major demographic episode. This is a ludicrously small sample by the standards
of modern population analysis, yet medievalists have to use such
information as is available, while remaining aware of the dangers of
basing too much on fragments of evidence. This examination of
deaths on the bishopric of Worcester manors is offered only as a
preliminary to a wider investigation based on dozens of court-roll
series. This further study would also involve series less broken than
those of the Worcester bishopric, which cover most of the years
between 1375 and 1540, but with gaps in the early fifteenth and
early sixteenth centuries.

The method of investigation has been to find the years in which the
largest numbers of tenant deaths occurred. A guide to the selection
of the worst years has been R. Schofield's definition of 'crisis
mortality'.[9] This was devised for use in analysing parish registers,
and applies to all years in which there was a doubling of the normal

⁹ R. Schofield, 'Crisis Mortality', *Local Population Studies*, ix (1972), pp. 10–22.

death-rate. As the normal rate was usually about thirty per thousand, crisis mortality was reached at about sixty per thousand. This has been applied to court rolls by calculating the number of deaths corresponding to 6 per cent of the tenant population, so that Kempsey, for example, where there were about eighty tenants, experienced crisis mortality when five or more died.

At Kempsey the court-roll series is fragmentary between 1394 and 1421, full from 1432 to 1518 and with patchy records between 1520 and 1539. The worst years for tenant deaths were 1455–6, 1464–5, 1471–2, 1488, 1499–1500, 1524–5, 1525–6, 1528–9 and 1536. In each case a twelve-month period is involved, but these often ran over the winter, so that, for example, the deaths of the first year mentioned are recorded in courts held in October 1455 and in January and April 1456. In each twelve-month period mentioned between five and eight tenants died, thus fulfilling the criteria for high mortality mentioned above. The average mortality among tenants recorded in the court rolls was about two per annum. The Kempsey figures suggest that there was an episode of high mortality in almost every decade covered by the documents, except in the 1430s, 1440s and 1510s, but with a concentration of years of high mortality in the 1520s.

At Hanbury, where the series begins earlier, the worst twelve-month periods were in 1442–3, 1452, 1453–4, 1465 and 1522–3. At Bredon the only year of high mortality recorded was in 1400, and at Whitstones, with a fuller series of records, the only bad year was in 1397–8. On the manors with more fragmentary records high tenant mortality occurred in 1462–3, 1473–4, 1503–4, 1524–5 and in the late 1530s.[10]

Our initial conclusion is that years with a high mortality cor-

[10] The years of high mortality are as follows. Each twelve-month period is followed by the number of deaths in brackets:

Kempsey 1455–6 (5), 1464–5 (6), 1471–2 (5), 1488 (5), 1499–1500 (5), 1524–5 (8), 1525–6 (5), 1528–9 (5), 1536 (5), 1545–6 (10)
Hanbury 1442–3 (6), 1452 (4), 1453–4 (4), 1465 (4), 1522–3 (4), 1545–6 (5)
Bredon 1400 (5), 1545–6 (7)
Whitstones 1397–8 (5), 1545–6 (9)
Wick 1473 (5), 1545–6 (4)
Hampton 1503–4 (4), 1545–6 (4)
Hartlebury 1473–4 (7), 1545–6 (4)
Henbury 1537–8 (10), 1538–9 (7), 1545–6 (9)
Cleeve 1462–3 (4), 1524–5 (5), 1538 (4), 1545–6 (13)

responding to or exceeding the 6 per cent figure mentioned above were a regular feature of our whole period. Their apparent absence in the early fifteenth century, and to some extent in the 1510s, could reflect lacunae in the series of documents. The episodes of high mortality were more frequent than in the early modern period investigated by Schofield. On the basis of this evidence no-one can deny that bouts of mortality, presumably associated with epidemics, played some part in keeping the late medieval population at a low level.

The evidence does not fully support some of the demographic theories outlined earlier. There is no sign of any great slackening of mortality in the late fifteenth century, or after 1520. If there was a respite in the first two decades of the sixteenth century, this was compensated by a concentration of bad years in the 1520s and 1530s. If episodes of high death-rates were the only force behind population change, then there would have been little scope for increase in the early sixteenth century. Indeed, it is doubtful if there would have been any expansion before 1570, in view of the plague of 1545 – the severity of which is reflected in our documents – and the sweating sickness and plagues of the 1550s and 1560s, attested by other sources.[11] The increased mortalities of the early sixteenth century can be found also in evidence of deaths among parish clergy. In Derbyshire, for example, of the six years with the highest numbers of deaths between 1400 and 1550, four occurred after 1500.[12]

The fifteenth-century mortalities do not seem to have been especially virulent. Most of the bad years at Kempsey involved the deaths of five tenants, the minimum needed for them to qualify as crisis mortality. The worst year known was at Hanbury in 1442–3, when six tenants, about a tenth of the total, died. In the case of almost every manor, the death-rate in 1545–6 was much higher than in any year in the previous century and a half. At Kempsey the 1545–6 epidemic claimed ten lives, double the number in most of the worst years of the fifteenth century. At Whitstones nine died, but there was not a single year when more than four deaths can be found in the period 1400–1540. Again, the death-rates among the parish clergy in the fifteenth century do not seem to have been

[11] Fisher, 'Influenza and Inflation', pp. 125–7; Shrewsbury, *A History of Bubonic Plague*, p. 200.
[12] Blanchard, 'Economic Change in Derbyshire in the Late Middle Ages', pp. 475–8.

particularly high, nor those found in contemporary continental sources, in the Lyonnais or at Arezzo.[13] It has sometimes been assumed that there were a series of 'national' plagues after the first fourteenth-century outbreaks, which became less frequent and less virulent in the late fifteenth and early sixteenth centuries.[14] Some of our years of high mortality coincide with these national epidemics recorded by chroniclers, notably in 1400, 1464–5 and 1471–3. Some supposed national plagues, such as those of 1375, 1479 and 1513, find no echoes in our documents. Instead, the 1545–6 epidemic stands out, with its high death-rate and geographical extent; here indeed was a national plague, but in the mid-sixteenth century.

To sum up, periods of exceptional mortality can be shown to have played an important rôle in the demographic history of the later middle ages. Before our court-roll series begins, the great plague of 1348–9 probably killed at least 40 per cent of the bishopric tenants (the evidence is discussed in Chapter 10). A very high mortality in the plagues of the 1360s is reflected in the deaths among the Worcester diocesan clergy and the tenants of neighbouring west-midland estates.[15] These epidemics helped to bring the population down to a low level by the 1370s. Recovery in the next century and a half must have been inhibited by recurrent mortality. But the fifteenth-century epidemics tended to be localized and not very virulent, and they intensified in frequency and severity in the 1520s and 1530s. As all of the available evidence suggests that the second quarter of the sixteenth century was a period of population growth, it appears that epidemics cannot be used as the sole explanation of demographic trends.

Court rolls do not generally record the cause of the tenant's death. The only exceptions in our series are one tenant who was murdered, two cases of judicial execution and two accidental drownings. We can make some inferences, however, from analysis of the seasonal

---

[13] Blanchard, *ibid.*; Hatcher, *Rural Economy and Society in the Duchy of Cornwall*, pp. 292–4, shows that the annual total of institutions to Cornish benefices never rose above eight (5.2 per cent) between 1400 and 1460; Lorcin, *Les Campagnes de la Région Lyonnaise*, pp. 211–20; and the mortality recorded at Arezzo between 1373 and 1531, J.-N. Biraben, *Les Hommes et la Peste en France et dans les Pays Européens et Mediterranéens* (Paris, 1975), p. 193.

[14] Hollingsworth, *Historical Demography*, pp. 358, 385.

[15] Reg. Bryan, i, fos. 85–6; GRO D678/99; WCL E20.

pattern of mortality, as the month of death is recorded in the court rolls up to 1490 (see Fig. 4).

Students of English parish registers find that the normal pattern is a peak of burials in the spring, followed by a falling number in the summer, rising again in the late autumn and winter.[16] The month of March often saw the highest death-rate, and August and September the lowest. As some infectious diseases, notably bubonic plague, were most active in the late summer, the seasonal distribution of deaths in epidemics often stands out in contrast to normal years.

Some of the years of high mortality listed can be shown to be concentrated in the late summer: for example, in 1400 at Bredon, and on a number of manors in 1471-3. This latter outbreak was probably not plague but dysentery, judging from the description of symptoms by a contemporary chronicler. A Henbury account of 1472-3 refers to a drought in the summer of 1473, and dysentery could well be associated with hot, dry weather.[17] In 1488 and 1499-1500 deaths are found in the winter period, which would be consistent with the development of influenza as a cause of death.

If the seasonal pattern of all recorded deaths, rather than those occurring in the worst years, is examined, the importance of summer infections, perhaps in endemic rather than epidemic form, is readily apparent. All recorded deaths in ten-year periods are gathered together in Fig. 4; this is necessary in order to obtain samples of adequate size. In every case a spring peak occurs, often in March, but sometimes in February, April or May; this is the 'normal' pattern. But in most decades a late summer or autumn peak in August, September or October exceeds that of the spring. The two exceptions are the 1430s, with no autumn peak, but an unusual proportion of deaths in June, and the 1480s, with an entirely 'normal' pattern. It seems likely then, that summer infections such as dysentery or plague were a significant cause of deaths for most of the period 1375-1480. This was also J. C. Russell's conclusion from an examination of the season of upper-class deaths recorded in Inquisitions post-mortem.[18] Our figures show a reduction in

[16] L. Bradley, 'An Enquiry into Seasonality in Baptisms, Marriages and Burials', *Local Population Studies*, vi (1971), pp. 15-30.

[17] C. Creighton, *A History of Epidemics in Britain*, 2nd edn (London, 1965), i, p. 231; Henbury AR, 1472-3.

[18] Russell, *British Medieval Population*, pp. 195-9.

J F M A M J J A S O N D
1375–99

= 1 recorded death

J F M A M J J A S O N D
1460–9

J F M A M J J A S O N D
1430–9

J F M A M J J A S O N D
1440–9

J F M A M J J A S O N D
1470–9

J F M A M J. J A S O N D
1450–9

J F M A M J J A S O N D
1480–9

4 Seasonal distribution of deaths. The deaths for which the month is recorded
have been brought together, from all manors, in periods, where possible, of ten
years

the number of deaths in late summer in the 1480s and Russell found the same phenomenon in the last quarter of the fifteenth century.

It would then be a plausible argument that endemic disease slackened after about 1480, thus allowing a growth in population. However, this was a short-lived phenomenon, as the high death-rates of the early sixteenth century show. Leaving aside the episodes of high mortality, the overall recorded death-rate after 1520 rises at Kempsey, for example, from an average of 1.9 per annum between 1430 and 1510 to 3.5 per annum in 1520–40. It is, however, hazardous to use such figures, as the number of deaths recorded could be distorted by such factors as changes in retirement patterns.

It is unlikely that many deaths can be connected with starvation in the period. A correlation between poor harvests and increased mortality has been demonstrated both before 1350 and after 1540.[19] We can identify the years of dearth between 1375 and 1540 (using Hoskins' and Harrison's definition of a dearth as a harvest year with prices 50 per cent or more above average) as 1390–1, 1409–10, 1437–8, 1438–9, 1482–3, 1520–1 and 1527–8.[20] This is based on Thorold Rogers' price series; using a Worcester series based on wheat valuations it is possible to add the years 1439–40 and 1469–70. The only significant relationship between these years and mortality occurs in 1437–40. Although these years do not qualify as a period of crisis mortality as defined above, there was an above average death-rate among tenants at Whitstones and Hanbury: of twelve deaths, seven were tenants of smallholdings of 3 acres or less, four had inadequate heriots, suggesting poverty, and some of the deaths occurred in the months of May, June, and July, when grain would have been in short supply. We can perhaps regard the dearth of the late 1430s as the last serious medieval famine; there were few dearths and little connection between them and mortality between 1440 and the mid-sixteenth century.

[19] Postan and Titow, 'Heriots and Prices on Winchester Manors', in *Essays in Medieval Agriculture and General Problems*, pp. 150–85; A. B. Appleby, 'Disease or Famine? Mortality in Cumberland and Westmorland, 1580–1640', *Econ. Hist. Rev.*, 2nd ser., xxvi (1973), pp. 403–32.

[20] W. G. Hoskins, 'Harvest Fluctuations and English Economic History, 1480–1619', *Ag. Hist. Rev.*, xii (1964), pp. 28–46; C. J. Harrison, 'Grain Price Analysis and Harvest Qualities, 1465–1634', *Ag. Hist. Rev.*, xix (1971), pp. 135–55.

The argument advanced so far, doubting that death-rates can provide the sole explanation for demographic change in the later middle ages, can be considered also in the light of data on the expectation of life. Court rolls make it possible to construct biographies of male tenants, from the point when they entered their first holding until their deaths. In theory, it should be possible to draw up many hundreds of biographies, but interruptions in the series of documents, and the incidence of migration and retirement, reduce the number to eighty-one from the three most fully documented manors.

The age at which tenants entered their first holdings can be calculated in a few cases where the date of 'swearing into assize' is also known. This inclusion in the tithing system happened at the age of twelve, and the gap between this event and the same individual taking on land for the first time varies from six to twenty-one years. The median period is eleven years; that is when the tenant was aged twenty-three. The lengths of tenancies are indicated in Table 33.

The conclusion must be drawn that a male tenant who survived until his early twenties could expect to live for another twenty-three to twenty-five years. These figures derive from a lengthy period, and include men born between 1410 and 1480. The majority were born before 1450, so they lived through the period of population stagnation of the mid-fifteenth century. The figures must represent a minimum: the most long-lived tenants would tend to have retired, so that their deaths would not be recorded. Even so, the life-expectation of peasants calculated here is only slightly below the figures of twenty-seven to thirty at the age of twenty calculated by Russell and Thrupp for contemporary tenants-in-chief and merchants. It is comparable with the figure of twenty-four at the age

Table 33. *Length of tenancies as an indicator of life-expectation, 1447–1522*

Manor	No. of tenants	Average length of tenancy in years	Date range of deaths
Hanbury	15	23.6	1447–89
Kempsey	48	23.0	1452–1522
Whitstones	19	24.8	1453–1505

of twenty found in mid-thirteenth century England, in a period of population growth.[21]

Any demographic analysis must consider the birth-rate and the size of families, but these are notoriously difficult to quantify in our period. By a combination of circumstances, resulting from the perpetuation of serfdom on the estate into the sixteenth century, a number of censuses of serfs have survived in the court rolls. The first evidence of a census comes from 1450, but the main body of material relates to the year of Bishop Alcock's succession in 1476, and sporadically in the early sixteenth century, in 1514, 1520 and 1536–9.[22] Most of the serfs lived at Kempsey and Whitstones, but the censuses cover seven manors. The serfs were socially diverse, including tenants of holdings of various sizes, and some who were apparently landless.

The census entries normally state the name of the father and of his children, including those living away from home. The purpose of the census, it should be remembered, was to record the legitimate blood ties by which the servile condition was transmitted. The census figures are given in Table 34. More sons than daughters are recorded; this is a well-known phenomenon in medieval documents, taken to reflect the low status of women. As well as the average number of recorded children per family, a corrected average has also been given, based on the assumption that in reality the balance of the sexes was roughly equal. It is possible that there were really fewer girls than boys, the result of such a factor as a lower standard of care of females in infancy. Figures are also given derived from wills of inhabitants of the bishopric manors, most of them tenants of the bishops, again with averages of the numbers of children actually mentioned by the testators, and a corrected average for daughters.

The samples are again too small for a great deal to be built on them, but they can be supported from other sources. In 1476 the uncorrected average of 1.92 would indicate a population failing to

[21] Russell, *British Medieval Population*, p. 186; S. Thrupp, *The Merchant Class of Medieval London* (Michigan, 1962), pp. 194–5; Postan and Titow, 'Heriots and Prices on Winchester Manors', p. 154.

[22] Hampton CR, Oct. 1476, July 1514; Kempsey CR, Oct. 1476, July 1514, Oct. 1536; Whitstones CR, Oct. 1476, Sept. 1520, Oct. 1536, Jan. 1538; Bredon CR, May 1520, Oct. 1538; Ripple CR, April 1520, April 1538, March 1539; Fladbury CR, Sept. 1537.

Table 34. Family sizes, 1476–1540

1. From censuses of serfs, 1476–1539

Date	Number of families	Number of children recorded	Average number of recorded children per family	Number of children, corrected*	Corrected average number of children per family
1476	38	73	1.92	88	2.32
1514–20	34	93	2.74	114	3.35
1536–9	25	62	2.48	68	2.72

2. From wills of inhabitants of bishopric manors, 1511–40

Number of testators	Number of children recorded	Average number of recorded children per testator	Number of children corrected*	Corrected average number of children per testator
38	101	2.66	110	2.89

*Correction is achieved by allowing for unrecorded daughters, assuming equal numbers of sons and daughters.

replace itself. After correction, though producing an average still relatively small (2.32), a modest capacity for growth is implied. Both figures are higher than the replacement rates calculated by Professor Thrupp from rather earlier fifteenth-century court rolls, but these are not really comparable.[23] It is still likely that these figures are greater than those prevailing for much of the fifteenth century and could indicate the beginnings of the upward movement in population in the 1470s postulated by Professor Postan.

By the early sixteenth century the average number of serfs' children had risen to 2.74 and 2.48 (observed average) or 3.35 and 2.72 (corrected average), an increase of between 20 per cent and 40 per cent. The wills, most of which belong to the 1530s, produce figures similar to the census figures of that decade. A similar pattern of rising family size affected the inhabitants of the city of Worcester in the early sixteenth century, but a decade or so later than is implied by this evidence. The only medieval English serf census with which comparison can be made is that of the Spalding Priory manors in Lincolnshire in the late thirteenth century. This gives an average of 4.68 for the whole family – that is, 2.68 children – and so is comparable with our figures for the 1530s. Both clearly belong to periods of population growth.[24]

The conclusion that can be drawn from the evidence presented here must be that no single factor will explain the demographic trends of the later middle ages. Of course epidemics reduced the population in the period 1348–75, and their continuation made some contribution to the long-term stagnation after 1375. But the demographic situation was complex, and changes in family size, perhaps reflecting birth-rates, must be taken into account.

After 1540, when the evidence becomes more abundant, a combination of high birth-rates with large completed families counteracted the effect of a relatively high death-rate, producing an overall expansion in population.[25] This particular conjunction of factors could perhaps be pushed back to about 1520. In the fifteenth century death-rates could have been lower than in the sixteenth century,

[23] Thrupp, 'The Problem of Replacement Rates', pp. 110–14; for criticisms, see Hatcher, *Plague, Population, and the English Economy*, pp. 28–9.

[24] Dyer, *The City of Worcester in the Sixteenth Century*, p. 35; H. E. Hallam, 'Some Thirteenth Century Censuses', *Econ. Hist. Rev.*, 2nd ser., x (1958), pp. 340–61.

[25] Dyer, *The City of Worcester in the Sixteenth Century*, pp. 20–5.

but family sizes were also low, so that the population stagnated. Possible reasons for low family sizes are:

1 A high level of infant and child mortality. It is possible that some diseases, like plague, dysentery, or other summer infections, affected children more drastically than adults.[26]

2 A low level of nuptiality, with late marriage. A 'European' marriage pattern, with late marriage and a high rate of celibacy, may have been adopted in the fifteenth century.[27] References to prostitution, even in rural areas, in the bishopric records could reflect the frustrations resulting from such a marriage pattern (see Chapter 17).

3 Deliberate family limitation. The experience of Colyton in Devon in the seventeenth century, where after a catastrophic plague births were limited so that the population stagnated, provides a useful parallel.[28] Medieval writers were fully aware of the existence of contraceptive practices, which were recounted in detail by the inhabitants of the Pyrennean village of Montaillou to an episcopal inquisition in the early fourteenth century.[29] At Hartlebury in the fifteenth century the church court dealt with two cases of abortion. In 1408 Alice Kynvare was said to have 'poisoned a child in the womb of Alice Brayles', and Agnes Consall was accused in 1494 of administering to a single girl who was pregnant 'certain medicines with herbs to destroy the child in her womb'.[30] Unfortunately occasional references to contraception or abortion are not susceptible to quantification.

4 A low level of fertility within marriage as a result of disease or poverty.

All that we know of the economic climate in the fifteenth-century countryside makes poverty an unlikely cause of low rates of marriage, late marriage or low fertility. Such factors as readily available land and high wages should have led to frequent and early marriage, and high fertility. We have seen that very bad harvests and deaths

[26] This is suggested in Thrupp, *Merchant Class of Medieval London*, pp. 200–5.

[27] J. Hajnal, 'European Marriage Patterns in Perspective', in D. V. Glass and D. E. C. Eversley (eds.), *Population in History* (London, 1965), pp. 101–35.

[28] E. A. Wrigley, 'Family Limitation in Pre-Industrial England', *Econ. Hist. Rev.*, 2nd ser., xix (1966), pp. 82–109.

[29] J. T. Noonan, *Contraception, A History of its Treatment by the Catholic Theologians and Canonists* (Cambridge, Mass., 1965); E. le R. Ladurie, *Montaillou, Village Occitan, de 1294 à 1324* (Paris, 1975), pp. 247–9; English translation, London, 1979.

[30] WCRO ref. 009:1 BA 2636/11 43700, fos. 12, 81.

associated with hunger seem to have been rare occurrences. Were the peasantry still suffering from the low productivity of the soil, a long-term consequence of the ecological crisis of the early fourteenth century? The relative abundance of grain in the fifteenth century again counters this argument, and it also seems unlikely that the land would take so long to recover. The notion that the late medieval population was affected by a progressive climatic deterioration finds little support from the evidence.[31]

The most likely explanations are either that children suffered more than adults from disease, or that changes in marriage patterns or deliberate limitations on fertility led to a reduced birth-rate. These practices could have been the result of a collective psychological shock arising from the fourteenth-century disasters. More plausibly, peasants learnt the lessons of the fourteenth century and determined to husband their resources by encouraging later marriage and a low birth-rate.

Such speculation can only be proved or disproved by further work on court rolls, particularly those which can provide more information on marriage than is obtainable from the Worcester bishopric documents. The preliminary conclusions must be that births as well as deaths need to be taken into account to explain population changes in the period. The low population of the late fourteenth and fifteenth centuries was associated with recurrent episodes of mortality caused by epidemics, which for much of the period after 1375 had serious, but not disastrous effects. The adult expectation of life, though low by modern standards, is comparable with that found in a medieval period of population growth. However, seasonal patterns of death indicate the existence of endemic as well as epidemic disease. These diseases could have had a particularly serious effect on the population if they had attacked children more than adults, but changes in the birth-rate, with economic or even psychological causes, could have contributed to the overall combination of factors that kept the population low. There may have been some remission in endemic diseases towards the end of the fifteenth century, judging from the time of year at which deaths occurred. The size of families could have begun to rise by the 1470s. Epidemics

---

[31] Postan, *Medieval Economy and Society*, pp. 64–92, argues that the 'metabolism of the field system' was disrupted, but see Hatcher, *Plague, Population, and the English Economy*, p. 57; on climate see E. le R. Ladurie, *Times of Feasting, Times of Famine* (London, 1972), pp. 244–87.

seem to have become less frequent between 1500 and 1520, but returned with renewed vigour and frequency in the 1520s and the succeeding decades. The population expansion of the early sixteenth century, indicated by the growing size of both peasant and urban families, occurred in spite of the high death-rates.[32]

[32] R. S. Gottfried, *Epidemic Disease in Fifteenth-century England* (Leicester, 1978), appeared after this chapter was written. It shows, from the evidence of wills, that East Anglia experienced epidemics that often coincided with those recorded here – in the mid-1460s and early 1470s, for example. There was also a similar seasonal pattern of mortality. Although the author stresses epidemics as a demographic factor more than this chapter does, he also recognizes the importance of changes in fertility in the period.

10. The tenant population, 1348–1544

The demographic movements in the later middle ages consisted of decline in the fourteenth century, stagnation for much of the fifteenth, followed by expansion in the early sixteenth. The changes could be expected to have their main impact on the ratio between land and people, and so be reflected in fluctuations in the numbers of tenants.

In fact, influences other than demographic movements have to be taken into account in explaining trends in tenant numbers. For example, as is now generally accepted, the rapid recovery after the plague of 1348–9 on many manors, such as those of the bishopric of Winchester, does not necessarily mean that the pestilence caused a low mortality, but indicates that there was a sufficiently large number of survivors among the families of tenants and the landless population to take on the vacant holdings.[1]

On 6 August, 1349 Bishop Bransford died at Hartlebury. The temporalities came into the hands of the crown, and for three months, from 28 August to 28 November, they were administered by two keepers, Robert de Warthecap and Leo de Perton. Two years later a view of account was recorded on the Lord Treasurer's Remembrancer's Memoranda Roll.[2] The keepers had been expected to pay into the exchequer a total of £238 5s. 0½d., calculated on the basis of the exchequer's experience of previous vacancies (in the vacancies of 1352–3 and 1361–2 the sums collected in 1302–3 were used as a yardstick of the expected revenues).[3] Such expectations were of course very unrealistic; the keepers of 1349 managed to pay only £66 13s. 4d., and sought to excuse the remainder. The largest single item, £84 4s. 0½d., could not be paid 'because of the lack of tenants who used to pay the rents, and the lack of customers and workers who used to do the works, and who died in the mortal pestilence which flourished on the lands of the said

---

[1] A. E. Levett, *The Black Death on the Estates of the See of Winchester* (Oxford, 1916); Postan, 'Some Agrarian Evidence of Declining Population in the Later Middle Ages', in *Medieval Agriculture and General Problems*, pp. 208–11. A caution on reading too much into statistics of numbers of tenants is in Hatcher, *Rural Economy and Society in the Duchy of Cornwall*, p. 292.

[2] PRO E 368 124 mm. 256–9.

[3] PRO E 136 13/25a; 13/28a.

bishopric within the time of the said account and before'. The numbers of customary and free tenants on the manors were then listed. These can be supplemented by figures given by Leo de Perton for the vacancy of 1353, which in most respects were identical with those in the earlier view of account, but include some additional information.[4] Together the documents provide us with post-plague numbers of customary tenants on fifteen manors and free tenants on twelve.

Can these figures be trusted? There are clearly some errors, as when the clerk confused yardlanders with half-yardlanders. Minor tenants, those who held only 'forlands' and 'swynlands', were omitted. But the documents have an air of authenticity as they list free tenants by name, and give the names of the reeves. The 1353 figures must refer back to 1349; evidently Perton copied the figures from the 1349 vacancy documents. The information summarized in Table 35 therefore relates to the situation on the estate in the autumn of 1349, probably specifically at Michaelmas, when rents were due. The numbers of tenants had fallen between 1299 and 1349 from 1,346 to 781, a drop of 565, or 42 per cent. Some of the vacancy documents mention pre-plague tenant numbers, which are virtually identical with those of 1299, showing that the reduction in tenant numbers happened in the plague period, not over a longer time-span.

It would be tempting to infer on the basis of the vacancy documents that the plague caused a mortality of 42 per cent. This would be unjustifiable, as the figures reflect recovery in the aftermath of the epidemic. Judging from the institutions of clergy recorded in the bishop's registers, the plague, spreading northwards from its original entry-point at Melcombe, reached Bristol late in 1348, and was affecting the clergy of north Worcestershire in the summer of 1349. Deaths among the clergy were well past their peak by September 1349.[5] So by the time the keepers were noting

---

[4] PRO E 368/126.

[5] *Reg. Bransford*, pp. 294–426; *Reg. Sede Vacante*, pp. 223–56. The figures for institutions are:

1348	July	August	September	October	November	December	
	1	1	0	4	5	13	

1349	January	February	March	April	May	June	July	August
	13	12	14	14	39	45	67	43

	September	October	November	December
	15	21	15	9

Table 35. *Reduction in the number of tenants, 1299–1349*

Reflecting the effects of the plague of 1348–9

Manor	1299*	1349	Reduction, 1299–1349	Reduction
Alvechurch	99	56	43	43%
Aston	10	2	8	80%
Bibury	29	7	22	76%
Blockley (including Paxford)	98	45	53	54%
Bredon (including Welland)	101	40	61	60%
Cleeve	94	61	33	35%
Hanbury	86	31	55	64%
Hartlebury	99	80	19	19%
Henbury	132	107	25	19%
Kempsey	112	56	56	50%
Ripple	103	46	57	55%
Tredington	51	28	23	45%
Whitstones	159	125	34	21%
Wick	116	74	42	36%
Withington	57	23	34	60%
Total	1,346	781	565	42%

*These figures have been adjusted by excluding types of tenants not in the 1349 lists, such as those holding 'forlands' only. In some free tenants are omitted because there are no 1349 figures for them.

vacant holdings in the autumn of 1349 the worst of the plague was over. Nearly a year had elapsed since it had reached Henbury, and all of the manors had had at least a few months to recover. The differences between manors in Table 35 might mark variations in the virulence of the disease, but they are also explicable in terms of the different rates at which tenants took up vacant holdings. Recovery may well have been rapid at Henbury, Hartlebury and Whitstones, and relatively slow at Bibury and Hanbury, because land was in greater demand on the first three manors. This can also be demonstrated by showing that smallholdings tended to fall vacant more frequently than half-yardlands and yardlands. The number of yardlanders fell by 29 per cent, while smallholders were reduced by 49 per cent. Perhaps smallholders succumbed more readily to disease because of poverty and under-nourishment. It is also likely that smallholders had fewer children, and so there were no heirs to succeed them. Smallholders would also have been able to move into larger holdings as they became available, so some smallholdings could have fallen vacant in 1349 because their tenants surrendered them in order to move upwards in village society. An example of this promotion of tenants is provided by Tredington. In 1299 there had been fifty-one customary tenants, and these were reduced to twenty-eight in 1349. The numbers of cottagers and smallholders fell from twenty-one to five, but half-yardlanders were reduced from seventeen to ten, and yardlanders were unchanged at thirteen at both dates.

The 42 per cent fall in tenant numbers does provide some indication of the scale of the catastrophe in 1348–9. The numbers of re-occupations of vacant holdings and surrenders by smallholders are unknown, but they probably tended to cancel each other out, so the actual mortality among tenants could have been in the region of 42 per cent. The death-rate among the English clergy in the great plague was very similar, and mortality in Europe as a whole was probably in the range of a third to a half.[6]

In the second half of the fourteenth century most vacant holdings on the estate were filled by new tenants. The court rolls occasionally contain lists of tenements 'in the lord's hands'. Only at Hanbury were the numbers very large; in 1376 twenty-five customary holdings were vacant, but many of these were taken up soon afterwards. On other manors the peak numbers of vacant holdings were reached in the last two decades of the fourteenth century, with between four and eight at Bredon, Whitstones and Wick. Apart from Hanbury the most seriously affected manor was Bibury, where five vacancies in 1390 represented nearly a quarter of the customary holdings. Smaller numbers of untenanted holdings appear in fifteenth-century records, and references become rare after the 1430s. This does not necessarily mean that the demographic situation had changed between the 1390s and the 1440s. Vacant holdings could result from bargaining over rents between lord and tenants, so that in the late fourteenth century the lord's high demands made tenants reluctant to take land. This is suggested by the absence of relatively lightly burdened free tenements from the list of vacancies. An example of the circum-

---

[6] The figures for mortality among the clergy vary from 39 per cent to 49 per cent. See G. G. Coulton, *Medieval Panorama* (Cambridge, 1938), p. 496. On European figures, the most comprehensive survey is Biraben, *Les Hommes et La Peste en France*, pp. 155–230.

stances under which a vacancy could arise is provided by a composite
Whitstones holding of a messuage and cotland and a toft and a mol-
land, with a parcel of meadow, left without a tenant in 1393 when
Henry atte Feld died. Feld had paid a rent of 18s. 10d. per annum, but
the lord maintained that he had occupied the land 'unjustly and
without title', at too low a rent. The land lay 'in the lord's hands'
until 1398, when a new tenant accepted it on a six-year term at a
rent of 26s. 8d. The lord had been willing to let the holding lie vacant
for five years in order to obtain a higher rent.[7]

Long-term trends in tenant numbers on some manors can be
investigated by means of rentals and a list of tenants made in
1544 to check on court attendance.[8] They confirm the evidence
of vacant holdings that tenant numbers could recover between
1349 and the early fifteenth century. At Bibury and Hanbury, which
had suffered great losses in 1349, the tenants nearly doubled, and
Henbury, which had remarkably few vacant holdings in 1349,
was back to its pre-plague tenant population by 1419. This is probably also true of Whitstones. This provides evidence of Henbury's
and Whitstone's economic vitality, contrasted with the low demand
for land at Bibury and Hanbury, where even after recovery the numbers of tenants were well below those of 1299 (see Table 36).

Further proof of the importance of economic factors in determining tenant numbers is that they were static or declining in the fifteenth and early sixteenth centuries. Perhaps the downward trend

Table 36. *Numbers of tenants, 1299–1544*

Manor	1299*	1349	Fifteenth-century rentals		1544
Bibury	31	7	(1431) 12		12
Cleeve	94	61	(1474–5) 53		52
Hanbury	86	31	(c. 1410) 60	(1466) 52	47
Hartlebury	113	80	(1479–83) 66†		75
Henbury	132	107	(1419) 137		109
Whitstones	166	125	(1484–5) 120		70‡

* Omitting tenants by knight service.
† An incomplete rental
‡ This total may exclude tenants in Worcester city.

[7] Whitstones CR, April 1393, Oct. 1398.
[8] Bibury AR, 1430–1; WCRO ref. 009:1 BA 2636/161 92113 2/6; /9 43696, fos.
28–30, 162–3; /168 92332; /37 (iii) fos. 78–83; /185 92574b; /165 92226 4/7; Soc. of
Antiquaries Lib., Pratinton Coll., Worcestershire parishes, vii, pp. 39–46.

at Hanbury between c.1410 and 1466 reflects the consequences of disease and a low birth-rate, but the continued decrease between 1466 and 1544, paralleled by decline at Henbury and stable tenant numbers at Bibury and Cleeve, cannot be explained in demographic terms. There can be little doubt that the population as a whole was rising well before 1544, so it would appear that the tenant population was moving in opposition to demographic trends. A very similar picture of decline or stagnation in tenant numbers emerges from rentals of the Bolton Priory estate in the period 1473–1539.[9]

The declining number of tenants in the fifteenth century coincides with the disappearance of vacant holdings. Only a few tenements had ceased to exist by, for example, being taken into the demesne; the rest were absorbed into multiple holdings. When this happened, the buildings on some of the holdings were allowed to decay, hence an increase in the number of presentments of ruinous buildings in the mid-fifteenth-century courts. Some buildings fell into ruin because of the poverty or carelessness of the tenants, but it can often be shown that the tenants responsible had more than one holding, and were allowing one set of buildings to fall down. Once the buildings had gone, the plot of land was no longer described as a messuage or cottage, but instead was called a toft. An early example of this is Henry atte Feld's holding described above. The proportion of holdings with tofts rather than messuages or cottages (see Table 37) varied from manor to manor in line with the long-term changes in the tenant population, with very few at Henbury, but large numbers at Cleeve and Hanbury. The proportion of tofts tended to increase in the course of the fifteenth century: for example, at Hanbury from 32 per cent in c.1410 to 46 per cent in 1466. Tofts do not seem to have been built on again in the early sixteenth century.

The decay of buildings and the decline in the number of tenants could be seen as evidence of an unrelieved economic depression. In some cases, for example at Hanbury in the early fifteenth century, accumulation of holdings was undoubtedly made possible by a slack demand for land. This was not necessarily true of a similar trend on economically active manors like Henbury, where the reduction in tenant numbers in the late fifteenth and early six-

[9] *Bolton Priory Rentals and Ministers' Accounts, 1473–1539*, ed. Ian Kershaw (Yorks. Arch. Soc., Record Ser., cxxxii, 1969), pp. xvi–xvii.

Table 37. *Holdings with tofts in the fifteenth century*

Holdings described as having a toft, rather than a messuage or
a cottage, as a percentage of all holdings described in fifteenth-
century court rolls and rentals.

Manor	Source	% of holdings with tofts
Cleeve	1474–5 rental	40
Hampton	court rolls	17
Hanbury	c.1410 rental	32
	1466 rental	46
	court rolls	42
Hartlebury	1479–83 rental	24
	court rolls	19
Henbury	1419 rental	2
	court rolls	6
Kempsey	court rolls	20
Whitstones	court rolls	18
Wick	court rolls	21

teenth century could have been a by-product of the creation of
larger units of production in the context of economic growth. In
both cases economics, as well as demography, must enter into the
explanation.

The numbers of tenants did not necessarily change in line with
demographic trends. Our records show, rather fitfully, that there
were many people living on the bishopric manors who were not the
bishops' tenants. Their names are mentioned in the proceedings of
the views of frankpledge, but not in the rentals or records of land
transfers.[10] Even the bishops' serfs were not necessarily their
tenants. Of fourteen serfs who were said to live at Kempsey in 1476,
three do not appear as landholders in the court rolls. Such people
were a normal part of village society, so that some by-laws were
addressed to 'all tenants and inhabitants'. Some may have held
land as subtenants, some were craftsmen, but most were probably
wage-earners. In the 1524 subsidy, taxpayers were assessed on
either land, goods or wages. The numbers of those taxed on wages
varied from none of fifty-one at Hartlebury, to nine of fifty-one
at Whitstones. Many wage-workers would presumably have been
exempt from taxation, so that only the better-off minority are

[10] This problem is discussed in J. A. Raftis, 'Social Structures in Five East
Midland Villages', *Econ. Hist. Rev.*, 2nd ser., xviii (1965), pp. 83–99.

recorded. Most of those paying taxes on land or goods are recorded as landholders in the contemporary court rolls, but most wage-earners do not seem to have been tenants. At Kempsey there were fifty-seven paying tax on land and goods, of whom forty-three are known to have held land on the manor. Of the five wage-earners, only two are recorded as tenants. Two of the eight Whitstones wage-earners whose names are legible can be found among the landholders, whereas three-quarters of the other taxpayers were tenants.[11]

When the population increased in the early sixteenth century, the number of tenants did not rise. Instead it would have been the landless wage-earners whose numbers were swelled. This social group played an important part in late medieval rural society, and we must not forget their existence, in spite of the lack of detailed documentation relating to them.

[11] PRO E 179 200/128.

11. Deserted villages

The most extreme result of the fall in the tenant population was the disappearance of whole settlements. The bishopric estate lay in a region where many villages were deserted in the late medieval and early modern periods. Warwickshire, where 128 deserted villages are recorded, has one of the highest densities of desertions in England; forty examples are known from Worcestershire and sixty-seven in Gloucestershire.[1] Using the customary definition of a village as a settlement with at least six households, ten villages on the demesne manors of the bishopric have been deserted, and an eleventh has been severely shrunken. The sites are often still identifiable from the distinctive earthworks of former roads, toft boundaries and house sites, or by a scatter of medieval pottery on a site that is now under the plough.

All villages experienced a reduction in population in the later middle ages. Why did some lose all of their inhabitants? The general phenomenon has been explained in many ways. In Europe W. Abel has linked desertions with the agrarian depression, specifically the low price of cereals, while French and Scandinavian scholars emphasize the effects of declining population, the abandonment of marginal lands (which had been occupied in the period of land-hunger in the early middle ages) and the devastation of war. In England the pioneer of deserted village studies, M. W. Beresford, has associated most desertions with the movement after 1450 to depopulate villages in order to make way for more profitable sheep pastures.[2]

The first stage in explaining our deserted villages is to consider the history of each settlement, examining the villages before desertion, defining the date and circumstances of desertion, and the

---

[1] The Gloucestershire and Warwickshire deserted villages are listed in M. W. Beresford and J. G. Hurst, *Deserted Medieval Villages* (London, 1971), pp. 187–8, 204–6; for Worcestershire see C. Dyer, 'DMVs in Worcestershire', *Medieval Village Research Group Report*, xix (1971), pp. 5–7.

[2] Some typical European explanations are to be found in École Pratique des Hautes Études, VIe Section, *Villages Désertés et Histoire Économique* (Paris, 1965), pp. 152–90, 515–30, 581–605; the most recent expression of Professor Beresford's views is in Beresford and Hurst, *Deserted Medieval Villages*, pp. 3–75.

use of the land afterwards. The individual histories are arranged in approximate order of the date of desertion.

1 *Wontley* (in Bishop's Cleeve)

Wontley was a remote upland settlement, lying at a height of 900 feet on the Cotswold escarpment above Bishop's Cleeve. In *c*.1170 there were six tenants with a half-yardland each, and a vacant yardland. There was also 'new land' paying a rent of 8d. In 1299 there were again six half-yardlanders, and two tenants with a half-yardland with a smallholding held together, making a total of eight tenants. The inhabitants paid tax jointly with those of nearby Cockbury in 1327. The village was abandoned by 1372–3. The Cleeve manorial account of that year states that the tallage, common fine and rents of Wontley were not being paid 'because of death', and the pasture at Wontley was being rented for 10s. 0d. In 1393–4 the rent had been reduced to 6s. 0d., but underwood there was sold for 32s. 1d. In the early fifteenth century the Wontley pasture was leased with the Cleeve demesne, but in 1437 it was farmed separately for 13s. 4d. In about 1480 the Wontley pasture was 'enclosed with ditches and hedges', and leased to two Winchcomb men for £6 13s. 4d. The land was leased again at the same rent in 1498 and 1529.[3] Medieval potsherds found on a ploughed field to the west of Wontley Farm now indicate the village site.

2 *Upton* (in Blockley)

Both the documentary and archaeological evidence for the village have been thoroughly investigated. It is an upland Cotswold site, lying between 700 and 750 feet above sea level. It was first mentioned in a charter of 897, and had eleven tenants in *c*.1170, with sixteen, most of them yardlanders, in 1299. Upton's taxpayers numbered eleven in 1275, eight in 1327 and four in 1332. Its tax assessment was less than that of any of the other villages in Blockley parish. It can be assumed that Upton was deserted by

[3] *RBW*, iv, pp. 344–5, 351; *Gloucestershire Subsidy Roll, 1 Edward III, 1327* (Middlehill Press, N.D.), p. 29; Cleeve AR, 1372–3 *et seq.*; WCRO ref. 009:1 BA 2636/37 (iii) 43806, fo. 58.

1383–4, when the bishop paid its tax for the subsidy. In 1383 the lands of Upton were being used to pasture the bishop's sheep; by 1419 part of the lands, and after 1458 all of them, were leased out as sheep pasture. In 1472 and 1510 Upton Wold, together with the pastures of *Alrichesdoun* and *Lytildoun*, were leased for £9 6s. 8d.[4]

3 *Hatton* (in Hampton)

This village has also been discussed in detail elsewhere. It lay in the valley of the Avon, probably near the modern Hatton Rock farm. The hill nearby was the site of a palace in the middle Saxon period. In *c*.1170 there were nine tenants, and in 1299 seventeen, fourteen of whom held yardlands. Eighteen tax-payers contributed to the 1327 subsidy, and seventeen to that of 1332. The desertion of Hatton by its tenants is recorded in the manorial accounts between 1371 and 1385, by which date ten yardlands had been abandoned. The bishop contributed to the payment of its subsidy. In the 1370s and 1380s the vacant hold-ings were let to Hampton tenants, but after 1385 the lands were used as a demesne sheep pasture. In 1392 Hatton was again leased for £10 13s. 4d. The leases in 1450, 1464 and 1515 were for £8 per annum. A shepherd lived on the site in 1427, but by 1452 the Hatton tithing was reported to the Hampton court to have no presentments 'because no tenants remain'. John Rous of Warwick, writing in about 1486, included Hatton in his list of deserted villages in Warwickshire.[5]

4 *Penton* (in Alvechurch)

Penton was in the north-west corner of Alvechurch parish in a low-lying situation. It is first mentioned with the name *Pimenna* (perhaps a copyist's error) in *c*.1170, when there were six *operarii* holding half-yardlands and one other with a quarter-yardland. In 1299 there were at least nine tenants, one a free

[4] Hilton and Rahtz, 'Upton, Gloucestershire, 1959–64', pp. 75–86; WCRO ref. 009:1 BA 2636/37 (iii) 43806, fo. 25.

[5] P. A. Rahtz, 'A Possible Saxon Palace near Stratford-upon-Avon', *Antiquity*, xliv (1970), pp. 137–43; S. Hirst and P. A. Rahtz, 'Hatton Rock, 1970', *Trans. Birm. Arch. Soc.*, lxxxv (1972), pp. 160–77; Dyer, 'Population and Agriculture on a Warwickshire manor in the Later Middle Ages', pp. 113–27.

tenant with a mill, two other free tenants and six customary tenants. One holding was vacant. Five other customary tenants may have held land there, but the survey is not clear on this point. The only documentary clue as to the date of desertion is a note explaining the non-payment of the Alvechurch common fine and tallage in the account of 1419–20: 'Nothing, because all of the tenants who used to render the common fine are dead and their lands are rented out at a fixed rent.' The explanation is unusual, and may be a reference to a desertion. The wording is very similar to that used in the earlier Cleeve account to explain the non-payment of the Wontley rents. Many of the more substantial customary tenants of Alvechurch lived at Penton, and the abandonment of their holdings would explain difficulties in collecting dues owed specifically by customary tenants. Additional evidence for a relatively early date of desertion is provided by the scatter of pottery that marks the site of the village, which does not include any sherds of distinctively fifteenth- or sixteenth-century wares. The subsequent fate of the land is not known, except that two tofts in Penton were taken by an Alvechurch tenant in 1529, suggesting that the village lands had been absorbed piecemeal by tenants from other villages.[6]

5 *Craycombe* (in Fladbury)

This Avon valley village lay on rising ground to the north of Fladbury. There were nineteen tenants in *c.*1170 and fourteen in the incomplete survey of 1299. At the latter date eleven tenants held half-yardlands, another had eleven and a half acres and there were two smallholders. An account of 1506–7 records a rent payment of £5 14s. 1d., 'for twenty half-yardlands, one cotland and two acres of meadow in Craycombe, that have lain in the lord's hands through lack of tenants for sixty-eight years, now leased to tenants in the same lordship'. This dates the desertion of the village to some time before 1438–9. In the subsidy abatements of 1446 Craycombe's tax quota was reduced from 19s 0d. to 1s. 0d., confirming the almost total disappearance of the settlement. A Fladbury rental of 1537–8 has twenty entries for Craycombe,

[6] *RBW*, ii, pp. 212–14, 216–20, 233; WCRO ref. 009:1 BA 2636/9 43696, fo. 136; Alvechurch CR, Oct. 1529.

and names fourteen tenants, but all except one also appear as holding land in the neighbouring villages of Fladbury and Moor. The piecemeal acquisition of the vacant holdings by tenants who lived elsewhere meant that the old tenurial units survived, and the village fields, unlike those of Wontley, Upton or Hatton, did not become a single block of land. The boundaries of the tofts of the village survived into the eighteenth century. When the enclosure map was made in 1789 they were surveyed and drawn in as faint lines, and identified in the enclosure award as 'Craycombe Closes'. The 'ghost' of the village on the map (see Ill. 1) contains twenty closes, corresponding with the tofts of the twenty half-yardlands leased in the fifteenth century.[7]

6 *Upper Ditchford* (in Blockley)

Upper and Middle Ditchford lay in the eastern part of Blockley parish, the former on rolling clay hills. 'Ditchford' is mentioned in a lease of 1051 × 1055, and three tenants by knight service held land there in c.1170. The 1299 survey shows that although four hides were held in Ditchford for military service (probably in Middle Ditchford), there were also twenty customary yardlanders who were tenants of the bishop. These are listed in two groups of ten, so they may have been divided between the two villages, but it is more likely that they all held land in Upper Ditchford. Upper Ditchford had thirteen taxpayers in 1327, and fourteen in 1332.[8]

A useful indication of the changing fortunes of villages in Blockley parish is given by the fluctuations in the farm of the tithe-corn, which belonged to the bishop after the appropriation of the rectory in 1335. The evidence is summarized in Table 38. The total revenue from the tithes of the parish declined from 1384 to 1420, recovered a little in the mid-fifteenth century and then fell again. This reflects changes in the price of grain and the bargaining position of the farmers, and also the grain produc-

[7] *RBW*, ii, pp. 135–7, 145–7; Fladbury AR, 1506–7; *The Lay Subsidy of 1334*, ed. R. E. Glasscock (London, 1975), p. 351; PRO, E 179 200/83; Fladbury rental, WCL C 580; WCRO ref. 705:81 BA 351/62.

[8] Robertson, *Anglo-Saxon Charters*, pp. 208–9; *RBW*, iii, pp. 302–5, 314–16; *Subsidy Roll for the County of Worcester, 1 Edward III*, p. 2; *Lay Subsidy Roll, A.D. 1332–3*, ed. J. Amphlett (Worcs. Hist. Soc., 1899), p. 7.

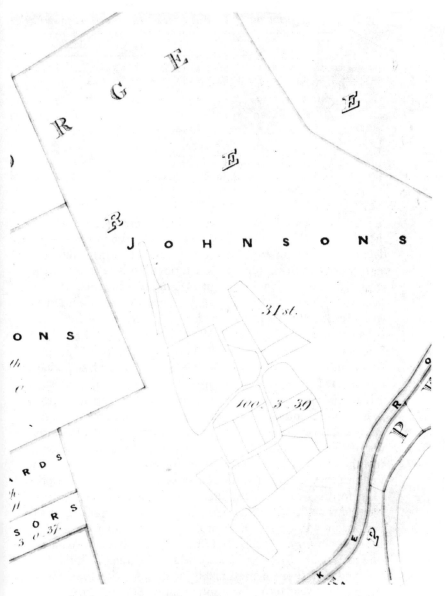

1 Enclosure map of Fladbury, 1789, showing Craycombe Closes, the 'ghost' of the deserted village of Craycombe (Worcester County Record Office)

Table 38. *Annual farms of the Blockley parish tithe-corn, 1383–1526*

	1383–4	1419–20	1458–9	1505–6	1525–6
Aston Magna	£8 13s. 4d.	£5 6s. 8d.	£6 13s. 4d.	£5 13s. 4d.	£5 13s. 4d.
Blockley	£3 0s. 0d.	£2 0s. 0d.	£4 13s. 4d.	£5 13s. 4d.	£5 13s. 4d.
Middle Ditchford	£2 0s. 0d.	£2 13s. 4d.	£3 3s. 4d.	—	—
Upper Ditchford	£7 6s. 8d.	£3 6s. 8d.	£4 6s. 8d.	—	—
Dorn	£6 13s. 4d.	£5 6s. 8d.	£3 10s. 0d.	£3 0s. 0d.	£3 0s. 0d.
Draycott	£2 10s. 0d.	£2 0s. 0d.	£2 16s. 8d.	£2 8s. 4d.	£2 8s. 4d.
Northwick	£4 6s. 8d.	£5 6s. 8d.	£4 10s. 0d.	£4 0s. 0d.	£4 0s. 0d.
Paxford	£8 0s. 0d.	£9 6s. 8d.	£6 13s. 4d.	£4 13s. 4d.	£4 13s. 4d.
Total	*£42 10s. 0d.*	*£35 6s. 8d.*	*£36 6s. 8d.*	*£25 8s. 4d.*	*£25 8s. 4d.*

tion of the eight villages involved. Upper Ditchford was one of the biggest grain-producing villages in the parish in 1383–4, but declined more than any of the others (except Dorn) in the early and mid-fifteenth century. This deterioration is reflected in the leasing of ten yardlands in about 1413 at reduced rents, seven of them to John Dide. The engrossing of so much land by one tenant was presumably associated with partial desertion, but grain production was continuing in 1458–9, as the tithe-corn was still being farmed. The only person mentioned in the Upper Ditchford tithing in the hundred court of 1457 was a shepherd, so perhaps the change from arable to pasture was then under way. The estate arrears rolls show that the Upper Ditchford tithe-corn had ceased to be farmed, and it is therefore reasonable to suppose that arable cultivation had been given up, in the period 1473–80. (The farmers of the tithe-corn always paid in arrears, and often failed to pay their farms in full, so the list of arrears of 1482 mentions all of the farmers two or three times, except the farmer of the Upper Ditchford corn.) The most likely date for the end of cereal production is 1475, when 'the demesne and tenants' holdings in the lord's hands in Upper Ditchford' were leased for £9 17s. 0d. to four people for fifty years. In 1507–8 it was leased in two halves, one to William Grevile, the lawyer, and the other to John Heritage and John Freman, presumably in anticipation of the expiry of the old fifty-year term, for a total rent of £18 10s. 0d. Grevile's indenture mentioned a hall with two chambers, a barn and two sheepcotes, so sheep pasture was clearly the main use of the site, and described the land as 'half of the enclosure of all the messuages, tofts, lands, holdings, meadows and pastures' in Upper Ditchford. Clearly the holdings had ceased to exist as separate units. When Thomas Wilkys (or Willys) of Blockley, one of the original lessees of 1475, made his will in 1512, he bequeathed his share of the lease as 'my pasture in Ditchford' to a relative, and Grevile in his will of 1513 left his sheep on his farm at Ditchford to Lanthony Priory.[9] The village earthworks and the ridge and furrow of its former arable fields are still visible, with the enclosure hedges which were probably laid out in the fifteenth century (see Ill. 2).

7 *Middle Ditchford* (in Blockley)

Middle Ditchford is first recorded as a distinct settlement in 1275, when nine taxpayers contributed to the subsidy. There were fourteen taxpayers in 1327 and ten in 1332. In the farms of the Blockley parish tithe-corn the village appears as the least important grain producer in the parish in 1383–4, suggesting that its cultivated area had declined at some time prior to 1383. However, alone among the eight Blockley villages its tithe-corn farm increased slightly but continuously between 1384 and 1459. The village still seems to have been active in 1457, when the tithing-men of Middle Ditchford presented two brewers and a miller to the hundred court of Winburntree, a contrast to the Upper Ditchford presentments. Rous reported 'the three Ditchford' (including Ditchford Friary, a hamlet in Stretton-on-Fosse) as deserted in about 1486. The farm of the tithe-corn ceased at some time between 1482 and 1497, so the date of the end of arable cultivation can be narrowed down to 1482–6. The end seems abrupt, and in view of the absence of evidence of a continuous decline in the fifteenth century it seems likely that some act of enclosure could have caused the final destruction of the village.[10]

[9] Blockley AR, 1458–9; WCRO ref. 009:1 BA 2636/164 92181; Arrears roll, 1473, 1482; Blockley AR, 1505–6; WCRO ref. 009:1 BA 2636/37 (iii) 43806, fos. 23–4; WCRO ref. 008:7 BA 3590, vol. ii, fo. 46; J. N. Langston, 'Priors of Lanthony by Gloucester', *Trans. Bristol and Glos. Arch. Soc.*, lxiii (1942), p. 134.

[10] *Lay Subsidy Roll for the County of Worcester circ. 1280*, ed. J. W. Willis Bund and J. Amphlett (Worcs. Hist. Soc., 1893), p. 76; *Subsidy Roll for... Worcester, 1 Edward III*, pp. 2–3; *Lay Subsidy Roll*, 1332–3, p. 7; Arrears roll, 1482; Rec. AR, 1497–8; J. Rous, *Historia Regum Angliae*, 2nd edn, ed. T. Hearne (Oxford, 1745), pp. 122–5.

2 Aerial photograph of the deserted village site of Upper Ditchford, from the
north. The small rectangles defined by banks and ditches in the centre of the
photograph are the tofts of the peasant holdings. The ridge and furrow of the
former arable fields surround the village site on all sides. The modern hedges,
coinciding partially with the boundary between the village and the ridge and
furrow, were probably laid out at the time of enclosure in the late fifteenth
century (Cambridge University Collection)

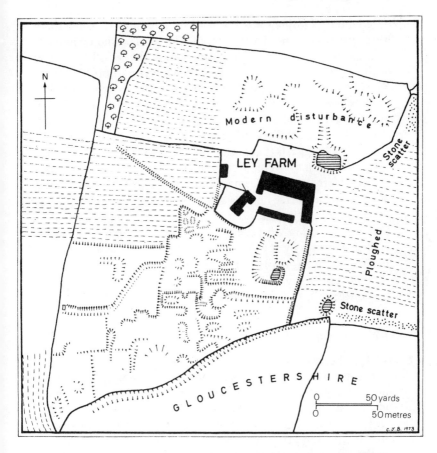

10 Sketch-plan of the deserted village site of Southley. The earthworks are less distinct than those at Upper Ditchford, but property boundaries and possibly the house sites are visible to the south-west of the modern farm, and ridge and furrow (plan by C. J. Bond)

8 *Southley* (in Ripple)

This village lay on rolling clay land east of Ripple. There were fourteen tenants in *c*.1170, eight paying money-rents, including a miller, five owing both money-rent and labour services, and one *avercman* with ten acres. The Ripple holdings in 1299 are not listed in a way that allows the tenant population of the village to be counted. Southley was taxed separately in 1275, when there were five taxpayers. The scattered Ripple manorial documents in the fifteenth century give no indication that Southley was in decline, except that the tithing-men had little to present at the Ripple courts apart from the failure of the Ormes family to repair their buildings. In 1520 there were two serf families called Ormes and Kewe living at Southley, of the five listed on Ripple manor, and they were still there in 1538 and 1539. The list of Ripple tenants in 1544 suggests that these two families were the only resident tenants left. There were no free tenants, and the three customary tenants were William Orme, Henry Kewe and Richard Leche-mere (who had a free holding nearby at Uckinghall, and probably lived there). Whereas Southley had been comparable in its tenant population with the other villages in Ripple manor in the twelfth century, by 1544 it was much the smallest, with even fewer tenants than at nearby Stratford, which had always been an insignificant hamlet. The surviving earthworks give some indication of the village's original size (see Maps 8 and 10).[11]

9 *Welcombe* (in Stratford)

Welcombe, the exact site of which is unknown, lay in a hilly district to the north of Stratford. Its decline was probably similar to that of Southley. There were eleven tenants in c.1170, and seventeen in 1299, all of them customary yardlanders and half-yardlanders. In 1327 eleven taxpayers contributed to the subsidy, and thirteen in 1332. In the Stratford court records of the late fifteenth and early sixteenth centuries the business of the Welcombe tithing, unlike that of the Old Stratford and Shottery tithings, was normally dismissed with the words 'all well'. There seems to have been some difficulty in finding a tithing-man in 1498, when John Wylmott agreed to serve on behalf of his widowed mother, an unusual incident suggestive of a shortage of resident tenants. However, there were still some tenants: three were presented for non-repair of buildings in 1498. Also the fields were still used as arable, as in 1501 and 1502 attempts were made to prevent the

[11] *RBW*, ii, pp. 167–8; *Lay Subsidy Roll...circ. 1280*, p. 27; Ripple CR, May 1451, May 1457, April 1520, April 1538, March 1539; WCRO ref. 009:1 BA 2636/18 43764–5, fo. 50.

ploughing of the common way leading from the village to Stratford parish church, and in 1507 there were complaints of trespass in the Welcombe corn fields.[12]

By the 1520s and 1530s the holdings at Welcombe were very large, with two of 2½ yardlands and one of 5 yardlands, so that two-thirds of the Welcombe land was in the hands of three tenants. Nor were the tenants resident. In 1539 a 2½ yardland holding and another of 6 acres were taken by William Clopton, and John Combes took 5 yardlands on customary tenure and, at about the same time, a further 2¾ yardlands on a ninety-nine year lease. Clopton and Combes were both important gentlemen with extensive property in the Stratford district. They may have sublet their Welcombe lands, but they could also have managed them directly and left the buildings associated with the yardlands unoccupied. Welcombe still survived as a 'town' with some land under the plough into the early seventeenth century, but between 1614 and 1619, in the teeth of local opposition, William Combe, John Combes' great nephew, enclosed much of his land in Welcombe, 'paled and stopped up the common street leading through the town of Welcombe', and was said to have depopulated the place. He was able to do this because of the concentration of lands into the hands of his family in the period before 1540, and we must assume that the village was in a state of decline long before the enclosure began.[13]

10 *Northwick* (in Blockley)

Earthworks show that a substantial village once existed on a hill in Northwick park. The bishops had only a few tenants there, as there was a sub-manor held for knight service. The tithe-corn figures show no drastic decline between 1383 and 1525, and there

[12] *RBW*, iii, pp. 252–4, 261; *Lay Subsidy Roll for Warwickshire of 1327*, p. 34; *The Lay Subsidy Roll for Warwickshire of 6 Edward III (1332)*, ed. W. F. Carter (Dugdale Soc., vi, 1926), pp. 85–6; Stratford CR, Oct. 1498, Oct. 1501, April 1502, July 1507.

[13] Stratford CR, April 1520, Oct. 1522, Oct. 1528, April 1529, Oct. 1538; *VCH Warks.*, iii, p. 264; WCRO ref. 009:1 BA 2636/37 (iii) 43806, fo. 206; on Clopton's and Combe's lands, and the enclosure of Welcombe, *VCH Warks.*, iii, pp. 262, 264, 267–8.

were twelve taxpayers in 1524. The desertion of the village was probably the result of post-medieval emparking.[14]

11 *Throckmorton* (in Fladbury)

This village was included in the bishopric manor of Fladbury until the early fifteenth century, when it was let at fee-farm to the Throckmorton family. Rentals made by the Throckmortons in 1476 and 1484 show that there was then a tenant population of twenty-seven, with no evidence of decline. Extensive earthworks now visible near the church show that Throckmorton has suffered severe shrinkage, but this could have been of post-medieval date.[15]

The villages listed here are the major settlements which are known to have been deserted. There were a number of minor settlements which also disappeared. For example, the sites of the hamlets of *Febley* and *Pyrley* in Alvechurch can now be identified only from field-names recorded on the 1840 tithe apportionment.[16] On the other manor, Hanbury, in the wooded part of north Worcestershire, there are indications of changes in the settlement pattern. In 1299 twenty free tenants were listed at Blickley on the eastern edge of the parish, eighteen of them with messuages. There is no village at Blickley now. Only two tenants are recorded as holding messuages there in the rental of 1466, though the location of free holdings is not always given. Tenant holdings were included with demesne land in the lease of Blickley Field in 1418, and it was described as 'hedged and ditched'. However, the area involved was small, judging from the low £3 0s. 0d. farm paid by the lessee. As a woodland settlement created by late assarting, Blickley in the thirteenth century probably consisted of scattered houses with much enclosed land, and so never existed as a compact village of the type discussed above. It is possible that there was some movement of settlement in other parts of Hanbury parish in the late middle ages, as buildings were decaying on some holdings while tenants were also building new houses 'on

---

[14] *RBW* iii, p. 297, 300; PRO E 179 200/128; R. Holt, 'Some Deserted Medieval Villages of North Gloucestershire' (University of Birmingham B.A. dissertation, 1969), p. 23.

[15] SBT, DR 5 3272-3.

[16] *RBW*, ii, pp. 212, 213; WCRO ref. f 760/7 BA 1572.

the lord's soil', but this would have involved the desertion of scattered farmsteads rather than a complete settlement.[17]

Other villages on the estate, though not deserted, experienced physical shrinkage, as is shown by the frequent references to tofts on which buildings had once stood. The earthworks that mark the sites of the decayed buildings can still be seen at a number of the estate's villages, notably at Aston (now White Ladies' Aston).

Why were these villages abandoned? A possible explanation that ought to be considered is that they reflect a withdrawal from marginal, late-colonized land. At first glance this theory seems to find support among our deserted settlements. Two of them lay in bleak situations high up in the Cotswolds. In most cases the first documentary reference to the name is in the late twelfth century. Names like Southley and Upton imply that they were secondary settlements, named in relation to another place.

There are many difficulties in accepting this argument. If it were correct, we would expect the main concentration of deserted settlements, both on the estate and in the country as a whole, to lie in the colonizing, woodland districts, such as north Worcestershire. In fact they are found mainly in old-settled areas. The villages are often not named in early documents because they were not manorial centres, and so would escape mention in charters or Domesday Book. Two are mentioned in pre-Conquest charters in any case, and there is archaeological evidence of Anglo-Saxon occupation at Hatton and Upton. An objective assessment of the quality of the land in the vicinity of the settlements is provided by the land classification of the modern Ministry of Agriculture, which uses criteria such as slope, drainage and soils to assess land quality. The classifications are listed in Table 39. Most of the villages lay on grade three land, which is predominant throughout the west midlands. It usually consists of clay, marl or limestone soils, described as having 'moderate' limitations, suited for both arable and pasture, and capable of 'giving reasonable yields under average management'. In no sense can our deserted villages, like those of Dartmoor or the Pennines, be said to lie on poor land suitable only for pastoral use. There are small areas of grade four land, which is poor, near

[17] WCRO ref. 009:1 BA 2636/168 92332; Hanbury AR, 1427–8; Hanbury CR, Nov. 1380, May 1381, Hanbury AR, 1386–7.

Table 39. *Settlement history of deserted villages*

Village (Manor)	Land classification of village area	whole manor	Distance from parish church (miles)	1327 tax lists No. taxed	Amount	1299 survey Free tenants	Customary tenants
Craycombe (Fladbury)	3	1–3	0.7	(taxed with Fladbury)		0	14
Middle Ditchford (Blockley)	3–4	3	4.0	14	£1 2s. 3d.	1	10*
Upper Ditchford (Blockley)	3	3	2.5	13	£1 1s. 8d.	0	10*
Hatton (Hampton)	2	2–3	1.6	18	£1 6s 4d.	1	16
Northwick (Blockley)	3	3	0.7	10	19s. 8d.	1	1?
Penton (Alvechurch)	3	3	1.5	(taxed with Alvechurch)		3	6(+5?)
Southley (Ripple)	3	1–3	1.2	5†	13s. 0d.†	—	—
Upton (Blockley)	3	3	1.0	8	12s. 2d.	2	13(+1?)
Welcombe (Stratford)	3–4	2–3	1.4	11	£1 1s. 0d.	0	17
Wontley (Cleeve)	3–4	2–4	3.5	5	6s. 3½d.	0	8
				(with Cockbury)			

* All of the Ditchford tenants may have been in Upper Ditchford
† 1275 tax-list

Middle Ditchford, Welcombe and Wontley but it must be stressed that most of their lands were of grade three. In the case of these three villages, and also at Craycombe and Southley, the land around the deserted settlement is somewhat inferior to that found on the rest of the manor, but the disparity was not very great.

So the deserted villages of the estate tended to be settlements of secondary importance, that often escaped mention in documents until the twelfth century. They were probably not the product of late colonization in the twelfth and thirteenth centuries, and most were well established by *c.*1170. Hatton and Welcombe seem to have grown considerably between *c.*1170 and 1299. The land on which they lay was not particularly poor, but in some cases it was inferior to that in the rest of the manor in which they were situated. These rather qualified generalizations would not give strong support to the marginal land explanation as the primary cause of desertion.

M. W. Beresford's argument, that most villages were depopulated by the creation of sheep pastures, finds only limited support from our examples. The sites of six of the villages did become enclosed pastures, and some of the dates, *c.*1480 at Wontley, *c.*1475 at Upper Ditchford, *c.*1482–6 at Middle Ditchford, fit Beresford's chronological scheme that puts most enclosure in the period after 1450. Three of our villages were specifically stated by a contemporary, John Rous, to have been destroyed by avaricious landlords.

The main objection to Beresford's hypothesis is that enclosure often followed desertion, and after a long time. Wontley was deserted by 1372, but the site was not enclosed for more than a century. Upper Ditchford was in decline by 1413, and enclosure was delayed until *c.*1475. The decaying state of Welcombe is apparent in the 1530s, but it was enclosed after 1614. The gap between desertion and enclosure at Hatton was much shorter, but there can be no doubt that desertion occurred first. The same story of declining villages preceding conversion to pasture is found in other villages in Oxfordshire, Warwickshire and Worcestershire.[18] The estate

---

[18] R. H. Hilton, 'A Study in the Prehistory of English Enclosure in the Fifteenth Century', in *The English Peasantry in the Later Middle Ages*, pp. 161–73; T. H. Lloyd, 'Some Documentary Sidelights on the Deserted Oxfordshire Village of Brookend', *Oxoniensia*, xxix/xxx (1964–5), pp. 116–28; C. Dyer, 'The Deserted Medieval Village of Woollashill, Worcestershire', *Trans. Worcs. Arch. Soc.*, 3rd ser., i (1965–7), pp. 55–61.

officials would not have removed villages or evicted tenants to make way for pastures. Eviction was a last resort for tenants who flagrantly violated their obligations. The official policy was conservative, seeking to maintain decaying holdings, even to the point of paying for repairs to buildings. The estate could obtain good money for enclosed pastures, and the leasehold rents of the pastures at Upper Ditchford, Upton and Wontley probably brought in more cash than the villages, if fully inhabited, would have done. But if the whole financial picture is taken into account, the long periods of decayed rents, the tax contributions paid by the bishop, and the eventual cost of enclosure, the transition from village to sheep pasture was not financially advantageous. There can be no doubt that the decay of settlements, as at Penton or Southley, which did not culminate in the creation of a pasture, caused considerable financial loss. It is difficult to argue that there could have been a profit motive for the lord to depopulate villages.

John Rous' evidence can be shown to have been unreliable in the case of Hatton, which was deserted long before his birth, so that he could have had no personal experience of its depopulation. He is a more reliable witness for the two Ditchfords, both of which ceased grain production shortly before he wrote against the destruction of villages.

At Upper Ditchford a dominant tenant could have made life difficult for any remaining villagers and so could have hastened total desertion and made enclosure possible. By 1413 such a tenant, John Dide, had engrossed seven yardlands. This was a common pattern of enclosure and depopulation in the early sixteenth century, and is well documented at Welcombe in the seventeenth century.[19] Such activities were most likely to succeed if the village was already in decline. Only at Middle Ditchford is it likely that a village was depopulated by a sudden act of policy. The bishops' tenants there in the late fifteenth century were members of the Clinton family, gentry who would have been more ready than the bishops to make drastic innovations, such as wholesale enclosure and conversion to pasture. In 1474, about ten years before the demise of Middle Ditchford, Elizabeth and Thomas Clinton were 'usurping' land in the neighbouring manor of Todenham.[20]

---

[19] Thirsk, *Agrarian History of England*, iv, pp. 200–1.
[20] *VCH Worcs.*, iii, p. 269; GRO 1099/31/M1.

With the exception of Middle Ditchford and Northwick, the deserted villages in our sample were either totally deserted or severely weakened in the later middle ages by the voluntary departure of the tenants. The well-documented desertion of Hatton shows the villagers leaving, one or two at a time, in the 1370s and 1380s. That this type of migration was a general phenomenon in the period is suggested by the concern of the keepers of the temporalities in the vacancy of 1433–5 that if tenants were pressed too closely to pay rents 'they would leave the lands, holdings and tenures of the... lordships vacant, to the great prejudice of the lord king and the final destruction of the aforesaid manors', or, 'all the tenants of the said manors... would leave the aforesaid manors immediately'.[21] Population decline was probably an indirect cause of desertion. Very few villages were wiped out immediately in the plague of 1348–9.[22] Population fell generally in the second half of the fourteenth century, but most villages recovered. Villages like Hatton, Upton and Wontley failed at this time because heirs or new tenants were not willing to move into the holdings which were left as tenants died or migrated, as happened in the villages which survived. The holdings were in some way unattractive, and population decline meant that better opportunities were opened up elsewhere.

A different pattern is found at Craycombe, Upper Ditchford, Southley and Welcombe. These villages also were affected by an extreme version of a general tendency of the fifteenth and sixteenth centuries, the slow reduction in the number of tenants and the acquisition of multiple holdings by some individuals. At Craycombe the holdings were taken by Fladbury tenants, so making the village itself redundant. Holdings at Upper Ditchford and Welcombe were engrossed into very large units, initially perhaps by residents, later by absentees. This suggests a lack of competition for land, which made the engrosser's task easy; he accumulated holdings, because they were uninviting to new tenants. This is indicated by the cheapness of some of the holdings, like the Upper Ditchford yardlands, which were paying a rent of 6s. 8d. each in the fifteenth century, though their works and rents together had been valued at 19s. 4½d. in 1299.[23]

If the villages declined because the tenants chose to leave, and

---

[21] WCRO ref. 009:1 BA 2636/174 92465, 92471.
[22] M. W. Beresford, *The Lost Villages of England* (London, 1954), pp. 155–63.
[23] Blockley AR, 1458–9; *RBW*, iii, pp. 302–4.

potential replacements were not attracted to their holdings, it ought to be possible to isolate the features of the villages that made them vulnerable to desertion. It has already been shown that the quality of their land could in some cases have led villagers to move to neighbouring settlements. All of the villages, with the possible exception of Penton, had land lying in open fields. Deserted villages were in general thinly distributed in old-enclosed or woodland districts, not just because they were immune to enforced enclosure, but because of the attractions of flexible agriculture in areas with ample resources of pasture. A number of villages that were deserted could have expanded arable cultivation in the period before 1349, so that little pasture would have remained. Certainly some of them, like Upton and Wontley, lacked access to much natural meadow-land.

The deserted villages on the bishopric estate, like the much larger sample analysed by M. W. Beresford, tended to be smaller and paid less tax than those that survived.[24] All but one of the deserted villages listed in Table 39 had fewer than fifteen taxpayers in 1327, and contributed less than 23s. 0d. The average Worcester-shire village in 1327 contained twenty-one taxpayers and contributed more than 32s. 0d.

The deserted villages tended to be subsidiary settlements, remote from such facilities as parish churches, which in most cases were more than a mile away (see Table 39). There were also peculiarities in their social structure. The surveys of 1299 show that the 'to-be-deserted' villages had an overwhelming predominance of customary tenants (see Table 39). There were no free tenants recorded at Craycombe, Upper Ditchford, Welcombe, and Wontley, though they made up more than a quarter of the tenants of the whole estate. Customary tenements were more heavily burdened with rents than free holdings, so the 'to-be-deserted' villages were more likely to lose tenants, though their level of customary rent was no higher than in villages that survived. The preponderance of customary tenure must have been particularly irksome to the tenants of Pen-ton, as the village lay in a manor with a majority of free tenants, and adjoined Bromsgrove, where the tenants enjoyed the privileges of tenure on royal demesne.[25] The situation is paralleled by three vil-

---

[24] Beresford and Hurst, *Deserted Medieval Villages*, pp. 21–6.
[25] *The Court Rolls of the Manor of Bromsgrove and King's Norton*, ed. A.F.C. Barber (Worcs. Hist. Soc., 1963), pp. 5–10.

lages in the Warwickshire hundred of Stoneleigh, which were the only places in the hundred in 1279 to have no free tenants at all, and were all deserted by the end of the fifteenth century.[26]

The size of holdings in the 'to-be-deserted' villages was unusually uniform. The surveys of 1299 take no account of sub-letting, but they must bear some relationship to reality. Most of the deserted villages consisted before abandonment of half-yardlands or yardland holdings. No smallholders at all are recorded at the Ditchfords, Welcombe and Wontley, and there were very few elsewhere, whereas more than a third of the customary tenants in the 1299 survey held less than a half-yardland. This presumably reflects the remoteness of the villages from influences that helped to create smallholdings: manorial centres and markets, for example. After 1349 the yardlanders of these villages must have been faced with particular difficulties in recruiting labour, as the few smallholders, together with any subtenants of smallholdings, would have tended to move into vacant holdings in the village or elsewhere. One effect of falling population was to create imbalances in the equilibrium between the social groups within the village.

No single cause led to the desertion of villages on the bishopric estate. Many villages were put at risk because of the falling population of the later middle ages; only a minority were deserted because of their economic and social weaknesses. Most of the desertions discussed here came about through the disintegration of a community under the strains that affected all villages, but became more acute for some. A few were undermined more deliberately, whether because of the activities of an engrossing tenant, or an enclosing or emparking landlord. The depopulation of a healthy village was unusual.

[26] The three villages were Biggin, Emscote and Newbold Comyn; I am grateful to Professor R. H. Hilton for allowing me to use his transcripts of the 1279 Warwickshire Hundred Rolls.

12. The relationship between lord and tenants, 1350–1540

The argument advanced in previous chapters is that while the declining population of the later middle ages greatly influenced social developments, some changes, like the movements in the numbers of tenants or the desertion of villages, cannot be explained solely by means of the demographic factor.

We have already seen that, particularly in the early and mid-fifteenth century, the bishopric estate experienced a decline in income from rents. This is an almost universal tendency of the period. Was it simply a reflection of population changes, or of the deteriorating market for agricultural produce, in other words, a response to changes in supply and demand? This seems unlikely, as lords possessed powers over their tenants, such as rights of jurisdiction or ownership of serfs, which would not necessarily be sensitive to market forces. It is therefore necessary to examine the development of the lords' powers, and their social relations with the tenants, in order to see whether these factors had any independent influence on the conditions of the late medieval peasantry.

We have seen earlier that the profits of jurisdiction deriving from the bishops' courts tended in the late fourteenth and early fifteenth centuries to be as high as or higher than in the period around 1300, but that they declined considerably by the middle of the fifteenth century.

The court records themselves show that changes in the jurisdictional powers of the bishops lay behind the fall in revenue.[1] The bishopric franchises declined in significance in the fifteenth century. The right to hang thieves, *infangentheof*, seems to have revived in the 1440s, when three separate cases are recorded at Kempsey, Henbury and Whitstones, but we hear of no more after 1447. Occasionally local officials paid for repairs to the bishops' gallows,

---

[1] D. A. Crowley, 'The Later History of Frankpledge', *Bull. of the Inst. of Hist. Research*, xlviii (1975), pp. 1–15, closely analyses the decline in seignorial courts in Essex in the fourteenth and fifteenth centuries.

as late as 1473–4 at Henbury and 1488 at Ripple, but we may suspect that by this date their function was symbolic.[2]

In the franchises, the old conflicts with rival jurisdictions continued. The boundaries between the episcopal manor of Whitstones and the city of Worcester were disputed in 1504; in 1450 the bailiff of the abbot of Cirencester's liberty of the Seven Hundreds was reported to be encroaching on the bishop's right on the manor of Bibury to return royal writs; at Wick in 1473 two tenants of Worcester Priory were said to have arrested a felon in the bishop's liberty and carried him into the Priory's area of jurisdiction.

Hundredal jurisdiction seems to have been concerned with relatively trivial cases. The Oswaldslow *tourns* of 1432–3 and the hundred court of Winburntree (one of the constituent hundreds of the liberty of Oswaldslow) in 1457 dealt with uncleaned ditches, breaches of the assize of ale and a small number of assaults and thefts. At one Oswaldslow *tourn* held at *Vernsycher*, north-west of Worcester, only five of the twelve jurors attended, and nine vills which owed suit were amerced for non-attendance.[3]

It was becoming increasingly difficult to ensure the attendance of representatives of the vills belonging to other lords at the bishops' views of frankpledge. Suitors from the Priory manors of Hallow and Grimley did not go to the view held at St Johns near Worcester; the vills of Southam, Brockhampton and Stoke Orchard were not represented at Cleeve; and the Hanbury views were ignored by the men of Broughton from 1511.[4]

The most important courts for the enforcement of the lord's control over his tenants were those held at manorial level. Manor courts could be held quite frequently in the late fourteenth and early fifteenth centuries, with as many as six sessions in a year on the larger manors. By the mid-fifteenth century a routine of four courts per annum had been established. The spring and autumn sessions combined both views of frankpledge and manorial courts, while manorial courts only were held in the summer and winter (often in July and January). The amount of business transacted at

[2] Kempsey CR, April 1443; Henbury AR, 1447–8; St Johns view, April 1447; Henbury AR, 1473–4; Bredon AR, 1487–8.
[3] WCRO ref. 009:1 BA 2636/193 92628 5/9; /193 92628 1/9; /164 92181.
[4] St Johns view, 1384; Cleeve AR, 1445–6; Cleeve CR, May 1451; Hanbury CR, April 1510; April 1513.

the summer and winter courts was often so small as not to justify the expense of sending officials to hold them, and in the 1520s this was finally recognized and the number of sessions each year was reduced to two. The small tenant population of Bibury generated so little business that only one annual session was held after 1520.

In theory, the jurisdiction of manor courts and views of frank-pledge were separate and distinct. The courts dealt with such seignorial business as land transactions and inter-tenant litigation, while the views, having originated from delegated royal jurisdiction, were concerned with petty crime, public nuisances (like uncleaned ditches), stray animals and the assize of bread and ale. In reality, the two types of jurisdiction were not strictly segregated, and it was not unusual for manor courts to deal with the assize of ale and even petty crime. A move towards stricter separation appears to have taken place on some manors in the first half of the fifteenth century.[5]

There were some important changes in the business coming before the courts. The court rolls of the late fourteenth and early fifteenth centuries contain many notes of proceedings in litigation between tenants, pleas of debt, trespass, broken contract and unjust detention of chattels, involving sums of a few shillings or even pence. The procedures used were rather slow and cumbersome, and each stage allowed the lord to collect a few pence from the parties in amercements. However, in comparison with other courts, the manor court must have provided a convenient means of settling minor disputes between villagers. By the 1420s and 1430s pleas between tenants had virtually disappeared from the courts of Hanbury and Whitstones. They were still numerous at Kempsey in the 1430s, but declined in the 1440s, and are rarely found after 1450. They still appear on the Henbury court records in the late fifteenth and early sixteenth centuries, and at other manors as late as the 1520s, but in relatively small numbers.

There is some evidence that tenants were turning to other courts in order to obtain satisfaction over debts and trespasses. As early as 1409 the steward ordered in the Kempsey court that, on pain of paying 6s. 8d., 'no tenants may bring a plea on others in courts other than the lord's court at Kempsey'. Two Kempsey tenants, Thomas and John Stonehale, were said in 1478 to have been to the

---

[5] Page, *The Estates of Crowland Abbey*, pp. 31–8, reveals similar problems.

hundred court of *Swinesherd*, part of the liberty of Oswaldslow, and there 'caused certain trespasses to be presented that belong to the lord's view in his liberty of Kempsey, concerning the lord and John Smyth of Stonehall'. Other tenants went to the royal courts, like John Kemys of Henbury, in a plea of trespass against another Henbury tenant in 1458, and Walter Lee of Kempsey in 1504 pursued a plea of debt against Thomas Legge of the same place 'in the king's court at Westminster'.[6]

As well as losing one important type of case from his courts, the lord was also deprived of some of his methods of enforcement. The late fourteenth-century court rolls contain constant references to the use of pledges, suitors appointed to ensure the presence in court of parties in inter-tenant litigation, to stand surety for payments of amercements, rents and fines, or to guarantee the good behaviour of others. Pledging has been seen as evidence for communal feeling and neighbourly co-operation, but as the same person often appears as pledge for large numbers of people who cannot all have been close associates, the institution can also be regarded as a method of enforcement imposed from above.[7] Pledging had died out on most manors by the 1440s, though it reappeared on a limited scale at Whitstones and Wick in the third quarter of the fifteenth century. A similar institution was the use of suitors to enforce court attendance. Many non-resident free tenants failed to do fealty for their holdings or perform suit of court, and other tenants were often ordered to compel them to come. The whole exercise sometimes seems ludicrous because of the disparity between the status of the parties involved; for example, two Bibury tenants were amerced 3d. in 1383 for failing to bring the abbot of Gloucester to do fealty.

In general, orders made by the courts were not readily obeyed. The same tenants were repeatedly presented for having ruinous buildings, not cleaning ditches, or for committing other offences, for many years. The relatives of serfs who had left the manor were constantly ordered to bring them back, but they rarely complied. This last practice was abandoned in the second half of the fifteenth century.

The main sanction available to the lord was the levying of amer-

  [6] For Kemys, *Cal. Pat. Rolls, 1452–61*, p. 447; Kempsey CR, Feb. 1409; Jan. 1478; Oct. 1504.

  [7] cf. Dewindt, *Land and People in Holywell-cum-Needingworth*, pp. 242–50.

cements from offenders, but we know that many of these were not paid. In one case a list of debts on a Bredon account of 1455–6 shows that £1 6s. 10d. of the total perquisites of courts of £1 10s. 9d. had not been paid. If typical, this could mean that the rather low totals of court profits in the mid-fifteenth century are really gross overstatements of the cash actually collected. Tenants might vigorously resist attempts to collect amercements: in 1481 at Kempsey Hugh Symonds assaulted the beadle with a drawn sword when he sought payment of an amercement of 2d. Amercements could be levied by distraint, but this was also resisted. In 1500 William Hawford of Whitstones would not allow the bailiff to take a distress for an unpaid amercement. The court replied with the rather futile device of imposing extra amercements, totalling 3s. 6d., which were presumably also ignored.[8]

The attitudes of the tenants towards the courts, and through them to the lord's authority, cannot easily be judged from the formal language of the court rolls. Most tenants, especially those with customary holdings, attended the courts. Occasionally they were amerced for arriving late or leaving before the end. At Stratford a suitor offended against normal practice by listening to the deliberations of the jury, which probably took place in a separate room of the court house. References to outbursts of high feelings remind us that, in spite of their declining authority, courts were dealing with important and contentious matters, and expressions of hostility could be roused towards the lord's steward or between tenants. Amercements were sometimes imposed on suitors who contradicted or insulted the steward, and in a remarkable case at Cleeve in 1462, Richard Smyth and his two sons addressed 'opprobrious words' to the steward, and physically assaulted him, an incident for which they were amerced a (symbolic) sum of £100, instead of the normal sum of between 2d. and 6d.[9]

Often disputes between tenants led to altercations in the court. Five Kempsey men 'disturbed' the court with 'illicit and quarrelsome words' among themselves, and another tenant of the same place assaulted his father-in-law in open court.[10] The court books of the 1530s contain the original notes made in court by the steward's clerk, including some verbatim quotations in English of comments

---

[8] Kempsey CR, Oct. 1481; Whitstones CR, Jan. 1500.
[9] Stratford CR, Oct. 1501; Cleeve CR, April 1452.
[10] Kempsey CR, April 1497; Oct. 1446.

made by suitors, which convey something of the atmosphere when disputed matters arose. Thomas Hyggyns of Bredon had evidently been asked to take a holding that he did not want; he 'said evil words against Richard Fysher in open court, namely "he should be hanged before he should enter the said land"', for which remark he was amerced 20s. 0d., later reduced to 6s. 8d. At Ripple William Hale came to the court to obtain a licence to sublet his holding, and in a very unusual procedure, the names of the subtenants and their terms of tenure were recorded on the court roll. This time-consuming activity apparently caused annoyance, as 'Richard Sowthall came into open court... and gave seditious words, and, said he, that William Hale had wrong... and caused the people to have a morning in the said court.'[11]

With the decline in certain types of business, like litigation between tenants and such cases as those involving escaped serfs, court rolls tended to become shorter in the course of the fifteenth century. Some compensation was provided by an increase in the number of by-laws and other regulations, often resulting from the tenants themselves seeking to control the agricultural activities of the villagers. They are very rare before 1400, appear occasionally in the mid-fifteenth century, and become frequent after about 1470. Presentments of offenders against these rules occupied little court time in the late fourteenth century, but bulk large in the records from the 1430s. This amounts to a change in the character of the courts, with the 'village meeting' aspect of the courts' work becoming more prominent.[12]

The institution of serfdom represented the lord's ultimate ability to control the lives of his subordinates. In the thirteenth century most of the customary tenants of the estate were of servile status. In the late fourteenth century, although most tenants still held land on customary tenures, not all of them were personally unfree.

By the fifteenth century the distinction in financial terms between the serfs and their neighbours with customary holdings was a narrow one. Both paid substantial money rents for their land, and could be liable to pay tallage and other customary dues. The main extra liability attached to serfdom was the payment of marriage fines, and

[11] WCRO ref. 009:1 BA 2636/18 43764–5.
[12] On the growing prominence of the vill as the lord's authority waned, see W. O. Ault, *Open-Field Farming in Medieval England* (London, 1972), p. 67.

serfs were also not supposed to leave the manor without permission. In spite of this the lord and the serfs themselves regarded servility as a major issue. When the clerks writing the court rolls came to the name of a serf they often noted his status, using the full title *nativus domini de sanguine*, which emphasized that serfdom was conferred by birth. Periodically between 1450 and the 1540s lists of *nativi* and their children were compiled, involving much time and trouble for estate officials and local juries. Manumissions were made with considerable formality, the grants being entered in both the bishops' and the priory registers. For their part the serfs occasionally denied their status or sought manumission, for which they presumably paid, though the sums involved are not recorded.

The numbers of *nativi* declined in our period and there was also a reduction in the disabilities of unfree status. In the reign of Richard II there must have been some hundreds of servile families living on the estate; by the 1530s there were fewer than thirty. Serfdom disappeared from some manors very early, so that the last Bibury serf was mentioned in 1383, and by the mid-fifteenth century there were only one or two servile families at Cleeve, Hanbury, Hampton and Henbury, and none remained on these manors at the end of the century. A few servile families survived at Blockley, Bredon, Fladbury, Hartlebury, Ripple, Tredington and Wick into the early sixteenth century. Kempsey and Whitstones retained the largest number:

Numbers of surnames associated with servile status at Kempsey and Whitstones, 1377–1540

	1377–99	1400–76	1430–76	1476	1514	1520	1538
Kempsey		19		10	5		
Whitstones	24		14	11		7	6

The reasons for the variations in the chronology of the decline of serfdom on different manors are uncertain. It would be tempting to argue that serfs remained longest on the manors near urban centres where the demand for land was most intense, but their relatively early disappearance at Henbury does not support this. Certainly the situation at Kempsey and Whitstones shows that proximity to towns and commercial influences did not necessarily erode servility quickly.[13]

---

[13] No particular geographical pattern is apparent in the areas where English serfdom survived in the sixteenth century, A. Savine, 'Bondmen under the Tudors', *Trans. Roy. Hist. Soc.*, new ser., xvii (1903), pp. 281–6.

A major reason for the decline in the numbers of serfs was that the families died out. No new serfs were created, and many lines of serfs were extinguished in much the same way as contemporary aristocratic families, either through childlessness, or by having families of daughters, who do not seem to have transmitted their status to their children.[14] For example, two names that disappeared from the lists of Kempsey serfs between 1476 and 1514 were Blake and Spenser. In 1476 Thomas Blake had three daughters, and Walter Spenser, who was in his 60s, had no children at all. Migration, either legally, with chevage payments to acknowledge their continued relationship with the lord, or more commonly by departing without permission, was another important factor in reducing serf numbers. Sometimes whole families moved. Three members of the Boys family of Wichenford in the manor of Wick, the father and two sons, had moved to the nearby villages of Kenswick and Eastbury by 1452, though another member of the family remained on the manor until 1457. By the time of the 1476 census four male Boys were all living away from the manor, and the Wick jurors did not know the names of their children.[15] More commonly sons only migrated, reducing the chances of the continuation of the servile line. Richard Rok senior of Kempsey held a half-yardland in the second quarter of the fifteenth century. His two sons, Thomas and Richard Rok junior were reported as living at London and Worcester in the period 1435–58. Richard senior died in 1449, and his widow Alice married again and went to live at Wyre Piddle, forfeiting the holding. The sons did not take up the land. The last Rok mentioned in the Kempsey records, another Richard, perhaps Alice's grandson, was living at Piddle in the years 1455–61.

For those *nativi* who wished to remain on their holdings, manumission provided an alternative route to legal freedom. As the grants often included a serf's *sequela* or family, they effectively ended a whole line of servility. Some were rewards for 'good service', but most were probably purchased. The sums charged are not known, but those recorded on other estates were large, in the region of £10.[16] The purchasers were often the more substantial tenants; one reason for the continuation of serfdom at Kempsey and

---

[14] P. R. Hyams, 'The Proof of Villein Status in the Common Law', *Eng. Hist. Rev.*, lxxxix (1974), pp. 721–49, shows that it was established in the thirteenth century that a villein woman marrying a free man and living on a free holding would be enfranchised.

[15] Wick CR, Oct. 1452; Oct. 1457; Oct. 1476.

[16] Hilton, *The Decline of Serfdom in Medieval England*, pp. 51–2.

Whitstones could have been the predominance of smallholdings on those manors, which made the accumulation of such a substantial sum of money difficult. The motives of the estate officials in compiling serf censuses could have been a long-term expectation of restoring the rigours of serfdom, but a more practical aim was doubtless to make the maximum profits from manumissions. The censuses could have spurred the *nativi* to buy their freedom: a note was added to the 1514 Kempsey census that 'Richard Pantyng, after this court... purchased manumission for himself and for his whole *sequela*.' Seventy-four manumissions are recorded between 1380 and 1540, with the greatest concentrations between 1423 and 1439, and in 1450–79, when a total of fifty were granted, presumably reflecting both the lord's need for cash in a period of declining manorial profits, and the growing aspirations (and resources) of the remaining serfs.[17]

A few *nativi* attempted to deny their status. The enquiry of *c*.1450 revealed some cases. An investigation was ordered at Whitstones and Wick 'to enquire of those tenants living in the said lordship, who are free and who are *nativi*'. More specifically William Boys, who has already been mentioned, was living off the manor of Wick and 'denied his serfdom', but he had served as reeve and beadle, had 'done the service of a serf without any contradiction', and had a brother, (who admitted his servile status) still living on the manor. The Wick jury stated in 1457 that Boys 'is the lord's serf by blood... and all his ancestors are and were serfs time out of mind'. The decision went against Boys, but he achieved *de facto* freedom by staying away from the manor. The interest of the case lies in his desire to have his free status recognized even after his departure from Wick; *de facto* freedom was not enough. The enquiry of *c*.1450 also discovered Richard Seveger, originally from Fladbury, but then living at Kempsey, 'who denies his serfdom, affirming himself to be free'. He was able to win his case, by showing that he was a

---

[17] *Reg. Wakefield*, pp. 18, 67; Reg. Winchcombe, fo. 16; Reg. Morgan, fos. 94–6; Reg. Polton, fos. 31, 123, 136, 137; Reg. Carpenter, i, fos. 38, 52, 65, 67, 82, 91, 108, 124, 136, 142, 158, 162, 210, 223, 240; ii, fos. 13, 16, 34, 36, 47, 58, 60; Lib. Alb. Pri., fos. cclix, cccliiii, ccclxx, ccclxxxix, ccclxxxxiiii, ccccxvii, ccccxxiiii, ccccxxviiii, ccccxxxii, ccccxlviii, cccclix, cccclxii, cccclxiii, cccclxxxiiii; WCL, Dean and Chapter Reg. AVI(1), fos. 9, 38, 42, 49, 78, 79, 88; Reg.AVI(2), fos. 18, 30, 33, 44, 54, 93, 97, 152; Reg. AVI(3), fos. 17, 28. A similar chronology of manumissions is apparent on the Ramsey estate: see J. A. Raftis, *Tenure and Mobility* (Toronto, 1964), pp. 183–9.

bastard.[18] Much later, in 1505, a dispute over status seems to have arisen at Whitstones, because the homage ruled that 'Ralph Wethy, now dead, and John Wethy, his brother, and all by the name of Wethy are *nativi*', presumably in response to some claim to the contrary.

In the late fourteenth century serfs were subject to a number of restrictions and disabilities. They were unable to enter the church; for instance, John Egholf of Hanbury had to obtain manumission in 1379 so that his son could enter holy orders. In 1381 the son of a Whitstones *nativus*, Richard Bylford, received ecclesiastical orders, but was forbidden in the manor court to hold land in the manor or to officiate there.[19]

Serfs were restricted in their ability to hold free tenures. John Boys of Wick was reported in 1383 to have purchased a free holding consisting of a toft and three crofts. The land was seized by the lord, who then granted it back as a customary tenure, at an increased rent of 2d. per annum, and a fine of 3s. 4d. John Bylford of Whitstones also acquired a free holding in 1381, by marrying a free woman. The land, consisting of a messuage, croft and 3 acres, was supposed to pay a rent of only 1d., but the lord intervened and forced Bylford to take the land as a customary holding, for 2s. 0d. per annum and an entry-fine of 2s. 0d. The decision was modified in 1389, so that the 1d. rent was to be paid during the lifetime of the wife, and the increased rent would come into force on her death. In a similar case at Hanbury in 1377, John Elvyn was allowed to keep a free holding that he had inherited on payment of a fine of three capons and conversion to customary tenure. These suggest that the lord was seeking to control the growing social fluidity of the period, or at least to make some profit from it.

The old restrictions on the personal lives of serfs were also enforced. A Hanbury woman in 1380 who was *carnaliter violata* had to pay a *leyerwite* of 5s. 0½d. At Whitstones another incontinent woman lost her holding, and had to pay a fine of 3s. 4d. for its

---

[18] WCRO ref. 009:1 BA 2636/193 92627 10/12; Hyams, 'The Proof of Villein Status', p. 746, shows that the freedom of bastards was established in the fourteenth century.

[19] *Reg. Wakefield*, pp. 18, 178; Whitstones CR, Feb. 1381; the problems of serfs becoming clergy at an earlier date are discussed in A. L. Poole, *Obligations of Society in the XII and XIII Centuries* (Oxford, 1946), pp. 28–30.

restoration.[20] High *merchet* payments of £1 are recorded before 1381. In the 1380s and 1390s they were reduced to between 3s. 4d. and 13s. 4d. In the first half of the fifteenth century sums comparable with these, 3s. 0d.–6s. 8d., are found at Kempsey, but elsewhere the rate had fallen to 2s. 0d. or less. After 1450 payments of 1s. 0d. or 2s. 0d. became normal everywhere, but the number of examples diminishes because payment seems to have been avoided at Whitstones and Kempsey after the mid-fifteenth century. In 1500 at Whitstones and in 1537 at Hartlebury serfs were fined for failing to pay *merchet*; in view of the number of daughters recorded in the censuses these must represent the tip of an iceberg of avoidance of marriage fines.

Similarly, chevage payments could be quite high, as much as 3s. 4d. to 6s. 8d. per annum before 1400, but were reduced to a shilling or two, and became less common in the fifteenth century. Serfs were then leaving their manors in greater numbers without permission, and attempts to control them were futile.[21]

Clearly in the late fourteenth century efforts were made to enforce the full rigours of servility, which is in accord with our evidence from other estates of a 'seignorial reaction'.[22] The more irksome penalties on serfs gradually disappeared; no case of *leyerwite* is known after 1381, and the attempts to control servile tenure of free land seem to have been given up in the fifteenth century. Only *merchet* remained, and that declined in severity and could be avoided. No doubt serfdom was still socially disadvantageous; there is some evidence that serfs tended to intermarry. Few marriage partners are recorded, but of those at Whitstones, three involved Whitstones serfs marrying others on the same manor, and one Whitstones serf married a Kempsey serf. The choice of partners may have been restricted by the prejudices of the parents of free girls who would have been reluctant to see their grandchildren born into servility.[23]

In many respects the *nativi* of the fifteenth and sixteenth centuries behaved in a very similar way to their neighbours. They

[20] Whitstones CR, Feb. 1381; the phrase, literally translated, means raped, but in the context probably refers to voluntary incontinence.

[21] On the growing number of serfs leaving the manor after 1400, Raftis, *Tenure and Mobility*, pp. 139–66.

[22] Hilton, *The Decline of Serfdom*, pp. 36–43; R. H. Hilton, 'A Rare Evesham Abbey Estate Document', *Vale of Evesham Research Papers*, ii (1969), pp. 5–10.

[23] Savine, 'Bondmen under the Tudors', p. 267.

could accumulate large holdings or occupy important positions in the village hierarchy. When the lords preserved serfdom after 1450 they were keeping alive, not a burdensome source of large profits, but a social theory that must have been all the more irritating to its victims because of its irrelevance.

The erosion of the lord's coercive powers, exercised through his courts and over his serfs, was a slow process. If the main factor in causing this was the decline in population, or deteriorating demand for land, we might have expected the changes to have come sooner. The lords resisted change with some success in the late fourteenth century. They could only be expected to make major concessions if their power met with determined resistance from the tenants. Tenant action might also be necessary to forestall attempts to re-assert seignorial authority.

The earliest example of such action is recorded in 1352, when a commission of *oyer* and *terminer* was appointed by the crown to investigate a complaint by Bishop Bryan that at Henbury three men, who may have been tenants, carried away the bishop's goods, assaulted his servant and 'by conspiracy procured his bondmen and other tenants of the same town to refuse to do their services due to him, and so he had to expend a great sum before he could compel them by law to do the said services'.[24] Like other pre-1381 village revolts, the targets of discontent were rents and services, but, also like their contemporaries, the Henbury tenants apparently met with little success, as the Henbury manorial accounts show little diminution in the tenants' obligations.[25] The great revolt of 1381 may have had some indirect effects on the bishopric estate. The west-midlands region was not greatly affected by the revolt, though the prior of Worcester complained that his tenants were demanding manumission and refusing to do services.[26] Some reductions in the rate of *merchet* and entry-fines in the 1380s, notably at Whitstones, may reflect a realization on the part of the bishop of the dangers in maintaining such dues at too high a level.

In the fifteenth century there is evidence of widespread refusals by the tenants to pay their rents. In 1433–5, during a vacancy, the

[24] *Cal. Pat. Rolls, 1350–4*, p. 275.
[25] Hilton, 'Peasant Movements before 1381', pp. 78–85.
[26] *Chapters of the English Black Monks, 1215–1540*, ed. W. A. Pantin, iii (Camden Soc., 3rd ser., liv, 1937), pp. 204–5.

royal keepers complained that the tenants refused to pay the recognition, a collective tax due to each new lord. The keepers reported that the tenants would abandon their holdings if demands for payment were pressed. In the mid-fifteenth century tenants were denying payment of collective dues like recognitions, common fines and tallage, and individual rents, amercements and other dues. This led to a loss of revenue of about £80 per annum for the bishopric, and contributed to the accumulation of arrears, and the permanent removal of some unpopular dues.[27]

The rent-strikes can be paralleled from a number of estates in the west midlands, other parts of England, and Wales in both the fifteenth and early sixteenth centuries.[28] Their importance is that they show that tenants adopted a more assertive attitude towards their lords, and that they could achieve a good deal in terms of obtaining reductions or even the removal of rents. Lords could do little to counter the movement, because it was too widespread; even against individuals the lords' sanctions were often ineffective. The threat of forfeiture was sometimes used: for example, in 1470 Giles Lumbard of Hanbury was given a month to pay his rent, on pain of losing his holding. Such threats were sometimes carried out but only in extreme circumstances, when no rents had been paid and the holding neglected. When attempts were made to distrain a tenant, he could resist; at Hartlebury in 1480 Giles Harper, who owed some rent, was amerced 1s. 0d. for breaking into the lord's pinfold and driving away a horse which had been impounded there in distraint. A complex example of the same type of incident took place near Worcester in 1469: a free tenant, Thomas Norton of Bristol, failed to pay his rent of 21s. 6d., so the bishop's bailiff seized a parcel of his hay. William Grove of Worcester, a mercer, who may have been a subtenant or even a business partner of Norton, was amerced the unusually high sum of 3s. 4d. because '*ex presumptione*' he broke the arrest and recovered the hay 'to the no little prejudice of the lord'.[29]

It is probably significant that all of these cases, which show the

[27] Dyer, 'A Redistribution of Incomes in Fifteenth-Century England?', *passim*.
[28] Hilton, *The English Peasantry in the Later Middle Ages*, pp. 64–9; B. J. Harris, 'Landlords and Tenants in England in the Later Middle Ages', *P and P*, xliii (1969), pp. 146–50; Raftis, *Tenure and Mobility*, pp. 198–9; Jack, *Grey of Ruthin Valor*, p. 70; problems of rent-collection appear in the correspondence of the period, e.g. *Plumpton Correspondence*, ed. T. Stapleton (Camden Soc., iv, 1839), pp. 67–8.
[29] Whitstones CR, Sept. 1469.

estate managers at least attempting to enforce rent-payment, come from the later fifteenth century. Similarly the only case of the use of distraint against an indebted official, John Wodham, beadle of Stratford, is recorded in 1464.[30] Certainly arrears lessened and tenants paid more of their rents in the late fifteenth and early six-teenth centuries. The explanation must be that tenants could no longer threaten to leave their holdings, and threats of eviction became more effective, as the demand for land increased.

Tenants of all kinds – peasantry and gentry – refused to pay rents. However, their behaviour differed: for example, the gentry contin-ued to be reluctant to pay into the early sixteenth century, but the peasantry fulfilled their obligations more readily.

A similar mingling of peasantry and their social superiors is presented by the revolt of 1450 – Cade's rising. The main focus of the rebellion, in the south-east of England, has been interpreted variously by historians, some seeing it as primarily political, others stressing the undercurrents of social protest by the lower classes.[31] Many local risings took place all over England in 1450, and one is recorded at a bishopric court session held just outside Worcester. In the spring of 1450 a new direction was taken in the running of the courts, and the change of policy was probably associated with the recently appointed steward, William Nottingham. The court rolls throughout the estate for 1450 and 1451 were unusually lengthy and detailed, and contain references to attempts to discipline tenants in a manner which had not been known on the estate for fifty years. A Kempsey freeholder had been granted previously two closes by customary tenure, on condition that he put up a new building; as he had failed to do this, the holding was forfeit and granted to another tenant. At Hampton a customary tenant who had sublet his holding and was living away from the manor was ordered to produce evi-dence that he had permission to do this, or lose the land. A former estate understeward at Cleeve was found to have a holding without title, to have sublet it, and to have pulled down the roof of the hall. For these 'enormities and injuries to the great damage of the lord'

[30] Stratford CR, April 1464.
[31] The political aspect is emphasized by G. Kriehn, *The English Rising in 1450* (Strassburg, 1892), pp. 116–24; an element of social discontent is suggested by the Kent indictments, see *Some Ancient Indictments in the King's Bench referring to Kent, 1450–2*, ed. R. Virgoe (Kent Arch. Soc. Records, xviii, 1964), pp. 227, 233–4; see also Du Boulay, *The Lordship of Canterbury*, pp. 190–1; Searle, *Lordship and Community*, pp. 397–9.

the land was seized by the lord and the offender ordered to pay £5 6s. 8d. Another Cleeve tenant forfeited his holding because he had failed to carry out a building agreement made six years earlier. At Bibury various illicit occupations of land and unpaid rents were discovered, and forfeiture ordered. For the first time lists of serfs were compiled at Cleeve, Hampton and Ripple.

None of the offences were unusual. The innovations in Nottingham's first year or two were the quantity of offences revealed at once, and the severe treatment of those involved.

The most extraordinary episode in Nottingham's campaign took place at the view of frankpledge held at St Johns for the inhabitants of the two manors of Whitstones and Wick on 12 April, 1450. Three women were presented respectively as gossip, brothel-keeper, and prostitute. Instead of the usual amercement, they were ordered to leave the lordship within two months, on pain of paying 20s. 0d. each. Eight unauthorized exchanges of land were presented, and all the land was seized until evidence of title had been produced. Three acres of arable, said to be under illicit occupation for a rent of 3s. 0d., were taken into the lord's hands, and the reeve was ordered to answer on his account for a rent of 10s. 0d., which was thought to be the land's true value. Another smallholding was declared forfeit because the tenant had neglected to pay a fine.

The tithing-men must have made these presentments under close questioning, as some of the offences had happened some time before, but had not been mentioned in previous courts. The next stage after the presentments was for the bailiff to bring forward a jury, composed of tenants from both manors, who were sworn in and asked to say, in the normal way, 'whether the tithing-men had presented well or concealed anything'. The jury, 'armed in a warlike manner, with sticks, spears and glaives, as insurrectionists and rebels against the peace of the lord king', came to the steward. He told them to give their verdict, stressing that the view derived from royal jurisdiction: 'he ordered and commanded them, *ex parte domini Regis*':

> On this, Robert Spechesley, one of the jurors, taking on himself the burden of giving the verdict for himself and his fellows, said that neither himself, nor his fellows, would, by order of the said steward, act, do, nor present, on account of which the steward ordered Robert and his fellows to comply with his order, under the penalty for each of them contradicting the orders of £20.

They still refused to bring a verdict, so the penalties were recorded, and the steward, 'to avoid a breach of the peace', ordered them to return the next day. They did so, but still refused to co-operate. The hostility of the jurors must have been caused by the high-handed behaviour of the new steward. In particular, the seizure of land and the threats of forfeiture must have been seen as a danger to all tenants. But this disturbance, like the others elsewhere during 1450, probably had a political dimension. The jury included some substantial free tenants, even gentry, such as Richard Abyndon of Wichenford, who were particularly likely to have been in contact with national political developments. Nottingham, who had served as a justice and escheator since 1445 could have been identified with the unpopular Lancastrian régime.

The jury's action in the St Johns incident seems to have been effective. The subsequent court rolls of Whitstones and Wick contain no references to the offences presented in April 1450, and they are notable for their brevity, with frequent presentments of *omnia bene*. In the estate as a whole there was some stiffening of seignorial policy towards arrears and tenures in the next twenty years, but Nottingham probably moderated his originally draconian methods of 1450 in the light of the reactions of the St Johns jury.

By the early sixteenth century the bargaining position of the tenants had deteriorated because of the increasing demand for land. This did not prevent them from continuing their resistance to some unpopular dues and beginning new rent strikes if confronted with unreasonable demands. When the bishopric was under royal control in 1533 the receiver, John Hornyhold, wrote to Thomas Cromwell and his associate, Anthony Bonvisi, complaining that Nicholas Poyntz, the Gloucestershire steward, was letting lands and taking fines 'at his pleasure', without the assent of other officials, 'as was never used before'. Trouble was concentrated at Henbury, where Poyntz had given orders that no tenants 'should appear at any time before my lord's officers', presumably to prevent them from complaining. The tenants were 'much annoyed', and refused to pay their rents, so that £60 due from the spring court session was not forthcoming. The difficulties continued in the autumn, and Hornyhold was unable to produce £200 owed.[32] Entry-fines seem to have been the main bone of contention. They had risen to an

[32] *Letters and Papers of Henry VIII*, vi (1533), nos. 533, 1274.

average of £3 per yardland at Henbury by 1530, but could be punitively high. In October 1530 a tenant paid £13 6s. 8d. (equivalent to about twenty years' annual rent) for a half-yardland, and such heavy exactions probably led to the 1533 rent strike.

Another disturbance, in 1504, apparently stemmed also from mismanagement by an estate official. The borough at Stratford-on-Avon was in theory administered by the bishops, but in reality the Guild of the Holy Cross had emerged by the fifteenth century as the virtual governing body of the town. The bailiffs, constables and other officials elected in the bishops' courts were prominent members of the guild.[33] In 1504 three Stratford townsmen caused a riot because they objected to the elections conducted by John Elys, the deputy steward. Elys had selected a jury of the 'simplest persons of the said town' some of whom were 'but men's servants', and had then appointed his own candidates as bailiffs and constables. Thomas Thomas, one of the objectors, was also involved in a dispute with Elys over a land transaction. There seems to be a similarity between Elys's actions and those of Poyntz; he was guilty, in the words of the rioters, 'of... misdealing contrary to their laudable customs of the said town'.[34] Some frictions evidently continued at Stratford because the tolls of markets and fairs which were supposed to be farmed for 20s. 0d. per annum were not paid between 1501 and 1519.[35]

The various troubles and disturbances on the bishopric estate seem minor affairs compared with the great rebellions that occurred elsewhere in the same period. However, they shared some common ground with other revolts. For example, they were not all mere village affairs: the refusal to pay recognition in 1433 must have been co-ordinated in some way by contact between the scattered villages of the estate, just as the risings on a regional scale in 1381 and 1450 needed communication and some organization.[36] The selective withdrawals of rent in the fifteenth century suggest a similar conception of a fair rent to that which lay behind the demand for rents of 4d. per acre in 1381. Refusals of dues could spill over into poli-

[33] VCH Warks., iii, p. 247; L. Fox, The Borough Town of Stratford-upon-Avon (Stratford, 1953), pp. 82–95.
[34] Select Cases before the King's Council in the Star Chamber, ed. I. S. Leadam (Selden Soc., xvi, 1902), pp. 230–4.
[35] Stratford AR, 1506–7, 1518–19.
[36] R. H. Hilton, Bond Men Made Free (London, 1973), pp. 214–20.

tical subversion. In about 1537 the bishop's bailiff at Blockley was collecting money to pay for troops sent to suppress the Pilgrimage of Grace. The villagers of Northwick, under the influence of Thomas Hunckes esquire, refused to contribute, and their potentially treasonable action came to the notice of the central government.[37]

There are many possible explanations of the lack of major rebellions in the west midlands, such as the absence of intense industrialization and market-orientation, compared with the south-east of England or other European areas affected by large-scale revolts. It was presumably no accident that incidents of friction on the bishopric estate tended to occur on those manors most influenced by the towns, Henbury and Whitstones.

The general conclusion must be that there was a good deal of tension between lord and tenants. No doubt there was a paternalistic aspect to the lord's attitude, implied by Bishop Wakefield's bequest of £100 to the tenants he had wronged, and deference on the part of the tenants, who, like the men of Stratford, accepted the established 'laudable customs'.

Was there an element of class conflict in the estate's troubles? The dividing line between the lord and the tenants was to some extent blurred by the presence of gentry who held land of the bishop, and acted as administrators, framing and implementing estate policies towards tenants. The ambiguity of their position is epitomized by Thomas Throckmorton, who acted as steward in the 1460s, while refusing to pay his fee-farm for the manor of Throckmorton. Some actions by tenants, such as the withholding of rent and the Whitstones dispute of 1450 involved both peasants and gentlemen tenants, and so cut across conventional class divisions. On the other hand, the economic interests of lords and tenants were most clearly opposed on the issue of rent-payment. The heaviest burden of rents was borne by the customary tenants, and they were most liable to extra dues, some of them incurring the charges associated with serfdom. The bulk of the customary tenants were peasants, and they sometimes behaved in a manner that seems especially characteristic of peasants, using collective action against rents they regarded as unjust. There is no suggestion that the rent-

[37] *Letters and Papers of Henry VIII*, xiii, part 2, no. 34.

strikes were led by the gentry, or even that there was any co-ordination between the two groups.[38]

Developments in lord–tenant relations were influenced by the general economic situation. The tenants took the initiative in the early fifteenth century after the lord's position had been weakened by the low demand for land, while the estate officials were causing resentment after 1500 by ignoring old customs when the demand for land was increasing and the tenants' bargaining position was being eroded. However, social relations were not governed entirely by economic circumstances. In the late fourteenth century some rents were reduced and services commuted, but in spite of the apparently unfavourable economic environment the lord was able to maintain judicial profits and servile dues. After many concessions had been made in the early fifteenth century William Nottingham attempted to mount a seignorial reaction, but he chose the worst possible moment to do this, the year of Cade's rising; he suffered a rebuff and his campaign achieved only a limited short-term success. In the early sixteenth century the economic revival did not lead to a great increase in rents and manorial profits. It has already been argued that the administrators lacked enthusiasm for their work, but the resistance of the tenants must also have inhibited them in pressing the lord's interests too hard.

---

[38] On gentry leadership in sixteenth-century rebellions, M. E. James, 'Obedience and Dissent in Henrician England: the Lincolnshire Rebellion 1536', *P and P*, xlviii (1970), pp. 3–78.

13. Lord and tenant relationships: rents and tenures, 1350–1540

So far the focus of attention has been on general trends in rents, but in order to assess their importance from the tenants' point of view, we need to examine changes in the rents of individual holdings, and see what light this throws on the economic position of the late medieval peasantry.

What did reductions in rents mean for the individual tenant? On some manors in the late fourteenth century labour services were still performed, but by 1400 commutation of services meant that the main obligation of all tenants became the payment of an assize rent in cash. When the administrators of the estate came to calculate the rent due from customary holdings as the final conversion to cash took place, they turned back to the survey of 1299. Cleeve yardlanders, according to the *Red Book*, had owed a cash rent of 8s. 0d. and works and customs valued at 14s. 1d., so when labour services at Cleeve were commuted, a rent of 22s. 1d. could be demanded. In some cases the Cleeve tenants settled for this sum, but on most manors the negotiations led to a smaller amount being fixed. There were very great variations in the rents that were paid, even between tenants on the same manor. At Hanbury, for example, in c. 1410 half-yardlanders were paying between 4s. 5d. and 10s. 0d. per annum, though their rents, works and customs were almost uniformly valued at 11s. 0d. in 1299.[1]

The rents went through a period of great fluidity in the late fourteenth and early fifteenth centuries. By the mid-fifteenth century they seem to have become fixed. Some adjustments led to small increments in the second half of the century: for example, the rents of some cottages at Hampton were pushed up by between 3d. and 1s. 7d., but on the whole rents of customary holdings were stable during the last century of our period.[2]

A comparison between the potential rents of 1299 (that is, the total of assize rent and valuation of labour services) and the rents

[1] WCRO ref. 009:1 BA 2636/9 43696, fos. 28–30.
[2] Hampton CR, April 1450, Jan. 1476, Oct. 1477, May 1481, April 1482.

of the same holdings in the fifteenth century shows that reductions varied from virtually nothing to 58 per cent (see Table 40).

It is impossible to generalize about the changes. In the case of Bibury and Henbury the disparity between these manors increased, while the slight reduction at Cleeve and substantial downward movement at Kempsey helped to close the gap between them.

The customs, such as aid, spenyngfee, pannage and so on, tended to disappear completely, sometimes because they were abolished, or through their theoretical absorption into the rent of assize. Aid, for example, was paid on eleven manors in 1393–4, on seven in 1419–20, and on five in 1506–7.[3] Common fines were more resilient, supposedly being paid on fourteen manors in 1506–7. Pannage also continued in theory, but was drastically reduced. In the late fourteenth century the existence of large herds of pigs owing ½d. or 1d. each led to pannage totals exceeding 10s. 0d. on some manors. Decline began as early as 1400 at Bredon, but became acute on manors like Kempsey and Henbury in the 1420s and 1430s. The Henbury tenants had paid 18s. 6½d. in 1379. This sank to 8s. 5d. in 1411–12, 2s. 9d. in 1437–8, and a derisory 5d. in 1448–9. There is no evidence for a decline in the number of pigs, so presumably the tenants evaded payment. The enquiry of c. 1450 found that the Henbury tenants were refusing to pay. At Kempsey, Whitstones and Wick the difficulties of collection were avoided by converting pannage into a ½d. rent paid by all customary tenants, regardless of the number of animals kept.[4]

Table 40. *Fifteenth-century assize rents for standard customary holdings compared with potential rents in 1299*

Manor	Holding	Median rent in 1299	Median rent in the fifteenth century	Change
Bibury	1 yardland	19s. 0d.	8s. 0d.	−58%
Bredon	1 yardland	24s. 9½d.	20s. 0d.	−19%
Cleeve	1 yardland	22s. 1d.	22s. 0d.	−0.4%
Hampton	1 yardland	13s. 2d.	9s. 0d.	−32%
Hanbury	½ yardland	11s. 0d.	8s. 0d.	−27%
Henbury	1 yardland	28s. 0½d.	25s. 0d.	−11%
Kempsey	½ yardland	17s. 10½d.	11s. 0d.	−38%
Whitstones	¼ yardland	12s. 0¾d.	9s. 0d.	−25%

[3] WCRO ref. 009:1 BA 2636/9 43696, fos. 33–8, 116–57; /176 92497–8.
[4] WCRO ref. 009:1 BA 2636/193 92627 10/12; Kempsey CR, Jan. 1448; Whitstones CR, Jan. 1441.

In general the manors with the highest assize rents, like Henbury, Whitstones, Wick and Cleeve, retained payment of customs longest, while they disappeared early, even before 1400, at Bibury, Hampton and Hanbury, manors with low assize rents for customary holdings.

The occasional payments that could make inroads on a peasant's savings were also either removed or reduced. We have already seen that the rate of *merchet* payments declined substantially after the late fourteenth century, and they were evaded in the late fifteenth and early sixteenth centuries. Tolls on the sale of animals, usually of 1d. or 2d., are recorded on a number of manors in the late fourteenth century, but there is evidence for them in the fifteenth century at Henbury only, where they disappeared after 1464. 'Attachments' were payments assessed by the woodward or messor to compensate the lord for damage to woods and fields. The woodward's attachments could amount to 10s. 0d. in the late fourteenth or early fifteenth centuries at Bredon. They are also recorded at Cleeve, Hanbury and Henbury in the same period, but disappear in the second half of the fifteenth century.

Heriots represented a major charge on the peasant holding. They were payable by both free and customary tenants on the death of the tenant, and customary holdings were liable on surrender also. The heriot was normally defined as the best beast or chattel, though at Hartlebury holdings of a half-yardland or more were liable to render an additional horse. The animal, once taken, was sold, added to the demesne stock, or even killed for the lord's larder. Sometimes the animal was sold back to the succeeding tenant.

A number of devices were used to reduce heriot payments in the fifteenth century. Some free tenants refused to pay them at all, or showed great reluctance by delaying the delivery of the animal. Cases of procrastination in heriot payment are particularly numerous at Welland, the remote part of Bredon manor where all of the tenants were freeholders. In 1418 three Welland tenants who had succeeded to holdings but had not rendered heriots were ordered 'to show why their holdings are not heriotable'.[5] Avoidance became more common from the late fifteenth century, partly through enfeoffment to uses, which exempted them as heriots were owed by free tenants only after death, not on transfer of land *inter vivos*. Other free tenants simply ignored the demands of the lord's

[5] Bredon CR, Oct. 1418.

officials: a list of 1533 shows that eleven heriots had not been paid on ten manors, all of these on free tenements, some going back fourteen years.[6]

Customary tenants do not seem to have used such direct methods of escaping from their liability to heriot, except, rarely, by fleeing the manor with all of their animals and chattels. Tenants may have concealed animals, but there is no direct evidence for such practices.

More commonly, a customary tenant who had a multiple holding made an agreement that the constituent parts should be regarded as one tenement for the purposes of heriot payment. This was particularly frequent at Kempsey and Whitstones, where many tenants held more than one of the smallholdings that predominated on those manors. A parallel development, especially after 1460, was an agreement that one of the holdings in a multiple tenement should pay only a cash heriot. This became so common by the early sixteenth century that it had the force of custom, justified by statements that only holdings with messuages should render the best beast; the second holding in a multiple tenement usually had an empty toft, the site of a messuage. Smallholders also secured agreements that they were liable to a cash heriot only.

Cash heriots were usually fixed when a tenant entered a holding, and the sums involved were generally favourable to the tenant. They rarely exceeded 6s. 8d., and could often be as low as 2s. 0d. or 3s. 4d., even for holdings like half-yardlands, the tenants of which would usually own cattle worth 5s. 0d. to 10s. 0d. in the late fifteenth century.

Heriots on customary holdings could be completely avoided by the device, in the case of *inter-vivos* transfers, of including the former tenant's heriot with the incoming tenant's entry-fine. This is recorded as early as the 1370s, but it became common after 1450. It is possible that some early combined fines and heriots were fixed at a level that genuinely repaid the lord for the loss of the separate heriot. There can be little doubt that the later fines that supposedly included heriots were no higher than normal fines, so the heriot had in effect been removed.

The consequence of these arrangements was a substantial reduction in the number of heriots. In the period 1440–9, there were

[6] WCRO ref. 009:1 BA 2636/191 92625 6/12.

thirty-six transfers of holdings at Kempsey on which heriots would normally have been due. Twenty-nine were actually paid. By 1470–9, the number of transfers rose to forty-six, but only twenty heriots were forthcoming.

Two changes compensated the lord to some extent for the decline in heriots. First, the numbers of tenants with animals increased in the fifteenth century, so the lord was less likely to receive a chattel of low value when a tenant died. Second, as heriots represented the last survival of payments in kind, their value rose with the inflation of the early sixteenth century, while fixed cash rents declined in real terms (see Table 50).

All of the movements in rents and dues mentioned so far tended to be sluggish and changed in the long term only. The differences between manors suggest that supply and demand played some part in determining the level of rents, but the force of the lord's authority and the influence of custom meant that tenants did not enjoy the maximum advantage of reductions until the mid- to late fifteenth century. Once rents had been reduced or removed, reimposition does not seem to have been possible. The only tenant payments that were flexible were the entry-fines due when a tenant took up a new customary holding. These have been calculated at a rate of £s per yardland, and the averages in ten-year period are given in Fig. 5. It is often assumed that the rate of fine was determined by the demand for land. Other factors were also influential, as in individual cases when the fine was waived 'for good service', or when the tenant's capacity to pay clearly influenced the amount of the fine: for example, a Worcester goldsmith who took a Whitstones holding paid nearly three times the normal rate.[7] Non-economic factors may also lie behind the halving of the rate of fine at Whitstones between the 1370s and 1380s; this could have been influenced by the events of 1381, and the high arbitrary fines disputed at Henbury in the 1530s have already been mentioned.

High rates of fine, at £1 per yardland or more, prevailed on the estate, except at Bibury and Bredon, in the late fourteenth century. At Kempsey high fines continued into the first two decades of the fifteenth century. Fines were generally low between 1430 and 1470, with a substantial proportion of transactions in which no fine was paid, or only nominal fines in the form of a few poultry. Cash fines

[7] St. Johns view, May 1462.

were normally less than a year's rent, usually below £1 per yardland.

Fines began to increase in the 1470s and 1480s, and by the first decade of the sixteenth century were often well above the mid-fifteenth century nadir. They tended to fall in the 1510s, but a rising trend is again apparent by 1530. In the 1530s fines exceeded £3 per yardland at Kempsey, £5 at Whitstones and £8 at Henbury. The main divergence from these trends was at Hampton, where fines remained low throughout the late fifteenth and early sixteenth centuries. There in the 1520s five fines were recorded as nil; in each case the explanation was given that the buildings on the holding were ruinous.

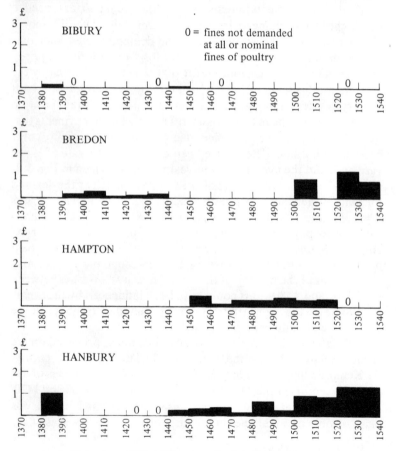

5 Entry-fines, 1370–1540, per yardland, in decennial averages.

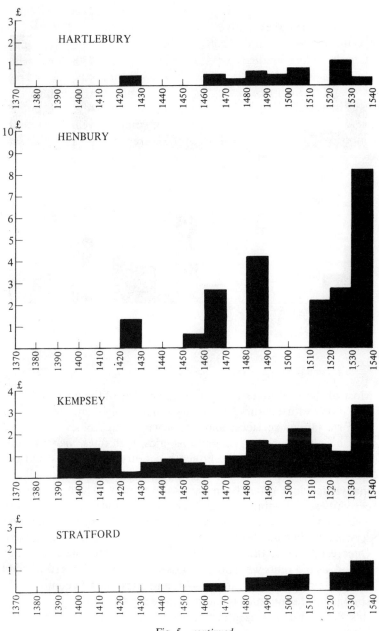

Fig. 5 – *continued*

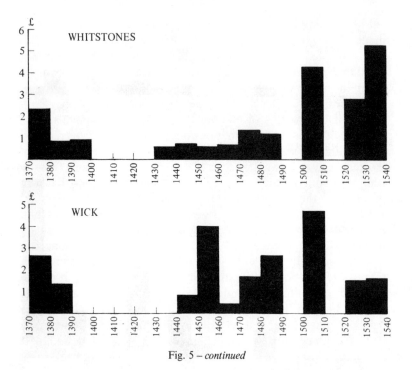

Fig. 5 – *continued*

Most of these changes were to the advantage of the tenants. In the late fourteenth century customary tenants might still be liable to perform labour services, and pay a wide range of extra and occasional dues such as recognitions, aids, high fines, *merchet*, tolls and pannage. By the mid-fifteenth century assize rents had declined and had been fixed, and regular extra payments like aid and spenyngfee had often been removed entirely. Much of the uncertainty surrounding rents and services had gone. Labour services had been commuted, recognitions removed, amercements and servile dues became less frequent, entry-fines and pannage reduced. Once established, these conditions remained until the end of our period, as old rents were not reimposed. Only entry-fines responded to new circumstances after 1470, and these had become a substantial burden on some manors by the early sixteenth century. Even this development was offset to some extent by the reduction in liability to heriot.

Life was made easier for tenants in the sense that their rents made fewer inroads on their annual income, so that more produce was available for consumption by the peasant and his family, and smallholders would not need to earn so much from wage work in order to pay rent. For the better-off tenants the removal or reduction of rent and occasional dues gave them more opportunity to accumulate capital for buildings, equipment and animals.

Some of the social distinctions between tenants were reduced. The number of serfs declined. The gap between free and customary tenure was less marked, as free rents did not change greatly, while customary rents declined, and many of the dues that were peculiar to the customary tenants disappeared.

Rents can also tell us about variations in the demand for land. In view of the other evidence of seignorial pressure on tenants in the late fourteenth century, we must be uncertain about the significance of the high entry-fines for that period. With the relaxation of the lord's social controls in the fifteenth century, it may be assumed that fines responded in that century primarily to the demand for land. Their movements, which can be paralleled in other parts of England, imply a very slack competition for holdings in the mid-fifteenth century, with a definite upturn in the 1470s and 1480s on a number of manors, which was sustained, after a set-back, in the early sixteenth century.[8] The considerable geographical disparities in the rate of fines point to variations in economic vitality over the manors of the estate (see Table 41). These coincide to a large extent with the different levels of assize rents in 1299 (see Table 10) and the fifteenth century. Proximity to large towns seems to have determined the high demand for land at Henbury, Whitstones, Wick and Kempsey. In view of the growth in Worcester's relative importance in the later middle ages and Bristol's decline in the early sixteenth century, it might be expected that the rate of entry-fines would show a narrowing of the gap between Henbury and the Worcester group of manors, but no such trend is apparent. Perhaps the crucial factor was the size of the nearby city, as Bristol in the 1530s still had more than twice Worcester's population.[9]

[8] Blanchard, 'Population Change, Enclosure, and the Early Tudor Economy', pp. 433–5.
[9] H. C. Darby (ed.), *A New Historical Geography of England before 1600* (Cambridge, 1976), p. 243; Dyer, *The City of Worcester in the Sixteenth Century*, p. 27.

Table 41. *Ranking order of manors by level of entry-fines*

Entry-fines per yardland

Manors	Highest average in any one decade, 1500–40
Henbury	over £8
Whitstones Wick	over £4
Kempsey	over £3
Bredon Cleeve Hanbury Hartlebury Stratford Tredington	£1–£2
Alvechurch Bibury Blockley Fladbury Hampton Ripple Withington	under £1

At the bottom end of the scale we gain the impression that some of the villages on the estate were in a very depressed state, with little demand for land, even in the early sixteenth century. Land was still being granted for no entry fine at all at Bibury and Hampton in the 1520s and 1530s.

There were also important changes in the tenures by which lands were held in the later medieval period. In the thirteenth century, with the exception of the minority who received leases of holdings for cash rents, customary tenants held on uniform hereditary tenures. In the late fourteenth century the lord often found himself with customary holdings on his hands, and had to find ways of securing tenants for these, with the least loss of rent. They were often leased for terms of years, or let 'at will'. The normal term for leasehold was short, often nine or twelve years. Tenancies 'at will' were of course terminable at any time. Tenants were attracted to these short-term lettings by low entry fines, some reduction in rent, and by the absence of labour services. Both types of tenure could protect the lord from permanent loss of rent in the event of a rise in land values, and the tenants also might accept them in the expectation of an eventual fall in rent.[10] These forms of tenure were used throughout our period for demesnes and mills, but after frequent references to them in connection with customary holdings in the late fourteenth and early fifteenth centuries, they disappear from the documents as they were converted back into hereditary customary tenures.[11] The Whitstones court rolls record fifteen tenancies for terms of years in the period 1378–98, ten of them for customary holdings, but only two after 1400. Of the seven customary tenements recorded as being held 'at will', four appear before 1400 and all before 1450. In one case the conversion of a leasehold tenancy to hereditary customary tenure is recorded when the tenant, John Joye, gave a fine of 1s. 0d. for the change to be made.[12] In other cases the change seems to have occurred when an heir took over a holding previously held on a short-term or precarious tenure.

The fluidity of late fourteenth-century tenures, followed by a reassertion of more stable forms, is well illustrated by the changes at Cleeve. In 1372–3 the tenants paid assize rents totalling £18 13s. 11d., not much less than in 1299, when the total had been £21 12s. 4¾d. The customary tenants were still performing most of their labour services, and works worth only £1 19s. 8¼d. had been 'sold' to the tenants. The simplicity of the situation in 1372–3 contrasts with the complexities of that in 1393–4. Most of the assize rent total was deducted in the 'allowance of rent' section, because thirty-one customary holdings were let at farm for terms of ten or twelve years or 'at will', and were listed individually as 'issues of the holdings of *nativi* in the lord's hands', or under the heading of 'farms'. Soon after 1394 the demesne were leased and the remaining labour services commuted, and by 1426 a transformation had taken place. All holdings were treated as normal customary tenements, paying assize rents and sums for commuted works, and only four holdings were held on lease.[13] The court records of Cleeve confirm that leasehold and 'at will' tenures had largely ceased to be used for custom-

[10] C. M. Gray, *Copyhold, Equity, and the Common Law* (Cambridge, Mass., 1963), pp. 9–12.

[11] For a similar movement from short-term or precarious tenures to hereditary tenures, see Harvey, *Westminster Abbey*, pp. 276–7; on other estates tenures 'at will' and for terms of years continued through the late medieval period, see Hilton, *Some Leicestershire Estates*, pp. 94–105.

[12] Whitstones CR, Oct. 1398.

[13] Cleeve AR, 1372–3, 1393–4, 1426–7.

ary holdings in the fifteenth century. A similar pattern of change on a smaller scale is apparent on the other manors, such as Henbury and Stoke, in about 1400. The Hanbury tenancies changed rather later. Sixteen of thirty-two customary holdings were 'at will' in c.1410, but none in 1466.

Copies of court roll held by the tenants as proof of their title are occasionally mentioned in the fifteenth century, and it is clear that hereditary copyhold tenure became the normal form of customary landholding on the estate. It became increasingly common for tenants in the late fifteenth century to surrender their lands and take them back as tenures for lives, usually specified as those of the tenant, his wife and a son. In the late fifteenth and early sixteenth centuries, reflecting the increased demand for land, would-be tenants acquired the reversion of holdings while a tenant, often a relative, was still living, so that the succession to the holding was secured for the future. In the long run, by the mid-seventeenth century, the form of copyhold on some manors became 'by copy of court roll for one life in possession and three lives in reversion'; that is, copyhold for lives rather than copyhold of inheritance, but this development probably came after 1540.[14]

Historians have long debated the extent to which copyholders enjoyed security of tenure.[15] It is important to examine the actual practice of lords, as recorded in court rolls, rather than to rely too heavily on the *dicta* of the great lawyers, or the relatively small number of cases that came before the royal courts. Evictions, or rather the forfeiture of holdings in the phraseology of the manorial courts, are recorded occasionally in the mid-fifteenth century, when attempts were made to tighten up the estate administration, and particular interest was being shown in maintaining tenants' buildings in good condition. Of the twenty cases known between 1440 and 1480, most were for neglect or destruction of buildings, but some were also for not living on the holding, illicit subletting, non-payment of rent, or for the tenant being 'badly governed'. Some tenants were accused of two or three of these offences together.

[14] T. R. Nash, *Collections for the History of Worcestershire*, 2nd edn (1781), i, pp. 97, 206.

[15] Notably R. H. Tawney, *The Agrarian Problem in the Sixteenth Century*, 2nd edn (New York, 1967), pp. 287–310; Gray, *Copyhold, Equity, and the Common Law, passim.*; E. Kerridge, *Agrarian Problems in the Sixteenth Century and After* (London, 1969), pp. 65–93.

Forfeiture was used sparingly in flagrant cases, or the number of tenants evicted for neglecting buildings or failing to pay their rents in full would have run into hundreds. Threats of forfeiture were often used to attempt to persuade tenants to observe their obligations, and a few actual evictions may have had some effect in encouraging the other tenants to take court orders seriously.

Forfeiture was rare after 1500. In 1529 a Kempsey tenant was found to have sublet almost all of his customary holding without permission, and the land was seized and granted to another tenant. A Henbury tenant, Edmund Wedon, who had a customary holding of a messuage and 5 acres, and 4 acres of demesne 'at will', was said in 1539 to have 'made an assault and affray' on Richard Brodebank, the lord's deputy steward, and took traps for catching wildfowl that belonged to the lord. For this, Wedon was 'discharged from his tenure and also from his demesnes'.[16]

The lord retained the right to remove tenants who breached custom, but the numbers of forfeitures diminished in the early sixteenth century. The same is true of the lord's rights to impose conditions on tenants, and to interfere in the succession to holdings. The most frequent extra obligation expected of some new tenants was that they would put up new buildings on their holdings, usually within a year or two of entering the land. Building agreements were rare before 1400; one tenant at Whitstones in 1388 was let off having to build a sheepcote on payment of a fine, as there were still some buildings on the holding. Building contracts for new tenants were most common in the period 1440–80, twenty-nine being recorded in those decades, but they cease to appear after 1490.[17]

To what extent was the lord able to choose his customary tenants? In the late fifteenth century it was still possible to use some discretion. In 1462 Alice Maunger of Whitstones surrendered a quarteryardland. Her son Richard, who would normally have had first claim on the land, was declared to be 'badly governed', so that 'his title and claim are forfeit' and the land passed to Alice's daughter and her husband. Another untrustworthy character at Wick, Richard Wody, was allowed in 1475 to take up a holding, but only

[16] WCRO ref. 009:1 BA 2636/18 43764.

[17] In Worcestershire in general there is a similar decline at the end of the fifteenth century in the number of building contracts: see R. K. Field, 'Worcestershire Peasant Buildings, Household Goods and Farming Equipment', *Medieval Arch.*, ix (1965), pp. 125–36.

under stringent conditions, that he would not 'act against the lord's tenants...in any illicit causes touching the ancient custom of the manor', on pain of paying 40s. 0d. and of forfeiting the land. He was also supposed to rebuild a barn and bakehouse on the holding.

In the early sixteenth century attempts were made by officials to influence the choice of tenants, but not without protest. In 1538 two tenants of Claines in Whitstones petitioned the king's council over the rights of daughters to succeed to customary holdings. Evidently the bishop's officials had decided not to allow inheritance by daughters, and the other Claines tenants supported them, saying 'that they never knew any man's daughter ever was adjudged to any customary tenement by their custom, or that ever they had any such custom', and 'that they never knew any wrong done unto any of the tenants there by any officer of the lord's.'[18] In fact a daughter had taken a customary tenement as recently as 1462, and not all of the bishopric tenants were as satisfied with the behaviour of officials. Mention has already been made of the dispute that arose at Henbury in the 1520s when Prior William More, the bishop's surveyor, favoured his brother by granting him a customary holding. The case resulted in a petition called a 'certificate', to the bishop from the Henbury tenants, which is the fullest statement that we have on the mutual obligations of lord and tenants. The tenants were to pay rents and other dues, repair their houses, choose a reeve and even make up the losses if the reeve made off with rent money already paid. The lord was reminded that he ought to allow tenants to 'buy' (that is, pay entry-fines) 'open in the court' and that new tenants should be approved by the other tenants, so that 'if my lord's tenants will not able any tenant that hath been taken tenant contrary to the custom, that then my lord's officers shall not admit him for no tenant of my lord's, but to discharge him, and his bargain to stand as void'. Lastly, if a holding became vacant, the former tenant's children or relatives should be able to take it for a reasonable fine. This Henbury 'certificate' emphasizes the overriding claims of inheritance in succession to holdings, and introduces the notion that the whole body of tenants could veto a choice made by the estate officials.[19]

These disputes show that the lord's officials had to be care-

[18] WCRO ref. 009:1 BA 2636/18 43763.
[19] GRO D1799, M28.

ful in their actions over tenures, or they could provoke trouble from the tenants. Both cases were taken to the Star Chamber, which indicates the power of the central government to interfere in disputes over copyhold. This must have acted as a check on the officials.[20]

As far as copyhold conditions after 1500 are concerned, we must conclude that tenure became more secure and less subject to seignorial interference. Of course, a ruthless lord could have exploited his residual powers of eviction, or the variable entry fines on the estate, to remove tenants and prevent heirs succeeding. Perhaps the attitude of the tenants to infringements of custom, and the potential power of the government to protect tenants, helped to prevent unscrupulous officials dealing more arbitrarily with copyhold tenants. The tenants' position on at least one manor seems not to have deteriorated after 1540, as a Whitstones jury of the mid-seventeenth century could not recall a case of forfeiture in living memory.[21]

The extent to which tenants controlled their copyholds by the end of our period is indicated by the bequests of customary land that appear in tenants' wills. For example, in 1539 John Edmonds of Westbury-on-Trym in Stoke left leasehold land and a tenement of unspecified status to his younger son, while he bequeathed a customary half-yardland called 'the Avyn house' to his eldest son and gave instruction on bargaining over the fine, 'and they to pay to my lord bishop's officers £12, or to agree with them the best cheap [that is, the cheapest] they can'.[22]

The peasantry had made significant advances in obtaining reduced rents and more secure tenures during the fifteenth century.

[20] Gray, *Copyhold, Equity, and the Common Law*, pp. 51–3, argues that the court of Chancery played a major role in extending protection to copyhold in the reigns of Henry VII and Henry VIII, while Star Chamber had a subsidiary function.

[21] Nash, *Collections for the History of Worcestershire*, i, p. 205.

[22] Worcester Wills 1538/46; Levett, *Studies in Manorial History*, pp. 208–34, shows an earlier origin, but then a decline, in the disposal of land by will.

14. *The land-market and peasant landholding*

As well as gaining greater control of their land and the product of their labour, the peasantry were able to increase the size of their holdings. There has been much discussion of the exact nature of the changing distribution of land among the late medieval peasantry. M. M. Postan argues that as a result of the declining population a process of 'economic promotion' took place, in which all groups within the peasantry tended to increase the size of their holdings. Others, influenced by Lenin's work on the origins of capitalism in nineteenth-century Russia, see differentiation at work, by which peasant society became more polarized between tenants of large holdings and wage-earning cottagers, foreshadowing the dichotomy between capitalist farmers and labourers in modern times.[1]

Neither explanation is fully satisfactory. The promotion theory is too simplistic, and fails to explain the development of some very large holdings, while the stagnant market for agricultural produce in much of the period would not have made an ideal environment for differentiation.

As well as the long-term structural changes, it is necessary to take into account the small-scale and short-term movements in the size of holdings. This factor has attracted more attention recently because of the translation into English of the writings of the Russian agricultural economist, A. V. Chayanov, who developed the concept of the peasant holding as a 'family farm', in which the consumption needs and labour contribution of the family helped to determine the amount of land cultivated. The development of the family farm was seen as a cycle, in which a young peasant began with a smallholding, which increased in size as his children grew older and consumed more, reaching a peak when the children were old enough to help with working the land, and then declined as

---

[1] See Postan, *The Medieval Economy and Society*, pp. 139–42 for 'promotion'; on differentiation see V. I. Lenin, *The Development of Capitalism in Russia*, Collected Works, iii (Moscow, 1964); Tawney, *The Agrarian Problem in the Sixteenth Century*, pp. 96–7; Hilton, *The Economic Development of some Leicestershire Estates*, pp. 94–105, 147–8.

children left home and the parents became less active in their old age.[2]

Of course, it is unlikely that ideas based on nineteenth-century Russia will be directly applicable to medieval England, as many circumstances – forms of tenure, agricultural techniques and the state of the market – were very different. However, some aspects of both societies are analogous, and an explanation is needed of how English tenants of, say, a yardland, managed to work their land at both the beginning and end of their land-holding careers.[3]

Rentals (see Table 42) indicate the trends in holding size in the long-term, when compared with the 1299 surveys.[4] Holdings are divided here into those of large, middle and small size; large holdings include yardlands and above, middling holdings those from a half-yardland up to a yardland, and the small category includes all those with less than a half-yardland. Professor Postan has pointed out that the choice of the categories influences the conclusions, but the dividing lines drawn here can be defended as they seek to distinguish as much as possible between different types of peasant economy.[5] The middle category consists mainly of half-yardlanders, those with sufficient land to keep their families, but not enough to produce a substantial surplus. The category of smallholders includes those who had to earn wages to supplement their income from land, and the large category includes those with substantial marketable surpluses and the tenants most likely to employ non-family labour.

The rentals show that in all cases both the numbers and proportion of tenants with large holdings increased dramatically. This may not be readily apparent in the case of Hartlebury, because there were many yardlanders there in 1299, and by the late fifteenth century many tenants accumulated two- or three-yardland holdings, of which there were twenty in 1479–83.

[2] A. V. Chayanov, *The Theory of Peasant Economy*, ed. D. Thorner, B. Kerblay and R. E. F. Smith (Homewood, Ill., 1966), pp. 53–61.

[3] Postan, 'The Charters of the Villeins', in *Essays on Medieval Agriculture and General Problems*, pp. 114–17, argues that such cycles lay behind the land-market in the thirteenth century on the Peterborough Abbey estate, but this interpretation is criticized in King, *Peterborough Abbey*, pp. 99–125.

[4] WCRO ref. 009:1 BA 2636/161 92113 2/6; /9 43696, fos. 28–30, 162–3; /168 92332; /37 (iii), fos. 78–83; /185 92574[b]; /165 92226 4/4.

[5] Postan, *Medieval Economy and Society*, p. 140.

Table 42. *Size of holdings in 1299 and the fifteenth century*

Cleeve	1299	1474–5	
large	10 (11%)	16 (30%)	
middle	29 (31%)	13 (24%)	
small	40 (42%)	21 (40%)	
unknown	15 (16%)	3 (6%)	
Total	94 (100%)	53 (100%)	
Hanbury	1299	*c.*1410	1466
large	0	12 (20%)	19 (36%)
middle	36 (42%)	10 (17%)	4 (8%)
small	17 (20%)	11 (18%)	4 (8%)
unknown	33 (38%)	27 (45%)	25 (48%)
Total	86 (100%)	60 (100%)	52 (100%)
Hartlebury	1299	1479–83	
large	57 (50%)	44 (67%)	
middle	23 (20%)	4 (6%)	
small	29 (26%)	10 (15%)	
unknown	4 (4%)	8 (12%)	
Total	113 (100%)	66 (100%)	
Henbury	1299	1419	
large	32 (24%)	49 (36%)	
middle	55 (42%)	40 (29%)	
small	37 (28%)	26 (19%)	
unknown	8 (6%)	22 (16%)	
Total	132 (100%)	137 (100%)	

The numbers of middling holdings, mainly half-yardlands, were reduced. In 1299 they represented between a fifth and a half of the tenants on our four manors; by the fifteenth century they had virtually disappeared at Hanbury and Hartlebury, and their numbers had fallen substantially at Cleeve and Henbury. This gives some support to the differentiation theory, but in order to confirm this the smallholders should increase, at least as a proportion of all tenants, but in none of our cases does this happen.

Our conclusion must be that the main development of our period was for large holdings to increase at the expense of both middling and smallholdings, which supports the promotion rather than the differentiation idea. However, we must be cautious in basing too much on the rentals. They survive for only some manors, and not in a complete form for those manors with many smallholdings, such as Kempsey or Whitstones, where the effect of promotion was to increase the number of middling holdings. Perhaps there is some artificiality in using the same standard of holding-size for manors with very different economies. Even those rentals that do survive have many defects, notably the high proportion of holdings of unknown size at Hanbury. Above all, the landless labourers, whose presence could strengthen the differentiation theory, are not recorded. The evidence of rentals is static, relating to a single year in a period of constant change; court rolls provide more evidence of continuous developments.

A more dynamic picture of landholding emerges from the land transactions recorded in the court rolls. The sheer volume of land transfers is impressive. The Henbury court rolls of the fifteenth century, for example, record an average of four land transactions in each court, or sixteen annually, so that more than 10 per cent of the holdings on the manor changed hands each year. At Kempsey, where it is possible to trace the descent of many holdings for a long period, most holdings were acquired by a new tenant every ten or fifteen years, and a cottage at Stonehall in Kempsey, for example, had no fewer than thirteen tenants in the forty-five years between 1441 and 1486. This phenomenon is found on many fifteenth-century manors.[6]

The evidence of land transfers is analysed in Table 43 from four of the fullest series of court rolls. The first column includes all transfers involving the lord as one of the parties to the transfer. All transfers of customary land involved the holding passing in theory into the lord's hands before going on to another tenant. Sometimes a court-roll entry simply states that a tenant had died, or withdrawn from the manor, or surrendered his holding, and the tenement 'lay in the lord's hands', no succeeding tenant being mentioned. There are also cases of tenants taking a holding from the lord, without reference to the death or withdrawal of the previous tenant, which implies that the land was in the lord's hands at the time of the new tenant's entry. All of these types of transactions are indicative of intervals between tenancies. These were not very long gaps, often

[6] For example, see A. Jones, 'Land and People at Leighton Buzzard in the Later Fifteenth Century', *Econ. Hist. Rev.*, 2nd ser., xxv (1972), pp. 18–27.

Table 43. *Analysis of land transactions, 1375–1540*

Dates	Transfers involving the lord	*Inter vivos* (non-family)	Transfers within family	Others	Total
Hanbury					
1376–94	13 (36%)	0 (0%)	9 (25%)	14 (39%)	36 (100%)
1420–39	21 (60%)	0 (0%)	6 (17%)	8 (23%)	35 (100%)
1440–9	6 (21%)	4 (14%)	10 (36%)	8 (29%)	28 (100%)
1450–9	14 (40%)	1 (3%)	11 (31%)	9 (26%)	35 (100%)
1460–9	4 (16%)	4 (16%)	10 (40%)	7 (28%)	25 (100%)
1470–9	3 (14%)	4 (19%)	6 (29%)	8 (38%)	21 (100%)
1480–99	3 (10%)	7 (22%)	4 (13%)	17 (55%)	31 (100%)
1500–19	4 (13%)	1 (3%)	11 (37%)	14 (47%)	30 (100%)
1520–40	1 (5%)	0 (0%)	17 (77%)	4 (18%)	22 (100%)
Kempsey					
1394–1421	6 (35%)	4 (24%)	4 (24%)	3 (18%)	17 (100%)
1430–9	10 (43%)	6 (26%)	2 (9%)	5 (22%)	23 (100%)
1440–9	25 (37%)	15 (23%)	8 (12%)	19 (28%)	67 (100%)
1450–9	17 (23%)	19 (26%)	8 (11%)	29 (40%)	73 (100%)
1460–9	9 (15%)	26 (43%)	4 (6%)	22 (36%)	61 (100%)
1470–9	6 (10%)	23 (37%)	11 (18%)	22 (35%)	62 (100%)
1480–9	0 (0%)	12 (40%)	4 (13%)	14 (47%)	30 (100%)
1490–9	5 (23%)	9 (41%)	2 (9%)	6 (27%)	22 (100%)
1500–9	10 (27%)	10 (27%)	6 (16%)	11 (30%)	37 (100%)
1510–20	0 (0%)	14 (40%)	9 (26%)	12 (34%)	35 (100%)
1521–40	4 (8%)	12 (24%)	13 (26%)	21 (42%)	50 (100%)
Whitstones					
1377–89	17 (31%)	14 (26%)	9 (16%)	15 (27%)	55 (100%)
1390–9	11 (27%)	8 (19%)	6 (15%)	16 (39%)	41 (100%)
1430–9	10 (45%)	1 (5%)	3 (14%)	8 (36%)	22 (100%)
1440–9	6 (21%)	13 (45%)	5 (17%)	5 (17%)	29 (100%)
1450–9	7 (54%)	1 (8%)	2 (15%)	3 (23%)	13 (100%)
1460–9	14 (40%)	7 (20%)	5 (14%)	9 (26%)	35 (100%)
1470–9	1 (3%)	11 (38%)	6 (21%)	11 (38%)	29 (100%)
1480–99	0 (0%)	14 (56%)	2 (8%)	9 (36%)	25 (100%)
1500–10	6 (19%)	9 (29%)	4 (13%)	12 (39%)	31 (100%)
1520–40	0 (0%)	2 (10%)	7 (35%)	11 (55%)	20 (100%)
Hampton					
1450–9	19 (59%)	7 (22%)	0 (0%)	6 (19%)	32 (100%)
1460–9	7 (41%)	2 (12%)	2 (12%)	6 (35%)	17 (100%)
1470–9	6 (60%)	0 (0%)	0 (0%)	4 (40%)	10 (100%)
1480–9	11 (64%)	3 (18%)	0 (0%)	3 (18%)	17 (100%)
1490–9	5 (36%)	2 (14%)	2 (14%)	5 (36%)	14 (100%)
1500–9	10 (50%)	5 (25%)	0 (0%)	5 (25%)	20 (100%)
1510–30	9 (41%)	5 (23%)	1 (4%)	7 (32%)	22 (100%)

no more than a few months between court sessions, but are still significant as they show a lack of eagerness on the part of tenants to acquire land the moment it became available. The transfers to and from the lord agree with the evidence of entry-fines, in that their frequency tended to be greatest when fines were low in the early and mid-fifteenth century, which was obviously a period of slack demand for land. (Unlike the fines, the figures suggest that there was low demand in the late fourteenth century, when entry fines were high, but this confirms the suggestion made earlier that fines were maintained at an artificially high level in that period.) The land transfers involving the lord became less common as demand for land picked up, after 1470 at Whitstones, from the 1470s and 1480s at Kempsey, and after 1460 at Hanbury. They revived around 1500 at Kempsey and Whitstones, and then virtually disappeared as demand intensified. Again this is broadly in line with the entry-fine evidence, just as the Hampton figures show a very high proportion of such transfers and a very low rate of fine throughout the period.

Another index of a growing demand for land on the more economically active manors is the development of the reversionary agreement. This method of acquiring land in anticipation of the death or retirement of the sitting tenant contains an element of speculation, and would suggest an anxiety to secure a title to land in a competitive market. Reversions are mentioned in the middle of the fifteenth century, increased in the last quarter of the century and accounted for as many as a third of all land transactions in the early sixteenth. Again Hampton was exceptional, in that only three reversionary agreements are recorded in an eighty-year series of court rolls.

The second column in Table 43 gives the numbers of transactions between living tenants who were not related: that is, when a holding was surrendered and immediately taken up by another tenant, or when the tenant surrendered the holding *ad opus* or *ad usum* of another. These have been picked out in order to reflect developments in the land-market, though it cannot be assumed that all such transfers resulted from the buying and selling of land. There is a clear rising trend of *inter-vivos* transfers at Hanbury, Kempsey and Whitstones in the late fifteenth century, suggesting an intensification of the land-market, but the proportion diminished in the early sixteenth century. No clear trend is apparent at Hampton, except that there was no decline in *inter-vivos* transfers after 1500.

The decline in the land-market, suggested by the falling off of *inter-vivos* transactions in the early sixteenth century, seems surprising. An explanation is apparently provided by the third column, which consists of transfers within the family. These figures are intended to isolate inheritance and transmission of land between generations, so the acquisitions of husbands' holdings by widows have been excluded. The court records are not sufficiently detailed to record the exact relationship between parties to land transfers, so the possession of the same surname has to be used as the main evidence that people belonged to the same family. This means that inheritance by brothers, and above all by sons, is reflected in the third column, but not inheritance by descendants in the female line, and sons-in-law. This will lead to an underestimation of the extent of inheritance, but the figures are still significant because they reflect the frequency of inheritance within the nuclear family. To some extent there was an inverse ratio between the *inter-vivos* and family transfers. Relatively few family transfers are recorded in the fifteenth century, sometimes fewer than 10 per cent at Kempsey and Whitstones, virtually none at Hampton, and a rather higher proportion at Hanbury, probably because of the large numbers of free tenants, who were involved in inheritance more frequently than customary tenants. After 1500 there was a marked increase in transfers within the family, up to 26 per cent at Kempsey, 35 per cent at Whitstones and 77 per cent at Hanbury. Hampton tenants behaved differently, and inheritance remained exceptional. The proportion of family transfers increased at Cleeve from 13 per cent in the fifteenth century to 32 per cent after 1500, and at Hartlebury the comparable figures were 20 per cent and 33 per cent.

Landholding was very fluid in the late fourteenth and throughout the fifteenth century, with land frequently changing hands. As the demand for land increased after 1470 the land-market became more active, with large numbers of transfers between unrelated parties. In the early sixteenth century there were more sons available to inherit or take over their fathers' land, and the greater shortage of land could have forced sons to wait for the family holding, rather than leave home and seek employment or land elsewhere, as often happened in the fifteenth century. An illustration of the transformation of the relationship between the family and its land is the fate of holdings at the death of Whitstones tenants. Between 1377 and 1499 the disposal of property at death (apart from holdings going to widows) led to more than half of the holdings passing to the lord or tenants outside the family. Only 45 per cent of holdings were inherited. After 1500 two-thirds of transfers after death went to relatives.

The frequency with which land remained in the family in the early sixteenth century should be regarded as a restoration of the normal pattern. Before 1349, on the closely comparable manors of Worcester Cathedral Priory, land transfers within the family accounted for 32 per cent of the total.[7] Under these circumstances, close links between the family and its land would be forged, as were common in other peasant societies. In the fifteenth century the traditional ties were broken, so that a typical rental entry reads: 'Thomas Yardington holds a messuage and six acres of land, formerly held by Thomas Wever, and before that by John Smythe'.[8]

The effect of the transfer of land on individuals can be investigated by preparing biographies of tenants from the court rolls. The most complete series, that for Kempsey, has been used. Apart from the inevitable gaps, even in the Kempsey series, there are many problems in assembling and interpreting the information. Subletting was only occasionally recorded, and could have taken place illicitly; tenants may have held land outside the manor; and some individuals cannot be disentangled when two or three members of the same family had the same christian names.

From the Kempsey records one hundred and nine biographies of tenants involved in more than one transfer of property can be compiled. At first sight, tenants with a relatively simple career of acquiring one holding, and then surrendering it or dying, seem to predominate. Fifty-six of the biographies are of this type. However, seventeen of these were widows, who acquired land as their free bench on the death of their husbands and with a few exceptions

[7] West, 'The Administration and Economy of the Forest of Feckenham', p. 229.
[8] On the traditional links, see T. Shanin (ed.), *Peasants and Peasant Societies* (Harmondsworth, 1971), pp. 30–5; on the weakening of family links, see R. Faith, 'Peasant Families and Inheritance Customs in Medieval England', *Ag. Hist. Rev.*, xiv (1966), pp. 77–95; C. Howell, 'Peasant Inheritance Customs in the Midlands, 1280–1700', in J. Goody, J. Thirsk and E. P. Thompson (eds.), *Family and Inheritance* (Cambridge, 1976), pp. 130–1; E. B. Dewindt, *Land and People in Holywell-cum-Needingworth* (Toronto, 1972), p. 134.

kept the land for only a few years before themselves dying or re-marrying. A further nine were cottagers with 3 acres or less, who doubtless worked primarily as wage-earners and artisans rather than as peasant cultivators. So of the eighty-three male tenants who were most likely to have gained much of their income from the produce of their holding, fifty-three of the biographies show tenants involved in transfers of more than one property, and the remaining thirty were of the 'simple' type.

Kempsey yardlands contained 24 acres; after the division of holdings in the early middle ages units of 3, 6, and 12 acres were created, and these survived as the units in which land was trans-ferred in the fifteenth and early sixteenth centuries. They could be put together in a wide variety of permutations, defying rational explanation. William Dorling, for example, was involved in nine separate transactions over a thirty-five year period, and his bio-graphy is very confusing. A coherent pattern is discernible in most cases: fifteen tenants tended to increase the size of their holdings, nine seemed to experience decline, and fifteen accumulated land and then lost it.

Some examples will show that the fluctuations in the size of holdings can be related to the life-cycle of the tenant and his family. Walter Rushemere acquired his first holding, totalling 9 acres, from his widowed mother in 1456. He next appears in 1478, acquir-ing a half-yardland as a subtenant. At the time, as revealed by a census of 1476, he had a family of six children, and would need the extra land to feed them; he may well have received assistance from the older children. The subletting arrangement ended by 1488, and Rushemere died in 1506 holding his original 9 acres. We do not know Rushemere's date of birth, but if he acquired his first holding when he was in his twenties, as was common in the fif-teenth century, he expanded his holding in his forties, reduced it in his fifties, and died in his seventies. It seems likely that as he grew older his children either died or left home. Certainly none of his three sons succeeded him; the holding was taken by a Perceval Rawlins.

Thomas Pensham seems to have begun his landholding career by acquiring a parcel of the Kempsey demesne on lease in 1471. In 1472 he married a widow, Alice Sylvester, and so gained her 9-acre holding. In 1488 he acquired a share in a substantial holding of meadow-land for which he paid a rent of 20s. 0d. Expansion continued in 1497 and 1503, when his holding reached a peak of at least 30 acres. In 1511–12 he began to make arrangements for the disposal of his property, as other tenants acquired the reversion of his holdings. As with Rushemere, the pattern would fit the gaining of a first holding in Pensham's twenties, expansion in his late thirties and forties, and decline in his late fifties. Like Rushemere, no son succeeded him.

Sometimes the pattern of expansion and contraction can be followed for more than one generation. Thomas Bate's early career belongs to the period before the court-roll series begins. We find him in the 1450s with a multiple holding of more than 18 acres, but the holding was in decline, as in 1456 12 acres were declared forfeit because he did not live on that part of his lands. He died in 1464 holding only 6 acres. Thomas' son, Walter Bate, was sworn into assize at the age of twelve in 1450, so he was eighteen years old when he took over the 12 acres lost by his father in 1456. In 1470 he paid a fine to secure the reversion of his father's other 6-acre holding, then in the hands of his widowed mother. He also acquired a parcel of demesne on lease in 1471, and by 1477 held the farm of the rectory glebe. Walter seems to have reached his peak between the age of thirty-two and thirty-nine, which seems young, but he acquired his first holding, and perhaps married, in his teens, so that his family would have reached its maximum size in the 1470s. No children stayed to take over his holding. He evidently shed much of his land, like his father, for when he died in 1500 at the age of sixty-two, he had only a 6-acre holding on customary tenure, and he was succeeded by John Leverok.

The absence of sons has been suggested as an explanation of a declining pattern in a tenant's later years. It would obviously be difficult for an aged tenant to keep a large holding intact. For example, John Walker had acquired in the 1460s and 1470s a half-yardland, a six-acre holding, a messuage and appurtenances, and a parcel of demesne on lease. The total was probably in excess of a yardland. Between 1477 and 1500 he surrendered his customary holdings to three different and apparently unrelated tenants, John Byrte, Richard Buk and Thomas Pensham, all of whom were accumulating land at the time of Walker's decline. Walker had a son in 1476, but he was already established at the Kempsey hamlet of Stonehall away from his father's home at Draycott, and he inherited none of his father's land.

The examples given so far are of holdings which diminished in size in the old age of the tenant. How do we explain those that expanded, but did not decline? In some cases it is clear that the cycle of expansion and decline was interrupted by early death. John Beke began his landholding with 12 acres in 1453, and he added another 6 acres in 1459, but then died in 1466 holding 18 acres, after a career of only thirteen years. John Waren, also in a brief thirteen-year period, assembled a composite holding of more than a yardland and a half, and a parcel of demesne on lease, but died in 1474. Both Beke and Waren were succeeded by apparent non-relatives; Waren's large holding was split up on his death, one holding going to his widow, the others to William Sharpe and Walter Rogers. Presumably any children that such tenants had were too young to inherit. If they observed the normal peasant practice of marrying at the time that they took their first holding, the eldest child would have been less than thirteen years old.[9]

The cyclical nature of landholding, with tenants gaining and shedding land to suit the needs and labour resources of their families, helps to explain the large number of land transfers between families and the small proportion of inheritances and transfers within the family in the fifteenth century. This is in accord with Chayanov's theory of the development of the family farm; similar patterns can also be seen in the landholding careers of east-midland villagers recorded by Raftis and Dewindt.[10]

However, this is not the whole story; our examples refer to the holdings of individuals whose families did not survive or remain to inherit, so they tended to end their careers, if they lived to old age, with a smallholding. Some families, even in the mid-fifteenth century, established greater continuity, so that land passed intact from father to son.

In 1440 Richard Hervey of Kempsey retired and handed over his half-yardland to his son Roger. Roger died in 1465 and was succeeded by his son John. He died in 1485, and it was only then that the holding passed into the hands of another family.

Although land was relatively plentiful in the fifteenth century, it was not available to all. As has been noted already, cottagers often

---

[9] G. C. Homans, *English Villagers of the Thirteenth Century*, 2nd edn (New York, 1970), pp. 144–59.

[10] Raftis, *Warboys*, pp. 179–92; Dewindt, *Land and People in Holywell-cum-Needingworth*, pp. 117–21.

acquired no extra land in the course of their lives. Young men who began building up their holdings with a small parcel of land often came from tenant families who may well have provided them with assistance. Parents might acquire holdings on behalf of their sons. For example in 1463 Walter Rogers, already the tenant of an 18-acre holding, took a further 6 acres which was stated to be for his son when he reached the age of twenty-one. Others may have helped their sons with cash, which would have been needed to pay entry fines and to obtain equipment and stock, but this is not recorded until the early sixteenth century, when wills of our tenants are available.

A variety of arrangements existed by which land could be transmitted from one generation to another. We have already seen how Walter Bate gradually took over his father's holding. The Byrtes' arrangements ensured continuity for a longer period. In 1445 Thomas Byrte acquired a half-yardland from Walter Western, and in 1446 inherited another half-yardland from his widowed mother. His earlier career is obscure, but he evidently already had a mature family, as in 1448 he made over a half-yardland to his son John, and replaced it by taking a half-yardland surrendered by John Wattes, who was 'impotent'. So in 1448 the already middle-aged Thomas Byrte held a yardland and the young John Byrte had a half-yardland. In 1456 John added another 6 acres to his tenement (from John Kerewode), and his holding finally outstripped that of his father in 1464 when Thomas surrendered 6 acres to his son. Presumably John now had a growing family to keep, and Thomas' capacity to work his holding was declining. Thomas died late in 1464, still holding a half-yardland, which went to his widow. She remarried in 1466, and left the village, and the holding passed out of the family.

John Byrte had no need of his father's last holding, as he had already accumulated a yardland, three-quarters of it from his father during his life-time. Unlike Thomas, he was able to keep the yardland intact for twenty years, presumably with the help of his son, William. In 1488 John formally surrendered the holding in court, and took it back as a joint tenancy with his son. John probably died between 1489 and 1495 (when the court-roll series is interrupted), and the holding passed intact to William Byrte, who still held it in 1529.

A branch of the Herdman family was able to use joint tenancies to keep an 18-acre holding intact for more than sixty years. In 1454

John Herdman made a joint tenancy with his son Richard. Richard made a similar agreement with his son Robert in 1476, and Robert was still alive in 1514, with his son living with him, ready to take over the holding into the next generation.

Joint tenancies, which helped to bind the generations together and ensure inheritance, were more frequent towards the end of the fifteenth century. Of seventeen recorded in the court records studied, twelve belong to the period after 1470. By the early sixteenth century they were superseded by reversionary agreements within the family. At Kempsey between 1510 and 1540, of eighty-three land transfers, thirty-two involved reversions, of which a half were between relatives, usually between tenants or widows and their sons.

The whole question of inheritance became more important and contentious in the early sixteenth century. In the late fourteenth and fifteenth centuries the problem was to find an heir, not to settle quarrels between rival claimants. There is some evidence of a concern to protect the interests of the children of previous marriages, a common problem in an age of frequent remarriage. At Whitstones in 1388 the rule was declared that a widow would not qualify for free bench (tenure of her husband's holding) if they had been married for less than a year and a day, and she was not pregnant. This was presumably devised to prevent unscrupulous women marrying dying tenants, so depriving the children of an earlier marriage of their inheritance. Another custom at Wick in 1462 was that a tenant had an obligation to 'remain' a holding to a young heir of the previous tenant, probably when he came of age. In the absence of male heirs, a liberal policy towards inheritance by daughters prevailed; three cases are known at Whitstones in 1378, 1398 and 1462.[11]

By 1538 attitudes at Whitstones had changed, and the jury declared that daughters had never inherited customary tenements on the manor, in contradiction of the earlier court-roll evidence. Similarly a daughter had inherited a Hartlebury holding in 1428, but the custom in the early sixteenth century was that daughters could inherit but not keep the land: 'If any tenant have a daughter to be heir, when she cometh to lawful age she [is] to make surrender

[11] On inheritance by women, see Hilton, *The English Peasantry in the Later Middle Ages*, pp. 98–100.

to whom it please her.'[12] A daughter was allowed to take a holding at Stratford in 1538, but only after a struggle.

Primogeniture was the prevailing custom on the estate, but the joint tenancies and reversionary agreements of the late fifteenth and early sixteenth centuries were used to advantage younger sons. For example, Robert Herdman of Kempsey, who became the heir of an 18-acre holding in 1476 (as mentioned above), was the second son of Richard Herdman. The eldest son, William, was living independently of his father in 1476 and had two children of his own. In another branch of the Herdman family, in 1504, Richard Herdman, fourth son of John, took reversion of his father's half-yardland. Richard Pantynge junior, second son of Richard Pantynge, obtained the reversion of his father's 6-acre holding in 1517. Elder sons were still able to obtain a living away from their parents' holding, so their younger brothers benefited, and presumably stayed at home to assist on the land. The link between inheritance and continued co-residence with the parents is suggested by the will of Thomas Wilkys or Wyllys of Blockley, who left his extensive leasehold lands to William Wyllys 'now dwelling with me'.[13] The manipulation of inheritance customs in favour of the younger children still living in the family home is reminiscent of the systems of inheritance prevailing in parts of medieval France.[14]

As the number of surviving children increased, peasants must have been tempted to practise some form of partible inheritance. William Gibbes of Blockley did this in 1529, splitting up his lands in Blockley and Stretton-on-Fosse between his nephew and three sons. Normally early sixteenth-century wills show that the land passed intact to one heir, and other children were bequeathed goods or cash. On two occasions the heir was enjoined to provide for siblings; the prevailing aim was expressed thus by a Fladbury testator: 'my son shall have all my meses [messuages] and lands to himself whole and to his heirs'.[15]

The desire to keep holdings intact is reflected in the court rolls. As we have seen in the Kempsey biographies, holdings in the

[12] WCRO ref. 009:1 BA 2636/37 (iii) 43806, fo. 83.

[13] WCRO ref. 008:7 BA 3590/I, vol. ii, fo. 46.

[14] E. le Roy Ladurie, 'Family Structures and Inheritance Customs in Sixteenth-Century France', in *Family and Inheritance*, pp. 37–70.

[15] WCRO ref. 008:7 BA 3590/I, vol. ii, fo. 104; Worcester Wills, 1537/80; M. Spufford, 'Peasant Inheritance Customs and Land Distribution from the Sixteenth to the Eighteenth Centuries', in *Family and Inheritance*, pp. 157–63.

fifteenth century tended to be split up in the later life of the tenant, or the accumulation of land broke up on his death. Both of these tendencies diminished with the increased demand for land in the late fifteenth and early sixteenth centuries. This can be demonstrated at Whitstones by examining the proportion of tenants who still held multiple tenements when they died. Between 1377 and 1479 only 23 per cent of tenants had more than one holding when they died (many of these had held two or more in middle life). The corresponding figure in the period 1480–1540 was 47 per cent. In the early part of our period multiple holdings tended to be split up after death, but by the early sixteenth century fourteen out of fifteen passed intact to the next tenant, who was often an heir.

Larger holdings became more stable in the late fifteenth and sixteenth centuries, and this contributed to a structural change in the distribution of land among villagers. Some families established their control over multiple holdings that were transmitted complete from generation to generation. So at Kempsey some holdings reached the equivalent of a yardland-and-a-half or more in the mid-fifteenth century, but these were temporary accumulations. It was not until the sixteenth century that holdings of one-and-a-half or two yardlands passed intact from one tenant to another. This happened seven times between 1509 and 1530. There was a similar development at Bredon, with again seven very large holdings transferred complete between 1520 and 1538, but only one such transaction is recorded before 1520. There must be some uncertainty about this phenomenon at Hanbury and Whitstones, because the size of holdings was not always given in terms of yardlands. At Whitstones few holdings exceeded a half-yardland, and of the four cases of holdings of three-quarters of a yardland or more passing from tenant to tenant without being broken up, the first was in 1474, and the other three after 1500. Even at Hampton, although inheritance did not increase in the early sixteenth century, the first references to transfers of one-and-a-half or two yardland holdings (in a series of records that began in the 1440s) came in 1510 and 1522.[16] The evidence of the court rolls, then, suggests that the growth in the number of large holdings revealed by the rentals tended to continue after 1480, when no rentals survive. This would

---

[16] A similar pattern is apparent at Forncett (Norfolk) with an increase in large holdings from 1466, see F. G. Davenport, *The Economic Development of a Norfolk Manor, 1086–1565* (Cambridge, 1906), pp. 81–3.

be consistent with the evidence of the tenants lists discussed in Chapter 10, which shows that tenant numbers on some manors declined in the period up to 1544.

This throws some light on the problem of depopulation and decay of tillage in the early sixteenth century. When the Enclosure Commissioners conducted their enquiries in Warwickshire in 1517, they found a number of cases of tenants who had been expelled from their holdings at Hampton.[17] Of the four people accused, two, William Clerk and John Brogden, appear in the court rolls as customary tenants. Brogden accumulated holdings at Hampton from 1504 to 1522, and also held the demesne and fisheries on lease. In 1517, he was said to have allowed three messuages and a cottage to decay, in 1509 and 1512, as a result of which eighteen people were forced to leave the land. The actual holdings mentioned in the Commission's returns cannot be identified precisely in the court rolls, but the accusation of depopulation can be reconciled with the general character of Brogden's career as a tenant. He was an absentee, as Minister of the house of Trinitarian Friars in the adjoining parish of Charlecote; when he took over customary holdings, he probably did not sublet them, but worked them with hired labour, so holdings that had previously kept a family became uninhabited. To the modern observer, Brogden was one of many tenants who increased the size of their holdings, aided at Hampton by the slack demand for land that enabled him to take holdings with ease. To contemporaries he was an engrosser and depopulator, building up a large agricultural unit at the expense of lesser men. The tensions caused by the accumulators of larger holdings would increase in the period of growing population, as the number of holdings available diminished, but demand for land increased.

There are two obscure areas which must be mentioned in a discussion of holding size. The first is subletting, which is mentioned occasionally when tenants obtained permission to sublet, or when illicit subtenancies were discovered. If concealed subletting was rife, then the records of 'official' landholding could be misleading as evidence of the real distribution of land. When subletting was revealed, it often consisted of short-term contracts for small parcels,

[17] *The Domesday of Inclosures*, ed. I. S. Leadam (Royal Hist. Soc., 1897), ii, pp. 427–8, 671.

rather than complete holdings. Tenants sometimes obtained licences to sublet when they took over new tenements: this could mean that letting out part of the holding helped a young tenant to cope in the early stages of the cycle of landholding. There is also evidence of absenteeism, especially in the numbers of clergy, gentry and wealthy townsmen who became tenants of customary holdings from the late fifteenth century. These include (apart from John Brogden already mentioned) Mr James Botiller, notary public and estate receiver, who acquired the reversion of eight holdings at Whitstones and Wick in 1488; John Hornyhold, the receiver, who had large customary holdings at Alvechurch, Hartlebury and Wick; and a number of gentry, as many as four among the thirty-seven customary tenants at Wick recorded in the lists of tenants of 1544. A mercer of Worcester, Edward Crompe, held a half-yardland at Whitstones in 1522. Such tenants are likely to have sublet their land. The fact that tenants of high status were interested in holding land on customary tenure suggests the extent of the land shortage towards the end of our period.

The second area of uncertainty is the use of wage labour. In the fifteenth century employees were scarce and expensive, but in the absence of sons they could have been used to keep a holding cultivated, almost as substitutes for sons, as has been shown among the peasants of eighteenth-century Austria.[18] For example, John Pantynge of Kempsey, who employed a servant in 1442 (mentioned because he was involved in an assault), held a half-yardland. He was clearly near the end of his active life, as he surrendered the half-yardland in 1443 and obtained a smallholding instead, and he died in 1445. He also lacked the help of a son, judging from the fact that none came to take either of his holdings. Other elderly tenants also employed servants and were thus able to keep their holdings going. William Churchyard of Whitstones died in 1513 and his widow Joan succeeded him as tenant of a double holding of a nook (quarter yardland) and an *arkeland* (probably of comparable size), and she maintained the holding for eleven years. Their wills mention no children, but Joan employed at least two servants. John Nurton,

---

[18] L. K. Berkner, 'The Stem Family and the Developmental Cycle of the Peasant Household: an Eighteenth-Century Austrian example', *Amer. Hist. Rev.*, lxxvii (1972), pp. 413–16.

also of Whitstones, maintained two nooks until his death, and employed three servants.[19]

On those manors where yardland or larger holdings predominated, there would have been a much greater need for employees than on manors like Kempsey and Whitstones, where holdings only occasionally exceeded a yardland. Hartlebury, with its numerous two- and three-yardland holdings, had a large servant population, according to the proceedings of its church courts.[20] In the early sixteenth century the growing population provided the tenants of larger holdings with greater quantities of both family and wage-labour.

The instability of landholding among the late fourteenth- and fifteenth-century peasantry meant that large holdings could be created, but then dissolved. The cycle of the family farm should be seen in the context of the weakening of the bonds of the family, and the economic circumstances of a low demand for land and its produce. From about 1470 demand for land picked up, and by the early sixteenth century families grew larger and the population increased. Landholding became more stable and continuous, and holdings tended to grow larger. The counterpart to the larger holdings in the early sixteenth century could have been an increase in the number of landless labourers, which would allow us to characterize at least the latter part of our period as one when peasant society was affected by differentiation.

[19] WCRO ref. 008:7 BA 3590/I, vol. ii, fos. 110–11; Worcester Wills, 1534/146.
[20] WCRO ref. 009:1 BA 2636/11 43700.

15. *The peasant holding: agriculture*

Changes in the ratio between land and people, the leasing of some demesnes, the adjustments in rents and tenures, all favoured the late medieval peasants. They were able to acquire larger holdings, either temporarily or, as became increasingly common in the early sixteenth century, as units that were passed from generation to generation. Was the period also one of economic growth, in that peasants invested in agricultural improvements and introduced new techniques? A number of scholars, both English and European, subscribe to the view that the fifteenth century was a relatively comfortable period for wage earners and peasants alike, but that real economic advances were not possible. In M. M. Postan's memorable phrase, this was a time 'of economic decline and... the golden age of English peasantry'.[1] In this view large holdings developed by default, because demographic decline left land empty and easily available. The main limiting factor on peasant enterprise, stressed for example by W. Abel, was the low price of grain; Ladurie also emphasizes the labour shortage that prevented peasant employers from cultivating large areas.[2] Accordingly there has been a tendency to downrate the extent of technical improvements in peasant agriculture, even by A. R. Bridbury, who in other respects sees the fifteenth century as a period of economic growth and rising *per capita* production.[3] Professor Postan argues that the land itself continued to suffer from its misuse in the thirteenth and early fourteenth centuries, so that there could have been no great advance in agricultural productivity.[4]

The quantitative data that could be used to test these generalizations are lacking; peasants did not keep accounts until the sixteenth and seventeenth centuries.[5] Court rolls have been used in the past

[1] Postan, *Medieval Economy and Society*, p. 142.
[2] W. Abel, *Crises Agraires en Europe (XIIIe–XXe siècles)*, (Paris, 1973), pp. 103–12; E. le Roy Ladurie, *The Peasants of Languedoc* (Homewood, Ill., 1974), pp. 11–50.
[3] A. R. Bridbury, 'Sixteenth-Century Farming', *Econ. Hist. Rev.*, 2nd ser., xxvii (1974), pp. 550–3; A. R. Bridbury, *Economic Growth: England in the Later Middle Ages* (London, 1962), *passim*.
[4] Postan, *Medieval Economy and Society*, pp. 64–72.
[5] B. H. Slicher van Bath, 'Accounts and Diaries of Farmers before 1800 as sources for Agricultural History', *Afdeling Agrarische Geschiedenis Landbouwhogeschool, Bijdragen*, viii (1962), pp. 5–33.

to show that peasants were keeping more animals, and many historians have accepted this as evidence of a significant technical
development.[6] Recent studies have emphasized strong regional
variations in the period, and this factor must be taken into account
in examining the bishopric estate sources.[7]

At the centre of the peasant holding lay its domestic and agricultural
buildings, and their construction and upkeep represented a major
item in the peasant farmer's expenditure. The holding could be
provided with buildings with many different functions; among those
listed as ruinous, apart from dwelling houses, are barns, granaries,
byres, sheepcotes, pigsties, wainhouses, 'shops', bakehouses,
maltkilns and kitchens. In many cases these seem to have been
separate structures, not divisions within a single building. The
type of peasant building known as a long-house, in which people
and animals were accommodated under the same roof, is mentioned only once, at Kempsey in 1408, when a tenant agreed
to maintain 'a building for his hall and byre, and a barn for grain'.
Long-houses are likely to have been more common in the thirteenth century, as suggested by archaeological excavations
in various parts of England. On the bishopric estate a long-
house was built at Upton in Blockley in the early thirteenth century, but when a new group of buildings were put up on the holding
in c.1300, the dwelling house was separated from the agricultural
buildings.[8]

Even smallholders are known to have provided themselves with
two agricultural buildings, one for crops (a barn or granary), and
another for animals (often a byre or sheepcote). A 1-acre holding
at Wick in 1466 had a hall, a barn and a sheepcote, described in
detail after the tenant had abandoned the land. A maintenance
agreement drawn up when a tenant retired at Kempsey in 1474
shows that his holding of 3 acres had a hall and chamber, a granary
and a byre. Specialized structures like bakehouses and wainhouses
were usually confined to larger holdings. The messuage of a peasant
holding must be envisaged as resembling a modern farm (though on

---

[6] e.g. Davenport, *The Economic Development of a Norfolk Manor*, pp. 80–1;
J. R. Ravensdale, *Liable to Floods* (Cambridge, 1974), pp. 69–84.

[7] H. S. A. Fox, 'The Chronology of Enclosure and Economic Development in
Medieval Devon', *Econ. Hist. Rev.*, xxviii (1975), pp. 181–202.

[8] Beresford and Hurst, *Deserted Medieval Villages*, pp. 104–13; Rahtz, 'Upton,
Gloucestershire, 1964–1968', pp. 93–8.

a much smaller scale), with three or four buildings grouped around a yard, or built in line.

The size of buildings on the Worcestershire manors of the estate has been shown by R. K. Field to have been normally specified in building agreements as two or three bays, that is approximately 30 by 15 feet, or 45 by 15 feet.[9] The same sizes predominated on the Gloucestershire and Warwickshire manors. They were usually one-storey structures; when a house was partitioned between a retired tenant and his or her successor, the agreements specify a horizontal division only: 'there should be reserved [for a widow] three couples [that is, two bays] of one building of the holding lying near to the street', according to a Hampton custom declared in 1455. The only evidence of a two-storey house is an agreement registered at Henbury in 1483, when William and Margery Rous were provided with 'a lower and upper chamber in the upper part of the hall'.

Some historians and archaeologists tend to dismiss peasant buildings as rough and flimsy, put up by the amateur labour of the tenants.[10] This is not supported by the evidence of the surviving buildings, which must have been built by professional carpenters working in a specialized vernacular tradition, who produced sturdy structures of high quality.[11] The peasant buildings in our documents were built with the use of crucks (called 'couples' or 'forks' in the court rolls). Even agricultural buildings on smallholdings contained crucks; a survey of the buildings on Thomas Hunte's 1-acre tenement at Wick in 1466 mentions a decayed 'forke legge' on the north side of a sheepcote. Crucks were made from specially selected timbers, and when the lord provided them, in the mid-fifteenth century, they sometimes came from the remaining large woodlands of the estate, from Bushwood in Lapworth or Malvern Wood. No doubt the peasant himself joined in the less skilled work of building, such as digging foundations or daubing the panels between the timbers, but the carpentry would have involved paying a professional. Even thatching might have been done by a specialist, as indicated by a plea of broken contract at Whitstones

[9] Field, 'Worcestershire Peasant Buildings, Household Goods and Farming Equipment in the Later Middle Ages', pp. 112–21.

[10] R. Roehl, 'Patterns and Structure of Demand, 1000–1500', in C. M. Cipolla (ed.), *The Fontana Economic History of Europe* (London, 1972), i, p. 118; Beresford and Hurst, *Deserted Medieval Villages*, pp. 89–100.

[11] F. W. B. Charles, *Medieval Cruck-Building and its Derivatives* (Medieval Arch. Monographs, ii, 1967), pp. 1–25.

in 1391, in which a tenant alleged that he had suffered damages of 10s. 0d. because Richard Red had failed to thatch a house and barn.

Construction must have involved a considerable outlay by the peasant in terms of cash. When the lord gave money to his tenants to pay for buildings the sums varied between 3s. 4d. and £1 0s. 0d., and these were for repairs only. The damages on the buildings of a Whitstones holding in 1479 were assessed at £3 0s. 0d. The cost of a completely new building would have been at least £3 or £4, and except for the period in the middle decades of the fifteenth century when the lord contributed cash and materials, the tenant would have borne the whole cost.[12]

A great deal is known about late medieval buildings because the lord was attempting to order his tenants to carry out repairs on ruins, making the construction of buildings a condition of new tenancies and even helping the tenants with money and timber; this knowledge might suggest that the period was solely one of deteriorating capital assets. Yet, there was a positive side to the decay of peasant buildings, in that many of the ruins can be shown to have belonged to tenants of multiple holdings, who were living on one holding and allowing the buildings on the others to fall down. The lord objected to this because it made the eventual separate renting of the individual holdings more difficult, but the tenant gained from the greater efficiency of maintaining one set of (presumably larger) buildings on one messuage. One of the problems of peasant farming was the wasteful duplication of under-utilized capital equipment. This was to some extent rectified by the growing proportion of holdings with empty 'tofts' as the numbers of tenants were reduced in the later middle ages. It is also likely that when a tenant did rebuild, he put up a high-quality structure, judging from the many peasant buildings of the period still surviving in much of England.[13] As well as providing a higher standard of housing for the peasant family, the agricultural buildings would have contributed to the efficiency of farming by providing secure shelter for crops, animals and equipment.

[12] Alcock, 'The Medieval Cottages of Bishop's Clyst, Devon', pp. 146–53. The cost of building in the late medieval period is discussed in T. H. Lloyd, *Some Aspects of the Building Industry in Medieval Stratford-upon-Avon* (Dugdale Soc. Occasional Papers, xiv), pp. 13–25.

[13] E. Mercer, *English Vernacular Houses* (London, 1975), pp. 3–4. An example on the estate is a cruck building of probable medieval date, now used as a public house, which stands near the church at Claines (Whitstones).

Arable cultivation declined in the later middle ages, but remained as a major element in the economy of most peasant households. Occasional references to vacant tenant holdings lying uncultivated are found on a number of manors, particularly in the late fourteenth and early fifteenth centuries, and we have seen that large areas reverted to waste or were converted to pasture on the sites of the deserted villages. However, such evidence as the substantial quantities of tithe-corn collected from the parishes of Blockley and Cleeve show the continued importance of arable cultivation, and it seems likely that there was a higher acreage under the plough in proportion to the population than in the thirteenth century. There is some evidence which indicates that the area of arable was being extended towards the end of our period; for example, at Hanbury in 1500 and 1503 the manorial courts attempted to stop a widespread ploughing-up of the grass baulks that divided the arable strips in the open fields.

The peasants, like the demesne managers, tended to concentrate on spring-sown crops. Walter Shayl of Hatton in Hampton planted 57 per cent of his holding with barley, oats and peas before he fled from the manor in June 1377, leaving his crops to be harvested by the lord and so to be recorded in the manorial account (see Table 44). When William Boys abandoned his holding at Wick in the summer of 1473, he had sown 4 'day-works' (meaning the amount of land one could work within a day) with wheat and drage, and 4 'day-works' with vetch, so that the spring-sown drage and vetch occupied a greater area than the wheat. Chance references in court records provide a rough indication of the relative importance of different crops; spring-sown crops predominated at both Kempsey and Whitstones, with a notable preponderance of barley and legumes at Kempsey.[14] (See Table 44.)

The attraction of these crops lay in their versatility, so that they could be used as either human or animal foodstuffs. The emphasis on lower-priced crops, rather than wheat, could reflect a greater concern with the internal consumption needs of the peasant

---

[14] The references to crops occur when animals trespassed in crops, when crops were stolen, or when a tenant left his holding and the crops were valued. Winter-sown crops were in the fields longer, and the more highly priced winter grains would have been more attractive to the thieves, so the large numbers of references to spring-sown crops are all the more significant. See also Hilton, *The English Peasantry in the Later Middle Ages*, pp. 41–2, with examples of holdings with both similar and dissimilar patterns.

Table 44. *Peasant crops, 1376–1540*

1. Walter Shayl. Hampton 1376–7, sown acreage

	Wheat	Rye	Barley	Oats	Peas	*Total*
No. of acres	8	7	12	1	7	35
%	23%	20%	34%	3%	20%	100%

2. Kempsey court rolls. References to crops, 1394–1540.

	Wheat	Rye	Barley	Drage	Oats	Peas (& pulse)	Malt
No. of references	4	5	10	1	3	8	2

	Total	Winter: Spring
No. of references	33	9 : 24

3. Whitstones court rolls. References to crops, 1377–1540

	Wheat	Rye	Barley	Drage	Oats	Peas (& pulse)	Vetch
No. of references	3	1	5	1	2	2	1

	Total	Winter: Spring
No. of references	15	4 : 11

household and farm, rather than with the production of grain for sale. Also, if the area under wheat and rye was kept as small as possible, more of the arable fields would have been available for winter grazing.

In some parts of Europe, peasants in the later middle ages grew more industrial crops, which provided a better return in the market than cereals.[15] Flax is mentioned in the fifteenth century at Cleeve, Hartlebury, Kempsey and Wick; the Cleeve reference is to a tenant polluting the water supply by retting his crop in a common stream. At Hanbury the crop was clearly an important one, as on six separate occasions between 1447 and 1486 two, three or four tenants were presented for ploughing up waste and common pasture in order to plant flax. Flax was ideal for newly ploughed-up grass-land, and though its preparation required a good deal of labour, the flax harvest would have fallen in the slack period between the haymaking and the corn harvest.[16]

[15] A. Verhulst, 'L'économie rurale de la Flandre et la dépression économique du bas Moyen Age', *Études Rurales*, x (1963), pp. 76–7.
[16] Cleeve CR, May 1414; Kempsey CR, Oct. 1458; Wick CR, Oct. 1481; WCRO ref. 009:1 BA 2636/11 43700, fo. 23; Hanbury CR, April 1447; Oct. 1451; April 1466; April 1482. E. Estyn Evans, *Irish Folk Ways* (London, 1957), pp. 151, 157–9; Chayanov, *Theory of Peasant Economy*, p. 148.

New variations in crop rotations were employed in the fifteenth century. In the thirteenth century the peasant lands, presumably like the demesne, followed a two-course rotation. This was still in use at Shottery in Stratford in the early sixteenth century, when a jury described two large areas of arable as 'every other year land': that is, 'one year fallow and another year sown'.[17] However, by 1465 a three-course system was in use at Hartlebury, as in that year William Ballard was holding a parcel in severalty that 'is common every third year', and a similar incident at Hanbury in 1444 shows that five crofts there were also supposed to be fallow every three years. In 1468 a holding was surrendered at the Cleeve hamlet of Woodmancote, and the incoming tenant allowed his predecessor to retain 'three acres of land... in three fields'.[18]

Such a reorganization implies that peasant cultivation was becoming more intensive, which is the opposite of what might be expected in a period of low prices. However, there are references to individuals on other manors sowing the fallow, which also implies greater intensity of cropping: Roland Bocher of Welcombe in Stratford, who in 1464 sowed 6 acres of pulse in the fallow field, and Thomas Sharewyn of Whitstones who ploughed and sowed a parcel 'in the field called Northfield in the fallow time' in 1487. The demesne farmer of Bredon in 1409 should have left 180 selions fallow, but sowed 20 of them. Similar actions probably lay behind a presentment at Hanbury in 1487 that 'various tenants cultivated certain fields against the old cultivation... They must occupy the fields according to the old cultivation.' Only at Hampton is there clear evidence that changes in methods of cultivation led to a lower frequency of planting on the arable, so that tenants were ordered to cultivate their lands, and in 1460 an ordinance stated that 'they must hold and keep each year one field fallow together, and all other fields sown', on the unusually severe penalty of forfeiture of their holdings.

Whether the peasants improved arable yields in the later middle ages is not known. The feeble performance of Walter Shayl's crops in 1376–7, which yielded less than the mediocre achievements

[17] SBT, Wheler Papers, i, no. 99.
[18] The dates of the changes could have been long before the 1440s or 1460s. A puzzling survey of the demesnes of the estate claims that they were all cultivated on a three-course rotation in 1364, but this was an escheator's survey, and is suspiciously stereotyped, PRO SC11 724; Brit. Lib. Add. MS. 6165, fos. 81–3.

of the lord's demesne, can hardly be regarded as typical, as Shayl's land lay in the fields of the declining village of Hatton.[19] The shortage of labour on larger peasant holdings could have led to the neglect of such time-consuming practices as fallow ploughing, as is recorded on the demesnes. On the other hand, greater quantities of manure were available, and legumes were planted, so the fertility of the soil should have improved.

Much of the evidence for animal ownership confirms that all peasants benefited from the changes of the later middle ages, apparently supporting the arguments of Postan and Ladurie. The heriots taken by the lord indicate whether tenants had any animals at the time when they died or surrendered their holdings. The figures in Table 45 derive from those holdings where an animal heriot was due, not from those exempted through an agreement to pay cash.

The late fourteenth-century percentage of those who lacked animals is comparable with those found on other estates before 1350, such as the St Albans manors (42 per cent), the Winchester manors (45 per cent) or the Chertsey Abbey estate (26 per cent).[20] The bishopric tenants in the late fourteenth century often had inadequate animals, like a piglet or 'a sick mare', as their best beast, so that only thirty-three of the sixty-six tenants rendering heriot had a really valuable animal. The improvement after 1400 (mainly after 1430, as most of the records survive from that date) is not just a documentary illusion, created by the substitution of cash payments

Table 45. *Proportions of tenants with and without animal heriots, 1376–1540*

(from all documented manors)

	Animal heriots	No animal heriots	Total (100%)
1376–99	43 (65%)	23 (35%)	66
1400–99	330 (88%)	46 (12%)	376
1500–40	152 (89%)	19 (11%)	171

[19] Hilton, 'Rent and Capital Formation in Feudal Society', in *The English Peasantry in the Later Middle Ages*, pp. 201–2.

[20] A. E. Levett, 'The Black Death on the St. Alban's Manors', in *Studies in Manorial History*, pp. 256–84; Postan and Titow, 'Heriots and Prices on Winchester Manors', in *Essays on Medieval Agriculture and General Problems*, p. 182; *Chertsey Abbey Court Roll Abstracts*, ed. E. Toms (Surrey Record Soc., xxxviii, 1937, and xlviii, 1954), *passim*.

in the fifteenth century. Those who negotiated to pay in cash were often the wealthier tenants, not those without animals, so it is unlikely that their exclusion has distorted the figures.[21]

In the late fourteenth century many tenants, most of them smallholders, had either no animal at all, or one of little value. In the fifteenth and early sixteenth centuries only 11 per cent or 12 per cent of tenants had no animals. They included many elderly, sick or widowed tenants, who had reached the end of their active lives before they became liable to pay a heriot. The heriot evidence reflects the state of a holding at the lowest point of the tenant's career; after 1400 the number of tenants in their prime who lacked animals must have been very small indeed.

This is supported by the evidence of maintenance agreements that even retired tenants would be expected to keep some stock, from as little as one cow in the case of Richard Reve of Cleeve, up to the pig, horse, and thirty sheep for which a Henbury couple were allowed food and pasture.[22] Cottagers were limited in the early sixteenth century at Bredon and Hampton to having one or two animals on the common, a rule presumably made necessary because some had more than this (see Table 46). Even the landless had animals: Richard Holy, a Ripple serf who had no holding, was drowned in the Severn estuary in 1451, and among the goods seized 'on account of his bondage' were a cow and calf, valued at 6s. 8d. At Kempsey in 1508 sixteen sheep belonging to a tenant's former servant were stolen from the common pasture. By-laws regulating the use of commons were sometimes addressed to 'all tenants and inhabitants', implying that non-tenants owned animals, and servants at Whitstones and Wick were specifically forbidden to keep animals on the common in 1447.

All of this suggests that, in contrast with the situation before 1350 on other comparable estates, the ownership of animals after 1400 was widely disseminated throughout village society. The key problem is whether the function of these animals was to provide for the consumption needs of the peasant household, or whether they signified a move towards large scale pastoral farming with a commercial orientation.

[21] Even if all tenants who paid in cash are assumed to have had no animal (a most unlikely supposition), the proportion of tenants without animals would still decline after 1400 – for example, for Hanbury from 44 per cent to 21 per cent.
[22] Cleeve CR, Oct. 1468; Henbury CR, Jan. 1483.

Table 46. *Stints, 1443–1539*

Manor	Date	Size of holding or type of tenant	Allowance of animals
Bredon	1501	cottager	1 'animal'
Cleeve	1538	1 yardland	30 sheep
Fladbury	1537	1 yardland	60 sheep, 6 oxen
Hampton	1488	1 yardland	60 sheep, 4 oxen, 3 horses, 2 cows
	1504	cottager	1 cow or 'animal', 1 sow or pig
Hanbury	1478	1 yardland	2 untethered horses
Hartlebury	1462	rector	100 sheep
	1479	1 yardland	60 sheep
	1504	1 yardland	60 sheep, 12 pigs and 1 sow, 12 avers
	1539	1 yardland	10 pigs
Kempsey	1443	all tenants	3 2-year-old horses or mares after Michaelmas
	1505	1 yardland	60 sheep
Ripple	1520	½ yardland	15 sheep
Stoke	1539	1 yardland	80 sheep
Stratford	1499 1501	1 yardland	50 sheep, 8 cattle and horses
Whitstones & Wick	1447	1 yardland	120 sheep, 30 'beasts', 2 horses

Many peasants kept draught animals in order to carry out arable cultivation. This is shown by the animals selected as the best beast for rendering as heriots to the lord (see Table 47). At least one ox was owned by a majority of those with more than a half-yardland, half of the half-yardlanders, and a third of those with between 4 acres and a half-yardland, mostly quarter-yardlanders. Normally

Table 47. *Types of animals taken as heriots, 1375–1540*

Based on five manors, Hampton, Hanbury, Henbury, Kempsey and Whitstones

Size of holding	3 acres or less	4 acres–½ yardland	½ yardland	More than ½ yardland
Oxen	0	29 (31%)	43 (48%)	62 (63%)
Other cattle	18 (43%)	42 (46%)	30 (33%)	20 (21%)
Other animals	11 (26%)	10 (11%)	9 (10%)	10 (10%)
No animal	13 (31%)	11 (12%)	8 (9%)	6 (6%)
Total	42 (100%)	92 (100%)	90 (100%)	98 (100%)

an ox would have been the most valuable animal on a peasant holding (though some wealthy tenants owned high-quality horses), so that if no ox was taken as heriot, it can be assumed that the tenant had none. It should.be emphasized again that many of the tenants paying heriot were past their prime, and some may have sublet their holdings, so a higher proportion of tenants as a whole would have owned oxen. Only Thomas Charlecote of Kempsey, who held a free yardland, had more than a complete team of oxen; eleven were seized when he was accused of felony in 1447. Other substantial tenants, like John Best, a Hanbury felon who was hanged in 1433, or John Momeford, a customary yardlander of Hampton whose probate inventory was compiled in 1538, had six and five oxen respectively.[23] Many half-yardlanders and quarter-yardlanders, judging from lists of animals seized by the lord, from wills and from the heriots paid on multiple holdings, had one, two or three oxen. Perhaps Best and Momeford managed to plough their lands with their own animals; the others would have had to make up plough-teams by loaning or hiring animals to each other. The latter practice is recorded at Bredon in 1408, when William Frygge was said to owe a man of nearby Naunton 3s. 0d. for the hire of an ox for a year. Enough quarter-yardlanders owned oxen to show that some of them ploughed their holdings, even if they had no plough. Those with 3 acres or less never owned oxen, and they probably worked their land by hand.[24] There is little evidence of innovation here. It must be assumed that some method of pooling of beasts for ploughing continued, and there is no indication that more efficient horses were replacing oxen, though such tenants as Best and Momeford could have used mixed teams.[25]

Tenants of all kinds owned horses; yardlanders and half-yardlanders usually had two or three, judging from the allowance made for them when commons were stinted, from the lists of stock of felons and from the will inventories. John Momeford of Hampton had as many as five, and evidently bred his own, as he had two mares and two colts. Some smallholders, even those who lacked cattle, kept horses which were taken as heriots. The animals proclaimed as strays show that there was a large floating horse population in the villages of the estate (see Table 48). Both stray and heriot horses

[23] Worcester Wills, 1538/241.
[24] Field, 'Worcestershire Peasant Buildings...in the Later Middle Ages', pp. 123–4.
[25] Titow, *English Rural Society*, pp. 38–9.

Table 48. *Stray animals at Cleeve, Hanbury and Kempsey,* *1376–1510*

	Cattle	Horses	Sheep	Pigs	Others and Unknown	Total (100%)
Cleeve	3 (3%)	17 (17%)	64 (63%)	18 (17%)	0	102 (100%)
Hanbury	26 (15%)	103 (61%)	23 (14%)	17 (10%)	0	169 (100%)
Kempsey	43 (12%)	213 (61%)	44 (13%)	44 (13%)	6 (2%)	350 (100%)

were often valued at only a shilling or two, and were clearly beasts of very low quality, 'olde nagges', in the words of a Cleeve inventory. The horses of more substantial tenants were, like the oxen, ancillary to arable cultivation, pulling carts and harrows. The cottagers probably rode their animals, as they would not have owned horse-drawn implements or vehicles; this would have helped them to find employment beyond their own villages.[26]

Most tenants owned a cow. Stints, maintenance agreements and heriots all show that cottagers often kept one, while more substantial tenants commonly had two. Their function was primarily to provide for the consumption needs of the peasant's family, the 'white meat' (dairy produce) which traditionally formed a part of peasant diet.[27] Cattle were more numerous on river-valley and woodland manors than in the Cotswolds, judging from the numbers of strays recorded (see Table 48). A few tenants can be shown to have developed dairying and cattle rearing on a commercial scale. Thomas Charlecote of Kempsey had seven cows in 1447, and a Hartlebury parishioner, John Thatcher, kept eleven. Such herds would have provided sufficient dairy produce to make a considerable cash income. When a Hartlebury tenant hired a cow, he received 3s. 0d. per annum for it, so that Charlecote and Thatcher could have earned annual profits of at least a pound or two from their animals.[28] They would also have produced calves beyond those

[26] Field, 'Worcestershire Peasant Buildings... in the Later Middle Ages', pp. 123–4. Horse-riding seems to have been widespread, and is occasionally mentioned in court rolls; for example Thomas Couper of Hampton 'trespassed by riding on the lands sown with grain with his horses', Hampton CR, July 1482.

[27] W. Harrison, *The Description of England*, ed. G. Edelen (Ithaca, New York, 1968), p. 126.

[28] The information on Hartlebury dairying comes from WCRO ref. 009:1 BA 2636/11 43700, fos. 14, 54.

needed to replace stock, which could have been sold. John
Momeford of Hampton, who had only three cows, had apparently
reared six calves from them in the two years before his death.

Pig-keeping was also widespread; many cottagers and retired
peasants owned one or two, so that they would have been self-
sufficient in bacon. Pannage figures from before the decline in payments show that more than a half of the Kempsey tenants in
1394 paid for grazing at least one pig. A few pig herds were large
enough to provide a substantial marketable surplus of meat; fourteen of the fifty Kempsey tenants who paid pannage in 1394 had ten
or more animals, and one had as many as eighteen. John Oneley
trespassed in the bishop's park at Hampton in the same year with
forty-eight pigs, and Thomas Elveyn of Hanbury had sixteen in
1383. Large pig herds were evidently causing concern at Hartlebury
in the early sixteenth century, as yardlanders were forbidden to keep
more than thirteen on the commons.

Sheep belonging to peasants were distributed more unevenly than
other animals. They tended to be most numerous on the Cotswold
manors. Within each village some tenants kept none, while others
had large flocks. The existence of substantial individual flocks led
to sheep being stinted more often than other animals, at rates of
between 30 and 120 per yardland, often at between 50 and 60. The
very high figure of 120 at Whitstones and Wick should be seen in
the context of the rarity of holdings as large as a yardland on those
manors, so that individual tenants, who often held no more than a
half-yardland, were in effect being limited to a maximum of 60 sheep
each (see Table 46).

Individual holdings of sheep could exceed the limits of the stints
by a large margin, so that two Bredon tenants in 1406 were presented
jointly for having a flock of 300; at Wick in the 1470s and 1480s two
flocks of 100 and one of 380 are recorded; a Stratford tenant in 1501
was accused of keeping 360 sheep on the common; and John
Lawrence of Cleeve also had 360 in 1523.[29] Peasant and non-
peasant demesne farmers can be presumed to have kept even larger
flocks on the enclosed pastures at Ditchford, Hatton, Stapenhill,
Upton and Wontley.

The cumulative total of peasant sheep flocks could be very large.

---

[29] All of the examples come from the court rolls except Lawrence, whose animals
were seized to pay a debt, PRO St. Ch. 2 18/276.

Tithes paid on lambs and wool in Cleeve parish at the end of the fourteenth century show that between 1,020 and 1,340 new lambs were born each year, and wool production could exceed fourteen sacks in a year, implying a sheep population of 3,000–4,000 in one parish, comparable with the total on all of the bishop's demesnes in the same period.[30]

This examination of peasant stock-keeping could be seen as confirming the hypothesis of general peasant well-being, as most of the evidence relates to the wider dissemination of animal ownership, rather than the concentration of stock into the hands of substantial tenants. There was nothing new about a few tenants having large sheep flocks, as is shown by thirteenth-century tax lists. However, it seems that some individuals had larger sheep flocks than are recorded on other west-midland manors before 1350.[31] These, together with those owning substantial herds of cattle or pigs mentioned above, show that some peasant graziers were producing wool, dairy produce and meat for the market in quantity.

Our knowledge of peasant stock-keeping depends largely on chance references. Court rolls can provide more systematic evidence of structural changes in the use of land.

By-laws, ordinances and other orders of the court, together with records of their enforcement, increase in quantity during the period. By-laws are rare in the court rolls before 1400, but become more frequent in the fifteenth century, especially after 1470, when on most manors at least one regulation appears every year. Most by-laws were initiated by the leading men among the tenants, often the twelve jurors, and reflect their concern for the maintenance of order in the life of the village. The majority dealt with agricultural matters; for example 122 of the 166 recorded at Kempsey.

These by-laws reveal the agricultural routine of the village. The greater part of the land was subject to communal control, even the closes and crofts on the north Worcestershire and Severn valley manors. The 'winter field' was enclosed in October or November, and the area sown in the spring was used for grazing until it was

---

[30] Corpus Christi College, Oxford, Cleeve Rectory AR, 1389–90, 1393–4, 1396–7.
[31] M. M. Postan, 'Village Livestock in the Thirteenth Century', in *Essays on Medieval Agriculture and General Problems*, p. 243; Hilton, *A Medieval Society*, p. 109; examples will appear in *The Agrarian History of England*, vol. ii.

closed off in March. The meadows would be fenced in February. Between March and June grazing was confined to the permanent common pastures and the arable that lay fallow, and at this time tenants had to be reminded to repair fences round the common, to prevent animals straying into the growing corn and hay. After the hay had been mown and the corn harvested, the meadows and arable were again available for common grazing, at first only for horses and cattle tethered on their owners' lands but more freely later when all crops had been carried. Night grazing on the stubble was forbidden, to protect unharvested grain. By Michaelmas all land was available for grazing, though sheep were sometimes kept off the stubble until November, to prevent close grazing before the other animals had been pastured. Commons were protected throughout the year from overburdening by individual tenants, encroachment by outsiders and the depredations of unringed pigs.

This ideal pattern of land use was that envisaged by the by-laws. The fact that they had to be made, and reiterated, shows that the rules were not strictly observed. In the mid-fifteenth century much court time was occupied with the presentment and amercement of offenders. In the late fifteenth and early sixteenth century on some manors less offenders were punished, but the increasing number of regulations does not suggest that the problems had been solved.

The earliest by-laws, like those on other manors investigated by W. O. Ault, reveal a preoccupation with the problems of the harvest.[32] A set of harvest laws made at Whitstones in 1383 regulated gleaning, forbade carrying sheaves by night (to prevent theft), ordered harvest workers not to seek work elsewhere until the Whitstones harvest was completed, excluded animals from the stubble while some corn remained and insisted on the removal of all sheaves from the fields by 8 September. This vital aspect of agrarian life was hardly mentioned in by-laws after 1400. Instead the emphasis shifted, again paralleled by Ault's collection, to regulating pasture and keeping grazing animals in check. The growing tension between the pastoral and arable interests of villagers must reflect a real change in the character of peasant agriculture. Among the Kempsey regulations, fifty-five were concerned with fencing arable

    [32] Ault, *Open-Field Farming in Medieval England*, pp. 27–38; W. O. Ault, 'By-laws of Gleaning and Problems of the Harvest', *Econ. Hist. Rev.*, 2nd ser., xiv (1961), pp. 210–17.

and meadow, thirty-four ordered the ringing and yoking of pigs, sixteen sought to keep animals out of the arable and meadow until the crops had been carried, eleven involved orders that tenants should make 'several' closes available for common pasture, and five imposed stints on the number of animals kept on the commons. Some of the rules were merely reminders to observe ancient practices; others, like the stints, seem to have been innovations made necessary by changing circumstances.[33]

A stream of presentments from the mid-fifteenth century shows constant friction over the maintenance of fences, trespass by animals, putting animals in the fields too early, night grazing, failure to ring pigs and overburdening the commons. Some indication of the height of feelings aroused is provided by the disputes over impounding straying animals, leading to presentments of 'unjust' impounding, or of breaking of the pinfold to release impounded animals. At Kempsey and Whitstones tenants occasionally drove animals off the manor and impounded them at the bishop's palace in the city of Worcester, presumably to draw attention to trespasses and to give the owners a good deal of inconvenience in recovering them.

Direct evidence that an increase in the animal population lay behind these laws and presentments was the declaration of stints. The earliest examples were at Kempsey and Whitstones in the 1440s, and they became more frequent between 1479 and 1540.[34]

These developments could have been the result of strains imposed by a shift in emphasis from arable to pasture, but not by any radical break with the traditional system of husbandry. On some manors important changes did take place, beginning in the middle of the fifteenth century and gathering pace towards the end of our period.

Since the early middle ages the Severn valley and north Worcestershire manors had contained a combination of open fields and parcels of enclosed land, called crofts and closes; many were held in severalty by individual tenants, but were subject to communal control, in that they were supposed to be opened to allow

[33] Field, 'Worcestershire Peasant Buildings...in the Later Middle Ages', pp. 105–6.

[34] Stints of similar type are recorded in the thirteenth century, see Trow-Smith, *A History of British Livestock Husbandry to 1700*, pp. 104–5; there must have been some limitations on animal numbers on the bishopric manors before the late fifteenth century, so the new declarations may be mere repetitions of old customary limits or may represent a change in the numbers allowed. See Table 46.

common grazing after the harvest and when they were lying fallow. A typical example was Palmer's croft, held by Roger Palmer, a freeholder, at Norton-juxta-Kempsey. The croft should have been open each year from Michaelmas (29 September) until the feast of the Conception (8 December). In 1441 Palmer was reported to have blocked the common way that gave access to the croft with a hedge and fence, and he was ordered to remove the obstruction on pain of paying 6s. 8d. He had not complied with this order in 1442, so the penalty was raised to 10s. 0d., and in the following year it was increased again to 20s. 0d. A further presentment was made in 1444, after which the case disappears from the records. We do not know who gave way, the court or Palmer, but we may suspect that it was the former. The size of the penalties indicates the seriousness with which the villagers regarded the erosion of their common pasture. The offenders defended their closes by ignoring the orders of the courts, and sometimes more directly, like Thomas Lee of Kempsey, who attacked Richard Blake with a pitchfork when he attempted to assert his common rights in Lee's croft in 1453.

Three or four presentments of refusals to open crofts were made each year at Kempsey in 1440–70, sometimes as many as six, but they became less frequent after 1471. The courts had not triumphed over the problem, but generalized by-laws replaced the specific presentment of offenders. In 1477 a by-law stated that 'various tenants of Broomhall and Brookend have various fields in severalty in the common time', and they were forbidden to keep them enclosed. In 1479 those who had land in severalty in which corn was growing were ordered to open it after the harvest, and in 1502 'sherdes' (gaps in the enclosures) were ordered to be opened 'at the common time', and 'each tenant of the lordship who has any land or pasture in severalty, except those who have a licence, must let them be open at the common time, by the feast of St Edward the King (13 October)'. A similar order was made in 1503.

At Whitstones before 1400 there were only three presentments of tenants denying common rights in their closes, but there were ten between 1442 and 1451, and they appear regularly after 1468. The attitude of the authorities influenced the presentment of cases, as in 1477 four tenants were elected 'to make a view of various parcels of land within the lordship enclosed by various tenants', and reported that thirteen tenants had enclosed a total of twenty pieces of land, mostly described as crofts. It is unlikely that they had all begun to deny common access to their lands in that year, but they had remained undetected until the special enquiry was made. Enclosures are recorded at Hanbury as early as 1394, but are mentioned most often in the 1440s. Presentments at Hartlebury were especially numerous in the 1460s and 1470s, and continued into the early sixteenth century.

The early enclosure cases often affected old crofts and closes that had previously been subject to common grazing. New enclosures were made possible by exchange and consolidation of parcels scattered in the open fields. Occasionally in the fifteenth century exchanges were carried out with the lord's permission, for example when Richard Gorle exchanged 2 acres of his customary holding for 2 acres of the free tenement of John Langeston at Kempsey in 1458. More exchanges probably went on without permission being granted. When William Nottingham held the ill-fated view at St Johns in 1450, eight exchanges involving more than 25 acres of land were discovered, and John Wode, who was a party in most of the exchanges was found to have enclosed a whole furlong (*cultura*) in severalty.

The final stage, the erection of fences around the consolidated land, sometimes caused disputes. In 1450 John Langeston of Kempsey was said to have dug a ditch 5 feet deep and planted a quickset hedge that encroached 20 feet on to neighbouring land.

The cumulative effect of enclosure involved large areas of land. Whole furlongs were enclosed at Hanbury, Hartlebury and Whitstones in the fifteenth century. At Hartlebury in 1460 John Croycer, and in 1487 Robert Parker, William Wyldon and Alice Bernard were all said to have enclosed all of their tenements. As Parker held a yardland, and Wyldon a yardland and a half, the area of enclosure must have been extensive. The steward ordered in the Whitstones court in 1455 that 'no tenant may make enclosures, except for two acres of land lying near their holdings'. This was a considerable concession, as most Whitstones tenants had only a half-yardland or less, and if they had all taken advantage of the order, more than a tenth of the land would have been enclosed.

By the early sixteenth century many of the villages of the estate must have presented a confused appearance, with areas of open arable interspersed with patches of consolidated and enclosed land (see Ill. 3). A Wick holding in 1537 consisted of ninety-two lands, butts, gores and headlands, of which forty-three were gathered in

3 Part of an estate map of Hanbury, 1731–2, showing a mixed pattern of
enclosure and open field (Worcester County Record Office)

groups of six or more parcels lying together (for example, 'seventeen butts together shooting up on two headlands of my lord's'),
presumably consolidated through exchanges. Bredon manor was
much less affected by these changes, so a holding there surveyed in
1544 had a high proportion of its arable dispersed over the open
fields in 'sundry parcels'; but twenty 'lands' of arable were 'together', nineteen 'lands or ridges of pasture' lay in a consolidated
group, and eight 'lands or ridges of pasture' were enclosed. The

references to ridges of pasture shows that conversion from arable to pasture was associated with exchange and enclosure.[35]

A radical change in the policy of the estate administration in the 1530s gave an impetus to the partly completed transformation of the estate's fields. In the fifteenth century the manorial courts had been used, albeit inconsistently and probably with little effect, to oppose enclosure. In 1538 and 1539 ordinances were made in the courts to encourage enclosure, and they make unusual references to the bishop, Hugh Latimer. He was a vociferous opponent of enforced enclosure, but would not necessarily have disapproved of voluntary enclosure agreements.[36]

The ordinance at Whitstones in 1538 stated:

It is ordered with the consent of all tenants of the same lordship, both free tenants and principal customary tenants of the lord Hugh bishop, lord there, that they should enclose all lands, namely meadows, wastes, pastures, and arable entirely. And moreover by the lord's grace all tenants may have licence to make exchanges one with another to the greater profit of the same tenants.

A similar order at Hanbury in the same year used much the same terms, emphasizing the permanence of the proposed change:

and keep several all lands, meadows and pastures of the aforesaid [lordship] in perpetuity.

At Stratford the order was confined to the townships of Old Town and Welcombe:

It is ordered with the consent of all tenants... [that they should] exchange with one another land for land, to the greater profit of all of the lord's tenants of the same, and thus remain several.

Two tenants at Bevere in Whitstones acted immediately on the order, so that one exchanged a holding of 22 acres of arable, 4 acres of meadow, a parcel of paddock and a parcel of pasture for an almost identical amount of land held by the other. At Hanbury in 1539 the tenants agreed to a list of 'closes that shall be kept several' drawn up by six men appointed for the purpose. The lands itemized amounted to 216½ acres, with some closes and a field of unknown size. They were held by twenty-three tenants, about a half of the total.[37]

---

[35] WCRO ref. 009:1 BA 2636/18 43763; /37 (iii) 43806, fo. 49.

[36] Latimer in his sermons blamed graziers and enclosers for depopulation, impoverishing the yeomen and causing Ket's rebellion, *Sermons by Hugh Latimer*, ed. G. E. Corrie (Parker Soc., 1844), pp. 99–102, 248–9.

[37] WCRO ref. 705:7 BA 7335/95 (iii).

The most complete example of peasant enclosure is provided by the Henbury demesne. Demesne farmers were in the vanguard of enclosure in the mid-fifteenth century, as we have seen, but they were usually members of the gentry. The Henbury and Stoke demesnes were leased in the early sixteenth century in parcels to peasant tenants. In 1299 82 per cent of the land had been arable, and lay in furlongs that were under a two-course rotation, presumably as part of the common fields of the surrounding villages. By the 1530s, 469 acres of the 745 acres of demesne were held in severalty. Land use had changed drastically; even in the late fourteenth century on the two demesnes a total of at least 100 acres were cultivated each year, but in the early sixteenth century there were only 44 acres of arable, and 86 per cent of the land was described as pasture and meadow. Some enclosed pastures consisted of the unploughed ridges and headlands of former arable.[38]

Enclosure was furthest advanced on the north Worcestershire and Severn valley manors of the estate. Apart from Hanbury, Hartlebury, Henbury and Stoke, Kempsey, Whitstones and Wick where the pre-1540 evidence is abundant, later documents, the glebe terriers, show much consolidation or enclosure at Alvechurch and Ripple by 1616. By contrast, the Avon valley and Cotswold manors were still unenclosed by the time of the glebe terriers of 1585–1635, and Tredington retained large areas of open field until the nineteenth century.[39] (See Ill. 4). The Hampton court rolls show that the traditional system of husbandry was decaying, but without any of the positive changes that affected other manors. There was only one presentment of enclosure and that was in 1457. In 1459 and 1460, the tenants were ordered to plough all of their selions in the cornfields, as if strips were being allowed to revert to waste. In 1474 the yardlanders were ordered to plough the headlands near their lands, a normal practice in open field villages. Dozens of presentments were made of tenants allowing their animals to trespass on the corn-

---

[38] WCRO ref. 009:1 BA 2636/37 (iii) 43806, fos. 115–19; conversion of arable to pasture is implied by descriptions such as 'two several pastures called the Busshopeslonds... one of twenty ridges and two headlands... the whole of that pasture containing four and a half acres, the other of twenty-two ridges and two headlands'.

[39] WCRO ref. 721:091 BA 2358/1 no. 6b, /2 no. 31a, 34a, /5 no. 87a, 98a, /6 no. 100a; ref. 721:091 BA 2735/1 no. 158a; Gloucester Public Lib., no. 45T; *Ecclesiastical Terriers of Warwickshire Parishes*, ed. D. M. Barratt, i (Dugdale Soc., xxii, 1955), pp. 100–1; ii (Dugdale Soc., xxvii, 1971), pp. 78–86; WCRO ref. b 009:1 BA 5403/20.

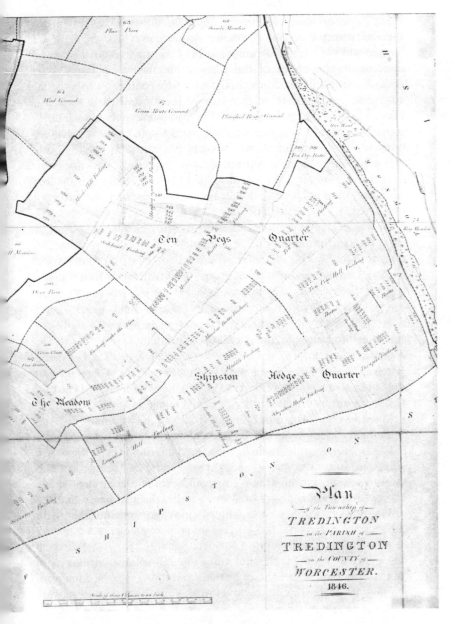

4   Part of an estate map of Tredington, 1846, showing extensive surviving open fields (Worcester County Record Office)

fields, probably because cultivated and uncultivated land lay interspersed, without adequate fencing. As early as *c.*1450 the demesne
farmer had threatened to abandon his lease unless something was
done about the beasts of the villagers damaging his crops. This
should be seen in the context of the very low demand for land that
affected the manor throughout the fifteenth and early sixteenth
centuries. Here apparently was the economic decline which is
sometimes regarded as typical of the period, with uncultivated land,
unenterprising peasants and rock-bottom rents. The village was
vulnerable to the enforced enclosure which the enclosure commissioners found in 1517, because its inhabitants had not been able
to carry out gradual and piecemeal enclosure in the fifteenth
century.

How can the divergence between the Severn valley and north
Worcestershire manors on the one hand, and the Avon valley and
Cotswold manors on the other, be explained? The first group started
with the advantage of old enclosures and a stronger pastoral element in their economies that went back to the early middle ages.
Their innovation was to extend already existing enclosures. It would
have been much more difficult for tenants of manors with unbroken
expanses of open field and a great predominance of arable to un-
scramble their intermixed selions and introduce radical technical
changes. There was a much greater danger that change would lead
to the collapse of the economy of the village, as happened at Hatton,
Upton, Wontley and the other deserted villages.

Much has been written about the vitality of the woodland districts
in the early modern period.[40] Their pastoral economy was associated with more individualism among their inhabitants, while the
village community was a stronger and more restrictive force in
the old-settled, arable areas. This could explain the progress made
by enclosure at Hanbury or Alvechurch. It is also likely that the
urban market stimulated technical innovation on the manors in
the vicinity of Bristol and Worcester. To take an obvious example,
urban butchers needed to use pastures near the towns, and villagers
co-operated with them, subletting their crofts, according to a
Whitstones by-law in 1477, or by taking animals on to the commons,
leading to presentments of 'overburdening the common pasture
with the beasts of strangers'.

[40] Thirsk, *Agrarian History of England*, iv, pp. 109–12.

The more substantial tenants were often those responsible for enclosure. Of ten Hartlebury tenants presented for enclosing in the 1470s and 1480s whose holdings are known, seven held 2 yardlands or more. Nine of eighteen Kempsey enclosers in the mid-fifteenth century had a yardland or more, and only two were smallholders.

The development of the market in the later part of our period would have given an impetus to peasant enclosure on the larger holdings by providing greater opportunities to accumulate capital and an incentive for higher production. How do we account for the technical changes in the mid-fifteenth century, when the market was relatively depressed? A possible answer lies with the shortage of both family and hired labour, again most acute on the larger holdings, as consolidation and conversion to pasture would have reduced the amount of labour needed. It should also be remembered that the mid-fifteenth-century generation of peasants were feeling the full benefit of reduced rents.

Peasantry of all kinds benefited from the changes in agricultural techniques of the fifteenth century, particularly the shift towards pastoral farming, which should be seen as rectifying the imbalances of the earlier period. Many of the developments raised the general level of subsistence by introducing more flexibility in cultivation, by broadening the distribution of sources of meat and dairy produce, and by providing greater quantities of manure. There were also significant advances in pastoral husbandry on a commercial scale, and in technical improvements such as consolidation and enclosure of holdings affecting mainly the more substantial tenants on the western and northern manors of the estate. These changes probably accelerated in the late fifteenth and early sixteenth centuries, but the mid-fifteenth century should not be underrated as a period of innovation.

16. The peasant economy: the market, getting and spending

The trends in the late medieval market economy are well known. International trade declined, reaching a low level in the mid-fifteenth century, and then recovered. Prices of agricultural produce tended to decline and then stagnate up to the early sixteenth century, while wages and the prices of manufactured goods moved upwards, especially up to the middle of the fifteenth century.

The declining market for agricultural produce on the bishopric estate cannot be documented with actual prices after the leasing of the demesnes. The main trends in grain prices can be indicated through the values put on customary wheat rents and allowances of wheat made to officials, which were clearly influenced by market prices until they became conventionalized in the 1480s (see Table 49). Apart from a few exceptional years, like the famine of the late 1430s, they seem to reflect the same sluggishness as price series derived from sources showing actual market prices. The valuations of oxen taken as heriots also indicate the decline of the fifteenth century, followed by recovery in the sixteenth, which became pronounced in the 1530s (see Table 50). The valuations reflect the higher prices of both grain and animals at Henbury, showing the influence of Bristol's demand for foodstuffs.

Another indication of a deteriorating market is provided by the tolls and profits collected by the bishops from the fairs held annually at Blockley. These were worth £4 to £6 around 1300, but fell to between £1 and £3 in the period 1383–1465. The decline continued until the fairs produced as little as 15s. 4d. in 1524–5. Similar figures can be found for other fifteenth-century markets and fairs, and are usually taken as evidence of dwindling local and regional trade.[1] However, as tolls were seignorial dues, there may have been an increase in evasion, as happened with other payments to lords in the period. It is unlikely that west-midland trade in general declined as much as the Blockley figures might suggest. The region's taxable

---

[1] e.g. Cheltenham (Glos.) market tolls declined from £3 in the fourteenth century to £1 5s. 1d. in 1421 and 6s. 8d. in 1466: see G. Hart, *A History of Cheltenham* (Leicester, 1965), p. 42.

Table 49. *Wheat valuations per quarter, 1407–89*

These are valuations of customary payments of wheat, or of wheat paid to officials. Figures in parentheses are those which seem to have a fixed valuation

	Bibury	Bredon	Cleeve	Henbury
1407–8	4s. 0d.			
1408–9				
1409–10				
1410–11				
1411–12		3s. 4d.		
1412–13				
1413–14				
1414–15				
1415–16				
1416–17				
1417–18				
1418–19				
1419–20				
1420–1				
1421–2		2s. 10d.		
1422–3				
1423–4				
1424–5				
1425–6	3s. 4d.			
1426–7			2s. 8d.	4s. 8d.
1427–8	2s. 8d.	2s. 8d.		4s. 8d.
1428–9				
1429–30				
1430–1	4s. 0d.			
1431–2				7s. 0d.
1432–3				
1433–4				
1434–5				
1435–6	4s. 0d.			
1436–7	4s. 0d.			
1437–8	8s. 0d.	6s. 8d.		10s. 8d.
1438–9	13s. 4d.		8s. 8d.	(7s. 0d.)
1439–40	8s. 0d.			(7s. 0d.)
1440–1				
1441–2				
1442–3				
1443–4		2s. 8d.		
1444–5	3s. 4d.			
1445–6	3s. 4d.		3s. 4d.	
1446–7				
1447–8	5s. 4d.	4s. 0d.		
1448–9	4s. 8d.			
1449–50	4s. 8d.			
1450–1	4s. 8d.			
1451–2				
1452–3	4s. 8d.	5s. 0d.		

Table 49 – *continued*

	Bibury	Bredon	Cleeve	Henbury
1453–4				
1454–5	3s. 4d.			
1455–6	3s. 4d.	2s. 8d.		
1456–7	3s. 4d.			
1457–8	3s. 4d.			
1458–9	6s. 0d.			
1459–60				
1460–1	6s. 0d.	6s. 0d.		
1461–2	3s. 8d.			
1462–3				
1463–4		2s. 8d.		
1464–5	3s. 4d.			
1465–6				
1466–7	4s. 4d.		3s. 4d.	
1467–8	4s. 4d.			
1468–9		5s. 4d.		
1469–70	6s. 8d.	8s. 0d.		
1470–1	6s. 4d.			
1471–2	4s. 5d.			
1472–3				
1473–4	3s. 8d.			
1474–5	4s. 0d.		3s. 0d.	
1475–6				
1476–7	4s. 0d.			
1477–8	5s. 4d.	4s. 8d.	5s. 4d.	
1478–9	4s. 0d.			
1479–80	3s. 4d.			
1480–1	4s. 0d.			
1481–2	4s. 0d.			
1482–3	4s. 0d.			
1483–4	5s. 4d.			
1484–5		3s. 6d.		
1485–6				
1486–7	(4s. 0d.)		4s. 0d.	
1487–8	(4s. 0d.)	3s. 4d.	4s. 4d.	
1488–9	(4s. 0d.)	2s. 8d.	3s. 4d.	

wealth grew more than that of many other parts of England between 1334 and 1515, particularly because of the growth in the cloth industry at Worcester and in south Gloucestershire.[2] This ought to

[2] R. Schofield, 'The Geographical Distribution of Wealth in England, 1334–1649', in R. Floud (ed.), *Essays in Quantitative Economic History* (Oxford, 1974), pp. 96–102.

Table 50. *Valuations of heriot oxen, 1376–1540*

	Bredon	Hampton	Hanbury	Hartlebury	Henbury	Kempsey	Whitstones
1376–1400	11s. 5d.* (3)†						13s. 1d. (7)
1401–25	12s. 6d. (4)		10s. 0d. (1)		12s. 0d. (2)	7s. 6d.(2)	9s. 10d. (3)
1426–50			9s. 6d. (7)		13s. 5d. (4)	9s. 7d.(19)	9s. 3d.(14)
1451–75		8s. 11d.(6)	8s. 10d.(15)	8s. 6d. (7)	16s. 0d. (1)	8s. 9d.(28)	9s. 3d.(14)
1476–1500		8s. 2d.(3)	7s. 6d. (7)	7s. 6d. (8)	17s. 0d. (4)	8s. 9d.(10)	10s. 0d.(13)
1501–25	11s. 2d.(5)	9s. 6d.(2)	10s. 4d. (3)	12s. 5d. (3)	17s. 0d. (1)	11s. 6d.(17)	12s. 10d.(10)
1526–40	17s. 0d.(2)	15s. 0d.(1)		£1 0s. 2d.(4)	£1 7s. 4d.(12)	13s. 1d. (9)	16s. 0d. (6)

* averages.
† numbers of examples.

have generated some local demand for wool and foodstuffs, which would have had some effect in countering the underlying downward trend.

The different groups in rural society would be affected in varying ways by these movements. Obviously the wage-earners, both landless and smallholders, gained from rising real wages for much of the period. More problematical are the consequences for the tenants of middling and larger holdings. The middling tenants were to some extent insulated from changes in the market, as they could be self-sufficient in labour and food. They needed some cash to pay rents (now paid entirely in money) and taxes, but rents declined, and taxes became less onerous towards the end of the fifteenth century. The ambitious peasant with a very large holding ought not to have found the environment favourable for commodity production, in view of the low prices of agricultural produce.

Some peasants adapted themselves to the new situation by marketing goods for which demand had not slackened, or which used less labour to produce. The cultivation of flax and the shift of emphasis from arable to pastoral husbandry are examples of peasants responding to economic circumstances. Similarly the demand for fish seems to have expanded in the later middle ages, and there is evidence that peasants were also involved in fishing.[3] The Severn was a free river, so its fishing rights were not seignorially controlled like those of other rivers, and rents of fisheries do not appear, apart from some fish-traps, in our documents. A number of thefts at Kempsey in the years 1436–50 reveal that tenants there owned nets, boats called 'harde-vales', and a 'hook-line'. A century later a Kempsey man bequeathed 'my bell net with other engines that I have to fish with'.[4] On the Avon the lord's fisheries were almost the only assets on the estate to increase in value during the later middle ages: from 10s 0d. in 1299 to £1 0s. 0d. in the fifteenth century at Bredon; from 17s. 0d. to £2 0s. 0d. at Stratford; and from 18s. 0d. to £2 13s. 8d. at Hampton. At the last manor the fisheries were rented out piecemeal to many tenants in the mid-fifteenth century, sometimes combined with a smallholding ('a messuage and a fishery called an Avenewatter', 'a messuage and a toft and a pinkwater'), sometimes separately, so that in 1427–8 five tenants were each farm-

[3] Abel, *Crises Agraires en Europe*, p. 99.
[4] Kempsey CR, April 1436, May 1442, April 1448, April 1450; WCRO ref. 008:7 BA 3590/1, v, fo. 39.

ing between eight and twenty 'engines called veseles'. Later on the fisheries became concentrated in fewer hands, so that in 1481 one tenant took a messuage, 4 acres, two 'netwaters' and five 'pink-waters', which had previously been held by seven different tenants. In 1510 the Hampton fisheries were leased *en bloc* to Thomas Lucy, lord of the neighbouring manor of Charlecote, who may have sub-let them, or employed local labour as fishermen.[5]

The rents paid for the Hampton fisheries were equivalent in the early sixteenth century to those of four customary yardland holdings, and suggest that fishing made a substantial contribution to the economic resources of the village.

Some of the villages on the estate were also affected by the general spread of rural industry in the period. As in the thirteenth century, we are aware of the existence of an unquantifiable scatter of peasant craftsmen, like the Whitstones wheelwright who agreed to make a pair of wheels as part of his entry-fine for a quarter-yardland in 1444, or the tiler in 1462 who had a thousand tiles available as a heriot when he surrendered his quarter-yardland on the same manor. The cloth industry can, however, be shown to have expanded in the fourteenth and fifteenth centuries. Stratford had a fulling mill in 1252 and in the fifteenth century, presumably to serve the weavers of the town. Of the rural manors only Hartlebury had a fulling mill in 1299; in the fifteenth century this mill continued to function, while others are mentioned for the first time at Blockley, Tredington and Hampton. The fulling mill at Hampton was an innovation of 1462, added when that mill was rebuilt.[6]

The Hartlebury cloth-workers mentioned in the fifteenth century included tailors, weavers, fullers and shearmen. Only the two tailors seem to have been tenants on the manor, one of them holding at least 2 yardlands, while the other cloth-workers may have sublet cottages from among those engrossed by some tenants.

[5] Hampton CR, Oct. 1449, April 1450; Hampton AR, 1427–8; Hampton CR, Oct. 1481, Oct. 1510. The etymology of the names of different types of fisheries is obscure.

[6] WCRO ref. 009:1 BA 2636/ 37 (iii), 43806, fos. 28, 43, 200; / 11 43700, fos. 23, 48; Blockley AR, 1458–9; the Tredington mill seems to have been built between 1379 and 1412, see WCL E30, E46; Hampton AR, 1462–3. This follows E. Miller's argument that fulling mills were established in order to take advantage of an already existing industry: see E. Miller, 'The Fortunes of the English Textile Industry in the Thirteenth Century', *Econ. Hist. Rev.*, xviii (1965), pp. 71–3.

The cloth-workers at Hampton are hardly mentioned in the court rolls, but the lists of goods and chattels of two felons, Simon Workeman, who fled in 1459, and William Honnewell, whose inventory was recorded in 1474, included looms, scissors and cloth-shears. This shows, together with the building of the fulling mill, that the main processes of cloth manufacture were carried out in the village. The court rolls record that the Hampton cottages were occupied by a rather transient series of tenants, who probably included cloth-workers.

At Kempsey various Worcester city cloth-workers became tenants of parcels of land in the fifteenth century. Their presence may be connected with a village industry, as in 1464 a by-law sought to compel all those who fulled cloth in the common stream to give 4d. to the lord.

While there may have been a decline in large-scale trade over long distances in the fifteenth century, the history of retail trade at village level still needs to be written. Through the view of frank-pledge the lord exercised the right to enforce the assize of ale and the assize of bread, and to regulate the sale of meat and candles. The assize of ale was the most important, allowing the lord to amerce those who sold ale at more than the fixed price (1½d. per gallon instead of 1d. at Bredon in 1394, for example), and to deal with sellers of bad ale and those who dispensed ale with unsealed measures. Amercements were probably imposed on everyone sell-ing ale, hence the willingness of regular brewers to pay for licences to brew, to avoid the inevitable amercements. Thus the lists of those breaking the assize (and paying for licences) can be used as evidence of all those involved in this form of retail trade.

In any consecutive series of lists of brewers it is immediately ap-parent that there were both 'professional' brewers who were amer-ced regularly, and occasional brewers who sold ale only once in every two or three years. By the late fourteenth century the 'pro-fessionals' were established in some of the villages of the estate. At Hanbury in the 1380s a total of thirty-seven people were presented for breaking the assize; of these, twenty-seven appear once or twice only. Four of them are recorded in almost every surviving court roll, between thirteen and seventeen times. At Whitstones in the same period brewing was concentrated into the hands of the tavern keep-ers of the tithing of Whitstones, in effect a suburb of the city of Worcester.

Developments on the rural manors in the fifteenth century made their ale selling come to resemble the more 'urban' pattern of Whitstones. There was a reduction in the number of people brewing: at Hanbury in a quantity of documents in the 1460s and 1470s, comparable with those analysed above, there were only nine or ten brewers instead of thirty-seven. The reductions at Hampton were from twenty-seven in the 1450s to eleven in the 1500s, and at Kempsey from thirty-three in the 1440s to ten around 1500. The occasional brewers tended to disappear from the records, so that brewing activity became concentrated in the hands of the professionals. For example, at Kempsey the ten brewers mentioned in the period 1495–1503 consisted of eight who paid at least once for licences to keep taverns, and four of these broke the assize ten or more times. Only two of these brewers can be described as occasional sellers of ale. Individual brewers in the late fifteenth century tended to ply their trade over long periods, so that it is not uncommon to find a brewer appearing in the court records over a period of ten years; the career of Henry Pugge or Powche and his wife as licensees and breakers of the assize at Hanbury lasted continuously from 1441 to 1482.

Was the decline in the number and variety of brewers simply another symptom of the waning powers of the courts? This is unlikely, because the by-laws also reflect professionalization. In the early and mid-fifteenth century their aim was to establish a rota of brewing, so that the consumers could always obtain ale, but there would be no competition between sellers. So a Hampton order of 1459 states that 'no tenants may brew ale for sale while their neighbours are brewing'. Kempsey tenants were forbidden 'to brew on another', that is 'that no-one should make ale until his neighbours have completely sold their brew'.

Later on the professional brewer was accepted, so that Kempsey by-laws in 1479 and 1504 sought to establish the identification of ale houses by enforcing the erection of ale stakes. At Hampton in 1467 brewers had been ordered not to brew more than three quarters of malt at once; by 1500 the attempts to curb the activities of the major brewers had been forgotten, and instead, efforts were made to maintain regular supplies for the consumers by specifying a minimum, 'brewers henceforth may not brew less than one quarter of malt at one time'.

Licences to brew and keep taverns, already issued at Whitstones in the 1380s, became normal in the more rural manors in the course of the fifteenth century, and by the 1480s were regularly used everywhere.

In economic terms the rise of the professional brewer meant that ale-selling ceased to be a sideline of a large number of villagers. In the late fourteenth and early fifteenth centuries as many as a half of the tenant families were represented among the brewers at Hampton, Hanbury, and Kempsey. They included tenants of all kinds, and at Kempsey the miller and the demesne farmer. For the tenants of larger holdings, brewing was evidently a normal method of disposing of surplus barley. The numbers of brewers varied with the quality of the harvest, with many brewing in good years.

The holdings of the professional brewers who emerged in the late fifteenth century tended to be small. They might occasionally include a yardlander, like John Momeford, who sold ale at Hampton in the early sixteenth century, but among the Kempsey brewers a half were cottagers, and some had no record of landholding at all, and may have been subtenants. Certainly they lacked the landed resources to produce the large quantities of grain needed. These are recorded in the Hampton courts (because of the by-laws specifying quantities), and often exceeded four quarters of malt per brewer in a six-month period. Between October 1516 and October 1517 there were only three brewers in Hampton, but two brewed twelve and the third brewed fourteen quarters of malt, making a total of thirty-eight. If they followed the practice in upper-class households of obtaining sixty gallons from a quarter, the Hampton brewers produced at least 2,280 gallons, but they are likely to have brewed a greater quantity of a thinner drink.[7]

The pattern of self-sufficiency in ale production in the earlier part of our period by which many villagers took turns to brew their grain, was replaced by a more specialized and commercially organized system, in which smallholders or non-tenants bought grain and brewed it for sale as a full-time occupation. The large quantities of ale produced at Hampton would represent a substantial part of the needs of a small village, Hampton having only about thirty tenants at the time. Perhaps the better-off peasants continued to brew for their own needs, so the main customers at the ale houses

---

[7] e.g. *Household Book of Dame Alice de Bryene, passim*; *Documents Illustrating the Rule of Walter de Wenlok, Abbot of Westminster 1283–1307*, ed. B. F. Harvey (Camden Soc., 4th ser., ii, 1965), p. 248; for thinner ale see W. Harrison, *The Description of England*, pp. 137–8.

would have been the smallholders and wage-earners without brewing equipment, and those in search of entertainment.

This period saw not only the genesis of the English public house, but also the beginnings of the village shop. At Cleeve, Hanbury, Hartlebury and Kempsey, ale brewers are also recorded as selling bread, candles and meat, usually from the last quarter of the fifteenth century. An example is George Underhyll of Hartlebury, tenant of a modest holding (by the standards of his village) of three-quarters of a yardland, who sold ale, bread and meat simultaneously in the 1490s. There was competition from urban bakers and butchers, who sold their wares at some distance from their towns. Worcester bakers visited Kempsey regularly from 1467, and Hartlebury from 1474, but more commonly bread came to Hartlebury from Bewdley, Droitwich and Kidderminster, and meat from Bewdley and Kidderminster butchers. Winchcomb bakers sold bread at Withington. The development of retail selling, both by specialists within the village and by outsiders, tells us something about the sophistication of the late medieval economy. Cultivators sold their surplus produce to middle men and left the tasks of food preparation and retail selling to them.

All of these developments point to growing prosperity in the lower ranks of village society. At Hampton smallholders rented the fisheries for much of the period; more generally cottagers or the landless took employment as artisans in the cloth industry, and played an important part in the evolution of professional ale-selling. It is likely that the new areas of growth were at least partly satisfying the consumption needs of the smallholding and wage-earning element; they would have been able to buy food-stuffs, especially such comparative luxuries as ale, meat and fish, and the cheaper products of the rural cloth industry, in ever-increasing quantities as real wages rose in the late fourteenth and fifteenth centuries.[8] For them, low prices of grain meant plenty, with cash to spare for non-essentials. There were still poor people in the fifteenth-century countryside. They are mentioned in a general way in court rolls, for example when an elm tree was blown down at Cleeve in 1451, 'it was given

[8] On increased meat eating, L. Stouff, *Ravitaillement et Alimentation en Provence aux XIVe et XVe siècles* (Paris, 1970), pp. 169–94; on the links between lower class consumption and the cloth industry, E. M. Carus-Wilson, *The Expansion of Exeter at the Close of the Middle Ages* (Exeter, 1963), p. 8.

by the lord's council to be divided among the poor of the place by the bishop's reeve for firewood'. Who were the poor? In the period before 1350 the question seems easily answered: they were the smallholders and landless who suffered from low wages and under-employment, though the court records of the period contain references to tenants of large holdings surrendering them 'because he is poor'. After 1350 the wage-earners continued to lead a more precarious existence than those with middling or large holdings but they had more opportunity to work and for much higher rates of pay, and contemporaries tended to react against them as the 'undeserving' poor.[9]

The word 'poor' was often used in the estate records in a comparative sense, but it can be taken to mean 'near destitution' when it appears in explanation of a tenant's inability to render any heriot, sometimes when a holding was surrendered and the tenant was said to be no longer capable of working it. Of the ten tenants described as poor in these circumstances, five held a quarter-yardland or less, but three had half-yardlands, and two were yardlanders and above. We may suspect that at least some of the thirty-six other tenants, who had no heriot when they died or when they surrendered their holdings, belonged to this category of paupers, but the court rolls are not consistent in recording their condition. How could tenants of substantial holdings be described as 'poor'? The answer is suggested by the additional information sometimes supplied, that the dead or departing tenant was *senex* (old) or *impotens* (incapable), or, in the case of John Baty of Kempsey in 1452, *senex et decrepitus*.

The problem of the elderly poor was partly due to the absence of families to look after tenants in their declining years. Only one of the ten paupers mentioned was succeeded by a son, so the old tenants had to struggle to keep their holdings worked until they died or gave up in a state of destitution. Series of court rolls of the period before 1350 often contain detailed agreements by which new tenants, both relatives and non-relatives of the retiring couple or individual, agreed to maintain them for the rest of their lives. The formally registered maintenance agreements probably represent only a fraction of those carried out under unwritten, customary arrangements. They were entered in the court rolls if there were doubts that the new tenants would fulfil their obligations.[10] Only nine such

---

[9] M. Mollat (ed.), *Études sur l'Histoire de la Pauvreté* (Paris, 1974), ii, pp. 691–706.

[10] Raftis, *Tenure and Mobility*, pp. 42–6; Hilton, *The English Peasantry in the Later Middle Ages*, pp. 29–30.

agreements have been found in the many bishopric court records of the late fourteenth, fifteenth and early sixteenth centuries. Does this mean that there was greater trust between old people and their successors, so that informal agreements were sufficient guarantees of maintenance? It seems more likely that would-be tenants would avoid taking on holdings encumbered with an expensive and inconvenient obligation to maintain an old couple when there was less urgent pressure on land.

As the demand for land increased, old people could bargain for ample maintenance from their successors, as they had sometimes done before 1350. Most of the bishopric estate agreements gave the retiring tenant no more than a few acres of land from the holding, and part of the house. At Henbury in 1483, Helena Ludlowe gave up her half-yardland holding to John Meye, and received in return food and drink, the use of a chamber, 'fire to warm herself as much as she pleases', a special weekly allowance of a loaf, a cheese and 'a gallon of the best ale of Bristol town', and annually 6s. 8d. in cash, $2\frac{3}{4}$ yards of green woollen cloth at 10d. per yard, and half of the fruit from the orchard. Meye was clearly anxious to obtain the land and was willing to provide goods worth at least £1 per annum in order to do so. Widows on other manors, particularly in the early and mid-fifteenth century, could not have hoped to find successors willing to keep them in such style.

The position of the elderly tenants probably improved in the early sixteenth century. They were more likely to have children surviving, and the wills emphasize the responsibilities of the younger generation. John Ordridge and Thomas Blake both insisted that their widows should share equally in the holdings with the inheriting son, and John Momeford of Hampton enjoined his nephew to give 6s. 8d. each year to his widow, as long as she remained single.[11]

The wills make us aware of a large pool of poverty in the early sixteenth-century village. William Churchyard of Claines (in Whitstones) left money to distribute fifty pairs of shoes to the poor in winter, and John Momeford responded to the provisions of the 1536 Poor Law by leaving 5s. 0d. 'to begin the common box to the behalf of the poor people in the parish'.[12] By this date declining real wages were putting an end to the prosperity of much of the rural population.

---

[11] Worcester wills, 1537/ 80, 1538–9/ 45, 1538/ 241.
[12] WCRO ref. 008:7 BA 3590/ I, ii, fo. 51; Worcester wills, 1538/ 241.

How did developments in the market affect the tenants of middling and larger holdings? Some medievalists, such as W. Abel and G. Fourquin, have supposed that low prices were a major source of peasant discontent in the later middle ages, but their views are based on an exaggerated conception of the importance of the market in the peasant economy.[13] Even a yardlander would have consumed or used on his holding most of the grain that he produced. The long-term decline of 10 per cent–20 per cent in cereal prices did not reduce the yardlander's income by that amount. However, low prices could have inhibited a wealthy peasant from transforming himself into a large-scale commodity producer.

Similarly the high cost of labour would have acted as a brake on the peasant cultivating large areas of land. Family labour was in short supply, both because of the small family sizes, and because sons were attracted away from the family holding by opportunities provided by land and employment elsewhere. One example is John Smyth of Whitstones, son of Henry Smyth, who went to work for a chaplain of Claines in 1384. In 1387 Henry claimed 10s. 0d. in damages from the chaplain for detaining John 'out of his service' for three years. Economic developments, such as the rural cloth-industry, further increased the demand for labour; even an ale-house keeper, like Thomas Smyth of Kempsey in 1502, might employ as many as two servants.

These problems were not insuperable, as is shown by the number of peasants in the fifteenth century – almost a third of the total at Hartlebury, for example – who held two or three yardlands. Tenants of both middling and large holdings would have enjoyed plenty in terms of the produce of their own land, and there is no reason to doubt that they were able to accumulate money also. There is some evidence of cash in the hands of peasants, like the sum of 16s. 0d. found in the purse of a Ripple serf when he was drowned in 1451, or the £3 'in pennies' stolen from a Kempsey tenant in 1498, or the loans of cash of 6s. 8d. and 10s. 0d. advanced by a quarter-yard-lander and a half-yardlander at Whitstones in the 1470s. It has already been pointed out that the tenants of larger holdings had been able to enclose, and all tenants were able to obtain more stock by the middle decades of the fifteenth century. As has been stressed before, the best opportunities for the larger tenants lay in the vicinity of

[13] Abel, *Crises Agraires en Europe*, pp. 109–12; R. Fourquin, *Les Campagnes de la Région Parisienne à la Fin du Moyen Age* (Paris, 1964), pp. 232–3.

towns. Henbury tenants in particular were able to sell their produce at prices well above those obtainable on the other manors. Better prospects for commodity producers everywhere came with the upturn in prices in the early sixteenth century. Those who held lands that had been enclosed and converted to pasture in the previous century were in a particularly fortunate position when the demand for produce increased.

An indication of the standard of living of the peasantry at the end of our period can be obtained from their wills. The poverty of an elderly smallholder is indicated by the inventory of Margery Gardener of Whitstones, the tenant of an *arkeland*, who had been widowed at least eleven years before her death in 1539. The crops on her holding were valued at 10s. 0d., and her list of goods reveals a pathetic collection of old and nearly worthless possessions, clothes, sheets, old pots and pans, wooden trenchers and a few sticks of furniture, which brought the total valuation of her goods to 15s. 5d. The only animals that she owned were two pigs.[14]

Most of the other wills suggest a higher level of prosperity. Where possible examples will be given from those wills where something of the testator's landholding is known from the court records. The inventory of a Hampton yardlander was valued at £13 6s. 2d., while cash bequests of £4 2s. 8d. were made by John Nurton of Claines (in Whitstones), a half-yardlander, and £9 2s. 0d. by Thomas Wilkys, lessee of part of Ditchford pasture in Blockley. Numbers of stock varied from the six calves of a Wick half-yardlander, Henry Onyon, and five cattle of John Nurton, who had the same size of holding, to five horses, fourteen cattle, and four pigs owned by John Momeford, the Hampton yardlander, and the forty sheep and four cattle of Thomas Dyer, another yardlander of Blockley.[15] The main items of agricultural equipment mentioned were ploughs, carts and waggons. The most valuable possessions tended to be metal pots, pewter-ware (often six pieces at most), beds and clothing. William Churcheyard of Claines, who held about a half-yardland, had two furred gowns, and his wife bequeathed four silver spoons. Silver spoons seem to have had a symbolic value: those few who owned them may have made a point of bequeathing them. William Harri-

---

[14] Worcester wills, 1540/25.
[15] WCRO ref. 008:7 BA 3590/1, ii, fo. 46; Worcester wills, 1538/45, 1534/146, 1538/241, 1538/119.

son, writing in the 1580s, thought that peasants had begun to acquire them only in his own day.[16]

One group of five wills from Henbury stands apart from the others.[17] Three of them mention silver spoons, including one with a dozen. More remarkable were the amounts of cash bequeathed by Henbury tenants. Thomas Hort, a customary yardlander, left £100 'of my goods and chattels', to be divided among his four children. John Edmonds, who held a half-yardland by customary tenure and 96 acres on lease, also left £100 to be apportioned among his five children, and William Puffe left £30. These sums were not necessarily immediately realizable from the dead man's goods, but may have been guarantees to the children that they could call on their share from the heir in the future.[18] Nevertheless they show that Hort and Edmonds regarded their holdings as worth a great deal of money, much more than any of the tenants on other manors whose wills survive.

Market forces gave advantages to the bottom ranks of rural society in the late fourteenth and fifteenth centuries. We are most aware of poverty among the old and incapable. The depressed market for the products of peasant farming did not prevent new developments in the economic life of the village, in industry and retail trade. The extent and chronology of the growth of large-scale commodity production among the peasantry cannot be known, though its existence even in the mid-fifteenth century is implied by large holdings and technical innovations. Much depended on geographical factors as well as the long-term movements in prices; at the end of our period Henbury tenants of large holdings had achieved considerable wealth.

[16] W. Harrison, *The Description of England*, pp. 201–2.

[17] Worcester wills no. 84; 1538/46, 1538/130, 1540/59a, 1540/63.

[18] Spufford, 'Peasant Inheritance Customs and Land Distribution in Cambridgeshire', pp. 157–9.

17. *The village community*

The individual peasants and their families have been the primary concern of previous chapters, yet many references have been made to the village community, and some account of the impact of late-medieval changes on the village is necessary. The village community is often assumed to have been a potent force in the lives of individuals, yet little is known of its internal functions, though we are in debt to the investigations of W. O. Ault, and can learn something from comparisons with the modern communities investigated by historians and anthropologists.[1] A decline in the cohesiveness of the English village has been seen as early as the fourteenth century and in the early modern period, and an important area of investigation must be the extent of conflict between individuals and the community.[2]

What constituted the village community? We are concerned with both the formal organization of the vill, and the much less easily definable sense of common interest and identity shared by its inhabitants. As an institution the vill was to some extent separate from and independent of the manor. We hear, for example, of the vill of Bibury acting as a single body, although the village was divided in lordship between the bishops of Worcester and Osney Abbey.[3] Usually the bishopric manors included a number of villages and hamlets. In these circumstances long association together meant that the organization of the village community functioned at two different levels, involving both the constituent settlements and the

---

[1] Ault, *Open-Field Farming in Medieval England, passim*; W. O. Ault, 'Village Assemblies in Medieval England', in *Album Helen Maud Cam. Studies presented to the International Commission for the History of Representative and Parliamentary Institutions* (Louvain/Paris, 1960), pp. 11–35; J. Blum, 'The Internal Structure and Polity of the European Village Community from the Fifteenth to the Nineteenth Century', *Journ. of Modern Hist.*, xliii (1971), pp. 541–76; I. Chiva, *Rural Communities, Problems, Methods, and Types of Research* (UNESCO, Reports and Papers in Social Science, x, 1958).

[2] Pollock and Maitland, *The History of English Law*, i, pp. 620–33, doubted the strength of the community at any time, but legal historians generally accept its importance, see H. M. Cam, 'The Community of the Vill', in V. Ruffer and A. J. Taylor (eds.), *Medieval Studies presented to Rose Graham* (Oxford, 1950), pp. 1–14. On fourteenth-century decline, Raftis, *Warboys*, pp. 213–24; on later decline, A. Macfarlane, *Witchcraft in Tudor and Stuart England* (London, 1970), pp. 205–6.

[3] Bibury AR, 1375–6.

larger federation contained in the whole manor. For example, ten major hamlets and villages, and at least three minor settlements, lay within the manor of Kempsey. For taxation purposes eight of the major settlements were assessed separately in 1275, but in most subsequent subsidies the tax was levied on all of them under the heading of Kempsey.[4]

The key to the 'federal' organization of Kempsey seems to be provided by the arrangements for the bishops' view of frankpledge, with its 'village meeting' aspect. This was held at a single place for the whole manor, but each of the ten villages formed a separate tithing. An important function of the community, the regulation of the common fields, would involve individual villages because some had separate field systems; however most by-laws were made at the central courts for all of the tenants and inhabitants of the manor. Occasionally two villages conflicted, as when the tenants of Brook End were ordered not to despoil corn and hay in Stonehall tithing 'out of malice'; but it was more common for Kempsey men to complain about depredations by the inhabitants of neighbouring settlements outside the manor.[5] The other main focus of community organization, the parish, had boundaries coterminous with those of the manor, though one of the constituent villages, Norton, had a dependent chapel.

The other manors of the estate present much the same problems of constituent villages within large manors, but at Alvechurch and Hanbury the many small and scattered settlements cannot have formed separate vills. Alvechurch was divided into three 'yields' for rent-collecting and tithing purposes, but these may not have had any significance for regulating fields.

The village was used by the state as a unit of government, and some system of internal organization must have existed to carry out these functions. From 1334 the subsidy was assessed on each vill as a lump sum, and the inhabitants assessed and obtained individual payments among themselves. The vill also had military functions, so that a Kempsey tenant owed money to another in 1411 for 'the wages of the men in Wales', and a similar dispute arose at Hartlebury in 1413, when parish funds had been used to 'hire four men in

---

[4] *Lay Subsidy Roll for the County of Worcester c.1280*, pp. 79–81.
[5] Kempsey CR, July 1444.

Wales for the defence of the realm'.[6] In the early sixteenth century, in the views of frankpledge, orders were issued for the erection of butts and the provision of bows and arrows for target practice, and in 1539 the muster arrangements are recorded in rough notes made at the views.[7] Each parish had to provide a quota of armed men 'competent upon an hour's warning', and the notes give a rare glimpse of the villagers assessing each other's wealth and dividing up the responsibility accordingly. Hanbury had to provide four 'harnessed men': one wealthy villager provided a bowman, but the other three were equipped by pooling the resources of eighteen men: 'Henry Nasshe findeth a coat, William Hopkynes a sallett, . . . John Poyge and Edward Yate a bow and sheaf, Thomas Nasshe arrows. . . '.

Similar deliberations were needed in the sessions of the view of frankpledge on the vill's obligations to perform public works. The views decided if the whole vill, as distinct from individual tenants or the lord, was responsible for the upkeep of bridges and roads. When the vills apportioned road work in the 1520s it was related to the size of holdings, so that Bredon tenants had to carry three cart-loads of stone per yardland, and Cleeve tenants five waggon-loads per yardland.[8]

The lord also used the internal governing machinery of the vill. Some collective dues such as recognitions and common fines were assessed as lump sums on all customary tenants, which they had to levy themselves. The administration of courts depended on the co-operation of the suitors, who found officials from among their own ranks. The functions of the courts included a village meeting aspect which is not always easily distinguished from the court's work as an instrument of seignorial authority. The source of by-laws and other court orders usually has to be deduced from the interest served by them. An order against poaching, for example, was clearly initiated by the steward seeking to protect the lord's property; but most by-laws were concerned with agricultural matters, in which the lord had no direct interest after the demesne had been leased, and these emerged from the villagers themselves. As well as legislating, the

[6] Kempsey CR, April 1411; WCRO ref. 009:1 BA 2636/11 43700, fo. 16.
[7] Hampton CR, April 1502; Tredington CR, May 1538; WCRO ref. 009:1 BA 2636/18 43764.
[8] Bredon CR, Oct. 1528; Cleeve CR, April 1529; on the vill's liability to perform public works, *Public Works in Mediaeval Law*, ed. C. T. Flower (Selden Soc., xl, 1923), pp. xl–liv.

villagers played an important part in enforcement, as offenders were presented by the tithing-men, and sometimes special 'keepers of the by-laws' were appointed to make presentments. The community was thus able to act as a coercive body, using the authority of the lord's courts.

The vill also provided its members with communal facilities, of which the most fully documented is the common herdsman. Before the leasing of the demesnes the lord contributed to the pay of village herdsmen who looked after demesne animals along with those of the village. For example, in 1372–3 the Bibury herdsman was given 1s. 0d. for keeping the lord's oxen in the harvest period, and the village swineherd received 6d. By-laws occasionally ordered villagers to place their animals 'in the custody of the common herd', presumably because of trespasses that resulted from unsupervised grazing. The negligence of the herdsman could lead to mass trespassing, as when in 1450 the Hampton herdsman who was William Sclatter, the son of a ten-ant, trespassed with 'forty avers of the vill of Hampton', and the whole vill was held to be responsible. In the early sixteenth century there were difficulties in collecting the herdsman's pay; at Hampton the farmer of the rectory was failing to pay his share, and at Darlingscott in Tredington it was ordered that 'each tenant should allow his avers to go in the keeping of the common herd, and they should pay the wages of the herd daily and every day'.[9]

The vill could also act as a collective tenant, taking on extra land, usually pasture, for the use of the community. This is re-corded at Stratford and Blockley in 1299, and at Bibury in the 1370s.[10]

Outside the strictly agricultural sphere villagers acted in co-operation with the lord in exercising social control. Breaches of the peace were countered immediately by the collective action of the hue and cry, and the tithing-men and jurors presented assaults and petty thefts at the view of frankpledge. There were also attempts to prevent social behaviour thought likely to lead to crime. Illicit games, associated with idleness as well as crime, were forbidden in the 1480s: draughts, dice and cards at Kempsey; bowls, cards and

[9] Bredon CR, Oct. 1399, July 1501; Hampton CR, April 1450, July 1465, Oct. 1520; Tredington CR, Oct. 1520.
[10] *RBW*, iii, pp. 254, 300; Bibury AR, 1375–6.

football at Hampton.[11] In 1460 a Hanbury tenant was amerced for holding dice games in his house. On all manors 'scolds' and those who quarrelled with neighbours and disturbed the peace were amerced. 'Receiving suspicious strangers' was also forbidden by by-laws on a number of manors, a prohibition aimed at preventing crime, but also perhaps reflecting problems of labour supply, as some of the strangers were doubtless employees of a villager.

The problem of illicit immigrants was most acute at Whitstones, where one of the tithings, Whitstones itself, was a northern suburb of Worcester and caught up in the social problems of a large town. In 1474 the residents were forbidden to entertain 'suspicious men and women' for more than two days and nights. A similar order in 1499 reduced the length of the stay allowed to one day and night, and identified the strangers as 'skulking chapmen', presumably itinerant traders. Whitstones also had a prostitution problem, and an ordinance of 1445 forbade brothel-keeping, and four cases were presented in that year. Five years later a brothel-keeper and prostitute were ordered to leave the manor. Brothels were still being reported in 1457 and 1473.

'Suspicious strangers' and houses of ill-repute were not confined to urban areas. Attempts were made at Hampton to suppress these threats to public order, and the initiative can be shown to have come from the leading villagers, as a number of presentments were made by the jurors. Thomas Botiller, a brewer, was the main offender, and was said in 1458 to be keeping a brothel 'to the annoyance of his neighbours'. He was ordered to restore good order in his house, on pain of paying £5 and forfeiting his holding. In 1460 Botiller and Thomas Vyell were reported to be 'suspicious men, and live suspiciously among their neighbours, by which neighbours have damage both in geese, and capons, and poultry, and other goods'. Botiller also received strangers frequently, and in 1467 was receiving 'vagabonds'. Vyell was later to forfeit his holding because he wasted it, and was 'badly governed towards the lord and all of his tenants'. William Crosse in 1462 was presented for receiving 'badly governed' men and women, and two years later his wife was reputed to be a prostitute. In 1463 another tenant, William Bache, was said to have 'received a certain strange woman in his house, who one night

---

[11] Kempsey CR, Oct. 1480; Hampton CR, April 1488; on football as a threat to public order see G. G. Coulton, *The Medieval Village* (Cambridge, 1925), pp. 93–5.

made such a shout that all of the tenants there were so perturbed by the aforesaid shout that they feared that their houses were on fire'. The community, or at least its leading figures, were apparently attempting to curb the activities of a village underworld.

The social cohesion of the village, by which neighbours practised mutual co-operation, is not adequately documented. The pooling of draught animals for ploughing, for example, has been inferred from the small numbers of oxen and horses owned by individuals, but it is not directly recorded in our documents. Court rolls, by their very nature, depict conflict rather than co-operation, with villagers fighting, stealing, trespassing, owing money and failing to observe contracts. Wills are a more satisfactory source, as they originate from the individual's own words, and allow us to reconstruct the testator's range of social contacts. Wills contain many references to people outside the testator's family, such as godchildren, those appointed as overseers or executors, witnesses, and people receiving bequests (it is normally stated if the latter are creditors, rather than friends). Fig. 6 shows the interconnections between families in the parish of Claines (coterminous with the manor of Whitstones), disclosed by references in ten early sixteenth-century wills. It suggests a close web of friendship, mutual regard and responsibility, some people having links with up to seven other families. The connections cut across social division; the Alfords, Nurtons, Vernills and Wythys were all serfs, but they were associated closely with free neighbours. Disparities of wealth, indicated by the size of holdings recorded in court rolls, or the amount paid in the 1524 subsidy, did not prevent social links either. Testators sometimes provided their servants with bequests that were more than just tokens; William Churchyard left as much (6s. 8d.) to his servants as to his nephews and nieces. In making their wills, peasants showed a concern for the general well-being of their communities by leaving money for the poor of their parish, or for the mending of roads.[12]

Feelings of loyalty to the community would have been reinforced by ceremonies and celebrations involving large numbers of villagers.[13] These are rarely mentioned in our documents. A 'metes and bounds' procession, an annual progress to ensure that the parish boundary was known and remembered, is recorded at

[12] WCRO ref. 008:7 BA 3590/I, ii, fo. 51; Worcester wills, 1536/211, 1538/46, 1538/241.
[13] C. Phythian Adams, *Local History and Folklore* (London, 1975), pp. 17–30.

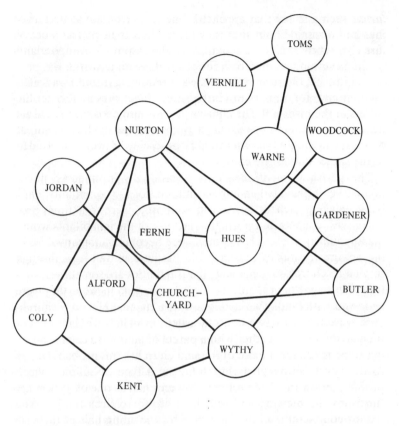

6 Diagrammatic representation of the family interconnections at Claines, from the wills of 1513–40 (only families with more than one link have been included)

Wichenford in 1462 because it led to a dispute over a boundary with the neighbouring villagers of Martley.

Bouts of communal drinking might also result in troubles that were noticed by courts. An enigmatic entry at Hampton records the death by drowning of seven people in a vat (*cumba*) on 5 January, 1477. Vats were normally used for brewing, and as the date falls within the 'orgy' of the twelve days of Christmas, it is tempting to infer that the incident was the tragic outcome of excessive revelry.

However, we know more about formally organized drinking sessions. By the late fourteenth century the lord's compulsory

fustale seems to have disappeared, but other communal ale drinkings still occurred. When many of the villagers helped with heavy
tasks, as when logs for a building were transported from Welland
to the Severn by people from Bredon in 1395–6, a wassail was provided. In 1392 the reeve and beadle at Bredon organized a wassail to
raise money for repairs to Hartlebury bridge, presumably on the
orders of the bishop.[14] The churchwardens also used communal ale
drinkings as a means of raising parish funds, and the lord's court at
Kempsey prevented competition by amercing brewers who traded
at the same time as the church-ale.

The parish is mentioned only occasionally in manorial documents, yet it provided an important focus for the community. Outlying villages, such as Norton in Kempsey, were sometimes provided with chapels, but normally the bulk of the inhabitants would
meet regularly at church. Laymen were becoming more involved in
the administration of the parish in the later middle ages through
service as churchwardens, and their activities are sometimes mentioned in seignorial records as they became tenants when they were
endowed with land. Two cottages which lay near Henbury churchyard were taken by two churchwardens in 1436 'with the assent of
the parishioners', together with a parcel of land 'for a certain building to be made for the use of the said church'. This probably refers
to the construction of a church-house, a type of building which
proliferated in the fifteenth century, and had as one of its primary
functions the brewing and selling of ale for church funds.[15] The
manor court could assist the parish by allocating half of the cash
raised from breaches of certain by-laws to the church, but the only
reference to this practice was at Cleeve in 1469.[16]

Much fuller information about the workings of the parish comes
from a stray ecclesiastical court book for Hartlebury kept among
the archives of the episcopal estate. In contrast with recent arguments that the late medieval parish lacked effectiveness as a centre
of religious life, this unusual document implies a very active paro-

[14] Bredon AR, 1392–3, 1395–6.

[15] *Churchwardens' Accounts of Croscombe, Pilton, Yatton, Tintinhull, Morebath, and
St. Michael's, Bath*, ed. Bishop Hobhouse (Somerset Record Soc., iv, 1890), pp.
xxi–xxiii.

[16] W. O. Ault, 'Manor Court and Parish Church in Fifteenth Century England',
Speculum, xlii (1967), pp. 53–67.

chial organization, in which large numbers of laymen were involved.[17]

Hartlebury parish, like the other parishes coinciding with episcopal manors, was an ecclesiastical peculiar, so that it was exempt from the jurisdiction of the archdeacon and rural deans, and separate church courts were held by an official appointed by the rector. The Hartlebury court book records proceedings between 1401 and the late sixteenth century, with the fullest coverage in the periods 1401–17 and 1443–1528. Some of the courts were called visitations, dealing with the state of the church fabric and goods (such as vestments and books), probate of wills and the failings of both clergy and laity. There were also 'chapters' (or consistories) concerned with the laity and probates. Court sessions were irregular, varying from four times a year (in 1401) to only once a year (the normal practice after 1477).

The procedures of the church court resemble those of the view of frankpledge. A panel of parishioners, varying from twelve to seventeen in number, represented villages and hamlets in the parish, and answered the articles of visitation, fulfilling a rôle similar to the tithing-men and jurors at the view. There were some coincidences of personnel between those making presentments in both lay and church courts. Orders were made, not unlike the by-laws and precepts of the manorial courts and views, and offenders were sometimes required to pay monetary penalties. The main differences were that compurgation survived longer as a means of defence than in the manor courts, and the normal punishments of offenders were the ecclesiastical sanctions of penance and excommunication.

The laity participated actively in parochial administration. As well as three churchwardens who were responsible for the upkeep of the church building and its goods, there were three wardens of the chantry of St Mary that had been founded in the church in 1325. The lay parishioners who reported to the courts on the morals of their neighbours do not seem to have been dominated by the clergy, as their complaints of clerical shortcomings reveal a highly critical attitude. John Smyth, one of the clergy, was reported in 1408 to have had sexual relations with four different women. In 1495,

[17] J. Bossy, 'The Counter-Reformation and the People of Catholic Europe', *P and P*, xlvii (1970), pp. 51–70; E. Mason, 'The Rôle of the English Parishioner, 1100–1500', *Journ. of Eccl. Hist.*, xxvii (1976), pp. 17–29.

William Lyrcock, the chantry chaplain, was said to gamble in taverns, and was involved in disputes in two houses, one of which belonged to a brewer, in the course of which he drew his hanger.[18]

Parishioners had a wide range of obligations. The courts attempted to enforce church attendance, though there were some persistent offenders. The villagers of Upper and Lower Mitton failed to attend in the 1480s and 1490s, understandably because they had to travel two or three miles. The courts sought to prevent working on Sundays, feast days and Saturday evenings; the demands of urgent work like harvest and fencing meant that breaches were regularly reported. Textile workers appear also among the offenders. Once in church, people were expected not to quarrel with neighbours, or again the court might deal with them.

There were attempts to enforce the payment of numerous dues for the support of the clergy and the maintenance of the church building. Tithes included payments not just on the major products of agriculture, but also on mill tolls, milk, profits from the sale of firewood and fish and even nuts. Not all parishioners paid in full, such as one who paid a twelfth, rather than a tenth, of his sheaves, but the main offenders seem to have been the millers, who negotiated to pay fixed annual sums in lieu of an exact tenth. Tithes gave the parishioners the right to enter into areas of economic regulation; for example, peasants were censured for failing to mow all of their hay, as this deprived the rector of his share. Beside the major payments of tithes and mortuaries, there were many minor dues. Those attending mass without receiving communion contributed 'holy loaves' that were later distributed to the poor; beekeepers were expected to give half of the wax and honey to the church; at wedding feasts 'henyng silver' was collected for the church; anyone wishing to be buried inside the church had to pay 6s. 8d. Parishioners were expected to maintain specific lengths of the churchyard wall.

As well as influencing the economic activities of the parishioners and ensuring that they paid their dues, the church court sought to deal with their personal morality. This took up much time; the visitation of October 1408, for example, dealt with eight cases of fornication and four of adultery, though numbers dwindled in the later fifteenth century so that some courts heard of no cases. The

18 WCRO ref. 009:1 BA 2636/11 43700, fos. 13, 83.

accusations show that sections of lay opinion, represented by the parishioners who informed on offenders, were willing to co-operate with the church authorities in imposing conventional moral standards. Any modern notion of privacy was clearly foreign to the parishioners in the court, who retailed the village gossip: 'Alice, servant of Agnes Ferans, is of bad reputation [*male fame*] with various men' or 'Peter ap Rice knew carnally a certain suspicious woman living with him ... and he walked with her suspiciously when she went to milk his cows in a certain pasture called Mytham'.[19] Often they investigated relationships within the household, including two cases of incest, and, much more often, sexual relations between male householders and their female servants.

Enforcement of morality brought the work of the church court near to the work of secular courts in seeking to maintain public order, and cases similar to those mentioned earlier appear in the Hartlebury book: brothel-keeping, 'disturbing neighbours at night', 'sowing discord', 'receiving men of ill-fame', and witchcraft are all mentioned.

The parish could also provide an organization for dealing with purely secular matters, such as paying troops provided for service in the Welsh wars, and the destruction of the 'meres' (boundary marks) on the parish boundary.

The Hartlebury parishioners also seem to have been involved in organizing education for the parish. Deeds of 1479 and 1480 show groups of laymen, ten in one case, twenty-two in the other, administering the endowment of St Mary's chantry. The chantry evidently had an educational function, as its lands were used to endow Hartlebury Grammar School in 1559, which was stated in its charter to be a refoundation. The post-Reformation school was run by twenty governors, corresponding to the laymen involved with the earlier chantry.[20]

The records of the Hartlebury church courts seem to show a serious decline towards the end of our period, notably after 1498, and business seems to have fallen into mere routine, with few cases of failure to attend church or reports of breaches of sexual morality.

The evidence examined so far suggests that the village community

[19] *ibid.*, 11 43700, fos. 76, 80.
[20] WCRO ref. 705:192 BA 5589/58; *The Old Order Book of Hartlebury Grammar School*, ed. D. Robertson (Worcs. Hist. Soc., 1904), pp. 209, 218–19.

performed many different functions through a variety of organizations. It was both a unit of government, with some coercive power, and a focal point of social co-operation.

Many late medieval developments helped to weaken the village community in both its governmental and social aspects. The inhabitants were conscious of the wider world beyond their own village, leading to constant migration from one village to another. This is a well-known phenomenon of the late medieval population in Europe as well as England, and can be measured by examining the changes in surnames recorded in rentals and court rolls.[21] No strong variations between villages are apparent: the normal pattern was for three-quarters of the surnames to change every forty to sixty years. For example, of the one hundred and three names recorded in the Kempsey documents in 1432–41, only twenty-five can be found in a comparable set of court rolls of 1499–1507.

The destinations of outward migrants are given for serfs leaving the manors, and those from Whitstones are depicted in Map 11. Most of the destinations of the serfs, fifty-three out of seventy-nine, taken from the records of all manors, were within ten miles of their home villages. A few were much more adventurous: a Whitstones serf went to Sussex, two Kempsey men were living at London and Salisbury, and one from Ripple was at Bicester in Oxfordshire. Long journeys are probably under-recorded, as those who made them were more likely to lose touch with their former village, and would be reported as living 'at an unknown place'. More than a third of the destinations were towns, twenty-nine of the seventy-nine, but this high figure is mainly due to the proximity of Worcester to Kempsey and Whitstones, from which most of the information comes. The emigrants normally went as individuals, mostly young men, not in family groups. They might find land in their new village, like Nicholas Hopkyns of Throckmorton, who took a Hanbury holding in 1431, but there is more evidence of them becoming servants or apprentices. Robert Strynge of Hanbury was apprenticed to a weaver, and John Porter of Hartlebury to a Coventry baker.[22]

Villagers commonly married outside their own village. The partners in first marriages are rarely recorded, but the remarriage of widows affected their right to retain their dead husband's holding,

---

[21] e.g. Morgan, *English Lands of the Abbey of Bec*, p. 111; Ladurie, *The Peasants of Languedoc*, pp. 29–31.

[22] Hanbury CR, Jan. 1431, Nov. 1379; Hartlebury CR, April 1428.

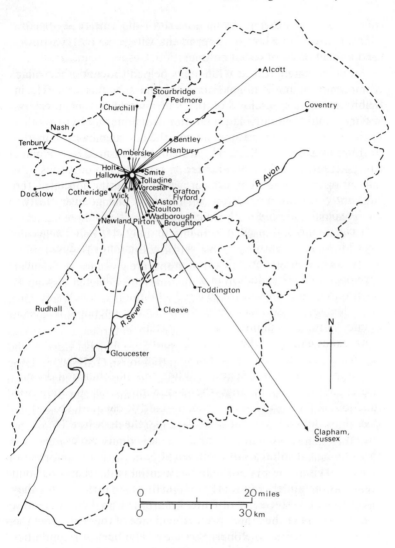

11 Migration of *nativi* from Whitstones, 1377–1540

so their new husbands are often named. Of thirty-five widows from Hampton, Hanbury and Kempsey, only ten married men from the same village. Most of the husbands came from villages within a ten-mile radius. The extra-marital sexual relations of the people of

Hartlebury also often involved partners from outside the parish.

Trade also led to contact beyond the village, so that a Throck-morton man sold a stack of pulse to a Whitstones tenant, a distance of ten miles, and another Whitstones peasant bought a horse and cart from Hanbury. William Fermor of Cleeve bought scythes from Belbroughton, a specialized centre of production thirty miles away, and then sold them in villages around Cleeve.[23]

There was nothing new about migration, exogamous marriage or trade outside the village. The scale of migration, however, must have increased in the late fourteenth and fifteenth centuries with the lifting of population pressure and seignorial controls. The constantly moving population can only have had an adverse effect on the social cohesion of the village.

It can be argued in general that economic and social adversity strengthened the early medieval village community. Social soli-darity increased under seignorial pressure, and the community developed its self-regulation in order to manage the common fields when population growth led to a reduction in pastures.[24] As seign-orial demands were relaxed and population declined, the com-munity's functions diminished in importance.

An examination of the late medieval by-laws seems to belie this argument, as the by-laws themselves became more frequent in the course of the fifteenth century. While this phenomenon demon-strates beyond doubt that the community's organization was functioning throughout our period, it would be dangerous to assume that the continuous repetition of rules reflects a healthy village society. By-laws were needed because individuals and groups were threatening the interests of their neighbours.

Who devised the by-laws? One influential group that lay behind them was the jurors, and some are directly attributed to them. They also brought verdicts on offenders presented by the tithing-men, and might make their own presentments. Service on the jury was not confined to the wealthiest stratum of the peasantry, but there was undoubtedly a tendency for jurors to belong to the more sub-stantial families. Of twenty-one men who were jurors at Han-

---

[23] Whitstones CR, July 1397, March 1388, Oct. 1391; Worcester wills, 1538/129.
[24] J. Blum, 'The European Village as Community: Origins and Functions', *Agricultural Hist.*, xlv (1971), pp. 161–7; a similar argument has been used to ex-plain the development of the continental mark, see B. H. Slicher van Bath, 'Manor, Mark, and Village in the Eastern Netherlands', *Speculum*, xxi (1946), pp. 121–5.

bury in the years 1465–8, fourteen appear in the 1466 rental as paying 10s. 0d. or more in rent, although most tenants had holdings paying less than 10s. 0d. Of the twelve male tenants holding a yardland or more in 1466, eleven served on the jury. At Kempsey three-quarters of the jurors of the years 1485–1509 held a half-yardland or more, in a manor where there were many quarter-yardlanders and cottagers. None of the ten tenants with less than a half-yardland listed in the Hartlebury rental of c.1480 ever became jurors.

The bias of the better-off tenants is evident in some of the by-laws: for example, restrictions on gleaning at harvest time or on the collection of rushes for sale, both activities of the poor. Wage-earners were not allowed to seek work elsewhere until the local harvest was over, and servants were forbidden to keep animals on the commons (both of these by-laws were implemented at Whitstones). Cottagers were very tightly restricted in the number of large animals that they could keep on the commons: one or two at Bredon and Hampton, none at Blockley.[25] Some of the apparently general regulations, such as those on fence breaking or morality, were probably directed at the poorer tenants.

Social bias is not evident in most agrarian by-laws, the primary purpose of which was to keep the common fields functioning. Many of the problems, like failures to mend fences or ring pigs, could have been the result of negligence or bad management. Others arose from deliberate acts by individuals who allowed their own interests to override those of the whole community. Perhaps the most heinous offence that a villager could commit against his neighbours was to ally with outsiders by allowing them to use the common pastures. Near towns the animals involved would belong to butchers. At Hartlebury in 1473 William Cokes entertained Welshmen and their cattle, presumably drovers on their way to urban markets. Cases are not very numerous, but they tended to increase in the late fifteenth century; of the ten recorded, eight fall in the years 1473–95.

More frequent, but also corrosive of the community's management of the fields and the ability of all tenants to gain access to pastures, were the enclosure of land and the denial of common grazing, and overstocking the common pastures. Those responsible were

[25] Whitstones CR, July 1383; St Johns view, April 1447; Kempsey CR, Oct. 1457, April 1499; Bredon CR, May 1501; Hampton CR, April 1504; Blockley CR, Oct. 1538.

often tenants of larger holdings, from the same social group as the jurors who influenced the conduct of the courts. They can be found sitting on the jury in the court that heard presentments of their wrongdoing. This ambiguity may explain the ineffectiveness of the later by-laws, especially after 1470, when rules were often made and repeated, but the numbers of presentments of offences declined. It must be stressed that in spite of the double standards of some tenants, the by-laws show that some community of interest in maintaining common rights survived. The disapproval of the villagers may even have had some inhibiting effects on enclosers, particularly in the areas of large nucleated villages and extensive open arable fields, such as in the Avon valley.

Another indication of social tensions within the village is the frequency of personal violence. Fig. 7 shows that there was a considerable increase in the number of assaults at Kempsey in the period 1445–67. This could reflect increased vigilance by the court, but if the statistics have any validity, they would coincide with contemporary complaints that serious crimes were increasing on a national scale.[26] Analysis of those involved does not suggest any clear social pattern: rich and poor, men and women, clergy and laity, neighbours and strangers, were all involved. Sometimes those accused of assault can be found to have been parties in other disputes. John Howton sued William Gorle in 1432 for carrying off his firewood, and they were presented for assaulting each other in 1432 and 1433. In 1446 Walter Taverner was presented for enclosing a meadow, and in the same court his servant was said to have assaulted various tenants. Thomas Brid junior and Thomas Brid senior were in dispute over a boundary mark in 1447, and the elder's servant was involved in a fight with the younger. There were also attacks on those in authority, with two assaults on tithing-men in 1450, a peak year for violence, perhaps to be associated with the high level of social and political troubles of that year. In 1461 William Benet attacked the village constable with a pitchfork, and Robert Woderuff hit the vicar with a stick.

These examples suggest that violence could stem from real clashes of interest and can be seen as a method of resolving disputes, or at least giving vent to strong feelings, when other methods of

---

[26] J. G. Bellamy, *Crime and Public Order in England in the Later Middle Ages* (London, 1973), pp. 27–8.

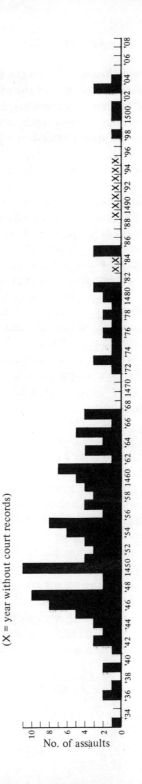

7 Assault cases at Kempsey, 1433–1508

redress, such as action through the courts, were going out of use. Assault cases became rare after 1495, but this does not mean that village society became more harmonious. Perhaps the courts had given up the attempt to control violence, or cases previously handled by the view of frankpledge were being heard by the justices of the peace.

It would be difficult to argue that village society had become polarized between the tenants of large holdings and wage-earners, as in most villages there was still too much middle ground between the two extremes. Particularly in the fifteenth century, tenure of both small and large holdings might be the experience of a tenant in one lifetime. The son of a Hartlebury tenant of two yardlands married his father's servant, suggesting that there was no unbridgeable social gulf between employers and employees.[27]

The village community continued to function as a unit of government and a social focus up to the end of our period. The troubles of the later middle ages show that the seeds of destruction of the village had already been sown. In the long run, the undermining of the common fields, the declining effectiveness of the village's internal government and the development of a distinct group of wealthy tenants, would lead to the triumph of individualism over the interests of the community.

[27] WCRO ref. 009:1 BA 2636/11 43700, fo. 71; see also Hilton, *The English Peasantry in the Later Middle Ages*, pp. 37–53.

Conclusion

The long-term social and economic changes on the estates of the bishops of Worcester can be conveniently summed up by examining the experiences of different social groups.

The bishops themselves acquired rights over great tracts of land in the two centuries after the foundation of the see, and then went through a difficult period in which they lost a good deal of property. Their position stabilized in the twelfth century, and they were able to expand their income dramatically in the thirteenth. By the early fourteenth century they had reached a turning point, and the trend in the later middle ages was towards a slow erosion of income. The 'Indian summer' of the late fourteenth century delayed decline, and administrative measures in the mid-fifteenth century paved the way for a small recovery in the later years of the fifteenth century; but the last decades before 1540 saw a combination of rising prices and increased taxes eating into the bishops' real income. However, declining revenues at no time reduced the bishops to penury, and in the fifteenth century they were still able to afford a lordly lifestyle.

The smaller lay landowners appear as a group gaining a good deal from the estate for most of the medieval period. The thegns and knights of the tenth to the twelfth centuries were granted almost half of the estate's lands in return for services. In the thirteenth century we are aware of the decline of small landowners such as William Wasthull and the Spineys. This contrasts with the ability of the Throckmortons and John Hornyhold to thrive in the fifteenth and early sixteenth centuries, when gentry officials obtained substantial rewards from the estate, and members of the gentry took over the demesnes on lease. The evidence from the estate seems to confirm the idea that small landowners in general did well in the fifteenth century, but the case of the indebted Thomas Wybbe is a reminder of the dangers of generalization about this varied social group.

We know little about the estate's peasants in the period before the twelfth century, but there are hints of their dependence and heavy obligations by the tenth century, which could have originated in a much earlier period. In the early and mid-twelfth century there is evidence of the disappearance of slavery, the spread of commutation, the renting out of parcels of demesne to peasant tenants and peasant assarting. This amelioration of tenant conditions was reversed in the thirteenth century, when assarting, developing market opportunities, and the slow spread of leasehold tenures, only partly compensated tenants for a general tendency for a growth in the demands by the lord, and some fragmentation of their smallholdings. The improvement in peasant conditions in the late fourteenth and fifteenth centuries was a long-drawn-out process, with major rent reductions in the years between 1400 and 1450, and advances in the economy of the peasant holdings apparent from the middle of the fifteenth century. Peasant opportunities depended on such factors as the location of their holdings, the size and structure of their families and the state of the market. All peasants, as well as wage-earners, achieved a higher standard of living in the fifteenth century, but significant advances by tenants of larger units towards stability of landholding and greater profitability, were most likely to occur in the period after 1470.

The geography of the estate clearly exercised a strong influence on its social and economic development. The manors were acquired at much the same time and experienced a unified and continuous lordship for most of our period. Accordingly differences between manors in land use, settlement patterns and social structure, apparent for example in the varied pace of enclosure at the end of our period, can be attributed to geographical factors. A further complicating factor lay in the uneven influence of market forces, varying from manor to manor, depending on the proximity of large urban centres.

What were the motors that propelled society along the lines indicated above? The more impersonal explanations, based on such external factors as ecology or epidemics, cannot provide the whole answer. The suggestion has been made that the declining population of the later middle ages should be seen as partly determined by social conditions, not as an independent force. The effect of the decline was not a simple adjustment in the ratio between land and people. The reduction in the size and cohesion of the peasant family had repercussions on the economy of the peasant holding, influencing the amount of land held and the pattern of retirement. The fall in tenant numbers was determined by complex economic and social circumstances, not just by demographic decline.

The influence of the market should not be underrated. The existence of a monetary element in the estate's economy can be seen as early as the ninth century. The growth of commodity production in the twelfth and thirteenth centuries enabled the lords to draw an increased income from the demesnes, but above all to increase the cash payments of the tenants. An expanding market was not a liberating force for most of the peasantry, as the lords were able to levy higher rents, particularly from those with ready access to urban centres. The declining market of the fourteenth and fifteenth centuries led to the end of direct management of the demesnes, but inhibited the new commodity producers, the demesne farmers and the peasants with very large holdings, from taking full advantage of their new assets. However, those who lived near large towns enjoyed economic opportunities at all times.

Developments in the consumption side of the market economy also promoted change. Examples are the demands of the lords for luxuries and manufactured goods in the early middle ages, which fostered urban growth, and which doubtless impelled the increase in seignorial incomes in the thirteenth century, and the more modest expansion of retail selling to satisfy the needs of villagers in the fifteenth century. We must beware of giving the market too much prominence as an agent of change. Even the bishops, such as Cantilupe and Wakefield, lived off the produce of their estates. Self-sufficiency among the peasantry limited the impact of market forces on them. One explanation of low cereal prices in the fifteenth century is the high proportion of the rural population who grew their own corn.

Social relationships can be regarded as an independent force, influenced but not determined by changes in population or the market. The institutions of feudal society, the manor, private jurisdiction and personal dependence were all established before the full development of the market. Rising population and prices strengthened seignorial control in the thirteenth century, but the exercise of the lord's power also pushed up rents. Perhaps they were increased too much, helping to precipitate the fourteenth century troubles. Rents and dues did not fall automatically with population and prices in the late fourteenth century, and a long process of readjustment, with pressure being applied by both sides, was needed before the peasantry gained concessions on rents and tenures. The lord retained some authority, such as the vestiges of serfdom, and the ability to levy variable fines, but attempts to reassert old powers in the mid-fifteenth and early sixteenth century were rebuffed. The permanent gains made by the tenants put them in a better position to benefit fully from the new market opportunities of the early sixteenth century.

Finally, political events had a considerable influence on social and economic developments. Bishops, more than any other magnates, enjoyed a close relationship with the monarchy. The estate was created by the emergent Mercian kingdom for a combination of political, social and religious ends. The state under the late-Saxon and Norman rulers seems to have been less beneficent in that the estate was truncated to provide for lay tenants. In the twelfth and thirteenth centuries the powers of jurisdiction of the bishops and other magnates were more closely defined. Particularly from the end of the thirteenth century, the growing demand for taxation reduced the resources of both lords and peasants, and the resulting popular interest in politics had repercussions on the estate in 1450. At the end of our period the state's involvement in the affairs of landlords increased, as the royal courts extended their jurisdiction, even to the point of offering protection to copyholders. State action eroded the episcopal finances in the 1530s, and shortly after the end of our period the bishops began to lose manors to laymen, after four centuries of territorial continuity.

Do all of these changes amount merely to a shift in the balance of society, or to some more profound structural change? In 1540 much remained as it had for centuries. The institutions, the social divisions and the premises on which medieval society had developed were still present. Bishop Bell, like his predecessors, occupied his palace and manor-houses, surrounded by an entourage of clergy and gentry, while his hundreds of peasant tenants laboured beyond the gates. But some important developments had taken place. The great magnates had lost their former economic initiative, and with it their primarily extractive management policies. Acquisitive gentry lessees had gained control of many demesnes on cheap, long leases. Some peasants had consolidated control of large holdings on copyhold tenure, had enclosed land, and had begun to break out of the restrictions of the village community. The market was beginning to expand once more, and some elements in rural society were poised to take advantage of the new era.

Appendix 1
Major officials of the bishopric estate, 1200–1540

Date in office	Name	Source	Biographical information
STEWARDS*			
1200 × 1212	William de Wara	White Book, fo. 62	—
1218 × 1236	Henry de Buteyate	White Book, fo. 60	—
1249	Jordan de Aldeswell	White Book, fos. 66, 72.	Rector of Withington, 1219 × 31 (*RBW*, ii, p. 143)
1262	Thomas de Molinton	White Book, fo. 66	Rector of Alvechurch (*VCH Worcs.*, iv, p. 447)
1237 × 1266	Peter de Butteville	Davies, *Administration of the Diocese of Worcester*, p. 300	—
1237 × 1266	Walter de Colingham	White Book, fo. 55	—
1269	John de Mething	Davies, pp. 300–1	—
1273	Nicholas de Wodeford	*Reg. Giffard*, p. 54	Chaplain and steward to Walter Giffard, archbishop of York, 1267. Rector of Kinwarton, 1270. Canon of Westbury, 1270. Rector of Fladbury, 1273. Rector of Chipping Norton, 1276. Comm. of *oyer* and *terminer*, 1279. Royal inquisition, 1283. Canon of Wells, 1284. (A. L. Browne, 'A Thirteenth Century Rector of Fladbury,' *Trans. Worcs. Arch. Soc.*, xi (1934), pp. 131–8; Davies, pp. 766–9)

*(Note that in most cases the officials listed here were stewards of the lands, rather than stewards of the household. However, the offices were not clearly distinguished in the documents in the thirteenth century, especially before 1266, and so some household stewards may be included here.)

377

Date in office	Name	Source	Biographical Information
1274–5	William de Causton	*Rotuli Hundredorum*, ii, p. 228	—
1284–7	Peter de Leicester	Davies, pp. 302–3	Rector of Preston Bagot, 1275. Rector of Budbrooke, 1282. Rector of Bishop's Cleeve, 1286. Clerk of receipt of exchequer, 1279. Justice of the Jews, 1289–90. Baron of exchequer, 1290–1303. (Davies, pp. 721–6)
1287	Nicholas de Mutton knt	*Reg. Giffard*, p. 327	Held manor of Mitton in Bredon. Comm. of *oyer and terminer*, 1288 (*VCH Worcs.*, iii, pp. 286–7; *Cal. Pat. Rolls, 1281–92*, p. 305)
1296	Walter de Berton	*Reg. Giffard*, p. 481	Rector of Bredon, 1286. Steward of the household, 1269–74, 1301. Bishop's chancellor 1298/9. Accused of pluralism, 1301. (Davies, pp. 703–7)
1296–9	William de Cherinton	*Reg. Giffard*, p. 481; *RBW*, iv, p. 398	Rector of Sezincote, 1279. Rector of Stoke Prior, 1281. Rector of Wotton-under-Edge, 1294. Bishop's sequestrator, 1283. Comm. of *oyer* and the *terminer*, 1293. (Davies, pp. 711–13)
1303	Simon de Greenhill	*Reg. Gainsborough*, pp. 66, 81	Sheriff of Worcs., 1286 (PRO *Lists and indexes*, ix, p. 157)
1303	Roger le Marescall	*Reg. Gainsborough*, p. 81	Rector of Thornbury, 1308–12 (*Reg. Reynolds*, pp. 51, 160)
1308–11	Milo de Redbourn	*Reg. Reynolds*, p. 2; *Lib. Alb. Pri.*, p. 34	Justice of gaol delivery, 1312 (*Reg. Reynolds*, p. 50)
1311–13	Robert de Cliderowe	*Reg. Reynolds*, pp. 20, 69	Comm. of *walliis et fossatis*, 1307–8. Comm. of *oyer and terminer*, 1311–14. Escheator north of the Trent, 1315. Steward of archbishopric of Canterbury, 1313–14. (*Cal. Pat. Rolls, 1307–13*, pp. 41, 165, 252, 371; *1313–17*, pp. 144, 245, 254, Du Boulay, *Canterbury*, p. 393)
1324	Stephen de Bramptone	*Reg. Cobham*, p. 181	—
1328	Richard de Bykerton	*Reg. Orleton*, fos. 99–100	Bishop's attorney, 1332, 1333 (*Cal. Pat. Rolls, 1330–4*, pp. 373, 472)

Date	Name	Source	Notes
1337	Nicholas de Stratford	*Registrum Prioratus*, ed. W. H. Hale (Camden Soc., 1865), p. 6	—
1339 (Worcs. & Warks.)	Peter de Grete	*Reg. Bransford*, p. 7	Held manor of Pirton Folliott. Sheriff of Worcs., 1346 (*VCH Worcs.*, iv, p. 182; *Reg. Bransford*, p. xxvii)
1339 (Glos.)	William de Cheltenham	*Reg. Bransford*, p. 13	Held lands in Pucklechurch and Hawkesbury, Glos. Comm. of peace in Glos., Herefs. and Worcs., 1344–61. M.P. Steward of Berkeley estate, 1350 (*Cal. IPM Glos.*, vi, pp. 5, 40; E. G. Kimball, 'Rolls of the Gloucestershire Sessions of the Peace', *Trans. Bristol and Glos. Arch. Soc.*, lxii (1940), p. 28; J. Smyth, *Lives of the Berkeleys*, i, p. 342)
1350	Walter atte Berough	Reg. Thoresby, fo. 12	Comm., 1350–3 (*Cal. Pat. Rolls, 1350–4*, pp. 28, 509, 517) Lands in Worcs., Warks., and Salop. Comm. on many occasions, 1335–56. (*Cal. Inq. Post Mortem*, x, pp. 281–2; *VCH Worcs.*, iii, pp. 24, 63, 192, 232; iv, pp. 8–10, 269, 329, 372; *Cal. Pat. Rolls, 1334–8*, p. 139, *et seq.*)
1351	Hugh de Cokesaye	Reg. Thoresby, fo. 63	
1369–75	William Churchehull	Henbury AR, 1369; Hanbury AR, 1375–6	
1375–81, 1383–7	John Brounyng	Hampton AR, 1375–6; Bibury AR, 1380–1, 1383–4; Henbury AR, 1386–7	Lands in three places in Glos. Sheriff of Glos., 1398 (*VCH Glos.*, viii, pp. 62, 92; x, p. 193; *PRO Lists and indexes*, ix, p. 50)
1381–3, 1387–96	Richard Thurgrym	Bibury AR, 1381–2, 1382–3; Hanbury AR, 1386–7; Henbury AR, 1395–6	Held Thorndon, Worcs., granted land in Wick. Comm. Escheator. J.P. (*VCH Worcs.*, iv, p. 158; *Cal. Pat. Rolls, 1377–81; 1385–9*, pp. 166, 464, 474; *1388–92*, pp. 10, 146, 342)
1396–7	Henry Wybbe	Henbury AR, 1396–7	Held land at Shell and Peopleton, Worcs. Comm. J.P. (*VCH Worcs.*, iii, p. 395; iv, p. 149; *Cal. Pat. Rolls, 1396–9*, p. 244; *1405–8*, p. 499)
1409–10	Thomas Throckmorton	Bredon CR, Oct. 1409, Feb. 1410	Held Throckmorton, Worcs. Beauchamp retinue, 1396. Escheator. Constable of Elmley (*VCH Worcs.*, iii, p. 356; Wedgwood, *History of Parlt.*, p. 851)

Date in office	Name	Source	Biographical Information
1413 1420–4	William Merbury William Woollashill	Cleeve CR, July 1413; Hanbury CR, April 1420; Henbury CR, May 1424	— Lands in seven Worcs. villages, including manor of Woollashill. Escheator. M.P. four times. J.P. Sheriff of Worcs. Attached to Beauchamps (Dyer, 'Deserted Village of Woollashill', pp. 56–8)
1425–48	John Wode esq	Misc. AR, 1425–6; Rec. AR, 1447–8	Lands in eight places in Worcs. and Warks. M.P. six times. J.P. Sheriff of Worcs. Lawyer. Attached to Beauchamps. (*Feudal Aids*, v, pp. 327–32; J. T. Driver, 'The Knights of the Shire for Worcestershire', *Trans. Worcs. Arch. Soc.*, xl (1963), pp. 43–4; *VCH Worcs.*, iv, p. 267)
1450–70 (Glos. only, 1460–70)	William Nottingham knt	St. Johns view, April 1450; Rec. AR, 1469–70	Held six manors and other lands in Glos. King's attorney, 1452–83. Baron of the exchequer, 1461–83. M.P. twice. J.P. Lawyer. (Wedgwood, *History of Parlt.*, pp. 642–3; notes provided by Dr E. Ives)
1459–70	Thomas Throckmorton esq	T. Habington, *A Survey of Worcestershire* (Worcs. Hist. Soc. 1895), i, pp. 426–7; Rec. AR, 1469–70	Lands in Worcs., Warks., and Bucks. Lawyer. M.P. twice. J.P. Sheriff of Warks. Lost offices in 1460s. (Habington, *Survey of Worcs.*, i, p. 427; Wedgwood, *History of Parlt.*, pp. 852–3)
1473	Humphrey Stafford esq	Reg. Carpenter, ii, fo. 34	Lands in ten counties. M.P. seven times. J.P. Sheriff of Worcs. for ten years. Rebelled and executed, 1486 (Wedgwood, *History of Parlt.* pp. 792–3; *Cal. Pat. Rolls, 1485–94*, pp. 111, 140, 151, 198–9, 231, 250, 257, 302).
1488–1519 (Glos.)	Robert Poyntz knt	Henbury AR, 1488–9, 1518–19	Held Iron Acton, Glos. Sheriff of Glos. in three years. On Enclosure Commission, 1517. Vice-chamberlain and chancellor to Catherine of Aragon (H. L. Thompson, 'The Poyntz Family', *Trans. Bristol and Glos. Arch. Soc.*, iv (1879–80), p. 76; I. S. Leadam, 'The Inquest of 1517', *Trans.*

Date	Name	Reference	Notes
1497–1506	Richard Croft knt	Rec. AR, 1497–8, 1505–6	*Royal Hist. Soc.*, new ser., viii (1894), p. 288; History of Parlt., unpublished biographies). Lands in Herefs., Salop, Worcs. M.P. three times. J.P. Sheriff of Worcs. and Herefs. Treasurer of the Household. Privy Councillor. Steward of Prince Arthur's Household. (Wedgwood, *History of Parlt.*, pp. 792–3).
1509–11	Gilbert Talbot knt	Rec. AR, 1509–10, 1510–11	Son of early of Shrewsbury. Lands in six counties. J.P. in six counties. Comm. M.P. seven times. Privy Councillor. Captain of Calais. Supported Henry VII in 1485 (Wedgwood, *History of Parlt.*, pp. 838–9; *Cal. Pat. Rolls, 1494–1509*, p. 595; Cal. of Talbot MSS. in British Museum, Birm. Reference Lib.)
1522–4	William Compton knt	Rec. AR, 1522–3, 1523–4	Lands in eighteen counties. Gentleman of the bedchamber under Henry VIII. Constable of Sudeley and Gloucester. Sheriff of Worcs. Military campaigns in France and Scotland (*DNB*, iv, pp. 908–9)
1523–30 (Glos.)	Anthony Poyntz knt	Rec. AR, 1523–4; Henbury CR, May 1530	Held Iron Acton, Glos. Served in royal household and military campaigns (for refs. see Robert Poyntz above)
1533–9 (Glos.)	Nicholas Poyntz knt	*Letters and Papers of Henry VIII*, vi, no. 533; WCRO ref. 009:1 BA 2636/18 43764	M.P. J.P. Sheriff of Glos. Steward of Kingswood Abbey. Groom of bedchamber. Wars in Ireland (1534) and North (1536). Protestant? (History of Parlt., unpublished biographies)
1528–40	George Throckmorton knt	WCRO ref. 009:1 BA 2636/177 92509; Rec. AR 1539–40	Lands in Worcs., Warks. and Bucks. M.P. J.P. Sheriff in three counties. Esquire and knight of the body. Steward of many estates, including Evesham Abbey. Opposed reformation legislation (History of Parlt., unpublished biographies)

RECEIVERS

Date	Name	Reference	Notes
1246–7	Thomas the Sacrist	Bodleian Lib., Worcester Rolls, no. 4	Sacrist of Worcester Cathedral Priory

Date in office	Name	Source	Biographical Information
1303	John de Stanwey	*Reg. Gainsborough*, p. 81	Rector of Mathon, 1281. Rector of St Helen's, Worcester, 1285. Rector of Weston-on-Avon, 1286. Rector of Bishop's Cleeve, 1288. Rector of Ripple, 1289. Rector of Fladbury, 1303 (Davies pp. 746–9)
1309–13	John de St Briavel	*Reg. Reynolds*, pp. 14, 25, 73. Reg. Maidstone, fo. 41	Sacrist of Worcester Cathedral Priory (*Reg. Reynolds*, pp. 14, 25)
1342	John le Botoner	*Reg. Bransford*, p. 97	Rector of Halford, 1339–49 (*Reg. Bransford*, pp. 54, 425)
1371–2	Robert Myle	Bibury AR, 1371–2	Rector of Chaddesley Corbett 1379. Rector of Chipping Norton, 1379–84. Warden of Straford College, 1384 (*Reg. Wakefield*, pp. 19, 162; *VCH Warks.*, ii, p. 124)
1375–88	Robert Broun	Hampton AR, 1375–6; Stoke AR, 1387–8	Rector of Hampton Lucy, 1382–9 (*Reg. Wakefield*, pp. 31, 76)
1388–92	John Clifford	Bibury AR, 1388–9, 1391–2	Rector of Whatcote, 1385, and/or Shenington, 1387 (*Reg. Wakefield*, pp. 46, 55)
1392–1413	John Newman	*Reg. Wakefield*, p. 103; Cleeve CR, July 1413	Rector of Weston-on-Avon, 1390–1, Upper Swell, 1391 (*Reg. Wakefield*, pp. 77, 93, 100)
1413–14	John Wedon	Cleeve CR, Dec. 1413, May 1414	Also surveyor (Arrears roll, 1412)
1417–20	Richard Thwayte	Bibury AR, 1417–18; Hanbury CR, April 1420	Rector of Grafton Flyford, 1430–5 (Nash, *Collections for a History of Worcestershire*, i, p. 469)
1425–7	Walter Eston	Bibury AR, 1425–6 Hanbury AR, 1426–7	Vicar of Blockley, 1419–33 (Nash, *Collections*, i, p. 104)
1427–8	Thomas Lowden	Bibury AR, 1427–8	'Clerk'
1430–2	Nicholas Mores	Bibury AR, 1430–1; Henbury AR, 1431–2	? Rector of Seven Stoke, 1450–9 (Nash, *Collections*, ii, p. 346)

1435–43	John Haye	Bibury AR, 1435–6; Stoke AR, 1443–4	Rector of Flyford Flavel, 1407–47 (Nash, *Collections*, i, p. 456)
1444–8	Mr Richard Ewen	Bibury AR, 1444–5, 1447–8	Rector of Bishop's Cleeve, 1447–8. Surveyor of the bishopric of Winchester, 1448–9 (Rec. AR 1447–8; N.S.B. Gras, *The Economic and Social History of an English Village* (Cambridge, Mass., 1930), p. 480)
1448–60	Thomas Arnold	Bibury AR, 1448–9; Hanbury AR, 1459–60	'Of Cirencester, gentleman, alias clothman, alias woolman, alias chapman'. Feoffee to convey William Nottingham's lands to Cirencester weaver's guild. (Postan and Power, *English Trade in the Fifteenth Century*, p. 53; J. D. Thorp, 'History of the manor of Coates', *Trans. Bristol and Glos. Arch. Soc.*, 1 (1928), p. 196)
1460–71	John Salwey	Bibury AR, 1460–1, 1470–1	Probably a relative of Humphrey Salwey, who held property in Worcs. Gentleman carver to Prior of Worcester (*VCH Worcs.*, ii, p. 110; iii, p. 472; iv, p. 342)
1471–5	Thomas Sybley	Bibury AR, 1471–2, 1474–5	? Owned property in Worcester city (*Original Charters relating to the City of Worcester* ed. J. H. Bloom (Worcs. Hist. Soc., 1909), p. 95.)
1476–85	William Plowmer	Bibury AR, 1476–7; Henbury AR, 1484–5	Rector of Fladbury, 1479–1503. (F. J. Thacker, 'The Monumental Brasses of Worcestershire, part II', *Trans. Worcs. Arch. Soc.*, iv (1926–7), pp. 155–6.)
1486–9	James Botiller	Bibury AR, 1486–7, 1488–9	Notary public (Wick CR, Sept. 1488)
1490–5	John Kent	Henbury AR, 1490–1; Bibury AR, 1494–5	—
1497–9	John Halsewell	Rec. AR, 1497–8, 1498–9	—
1500–3	John Payne	Rec. AR, 1500–1, 1502–3	—
1503–5	William Lane	Rec. AR, 1503–4, 1504–5	? Bailiff of Worcester city (*Original Charters relating to . . . Worcester*, ed. Bloom, p. 47)

Date in office	Name	Source	Biographical Information
1505–35	John Hornyhold	Rec. AR, 1505–6; *Valor Ecclesiasticus*, iii, p. 219	Family 'was by a female line come from the Earls of Ormond'. Lessee of Hanley Castle (Habington, *Survey of Worcs.*, i, p. 274; *VCH Worcs.*, iv, p. 96)
1538–9	Anthony Ailworth	Rec. AR, 1539–40	—
1539–40	Walter Blonte, esq	Rec. AR, 1539–40	Held Glasshampton manor, M.P. twice. J.P. 'moved only in local circles' (*VCH Worcs.*, iv, p. 236; History of Parlt., un-published biographies)

AUDITORS

Date in office	Name	Source	Biographical Information
1305	John Salemon	*Reg. Gainsborough*, p. 20.	
1309	William Merre	*Reg. Reynolds*, p. 6.	
1371–3	Roger Stanford	Bibury AR, 1371–2, 1372–3.	—
1382–7 1390–1	Richard Haym	Henbury AR, 1382–3, 1386–7, 1390–1.	—
1382–3 1390–1	John Chacombe	Henbury AR, 1382–3, 1390–1	—
1386–7 1392–3	John Clifford	Henbury AR, 1386–7, Bredon AR, 1392–3	Receiver, 1388–92 (see above)
1389–90	John Brounyng	Henbury AR, 1389–90	Steward, 1375–81, 1383–7 (see above)
1392–6	John Vampage	Bredon AR, 1392–3; Henbury AR, 1395–6	A Pershore man. Escheator (Habington, *Survey of Worcester-shire*, ii, pp. 239, 411)
1393–4	Henry Forster	Bredon AR, 1393–4	—
1453–9	William Pullesdon	Valor, 1454, 1459	M.P. Worcester city three times. Bailiff of Worcester (Wedgwood, *History of Parlt.*, p. 702)

1460–83	Thomas Arnold	Bibury AR, 1460–1, 1482–3	Receiver, 1448–60 (see above)
1505–35	Richard Rotsey	Rec. AR, 1505–6; *Valor Ecclesiasticus*, iii, p. 219	Auditor of Bordesley Abbey (*Valor Eccl.*, iii, p. 271)
1539–40	William Walter	Rec. AR, 1539–40	Of Turkdean, Glos. Lawyer. M.P. Son of a citizen of London (History of Parlt., unpublished biographies)

SURVEYORS

c.1410	Mr Thomas Baldyng	Arrears roll, 1412	Preceptor of the Hospital of St Wulfstan (Arrears roll, 1412)
1411–12	John Wedon	Arrears roll, 1412	Later receiver (see above)
1448–51	John Eddon	Hanbury AR, 1448–9, 1450–1	Rector of Kempsey, 1455 (Reg. Carpenter, i, fo. 134)
1463–6	John Salwey	Rec. AR, 1463–4, 1465–6	Also receiver (see above).
1497–1501	John Paul de Gigli	Rec. AR, 1497–8, 1500–1	Also procurator and factor, i.e. the bishop's representative in London. Richard Bukke acted as deputy-surveyor
1509–10	John Hornyhold	Rec. AR, 1509–10, 1522–3	Also receiver (see above)
1522–3			
1523–5	William More	Rec. AR, 1523–4; PRO St. Ch. 2 21/136	Prior of Worcester
1523	John Gostwick John Russell Thomas Russell	*Letters and Papers of Henry VIII*, iii, no. 2843	(for John Russell see below)
1533–40	John Russell knt	*Letters and Papers of Henry VIII*, vii, no. 1202; Rec. AR, 1539–40	Of Strensham. Lands in four counties. M.P. J.P. Sheriff of Worcs. In favour with Thomas Cromwell, but conservative in religion. (History of Parlt., unpublished biographies)

Appendix 2
Profits and arrears on individual manors, 1370—1540

The shaded bars on the profit diagrams represent profits (that is, liveries to the receivers, the lord himself, or foreign payments made on the lord's behalf) in cash. The unshaded bars indicate the value of liveries in kind, that is in grain, wool and stock. O shows that profits, and in the arrears diagrams, arrears, were nil in that year.

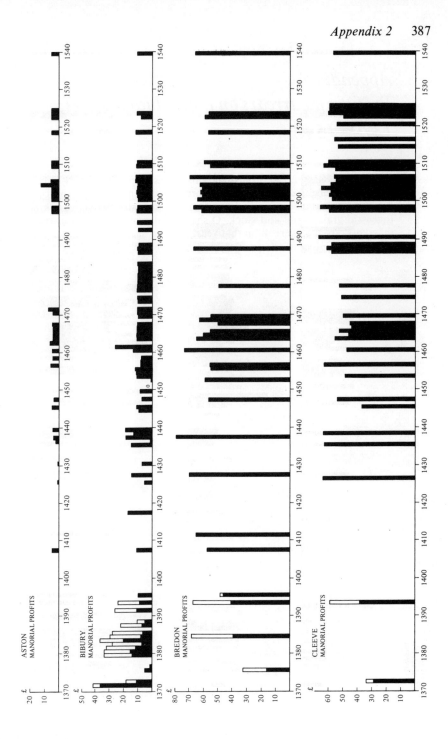

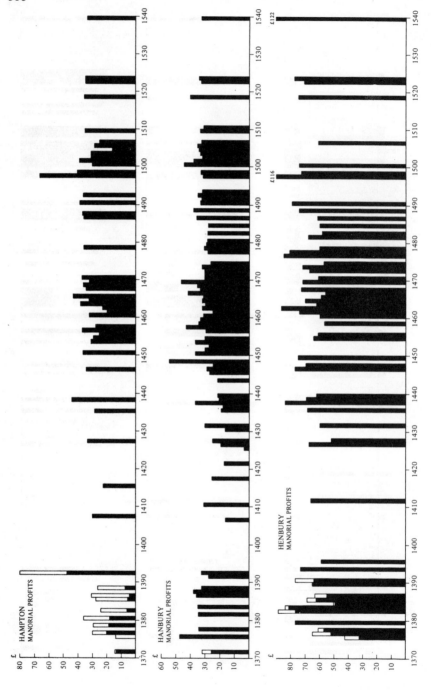

HAMPTON
MANORIAL PROFITS

HANBURY
MANORIAL PROFITS

HENBURY
MANORIAL PROFITS

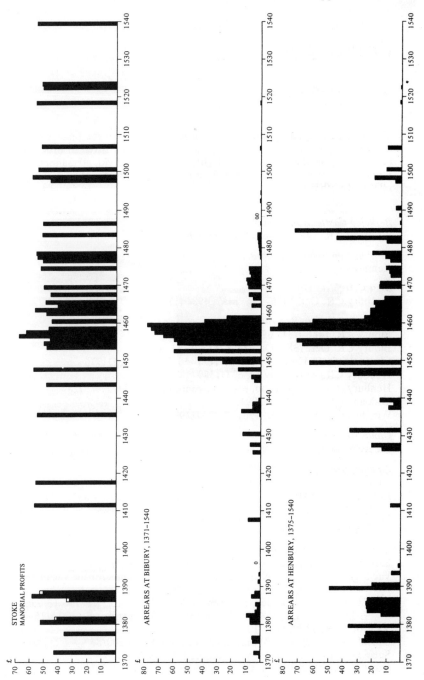

STOKE
MANORIAL PROFITS

ARREARS AT BIBURY, 1371–1540

ARREARS AT HENBURY, 1375–1540

Bibliography

MANUSCRIPT SOURCES

These are arranged in alphabetical order according to the place where deposited. Within each collection, the documents are listed in order of (a) records of the whole estate, (b) records of individual manors, in alphabetical order, (c) other records, both non-estate material and records relating to other estates.

Berkeley Castle Muniment Room
Stratford AR, 1464–5. Select Rolls no. 63

Birmingham Reference Library
Kempsey deeds. Zachary Lloyd MSS., nos. 73–80

Bristol Archives Office
Henbury CR, Oct. 1436–Jan. 1437. 4984 (1)

Gloucester County Records Office
Bibury AR, 1486–7. D 678/89
Bibury CR, Oct. 1382–Oct. 1498. D 678/63–4
Cleeve deeds. D 326 T139; D 1637 T6/1–15, T14/1–10; D1776
Henbury CR, April–July 1456. D1389
Henbury, tenants' petition, early sixteenth century. D1799/M28
Todenham CR, 1474. D1099/31/M1
Winchcombe Abbey CR, 1361–2. D678/99

Gloucester Public Library
Cleeve glebe terrier, 1589. no. 45T

London, British Library
Extents of the bishopric, 1364, 1407. Add. MS. 6165, fos. 81–3, 87
Alvechurch and Hanbury deeds. Egerton charters 1,829—1,832

London, Lambeth Palace Library
Bredon CR, Oct. 1406. ED. 284

London, Public Record Office
Extent of the temporalities of the bishopric, 1364. SC11 724
Vacancy documents, escheators' and keepers' accounts for the vacancies
    of 1317, 1349, 1352–3, 1361–2, 1363–4
        SC 6 1143/19, E 368 124 mm. 256–9, E 136 13/9, E 136 13/25a,
        E 357/3 m. 53, E 368 126, E 136 14/13, E 136 13/28a, E 136 14/16
Stratford AR, 1370. SC 6 1040/20
Subsidy abatements for Worcestershire, 1446. E 179 200/83
Subsidy of 1524 for Oswaldslow hundred. E 179 200/128
Star Chamber records. St. Ch. 2 26/36, 18/276, 15/310, 21/136

London, Society of Antiquaries Library
Pratinton Collection, Worcestershire Parishes, Vols. ii, v, vii, xvii

Oxford, Bodleian Library
Fladbury AR, 1246–7; Tredington AR, 1246–7. Worcestershire rolls no. 4
Bibury CR, April 1479 – April 1494 (Osney Abbey manor). Bodleian Rolls
    nos. 1,92; Ms. D.D.Ch.Ch.O.R. 127, 130

Oxford, Corpus Christi College
Cleeve Rectory AR, 1389–90–1417–18. B/14/2/3

Stratford-on-Avon, Shakespeare Birthplace Trust Records Office
Stratford CR, Sept. 1463–July 1507. DR 75 nos. 1–3, 5–6; ER 2/436
Stratford CR, April 1520–April 1539, transcribed by J. H. Bloom, 1903–4.
    ER 56/1355
Stratford Borough CR, Oct. 1499–Aug. 1500. DR 75 no. 4
'Order of the fields and meadows belonging to Shottery', early sixteenth
    century. Wheler papers, i, no. 99
Throckmorton rentals, 1476, 1484. DR5 3272–3

Worcester Cathedral Library
Fladbury rental, 1537–8. C580
Registers of Worcester Cathedral Priory. *Liber Albus*, Dean and Chapter
    Reg. A IV. Other registers, Dean and Chapter Reg. A VI(1), A VI(2),
    and A VI (3)
Worcester Cathedral Priory CR, 1346, E15; 1379, E30; 1412, E46

Worcester, County Record Office
The bulk of the documents used come from the collection of the Ecclesiastical Commissioners, deposited in the Record Office in 1959. They are
catalogued at Worcester under ref. 009:1 BA 2636, and documents from
the collection will be listed below simply under their parcel number,
followed by the five figure number assigned to them by the Commissioners,
e.g. 176 92486. It is necessary to give the numbers in full as the Commissioners listed the documents out of sequence, and made errors in
identifying manors and types of document. Manuscripts from other
collections are distinguished by giving the reference and bulk accession
numbers in full.

Liber Albus of the bishopric. Cartularies of *c.*1300 and the fifteenth century,
    with additional material, including the survey of rents of 1408. ref.
    821 BA 3814
Charters, 1199–1316. ref. 829 BA 3332 nos. 208–17
Book of charters, rentals, accounts, a valor, surveys of knight service
    and rents, fifteenth century. 9 43696
Lease book, late fifteenth-early sixteenth century. 37 (iii) 43806
Lease book, temp. Bishop Latimer. 37 (iv) 43807
Receivers' AR, 1433–1540. 192 92627 4/12, 175 92475, 175 92480, 168
    92313, 174 92470 4/6, 175 92483–4, 176 92493–4, 175 92485, 176
    92487, 174 92473, 192 92627 7/12, 191 92625 3/12, 192 92627 5/12,

191 92625 7/12, 192 92627 6/12, 191 92625 5/12, 191 92625 8/12, 192 92625 10/12, 176 92496, 176 92499–500, 177 92505, 177 92507, 178 92517

Valors, 1454–66. 175 92477, 175 92479, 175 92481, 174 92472, 174 92470 1/6, 191 92625 4/12, 176 92486

Arrears rolls, 1389–1533. 193 92628 4/9, 192 92627 8/12, 191 92625 2/12, 176 92488, 176 92490, 176 92489, 191 92625 6/12

Vacancy documents, 1302–3, 1433–5. 192 92626 7/12, 174 92465, 174 92471, 193 92628 8/9

Master shepherd's AR, 1449–50. 193 92627 9/12, 192 92626 8/12

Survey of the bishopric, c.1450. 193 92627 10/12

Accounts of all manors, 1506–7, 1518–19. 176 92497–8, 177 92503

Court rolls of all manors, April 1520–April 1538. 177 92504, 177 92508–9, 178 92510–11a, 178 92515

Court rolls of all manors, Sept. 1544–May 1546. 178 92514, 178 92516

Court books, Oct. 1528–May 1539. 18 43762–5

Post-medieval estate documents. Parliamentary surveys, 47 43955, 48 43964 etc. Surveyor's book, 9 43693

Alvechurch AR, 1510–25. 177 92501–2, 174 92470 3/6

Bibury AR, 1371–1499. 160 92050–1, 159 92049 3/7 and 4/7, 160 92052–4, 159 92049 6/7 and 7/7, 160 92055–60, 159 92049 5/7, 159 92049 2/7, 160 92061–4, 166 92266, 160 92065–79, 161 92080–4, 161 92099, 161 92085–92, 159 92049 1/7, 161 92093–92106

Blockley AR, 1383–1526. 157 92007–8, 177 92501, 170 92389, 177 92502, 174 92470 3/6, 157 92010

Bredon AR, 1375–1489. 158 92014–5, 158 92017, 157 92012 1/8, 158 92020, 158 92027, 159 92031, 158 92013 3/8, 159 92037, 159 92040–3, 157 92012 7/8, 158 92013 8/8, 157 92012 2/8, 174 92470 3/6, 159 92044–6, 157 92012 3/8, 158 92013 6/8, 158 92013 5/8, 157 92012 4/8

Bredon CR, Oct. 1389–July 1501. 158 92016, 158 92018–19, 158 92021, 193 92628 2/9, 158 92022, 158 92013 1/8 and 2/8, 158 92023–5, 158 92013 7/8, 158 92028, 158 92013 4/8, 158 92029–30, 157 92012 6/8, 157 92012 8/8, 159 92032–3, 158 92026, 159 92034–9, 193 92628 6/9, 165 92226 5/7, 159 92047–8

Cleeve AR, 1372–1526. 161 92113 5/6, 193 92627 12/12, 162 92114, 162 92116, 161 92113 1/6, 162 92123, 192 92626 11/12, 162 92118–19, 161 92113 3/6, 162 92120–1, 161 92113 6/6, 157 92009, 170 92388, 177 92501, 162 92124, 177 92502, 170 92386, 174 92470 3/6

Cleeve CR, Oct. 1412–July 1515. 162 92115, 193 92628 9/9, 174 92470 6/6, 162 92117, 192 92627 2/12, 192 92626 12/12, 192 92495, 162 92122, 161 92113 4/6

Cleeve rental, 1474–5. 161 92113 2/6

Fladbury AR, 1523–4. 177 92506

Hampton AR, 1371–1524. 163 92160, 163 92158 1/7, 163 92161–9, 163 92625 12/12, 164 92171–3, 163 92158 7/7, 164 92176, 163 92159 6/7, 164 92179, 163 92159 2/7, 164 92184, 163 92158 5/7, 163 92159 3/7, 163 92158 2/7, 163 92158 6/7, 163 92159 5/7, 164 92189, 165

92225 3/8, 164 92191, 191 92625 9/12, 163 92159 4/7, 163 92159 1/7, 164 92203–5, 165 92223

Hampton CR, Oct. 1394–April 1518. 164 92170, 164 92174–5, 164 92177–8, 164 92180–1, 164 92182–3, 164 92185–8, 164 92190, 164 92192–92202, 164 92206–22

Hanbury AR, 1371–1502. ref. 705:7 BA 7335/37–9, 75

Hanbury AR, 1377–8. ref. 705:7 BA 57

Hanbury AR, 1386–1524. 166 92254, 167 92276, 167 92282, 167 92285, 165 92225 2/8, 168 92321, 168 92325, 168 92336, 168 92342, 168 92344, 168 92348, 169 92351, 169 92355, 166 92268, 169 92369

Hanbury CR, Oct. 1375–April 1504. 165 92229, 166 92231–4, 166 92236–9, 166 92241–5, 166 92247–50, 166 92253, 166 92255, 166 92258–9, 166 92267, 169 92359, 167 92270, 166 92269, 167 92271–5, 167 92277, 167 92279–81, 167 92283, 192 92626 6/12, 167 92286–7, 167 92289–91, 167 92293–92300, 167 92302, 167 92307, 167 92304, 167 92306, 167 92309–12, 168 92314–15, 168 92318–20, 168 92323–4, 168 92327–8, 168 92331, 168 92338, 168 92345–6, 168 92349, 169 92353–4, 165 92226 3/7, 169 92358, 169 92356, 169 92361, 169 92363, 169 92366–7

Hanbury CR, Sept. 1488–April 1489. ref. 705:192 BA 5589/82

Hanbury CR, April 1433–Sept. 1530. ref. 705:7 BA 7335/64–5

Hanbury, list of enclosures, 1539–40. ref. 705:7 BA 7335/95 (iii)

Hanbury rental, 1466. 168 92332

Hartlebury CR, Oct. 1394–April 1505. 169 92372, 169 92371 1/4, 192 92627 3/12, 192 92627 1/12

Henbury AR, 1363–1524. 165 92227–8, 167 92308, 166 92230, 166 92235, 165 92226 2/7, 165 92225 6/8, 166 92240, 166 92246, 170 92387, 165 92226 6/7, 166 92251–2, 166 92256–7, 166 92260–4, 167 92301, 165 92225 5/8, 167 92278, 167 92284, 167 92288, 167 92292, 167 92301, 167 92303, 167 92305, 165 92226 7/7, 167 92308, 168 92316–17, 168 92322, 168 92326, 165 92225 1/8, 168 92329, 169 92368, 168 92330, 168 92333, 168 92335, 168 92337, 168 92340, 168 92341, 168 92343, 166 92265, 168 92347, 168 92350, 169 92352, 169 92357, 169 92360, 169 92362, 165 92225 8/8, 169 92364, 169 92365, 169 92368

Henbury CR, Nov. 1423–July 1517. 192 92626 9/12, 174 92470, 165 92225 7/8, 192 92626 1/12, 168 92339, 165 92225 4/8, 165 92226 1/7

Henbury rental, 1419. 185 92574[b], 165 92226 4/7,

Kempsey AR, 1505–26. 157 unnumbered, 170 92389, 170 92388, 177 92501, 170 92389, 177 92502, 170 92386, 170 92390, 174 92470 3/6

Kempsey CR, Oct. 1394–Oct. 1537. ref. 705:4 BA 54

Miscellaneous AR (i.e. accounts of the manors of Aston, Knightwick, Throckmorton, the Droitwich salt-works, the liberties of Oswaldslow and Pathlow, Hillingdon rectory, London rents, and the revenues from the tomb of St Wulfstan), 1407–1517.
172 92429–31, 172 92428 3/5–5/5, 172 92432–8, 172 92428 1/5, 172 92439–41, 172 92428 2/5, 172 92442–4, 177 92501–2

Ripple AR, 1456–7. ref. 899:24 BA 5561/1

Ripple CR, Dec. 1394–July 1457. ref. 899:24 BA 5561/1

St Johns views, see Whistones CR below

Stock and Bradley AR, 1516–25. 174 92502, 174 92470 3/6

Stoke AR, 1369–1487. 192 92625 11/12, 192 92626 10/12, 171 92415 4/8, 171 92416–19, 171 92414 1/6, 171 92415 1/8, 171 92415 6/8, 171 92415 3/8, 171 92414 6/6, 171 92415 8/8, 171 92414 3/6, 171 92420, 171 92415 7/8, 171 92421–3, 171 92415 5/8, 171 92414 5/6, 171 92424–7, 171 92414 2/6

Stratford AR, 1523–4. 192 92626 4/12

Tredington AR, 1523–4. 165 92223

Whitstones, AR, 1523–4. 177 92506

Whitstones CR (including Wick CR and St Johns views) Nov. 1377–April 1510. 173 92447–8, 175 92474, 175 92476, 175 92482, 176 92491–2, 192 92626 5/12

Withington CR, May 1521–Oct. 1521. 196 92495

Oswaldslow CR, Oct. 1432–May 1433. 193 unnumbered, 193 92628 5/9

Winburntree CR, April 1457. 164 92181

Commissary's AR, 1452, 1474–5. 10 43699, 190 92614

Extracts from the priory registers. ref. 821 BA 2437

Bishops' registers. ref. b 716:093 BA 2648
   Maidstone 1 (iv), Orleton 2 (ii), Montacute 2 (iii), Hempnall 2 (iv), Thoresby 3 (ii), Brian 3 (iii) and 3 (iv), Barnet 4 (i), Whittlesey 4 (ii), Lenn 4 (iii), Winchcombe 4 (v), Clifford 5 (i), Peverel 5 (ii), Morgan 5 (iii), Polton 5 (iv), Bourgchier 6 (i), Carpenter 6 (ii) and 6 (iii), Alcock 7 (i), Morton 7 (ii), Giovanni de' Gigli 7 (iii), Silvestro de' Gigli 8, Ghinucci 9 (i), Latimer 9 (ii)

Hartlebury court book of peculiar jurisdiction, fifteenth–sixteenth centuries. 11 43700

Wills, 1511–40. ref. 008:7 BA 3590/I vols. ii, v. Worcester wills nos. 40, 76, 84, 219, 1528/101, 1529/110, 1534/146, 1537/7, 1537/64, 1537/80, 1537/107, 1537/211, 1538/45, 1538/46, 1538/57, 1538/119, 1538/126, 1538/129, 1538/130, 1538/241, 1538/245, 1538/246, 1538/247, 1538/249–53, 1538/305, 1538/324, 1538/344, 1538/370, 1538/377, 1538–40/18, 1538–9/45, 1538–9/48, 1538–9/54, 1538–9/77, 1540/25, 1540/30, 1540/32, 1540/59a, 1540/63, 1540/70

Glebe terriers, 1585–1635. ref. 721:091 BA 2358/1 no. 6b, /2 no. 31a, 34a, /5 no. 87a, 98a, /6 no. 100a, 100b. ref. 721:091 BA 2735/1 no. 158a

Alvechurch tithe assessment and map, 1840. ref. f. 760/7 BA 1572

Fladbury enclosure map, 1789. ref. 705:81 BA 351/62

Hartlebury chantry deed. ref. 705:192 BA 5589/58

Kempsey estate map, c.1700. f.970.5:73 BA 940/1 (iv)

Tredington estate map, 1846. ref. b. 009:1 BA 5403/20

Vernon estate map, 1731–2. ref. f. 970.5:7 BA 1101/1

PRINTED SOURCES

These are arranged in alphabetical order by title, except for chronicles which appear under their authors, and modern anthologies (e.g. Robertson, Whitelock) which appear under their editors.

Some Ancient Indictments in the King's Bench referring to Kent, 1450–2,
ed. R. Virgoe (Kent. Arch. Soc. Records, xviii, 1964)

Anglo-Saxon Chronicle, ed. D. Whitelock, D. C. Douglas and S. Tucker
(London, 1961)

Annales Monastici, i, iv, ed. H. R. Luard (Rolls ser., 1864, 1869)

Bolton Priory Rentals and Ministers' Accounts, 1473–1539, ed. I. Kershaw
(Yorks. Arch. Soc. Record Ser., cxxxii, 1969)

The Book of Margery Kempe, 1436, ed. W. Butler-Bowden (London, 1936)

The Book of Nurture by John Russell, ed. F. J. Furnivall (Early Eng. Text
Soc., 1868)

Calendar of Charter Rolls

Calendar of Close Rolls

Calendar of Inquisitions Miscellaneous

Calendar of Inquisitions Post Mortem

Calendar of Papal Registers

Calendar of Patent Rolls

Calendars of bishops' registers, see under Registers below.

Cartularium Saxonicum, ed. W. de Gray Birch, 3 vols. (London, 1885–
93)

The Cartulary of Worcester Cathedral Priory (Register I), ed. R. R. Darlington (Pipe Roll Soc., lxxvi, 1962–3)

Chapters of the English Black Monks, 1215–1540, ed. W. A. Pantin, iii
(Camden Soc., 3rd ser., liv, 1937)

Chertsey Abbey Court Roll Abstracts, ed. E. Toms, 2 vols. (Surrey Record
Soc., xxxviii, 1937, and xlviii, 1954)

Chronicon Abbatiae de Evesham, ed. W. D. Macray (Rolls ser., 1863)

*Churchwardens Accounts of Croscombe, Pilton, Yatton, Tintinhull, Morebath
and St. Michael's Bath*, ed. Bishop Hobhouse (Somerset Record
Soc., iv, 1890)

The Court Rolls of the Manor of Bromsgrove and King's Norton, ed. A. F. C.
Baber (Worcs. Hist. Soc., new ser., 1963)

*Documents Illustrating the Rule of Walter de Wenlok, Abbot of Westminster,
1283–1307*, ed. B. F. Harvey (Camden Soc., 4th ser., ii, 1965)

Domesday Book (Record Commission, 1783)

The Domesday of Inclosures, ed. I. S. Leadam, 2 vols. (Royal Hist. Soc.,
1897)

D. C. Douglas and G. W. Greenaway, *English Historical Documents*, ii
(London, 1953)

The Duchy of Lancaster's Estates in Derbyshire, 1485–1540, ed. I. S. W.
Blanchard (Derbyshire Archaeological Soc. Record Ser., iii, 1967)

W. Dugdale, *Monasticon Anglicanum*, ed. J. Caley, H. Ellis, and B. Bandi-
nel, 6 vols. (London, 1849)

Early Worcester Manuscripts, ed. C. H. Turner (Oxford, 1916)

Ecclesiastical Terriers of Warwickshire Parishes, ed. D. M. Barratt, 2 vols.
(Dugdale Soc., xxii, 1955, and xxvii, 1971)

'Evesham A, A Domesday Text', ed. P. H. Sawyer, in *Miscellany I* (Worcs.
Hist. Soc., new ser., i, 1960)

Feudal Aids

Florence of Worcester, *Chronicon ex chronicis*, ed. B. Thorpe, 2 vols. (Eng. Hist. Soc., xiii, 1848–9)

Sir John Fortescue, *The Governance of England*, ed. C. Plummer (Oxford, 1885)

Die Gesetze der Angelsachsen, ed. F. Liebermann, 3 vols. (Halle, 1903–16)

Gloucestershire Subsidy Roll, 1 Edward III, 1327 (Middlehill Press, N.D.)

The Grey of Ruthin Valor, ed. R. I. Jack (Sydney, 1965)

T. Habington, *A Survey of Worcestershire*, ed. J. Amphlett, 2 vols. (Worcs. Hist. Soc., 1895, 1899)

F. E. Harmer, *Select English Historical Documents of the Ninth and Tenth Centuries* (Cambridge, 1914)

F. E. Harmer, *Anglo-Saxon Writs* (Manchester, 1952)

W. Harrison, *The Description of England*, ed. G. Edelen (Ithaca, New York, 1968)

Hemingi Chartularium Ecclesiae Wigorniensis, ed. T. Hearne, 2 vols. (Oxford, 1723).

Historia et Cartularium Monasterii Sancti Petri Gloucestriae, ed. W. H. Hart, 3 vols. (Rolls ser., 1863–7)

Historians of the Church of York, ii, ed. J. Raine (Rolls ser., 1886)

Household Book of Dame Alice de Bryene, ed. V. B. Redstone (Suffolk Institute of Archaeology and Natural History, Ipswich, 1931)

Household Roll of Bishop Ralph of Shrewsbury, ed. J. A. Robinson (Somerset Record Soc., *Collectanea*, lix, 1924)

Inquisitiones Nonarum (Record Commission., 1807)

Inquisitiones Post Mortem for Gloucestershire, ed. S. J. Madge and E. A. Fry (British Record Soc., 1903, 1910, 1914)

John of Worcester, *Chronicle*, ed. J. R. H. Weaver (Oxford, 1908)

Journal of Prior William More, ed. E. S. Fegan (Worcs. Hist. Soc., 1914)

The Lay Subsidy of 1334, ed. R. E. Glasscock (London, 1975)

Lay Subsidy Roll, Warwickshire, 1327, ed. W. B. Bickley (Trans. Midland Rec. Soc., vi, 1902)

Lay Subsidy Roll for Warwickshire of 6 Edward III (1332), ed. W. F. Carter (Dugdale Soc., vi, 1926)

Lay Subsidy Roll for the County of Worcester, circa 1280, ed. J. W. Willis Bund and J. Amphlett (Worcs. Hist. Soc., 1893)

Lay Subsidy Roll for the County of Worcester, 1 Edward III, ed. F. J. Eld (Worcs. Hist. Soc., 1895)

Lay Subsidy Roll, AD 1332–3, ed. J. Amphlett (Worcs. Hist. Soc., 1899)

Leland's Itinerary in England and Wales, ed. L. Toulmin Smith, 5 vols. (London, 1964, reprint)

Letters and Papers of Henry VIII

The Liber Albus of Worcester Priory, ed. J. M. Wilson (Worcs. Hist. Soc., 1919)

Memorials of St. Dunstan, ed. W. Stubbs (Rolls ser., 1874)

Ministers' Accounts of the Warwickshire Estates of the Duke of Clarence, 1479–80, ed. R. H. Hilton (Dugdale Soc., xxi, 1952)

The Old Order Book of Hartlebury Grammar School, ed. D. Robertson (Worcs. Hist. Soc., 1904)

Original Charters relating to the City of Worcester, ed. J. H. Bloom (Worcs. Hist. Soc., 1909)

Pipe Rolls: *Great Rolls of the Pipe* (Record Commission, 1844); *Pipe Rolls 5 Henry II – 2 Henry III* (Pipe Roll Soc., i, 1884–lxxvii, 1964)

Placita de Quo Warranto temp. Edward I, II, and III (Record Commission, 1818)

Placitorum Abbreviatio (Record Commission, 1811)

Plumpton Correspondence, ed. T. Stapleton (Camden Soc., iv, 1839)

Public Works in Mediaeval Law, ed. C. T. Flower, 2 vols. (Selden Soc., xxxiii, 1915, and xl, 1923)

Red Book of the Exchequer, ed. H. Hall, 3 vols. (London, 1896)

Red Book of Worcester, ed. M. Hollings, 4 parts (Worcs. Hist. Soc., 1934–50)

Register of Bishop Godfrey Giffard, ed. J. W. Willis Bund (Worcs. Hist. Soc., 1898–1902)

Register of Thomas de Cobham, ed. E. H. Pearce (Worcs. Hist. Soc., 1930)

Register of Walter Reynolds, Bishop of Worcester, 1308–13, ed. R. A. Wilson (Worcs. Hist. Soc., 1928)

Register of William de Geynesburgh, Bishop of Worcester, 1302–7, ed. J. W. Willis Bund and R. A. Wilson (Worcs. Hist. Soc., 1907–29)

A Calendar of the Register of Henry Wakefield, ed. W. P. Marett (Worcs. Hist. Soc., new ser., vii, 1972)

A Calendar of the Register of Wolstan de Bransford, ed. R. M. Haines (Worcs. Hist. Soc., new ser., iv, 1966)

Register of Richard Clifford, Bishop of Worcester, 1401–7, ed. W. E. L. Smith (Toronto, 1976)

Register of the Gild of the Holy Cross . . . of Stratford-upon-Avon, ed. J. H. Bloom (London, 1907)

Registrum Prioratus Beatae Mariae Wigorniensis, ed. W. H. Hale (Camden Soc., 1865)

Registrum Sede Vacante, ed. J. Willis Bund (Worcs. Hist. Soc., 1897)

Report on the Manuscripts of Lord Middleton (Hist. Manuscripts Commission, 1911)

A. J. Robertson, *Anglo-Saxon Charters*, 2nd edn, (Cambridge, 1956)

'Rolls of the Gloucestershire Sessions of the Peace', ed. E. G. Kimball (*Trans. Bristol and Glos. Arch. Soc.,* lxii, 1940)

Rolls of the Justices in Eyre for Gloucestershire, Warwickshire, and Staffordshire, 1221, 1222, ed. D. M. Stenton (Selden Soc., lix, 1940)

Rolls of the Justices in Eyre for Lincolnshire, 1218–9, and Worcestershire, 1221, ed. D. M. Stenton (Selden Soc., liii, 1934)

Rotuli Chartarum (Record Commission, 1837)

Rotuli Hundredorum, 2 vols. (Record Commission, 1812–18)

Rotuli Litterarum Patentium (Record Commission, 1835).

Rotuli Parliamentorum, 6 vols. (Record Commission, N. D.)

J. Rous, *Historia Regum Angliae*, 2nd edn, ed. T. Hearne (Oxford, 1745)

Select Cases before the King's Council in the Star Chamber, ed. I. S. Leadam (Selden Soc., xvi, 1902)

Sermons of Hugh Latimer, ed. G. E. Corrie (Parker Soc., 1844)

Statutes of the Realm, 11 vols. (London, 1810–28)
Taxatio Ecclesiastica auctoritate P. Nicholai IV, ca. 1291 (Record Commission, 1802)
Valor Ecclesiasticus, 6 vols. (Record Commission, 1810–34)
Vita Wulfstani of William of Malmesbury, ed. R. R. Darlington (Camden Soc., 3rd ser., xl, 1928)
Walter of Henley, ed. D. Oschinsky (Oxford, 1971)
D. Whitelock, *English Historical Documents*, i (London 1955)

SECONDARY WORKS BOOKS
(including pamphlets and unpublished theses)

W. Abel, *Crises Agraires en Europe (XIIIe–XXe siècles)* (Paris, 1973)
R. Allen Brown, *Origins of English Feudalism* (London, 1973)
M. Altschul, *A Baronial Family in Medieval England: The Clares, 1217–1314* (Baltimore, 1965)
J. Armitage Robinson, *St. Oswald and the Church of Worcester*, Brit. Acad. Supplemental Papers, v (1919)
W. O. Ault, *Open-Field Farming in Medieval England* (London, 1972)
A. R. H. Baker and R. A. Butlin (eds.), *Studies of Field Systems in the British Isles* (Cambridge, 1973)
J. F. Baldwin, *The King's Council in England during the Middle Ages* (Oxford, 1913)
F. Barlow, *The English Church, 1000–1066* (London, 1963)
J. M. W. Bean, *The Estates of the Percy Family, 1416–1537* (Oxford, 1958)
J. M. W. Bean, *The Decline of English Feudalism, 1215–1540* (Manchester, 1968)
J. G. Bellamy, *Crime and Public Order in England in the Later Middle Ages* (London, 1973)
M. W. Beresford, *The Lost Villages of England* (London, 1954)
M. W. Beresford, *New Towns of the Middle Ages* (London, 1967)
M. W. Beresford and J. G. Hurst, *Deserted Medieval Villages* (London, 1971)
J.-N. Biraben, *Les Hommes et la Peste en France et dans les Pays Européens et Mediterranéens* (Paris, 1975)
I. S. W. Blanchard, 'Economic Change in Derbyshire in the Late Middle Ages, 1272–1540' (Univ. of London, Ph.D. thesis, 1967)
A. R. Bridbury, *England and the Salt Trade in the Later Middle Ages* (Oxford, 1955)
A. R. Bridbury, *Economic Growth: England in the Later Middle Ages* (London, 1962)
Cambridge Economic History of Europe, i–iv (Cambridge, 1952–67)
E. M. Carus-Wilson (ed.), *Essays in Economic History*, i–ii (London, 1954, 1962)
E. M. Carus-Wilson and O. Coleman, *England's Export Trade, 1275–1547* (Oxford, 1962)
E. M. Carus-Wilson, *The Expansion of Exeter at the Close of the Middle Ages* (Exeter, 1963)

E. M. Carus-Wilson, *Medieval Merchant Venturers,* 2nd edn (London, 1967)

H. M. Chadwick, *Studies on Anglo-Saxon Institutions* (Cambridge, 1905)

D. S. Chambers, *Cardinal Bainbridge in the Court of Rome, 1509 to 1514* (Oxford, 1965)

F. W. B. Charles, *Medieval Cruck-Building and its Derivatives* (Medieval Archaeology monographs, ii, 1967)

A. V. Chayanov, *The Theory of Peasant Economy,* ed. D. Thorner, B. Kerblay, and R. E. F. Smith (Homewood, Ill., 1966)

H. M. Chew, *The English Ecclesiastical Tenants-in-Chief and Knight Service* (Oxford, 1932)

I. Chiva, *Rural Communities, Problems, Methods, and Types of Research* (UNESCO, Reports and Papers in Social Science, x, 1958)

C. M. Cipolla (ed.), *The Fontana Economic History of Europe,* i (London, 1972)

W. Cooper, *Wootton Wawen, its History and Records* (Leeds, 1936)

G. G. Coulton, *The Medieval Village* (Cambridge, 1925)

G. G. Coulton, *Medieval Panorama* (Cambridge, 1938)

C. Creighton, *A History of Epidemics in Britain,* 2nd edn (London, 1965)

H. C. Darby and I. B. Terrett, *The Domesday Geography of Midland England,* 2nd edn (Cambridge, 1971)

H. C. Darby (ed.), *A New Historical Geography of England before 1600* (Cambridge, 1976)

F. G. Davenport, *The Economic Development of a Norfolk Manor, 1086–1565* (Cambridge, 1906)

S. J. Davies, 'Studies in the Administration of the Diocese of Worcester in the Thirteenth Century' (Univ. of Wales Ph.D. thesis, 1971)

N. Denholm-Young, *Seignorial Administration in England* (Oxford, 1937)

E. de Moreau, *Les Abbayes de Belgique* (Brussels, 1952)

E. B. Dewindt, *Land and People in Holywell-cum-Needingworth* (Toronto, 1972)

Dictionary of National Biography

R. B. Dobson, *The Peasants' Revolt of 1381* (London, 1970)

F. R. H. Du Boulay, *The Lordship of Canterbury* (London, 1966)

G. Duby, *L'Économie Rurale et la Vie des Campagnes dans L'Occident Médiéval,* 2 vols. (Paris, 1962)

G. Duby, *The Early Growth of the European Economy* (London, 1974)

W. Dugdale, *The Antiquities of Warwickshire* (London, 1656)

A. D. Dyer, *The City of Worcester in the Sixteenth Century* (Leicester, 1973)

École Pratique des Hautes Études, VIe Section, *Villages Désertés et Histoire Économique* (Paris, 1965)

G. R. Elton, *The Tudor Constitution* (Cambridge, 1962)

E. Estyn Evans, *Irish Folk Ways* (London, 1957)

O. von Feilitzen, *The Pre-Conquest Personal Names of Domesday Book* (Uppsala, 1937)

R. K. Field, 'The Worcestershire Peasantry in the Later Middle Ages' (Univ. of Birmingham M.A. thesis, 1962)

W. J. Fieldhouse, T. May, and F. C. Wellstood, *A Romano-British Industrial Settlement near Tiddington, Stratford-upon-Avon* (Birmingham, 1931)

H. P. R. Finberg (ed.), *Gloucestershire Studies* (Leicester, 1957)

H. P. R. Finberg, *The Early Charters of the West Midlands* (Leicester, 1961)

H. P. R. Finberg, *Lucerna* (London, 1964)

H. P. R. Finberg, *Tavistock Abbey*, 2nd edn (Newton Abbot, 1969)

H. P. R. Finberg (ed.), *The Agrarian History of England and Wales*, i, part 2 (Cambridge, 1972)

R. Floud, *An Introduction to Quantitative Methods for Historians* (London, 1973)

G. Fourquin, *Les Campagnes de la Région Parisienne à la Fin du Moyen Age* (Paris, 1964)

L. Fox, *The Borough Town of Stratford-upon-Avon* (Stratford, 1953)

D. V. Glass and D. E. C. Eversley (eds.), *Population in History* (London, 1965)

A. E. Goodman, *The Loyal Conspiracy* (London, 1971)

J. Goody, J. Thirsk, and E. P. Thompson (eds.), *Family and Inheritance* (Cambridge, 1976)

J. E. B. Gover, A. Mawer, and F. M. Stenton, *The Place-Names of Warwickshire* (English Place-Name Soc., xiii, 1936)

N. S. B. Gras, *The Evolution of the English Corn Market* (Cambridge, Mass., 1926)

N. S. B. Gras, *The Economic and Social History of an English Village* (Cambridge, Mass., 1930)

C. M. Gray, *Copyhold, Equity, and the Common Law* (Cambridge, Mass., 1963)

H. L. Gray, *English Field Systems* (Cambridge, Mass., 1915)

G. B. Grundy, *Saxon Charters and Field Names of Gloucestershire* (Gloucester, 1935–6)

R. M. Haines, *The Administration of the Diocese of Worcester in the first half of the Fourteenth Century* (London, 1965)

C. R. Hart, *The Early Charters of Northern England and the North Midlands* (Leicester, 1975)

G. Hart, *A History of Cheltenham* (Leicester, 1965)

B. Harvey, *Westminster Abbey and its Estates in the Middle Ages* (Oxford, 1977)

P. D. A. Harvey, *A Medieval Oxfordshire Village* (Oxford, 1965)

J. Hatcher, *Rural Economy and Society in the Duchy of Cornwall, 1300–1500* (Cambridge, 1970)

J. Hatcher, *English Tin Production and Trade before 1550* (Oxford, 1973)

J. Hatcher, *Plague, Population and the English Economy, 1348–1530* (London, 1977)

P. M. Hembry, *The Bishops of Bath and Wells* (London, 1967)

D. Herlihy, *Pisa in the Early Renaissance* (New Haven, 1958)

R. H. Hilton, *The Economic Development of some Leicestershire Estates in the Fourteenth and Fifteenth Centuries* (Oxford, 1947)

R. H. Hilton, *A Medieval Society* (London, 1966)

R. H. Hilton, *The Decline of Serfdom in Medieval England* (London, 1969)

R. H. Hilton, *Bond Men Made Free* (London, 1973)

R. H. Hilton, *The English Peasantry in the Later Middle Ages* (Oxford, 1975)

R. H. Hilton (ed.), *The Transition from Feudalism to Capitalism* (London, 1976)

G. A. Holmes, *The Estates of the Higher Nobility in Fourteenth-Century England* (Cambridge, 1957)

T. H. Hollingsworth, *Historical Demography* (London, 1969)

C. Warren Hollister, *Anglo-Saxon Military Institutions* (Oxford, 1962)

G. C. Homans, *English Villagers of the Thirteenth Century*, 2nd edn (New York, 1970)

M. Howell, *Regalian Right in Medieval England* (London, 1962)

K. Hughes, *The Church in Early Irish Society* (London, 1966)

E. F. Jacob, *The Fifteenth Century* (Oxford, 1961)

M. K. James, *Studies in the Medieval Wine Trade* (Oxford, 1971)

E. John, *Land Tenure in Early England* (Leicester, 1960)

A. E. E. Jones, *Anglo-Saxon Worcester* (Worcester, 1958)

E. Kerridge, *The Agricultural Revolution* (London, 1967)

E. Kerridge, *Agrarian Problems in the Sixteenth Century and After* (London, 1969)

I. Kershaw, *Bolton Priory* (Oxford, 1973)

E. King, *Peterborough Abbey, 1086–1310* (Cambridge, 1973)

D. Knowles, *The Religious Orders in England*, 3 vols. (Cambridge, 1948–59)

E. A. Kosminsky, *Studies in the Agrarian History of England in the Thirteenth Century* (Oxford, 1956)

G. Kriehn, *The English Rising of 1450* (Strassburg, 1892)

E. le Roy Ladurie, *The Peasants of Languedoc* (Homewood, Ill., 1974)

E. le Roy Ladurie, *Times of Feasting, Times of Famine* (London, 1972)

E. le Roy Ladurie, *Montaillou, Village Occitan, de 1294 à 1324* (Paris, 1975. English translation, London, 1979)

J. R. Lander, *Crown and Nobility, 1450–1509* (London, 1976)

V. I. Lenin, *The Development of Capitalism in Russia*, Collected Works, iii (Moscow, 1964)

R. Lennard, *Rural England, 1086–1135* (Oxford, 1959)

A. E. Levett, *The Black Death on the Estates of the See of Winchester* (Oxford, 1916)

A. E. Levett, *Studies in Manorial History* (Oxford, 1938)

W. Levison, *England and the Continent in the Eighth Century* (Oxford, 1946)

T. H. Lloyd, *Some Aspects of the Building Industry in Medieval Stratford-upon-Avon* (Dugdale Soc. Occasional Papers, xiv, 1961)

T. H. Lloyd, *The Movement of Wool Prices in Medieval England* (Econ. Hist. Rev. Supplement, no. 6, 1973)

M. L. Loane, *Masters of the English Reformation* (London, 1954)

M.-T. Lorcin, *Les Campagnes de la Région Lyonnaise aux XIVe–XVe siècles* (Lyons, 1974)

F. Lot, *Études Critiques sur l'Abbaye de Saint Wandrille* (Paris, 1913)

H. R. Loyn, *Anglo-Saxon England and the Norman Conquest* (London, 1962)

W. E. Lunt, *Financial Relations of England with the Papacy*, 2 vols. (Cambridge, Mass., 1939 and 1962)

A. Macfarlane, *Witchcraft in Tudor and Stuart England* (London, 1970)

K. B. McFarlane, *The Nobility in Later Medieval England* (Oxford, 1973)

J. R. Maddicott, *The English Peasantry and the Demands of the Crown, 1294–1341* (P. and P. Supplement, i, 1975)

F. W. Maitland, *Domesday Book and Beyond* (Cambridge, 1897)

A. Mawer, F. M. Stenton, and F. T. S. Houghton, *The Place-Names of Worcestershire* (English Place-Name Soc., iv, 1927)

A. Meaney, *A Gazetteer of Early Anglo-Saxon Burial Sites* (London, 1964)

E. Mercer, *English Vernacular Houses* (London, 1975)

E. Miller, *The Abbey and Bishopric of Ely* (Cambridge, 1951)

H. A. Miskimin, *The Economy of Early Renaissance Europe, 1300–1460* (Englewood Cliffs, New Jersey, 1969)

M. Mollat (ed.), *Études sur l'Histoire de la Pauvreté*, 2 vols. (Paris, 1974)

M. Morgan, *The English Lands of the Abbey of Bec* (Oxford, 1946)

T. R. Nash, *Collections for a History of Worcestershire*, 2nd edn, 2 vols. (1781)

N. Neilson, *Customary Rents* (Oxford Studies in Social and Legal History, ii, 1910)

J. T. Noonan, *Contraception, A History of its Treatment by the Catholic Theologians and Canonists* (Cambridge, Mass., 1965)

F. M. Page, *The Estates of Crowland Abbey* (Cambridge, 1934)

S. Painter, *Studies in the History of the English Feudal Barony* (Baltimore, 1943)

C. Phythian Adams, *Local History and Folklore* (London, 1975)

F. Pollock and F. W. Maitland, *The History of English Law*, 2nd edn, 2 vols. (Cambridge, 1968)

A. L. Poole, *The Obligations of Society in the Twelfth and Thirteenth Centuries* (Oxford, 1946)

M. M. Postan and E. Power (eds.), *Studies in English Trade in the Fifteenth Century* (London, 1933)

M. M. Postan, *The Famulus* (Econ. Hist. Rev. Supplement, no. 2, 1954)

M. M. Postan, *The Medieval Economy and Society* (London, 1972)

M. M. Postan, *Essays on Medieval Agriculture and General Problems of the Medieval Economy* (Cambridge, 1973)

M. M. Postan, *Medieval Trade and Finance* (Cambridge, 1973)

M. Powicke, *Military Obligation in Medieval England* (Oxford, 1962)

M. Prestwich, *War, Politics, and Finance under Edward I* (London, 1972)

O. Rackham, *Trees and Woodland in the British Landscape* (London, 1976)

J. A. Raftis, *The Estates of Ramsey Abbey* (Toronto, 1957)

J. A. Raftis, *Tenure and Mobility* (Toronto, 1964)

J. A. Raftis, *Warboys* (Toronto, 1974)

J. R. Ravensdale, *Liable to Floods* (Cambridge, 1974)

H. G. Richardson and G. O. Sayles, *Law and Legislation from Æthelberht to Magna Carta* (Edinburgh, 1966)

J. H. Round, *Feudal England* (London, 1909)

Royal Commission on Historical Monuments, *Iron-Age and Romano-British Monuments in the Gloucestershire Cotswolds* (London, 1976)

J. C. Russell, *British Medieval Population* (Albuquerque, 1948)

L. F. Salzman, *Building in England* (Oxford, 1967)

I. J. Sanders, *English Baronies* (Oxford, 1960)

P. H. Sawyer, *Anglo-Saxon Charters, an annotated List and Bibliography* (London, 1968)

P. H. Sawyer (ed.), *Medieval Settlement* (London, 1976)

E. Searle, *Lordship and Community, Battle Abbey and its Banlieu, 1066–1538* (Toronto, 1974)

T. Shanin (ed.), *Peasants and Peasant Societies* (Harmondsworth, 1971)

J. F. D. Shrewsbury, *A History of the Bubonic Plague in the British Isles* (Cambridge, 1970)

A. H. Smith, *The Place-Names of Gloucestershire*, 4 vols. (Eng. Place-Name Soc., xxxviii–xli, 1964–5)

B. S. Smith, *A History of Malvern* (Leicester, 1964)

R. A. L. Smith, *Canterbury Cathedral Priory* (Cambridge, 1943)

J. Smyth, *Lives of the Berkeleys*, ed. J. Maclean (Gloucester, 1883)

F. M. Stenton, *The Latin Charters of the Anglo-Saxon Period* (Oxford, 1955)

F. M. Stenton, *The First Century of English Feudalism*, 2nd edn (Oxford, 1961)

F. M. Stenton, *Anglo-Saxon England*, 3rd edn (Oxford, 1972)

R. L. Storey, *Diocesan Administration in the Fifteenth Century* (St Anthony's Hall Publications, xvi, York, 1959)

L. Stouff, *Ravitaillement et Alimentation en Provence aux XIVe et XVe siècles* (Paris, 1970)

W. Stubbs, *The Constitutional History of England*, 6th edn, 3 vols. (Oxford, 1903)

R. H. Tawney, *The Agrarian Problem in the Sixteenth Century*, 2nd edn (New York, 1967)

J. Thirsk (ed.), *The Agrarian History of England and Wales*, iv (Cambridge, 1967)

A. Hamilton Thompson, *The English Clergy and their Organization in the Later Middle Ages* (Oxford, 1947)

J. A. F. Thomson, *The Later Lollards, 1414–1520* (Oxford, 1965)

J. E. Thorold Rogers, *A History of Agriculture and Prices in England*, 7 vols. (Oxford, 1866–1902)

S. Thrupp, *The Merchant Class of Medieval London* (Michigan, 1962)

J. Z. Titow, *English Rural Society, 1200–1350* (London, 1969)

J. Z. Titow, *Winchester Yields* (Cambridge, 1972)

R. Trow-Smith, *A History of British Livestock Husbandry to 1700* (London, 1957)

Victoria County Histories of Gloucestershire, Middlesex, Warwickshire, Worcestershire

P. Vinogradoff, *Villainage in England* (Oxford, 1892)

E. K. Vose, 'Estates of Worcester Cathedral Priory' (unpublished type-script, School of History, University of Birmingham)

J. M. Wallace-Hadrill, *Early Germanic Kingship in England and on the Continent* (Oxford, 1971)

J. C. Wedgwood, *History of Parliament. Biographies of the members of the Commons House, 1439–1509*, 2 vols. (London, 1936)

J. West, 'The Administration and Economy of the Forest of Feckenham during the Early Middle Ages' (Univ. of Birmingham M.A. thesis, 1964)

H. Wharton, *Anglia Sacra* (London, 1691)

L. White, *Medieval Technology and Social Change* (Oxford, 1962)

K. P. Witney, *The Jutish Forest* (London, 1976)

E. R. Wolf, *Peasants* (Englewood Cliffs, New Jersey, 1966)

E. A. Wrigley, *Population and History* (London, 1969)

SECONDARY WORKS: ARTICLES

N. W. Alcock, 'The Medieval Cottages of Bishop's Clyst, Devon', *Medieval Arch.*, ix (1965), pp. 146–53

A. B. Appleby, 'Disease or Famine? Mortality in Cumberland and Westmorland, 1580–1640', *Econ. Hist. Rev.*, 2nd ser., xxvi (1973), pp. 403–32

T. H. Aston, 'The English Manor,' *P and P*, x (1956), pp. 6–14

T. H. Aston, 'The Origins of the Manor in England', *Trans. Roy. Hist. Soc.*, 5th ser., viii (1958), pp. 59–83

I. Atkins, 'The Church of Worcester from the Eighth to the Twelfth Century', *Antiquaries Journ.*, xvii (1937), pp. 371–91; xx (1940), pp. 1–38

W. O. Ault, 'Village Assemblies in Medieval England', in *Album Helen Maud Cam. Studies presented to the International Commission for the History of Representative and Parliamentary Institutions* (Louvain/ Paris, 1960), pp. 11–35

W. O. Ault, 'By-laws of Gleaning and Problems of the Harvest', *Econ. Hist. Rev.*, 2nd ser., xiv (1961), pp. 210–17

W. O. Ault, 'Manor Court and Parish Church in Fifteenth Century England', *Speculum*, xlii (1967), pp. 53–67

P. A. Barker, 'The Roman Town' (of Worcester), *Trans. Worcs. Arch. Soc.*, 3rd ser., ii (1968–9), pp. 15–19

P. A. Barker *et al.*, 'Two Burials under the Refectory of Worcester Cathedral', *Medieval Arch.*, xviii (1974), pp. 146–51

J. M. W. Bean, 'Plague, Population, and Economic Decline in England in the Later Middle Ages', *Econ. Hist. Rev.*, 2nd ser., xv (1963), pp. 432–37

H. S. Bennett, 'The Reeve and the Manor in the Fourteenth Century', *Eng. Hist. Rev.*, xli (1926), pp. 358–65

L. K. Berkner, 'The Stem Family and the Developmental Cycle of the Peasant Household: an Eighteenth Century Austrian example', *Amer. Hist. Rev.*, lxxvii (1972), pp. 398–418

W. Beveridge, 'Wages in the Winchester Manors', *Econ. Hist. Rev.*, vii (1936), pp. 22–43

Lord Beveridge, 'The Yield and Price of Corn in the Middle Ages', in E. M. Carus-Wilson (ed.), *Essays in Economic History*, i (London, 1954), pp. 13–25

M. Biddle, 'The Development of the Anglo-Saxon Town', in *Settimane di Studio del Centro Italiano di Studi sull'alto medioevo*, xxi (Spoleto, 1974), pp. 203–30

J. R. Birrell, 'Peasant Craftsmen in the Medieval Forest', *Ag. Hist. Rev.*, xvii (1969), pp. 91–107

I. S. W. Blanchard, 'Population Change, Enclosure, and the Early Tudor Economy', *Econ. Hist. Rev.*, 2nd ser., xxiii (1970), pp. 427–45

I. S. W. Blanchard, 'Derbyshire Lead Production, 1195–1505', *Derbyshire Arch. Journ.*, xci (1971), pp. 119–40

I. S. W. Blanchard, 'The Miner and the Agricultural Community in Late Medieval England', *Ag. Hist. Rev.*, xx (1972), pp. 93–106

I. S. W. Blanchard, 'Commercial Crisis and Change: Trade and the Industrial Economy of the North-East, 1509–32', *Northern Hist.*, viii (1973), pp. 64–85

M. Bloch, 'Comment et pourquoi finit l'esclavage antique', *Annales ESC,* ii (1947), pp. 161–70

J. Blum, 'The European Village as Community: Origins and Functions', *Agricultural Hist.*, xlv (1971), pp. 157–78

J. Blum, 'The Internal Structure and Polity of the European Village Community from the Fifteenth to the Nineteenth Century', *Journ. of Modern Hist.*, xliii (1971), pp. 541–76

G. C. Boon, 'The Roman Site at Sea Mills, 1945–6', *Trans. Bristol and Glos. Arch. Soc.*, lxvi (1945), pp. 258–95

J. Bossy, 'The Counter-Reformation and the People of Catholic Europe', *P and P*, xlvii (1970), pp. 51–70

L. Bradley, 'An Enquiry into Seasonality in Baptisms, Marriages, and Burials', *Local Population Studies*, vi (1971), pp. 15–30

R. Brenner, 'Agrarian Class Structure and Economic Development in Pre-Industrial Europe', *P and P*, lxx (1976), pp. 30–75

A. R. Bridbury, 'The Black Death', *Econ. Hist. Rev.*, 2nd ser., xxvi (1973), pp. 577–92

A. R. Bridbury, 'Sixteenth-Century Farming', *Econ. Hist. Rev.*, 2nd ser., xxvii (1974), pp. 538–56

N. Brooks, 'The Development of Military Obligations in Eighth- and Ninth-Century England', in P. Clemoes and K. Hughes (eds.), *England Before the Conquest, Studies in Primary Sources presented to Dorothy Whitelock* (Cambridge, 1971), pp. 69–84

N. Brooks, 'Anglo-Saxon Charters: the Work of the Last Twenty Years', in P. Clemoes (ed.), *Anglo-Saxon England* (Cambridge, 1974), pp. 211–31

A. L. Browne, 'A Thirteenth Century Rector of Fladbury', *Trans. Worcs. Arch. Soc.*, xi (1934), pp. 131–8

H. M. Cam, 'Early Groups of Hundreds', in *Liberties and Communities in Medieval England* (London, 1963), pp. 91–106

H. M. Cam, 'The Community of the Vill', in V. Ruffer and A. J. Taylor (eds.), *Medieval Studies presented to Rose Graham* (Oxford, 1950), pp. 1–14

E. Carpentier, 'Famines et Épidémies dans l'Histoire du XIVe siècle', *Annales ESC*, xvii (1962), pp. 1062–92

E. M. Carus-Wilson, 'Evidences of Industrial Growth on some Fifteenth-Century Manors', *Econ. Hist. Rev.*, 2nd ser., xii (1959), pp. 190–205

E. M. Carus-Wilson, 'The First Half-Century of the Borough of Stratford-upon-Avon', *Econ. Hist. Rev.*, 2nd ser., xviii (1965), pp. 46–63

T. M. Charles Edwards, 'Kinship, Status, and the Origins of the Hide', *P and P*, lvi (1972), pp. 3–33

H. B. Clarke and C. C. Dyer, 'Anglo-Saxon and Early Norman Worcester: the Documentary Evidence', *Trans. Worcs. Arch. Soc.*, 3rd ser., ii (1968–9), pp. 27–33

W. J. Corbett, 'England, 1087–1154', in *Cambridge Medieval History* (Cambridge, 1926), v, pp. 521–53

P. Coss, 'Sir Geoffrey de Langley and the Crisis of the Knightly Class in Thirteenth-Century England', *P and P*, lxviii (1975), pp. 1–37

M. Creighton, 'The Italian Bishops of Worcester', in *Historical Essays and Reviews* (London, 1902), pp. 202–34

D. A. Crowley, 'The Later History of Frankpledge', *Bull. of the Inst. of Hist. Research*, xlviii (1975), pp. 1–15

B. Cunliffe, 'Saxon and Medieval Settlement-Pattern in the region of Chalton, Hampshire', *Medieval Arch.*, xvi (1972), pp. 1–12

R. R. Darlington, 'Aethelwig, Abbot of Evesham', *Eng. Hist. Rev.*, xlviii (1933), pp. 1–22, 177–98

R. R. Davies, 'Baronial Accounts, Incomes, and Arrears in the Later Middle Ages', *Econ. Hist. Rev.*, 2nd ser., xxi (1968), pp. 211–29

W. Davies, 'St. Mary's Worcester and the *Liber Landavensis*', *Journ. of the Soc. of Archivists*, iv (1972), pp. 459–85

W. Davies and H. Vierck, 'The Contexts of the Tribal Hidage: Social Aggregates and Settlement Patterns', *Frühmittelalterliche Studien*, viii (1974), pp. 223–93

M. Deanesley, 'Early English and Gallic Minsters', *Trans. Roy. Hist. Soc.*, 4th ser., xxiii (1941), pp. 25–52

J. T. Driver, 'The Knights of the Shire for Worcestershire', *Trans. Worcs. Arch. Soc.*, xl (1963), pp. 42–64

F. R. H. Du Boulay, 'Who were Farming the English Demesnes at the end of the Middle Ages?', *Econ. Hist. Rev.*, 2nd ser., xvii (1965), pp. 443–55

C. C. Dyer, 'The Deserted Medieval Village of Woollashill, Worcestershire', *Trans. Worcs. Arch. Soc.*, 3rd ser., i (1965–7), pp. 55–61

C. C. Dyer, 'Population and Agriculture on a Warwickshire Manor in the Later Middle Ages', *Univ. of Birm. Hist. Journ.*, xi (1968), pp. 113–27

C. C. Dyer, 'A Redistribution of Incomes in Fifteenth-Century England?', *P and P*, xxxix (1968), pp. 11–33

C. C. Dyer, 'D.M.V.'s in Worcestershire', *Med. Village Research Group Report*, xix (1971), pp. 5–7

C. C. Dyer, 'A Small Landowner in the Fifteenth Century', *Midland Hist.*, i (1972), pp. 1–14

R. Faith, 'Peasant Families and Inheritance Customs in Medieval England', *Ag. Hist. Rev.*, xiv (1966), pp. 77–95

D. L. Farmer, 'Grain Yields on the Winchester Manors in the later Middle Ages', *Econ. Hist. Rev.*, 2nd ser., xxx (1977), pp. 555–66

R. K. Field, 'Worcestershire Peasant Buildings, Household Goods and Farming Equipment', *Medieval Arch.*, ix (1965), pp. 105–45

H. P. R. Finberg, 'Some Early Gloucestershire Estates', in *Gloucestershire Studies* (Leicester, 1957), pp. 1–16

H. P. R. Finberg, 'The Genesis of the Gloucestershire Towns', in *Gloucestershire Studies*, pp. 62–83

H. P. R. Finberg, 'Continuity or Cataclysm?', in *Lucerna* (London, 1964), pp. 1–20

H. P. R. Finberg, 'Roman and Saxon Withington', in *Lucerna*, pp. 21–65

H. P. R. Finberg, 'Charltons and Carltons', in *Lucerna*, pp. 144–60

F. J. Fisher, 'Influenza and Inflation in Tudor England', *Econ. Hist. Rev.*, 2nd ser., xviii (1965), pp. 120–9

W. J. Ford, 'Some Settlement Patterns in the Central Region of the Warwickshire Avon', in P. H. Sawyer (ed.), *Medieval Settlement* (London, 1976), pp. 274–94

H. S. A. Fox, 'The Chronology of Enclosure and Economic Development in Medieval Devon', *Econ. Hist. Rev.*, 2nd ser., xxviii (1975), pp. 181–202

V. H. Galbraith, 'An Episcopal Land-Grant of 1085', *Eng. Hist. Rev.*, xliv (1929), pp. 353–72

V. H. Galbraith, 'Notes on the Career of Samson, Bishop of Worcester (1096–1112)', *Eng. Hist. Rev.*, lxxxii (1967), pp. 86–101

J.-P. Genet, 'Économie et Société en Angleterre au XVe siècle', *Annales ESC*, xxvii (1972), pp. 1449–74

P. Grierson, 'Carolingian Europe and the Arabs: the Myth of the Mancus', *Revue Belge de Philologie et d'Histoire*, xxxii (1954), pp. 1059–74

P. Grierson, 'Commerce in the Dark Ages: a critique of the evidence', *Trans. Roy. Hist. Soc.*, 5th ser., ix (1959), pp. 123–40

G. B. Grundy, 'Saxon Charters of Worcestershire', *Trans. Birm. Arch. Soc.*, lii (1927), pp. 1–183; liii (1928), pp. 18–131

A. D'Haenens, 'La Crise des Abbayes Bénédictines au bas Moyen Age, St.-Martin de Tournai de 1290 à 1350', *Le Moyen Age*, lxv (1959), pp. 75–95

R. M. Haines, 'Bishop Carpenter's Injunctions to the Diocese of Worcester in 1451', *Bull. Inst. Hist. Research*, xl (1967), pp. 203–7

R. M. Haines, 'Aspects of the Episcopate of John Carpenter, Bishop of Worcester, 1444–76', *Journ. of Eccl. Hist.*, xix (1968), pp. 11–40

J. Hajnal, 'European Marriage Patterns in Perspective', in D. V. Glass and D. E. C. Eversley (eds.), *Population in History* (London, 1965), pp. 101–43

H. E. Hallam, 'Some Thirteenth Century Censuses', *Econ. Hist. Rev.*, 2nd ser., x (1958), pp. 340–61

B. J. Harris, 'Landlords and Tenants in England in the Later Middle Ages', *P and P*, xliii (1969), pp. 146–50

C. J. Harrison, 'Grain Price Analysis and Harvest Qualities, 1465–1634', *Ag. Hist. Rev.*, xix (1971), pp. 135–55

B. F. Harvey, 'The Population Trend in England between 1300 and 1348', *Trans. Roy. Hist. Soc.*, 5th ser., xvi (1966), pp. 23–42

B. F. Harvey, 'The Leasing of the Abbot of Westminster's Demesnes in the Later Middle Ages', *Econ. Hist. Rev.*, 2nd ser., xxii (1969), pp. 17–27

P. D. A. Harvey, 'The English Inflation of 1180–1220', *P and P*, lxi (1973), pp. 3–30

P. D. A. Harvey, 'The Pipe Rolls and the Adoption of Demesne Farming in England', *Econ. Hist. Rev.*, 2nd ser., xxvii (1974), pp. 345–59

F. Heal, 'The Tudors and Church Lands: Economic Problems of the Bishopric of Ely during the Sixteenth Century', *Econ. Hist. Rev.*, 2nd ser., xxvi (1973), pp. 198–217

D. Herlihy, 'Church Property on the European Continent, 701–1200', *Speculum*, xxxvi (1961), pp. 81–105

R. H. Hilton, 'Peasant Movements in England before 1381', in E. M. Carus-Wilson (ed.), *Essays in Economic History* (London, 1962), ii, pp. 73–90

R. H. Hilton 'Y eût-il une crise générale de la Féodalité?', *Annales ESC*, vi (1951), pp. 23–30

R. H. Hilton, 'Gloucester Abbey Leases of the Late Thirteenth Century', in *The English Peasantry in the Later Middle Ages* (Oxford, 1975), pp. 139–60

R. H. Hilton, 'A Study in the Pre-history of English Enclosure in the Fifteenth Century', *ibid*, pp. 161–73

R. H. Hilton, 'Old Enclosure in the West Midlands', *Annales de L'Est*, 1959, pp. 272–83

R. H. Hilton, 'Rent and Capital Formation in Feudal Society', in *The English Peasantry in the Later Middle Ages*, pp. 174–214

R. H. Hilton, 'Freedom and Villeinage in England', *P and P*, xxxi (1965), pp. 3–19

R. H. Hilton, 'A Rare Evesham Abbey Estate Document', *Vale of Evesham Research Papers*, ii (1969), pp. 5–10

R. H. Hilton and P. A. Rahtz, 'Upton, Gloucestershire, 1959–64', *Trans. Bristol and Glos. Arch. Soc.*, lxxxv (1966), pp. 70–146

S. Hirst and P. A. Rahtz, 'Hatton Rock, 1970', *Trans. Birm. Arch. Soc.*, lxxxv (1972), pp. 160–77

M. Hollings, 'The Survival of the Five-Hide Unit in the Western Midlands', *Eng. Hist. Rev.*, lxiii (1948), pp. 453–87

J. C. Holt, 'Feudalism Revisited', *Econ. Hist. Rev.*, 2nd ser., xiv (1961), pp. 333–40

W. G. Hoskins, 'Harvest Fluctuations and English Economic History, 1480–1619', *Ag. Hist. Rev.*, xii (1964), pp. 28–46

C. Howell, 'Peasant Inheritance Customs in the Midlands, 1280–1700', in J. Goody, J. Thirsk and E. P. Thompson (eds.), *Family and Inheritance* (Cambridge, 1976), pp. 112–55

P. R. Hyams, 'The Origins of a Peasant Land Market in England', *Econ. Hist. Rev.*, 2nd ser., xxiii (1970), pp. 18–31

P. R. Hyams, 'The Proof of Villein Status in the Common Law', *Eng. Hist. Rev.*, lxxxix (1974), pp. 721–49

M. E. James, 'Obedience and Dissent in Henrician England: the Lincolnshire Rebellion 1536', *P and P*, xlviii (1970), pp. 3–78

E. John, 'The Imposition of the Common Burdens on the Lands of the English Church', *Bull. Inst. Hist. Research*, xxxi (1958), pp. 117–29

E. John, 'An Alleged Worcester Charter of the reign of Edgar', *Bull. of the John Rylands Library*, xli (1958), pp. 54–80

E. John, 'English Feudalism and the Structure of Anglo-Saxon Society', in *Orbis Britanniae*, pp. 128–53

E. John, 'St. Oswald and the Church of Worcester', in *Orbis Britanniae* (Manchester, 1966), pp. 234–48

J. E. A. Jolliffe, 'Some Factors in the Beginnings of Parliament', in E. B. Fryde and E. Miller (eds.), *Historical Studies of the English Parliament* (Cambridge, 1970), i, pp. 31–69

A. Jones, 'Land and People at Leighton Buzzard in the Later Fifteenth Century', *Econ. Hist. Rev.*, 2nd ser., xxv (1972), pp. 18–27

N. Kenyon, 'Labour Conditions in Essex in the reign of Richard II', in Carus-Wilson (ed.), *Essays in Economic History*, ii, pp. 91–111

N. R. Ker, 'Hemming's Cartulary: a description of the two Worcester Cartularies in Cotton Tiberius Axiii', in R. W. Hunt, W. A. Pantin and R. W. Southern (eds.), *Studies in Medieval History presented to F. M. Powicke* (Oxford, 1948), pp. 49–75

E. Kerridge, 'The Movement of Rent, 1540–1640', in Carus-Wilson (ed.), *Essays in Economic History*, ii, pp. 208–26

E. le Roy Ladurie, 'Family Structure and Inheritance Customs in Sixteenth-Century France', in Goody *et al.* (eds), *Family and Inheritance*, pp. 37–70

J. N. Langston, 'The Priors of Lanthony near Gloucester', *Trans. Bristol and Glos. Arch. Soc.*, lxiii (1942), pp. 1–144

I. S. Leadam, 'The Inquest of 1517', *Trans. Roy. Hist. Soc.*, new ser., viii (1894)

T. H. Lloyd, 'Ploughing Services on the Demesnes of the Bishop of Worcester in the Late Thirteenth Century', *Univ. of Birm. Hist. Journ.*, viii (1961), pp. 189–96

T. H. Lloyd, 'Some Documentary Sidelights on the Deserted Oxfordshire Village of Brookend', *Oxoniensia*, xxix/xxx (1964–5), pp. 116–28

E. Mason, 'The Rôle of the English Parishioner, 1100–1500', *Journ. of Eccl. Hist.*, xxvii (1976), pp. 17–29

A. May, 'An Index of Thirteenth-Century Peasant Impoverishment? Manor Court Fines', *Econ. Hist. Rev.*, 2nd ser., xxvi (1973), pp. 389–402

J. Melland Hall, 'The Will of Godfrey Giffard, Bishop of Worcester, A.D. 1301', *Trans. Bristol and Glos. Arch. Soc.*, xx (1895–7), pp. 139–54

D. M. Metcalf, 'How Large was the Anglo-Saxon Currency?', *Econ. Hist. Rev.*, 2nd ser., xviii (1965), pp. 475–82

D. M. Metcalf, 'Sceattas from the Territory of the Hwicce', *Numismatic Chronicle*, cxxxvi (1976), pp. 64–74

E. Miller, 'The English Economy in the Thirteenth Century: Implications of Recent Research', *P and P*, xxviii (1964), pp. 21–40

E. Miller, 'The Fortunes of the English Textile Industry in the Thirteenth Century', *Econ. Hist. Rev.*, 2nd ser., xviii (1965), pp. 64–82

E. Miller, 'England in the Twelfth and Thirteenth Centuries: an Economic Contrast?', *Econ. Hist. Rev.*, 2nd ser., xxiv (1971), pp. 1–14

R. O'Day, 'Cumulative Debt: the Bishops of Coventry and Lichfield and their Economic Problems, c.1540–1640', *Midland History*, iii (1975), pp. 77–93

H. E. O'Neil, 'Court House Excavations, Kempsey, Worcestershire', *Trans. Worcs. Arch. Soc.*, xxxiii (1956), pp. 33–44

E. H. Phelps Brown and Sheila V. Hopkins, 'Seven Centuries of Building Wages', in Carus-Wilson (ed.), *Essays in Economic History*, ii, pp. 168–78

E. H. Phelps Brown and Sheila V. Hopkins, 'Seven Centuries of the Prices of Consumables, compared with Builders' Wage-Rates', in Carus-Wilson, *ibid*, pp. 179–96

E. H. Phelps Brown and Sheila V. Hopkins, 'Wage Rates and Prices: Evidence for Population Pressure in the Sixteenth Century', *Economica*, xxiv (1957), pp. 289–306

A. J. Pollard, 'Estate Management in the Later Middle Ages: the Talbots and Whitchurch, 1383–1525', *Econ. Hist. Rev.*, 2nd ser., xxv (1972), pp. 553–66

M. M. Postan, 'The Chronology of Labour Services', in *Essays on Medieval Agriculture and General Problems of the Medieval Economy* (Cambridge, 1973), pp. 89–106

M. M. Postan, 'Some Agrarian Evidence of Declining Population in the Later Middle Ages', *ibid*, pp. 186–213

M. M. Postan, 'The Trade of Medieval Europe: the North', in *Medieval Trade and Finance* (Cambridge, 1973), pp. 92–231

M. M. Postan and J. Z. Titow, 'Heriots and Prices on Winchester Manors', in *Essays on Medieval Agriculture and General Problems*, pp. 150–85

M. M. Postan, 'The Charters of the Villeins', *ibid*, pp. 107–49

M. M. Postan, 'Village Livestock in the Thirteenth Century', *ibid*, pp. 214–48

J. O. Prestwich, 'Anglo-Norman Feudalism and the Problem of Continuity', *P and P*, xxvi (1963), pp. 39–57

J. A. Raftis, 'Social Structure in Five East Midland Villages', *Econ. Hist. Rev.*, 2nd ser., xviii (1965), pp. 83–99

P. A. Rahtz, 'Upton, Gloucestershire, 1964–8', *Trans. Bristol and Glos. Arch. Soc.*, lxxxviii (1969), pp. 74–126

P. A. Rahtz, 'A Possible Saxon Palace near Stratford-upon-Avon', *Antiquity*, xliv (1970), pp. 137–43

P. A. Rahtz and D. Bullough, 'The parts of an Anglo-Saxon mill', in P. Clemoes (ed.), *Anglo-Saxon England* (Cambridge, 1977), vi, pp. 15–37

B. K. Roberts, 'A Study of Medieval Colonisation in the Forest of Arden, Warwickshire', *Ag. Hist. Rev.*, xvi (1968), pp. 101–13

C. D. Ross, 'The Household Accounts of Elizabeth Berkeley, Countess of Warwick, 1420–1', *Trans. Bristol and Glos. Arch. Soc.*, lxx (1951), pp. 81–105

J. C. Russell, 'Late Ancient and Medieval Population', *Trans. Amer. Phil. Soc.*, xlviii (1958), pp. 3–152

A. Savine, 'Bondmen under the Tudors', *Trans. Roy. Hist. Soc.*, new ser., xvii (1903), pp. 235–89

P. H. Sawyer, 'Charters of the Reform Movement: The Worcester Archive', D. Parsons (ed.), *Tenth Century Studies* (Chichester, 1975), pp. 84–93

J. Scammell, 'Freedom and Marriage in Medieval England', *Econ. Hist. Rev.*, 2nd ser., xxvii (1974), pp. 523–37

R. Schofield, 'Crisis Mortality', *Local Population Studies*, ix (1972), pp. 10–22

R. Schofield, 'The Geographical Distribution of Wealth in England, 1334–1649', in R. Floud (ed.), *Essays in Quantitative Economic History* (Oxford, 1974), pp. 79–106

P. Sims-Williams, 'Continental Influence at Bath Monastery in the Seventh Century', in P. Clemoes (ed.), *Anglo-Saxon England* (Cambridge, 1975), iv, pp. 1–10

P. Sims-Williams, 'Cuthswith, Seventh Century Abbess of Inkberrow, near Worcester, and the Würzburg manuscript of Jerome on Ecclesiastes', in P. Clemoes (ed.), *Anglo-Saxon England* (Cambridge, 1976), v, pp. 1–21

B. H. Slicher van Bath, 'Manor, Mark, and Village in the Eastern Netherlands', *Speculum*, xxi (1946), pp. 115–28

B. H. Slicher van Bath, 'Accounts and Diaries of Farmers before 1800 as Sources for Agricultural History', *Afdeling Agrarische Geschiedenis Landbouwhogeschool, Bijdragen*, viii (1962)

B. H. Slicher van Bath, 'Yield Ratios, 810–1820', *ibid.*, x (1963)

A. H. Smith, 'The Hwicce', in J. B. Bessinger and R. P. Creed (eds.), *Franciplegius: Medieval and Linguistic Studies in Honour of Francis Peabody Magoun, Jr.* (London, 1965), pp. 56–65

C. N. S. Smith, 'Two Romano-British Sites', *Trans. Worcs. Arch. Soc.*, xxx (1953), pp. 81–2

C. N. S. Smith, 'A Catalogue of Prehistoric Finds from Worcestershire', *Trans. Worcs. Arch. Soc.*, xxxiv (1957), pp. 1–27

M. Spufford, 'Peasant Inheritance Customs and Land Distribution in Cambridgeshire from the Sixteenth to the Eighteenth Centuries', in Goody *et al.*, *Family and Inheritance*, pp. 156–76

F. M. Stenton, 'The Supremacy of the Mercian Kings', *Eng. Hist. Rev.*, xxxiii (1918), pp. 433–52

W. H. Stevenson, 'Trinoda Necessitas', *Eng. Hist. Rev.*, xxix (1914), pp. 689–703

E. Stone, 'Profit-and-Loss Accountancy at Norwich Cathedral Priory', *Trans. Roy. Hist. Soc.*, 5th ser., xii (1962), pp. 25–48

W. Stubbs, 'The Cathedral, Diocese, and Monasteries of Worcester in the Eighth Century', *Arch. Journ.*, xix (1862), pp. 236–52

C. S. Taylor, 'Early Christianity in Gloucestershire', *Trans. Bristol and Glos. Arch. Soc.*, xv (1890–1), pp. 120–38

C. S. Taylor, 'The Origins of the Mercian Shires', in Finberg (ed.), *Gloucestershire Studies*, pp. 17–51

F. J. Thacker, 'The Monumental Brasses of Worcestershire, part II', *Trans. Worcs. Arch. Soc.*, iv (1926–7), pp. 129–56

J. Thirsk, 'The Common Fields', *P and P*, xxix (1964), pp. 3–25

H. L. Thompson, 'The Poyntz Family', *Trans. Bristol and Glos. Arch. Soc.*, iv (1879–80), pp. 73–85

J. D. Thorp, 'History of the Manor of Coates', *Trans. Bristol and Glos. Arch. Soc.*, 1 (1928), pp. 135–274

S. Thrupp, 'The Problem of Replacement-Rates in Late Medieval English Population', *Econ. Hist. Rev.*, 2nd ser., xviii (1965), pp. 101–19

J. Z. Titow, 'Some Evidence of the Thirteenth Century Population Increase', *Econ. Hist. Rev.*, 2nd ser., xiv (1961), pp. 218–23

A. Verhulst, 'L'Économie rurale de la Flandre et la dépression économique du bas Moyen Age', *Études Rurales*, x (1963), pp. 68–80

J. F. R. Walmsley, 'The *Censarii* of Burton Abbey and the Domesday Population', *North Staffs. Journ. of Field Studies*, viii (1968), pp. 73–80

G. Webster and B. Hobley, 'Aerial Reconnaissance over the Warwickshire Avon', *Arch. Journ.*, cxxi (1964), pp. 1–22

D. Whitelock, 'Archbishop Wulfstan, Homilist and Statesman', in R. W. Southern (ed.), *Essays in Medieval History* (London, 1968), pp. 42–60

M. Wilson, 'The Hwicce', *Trans. Worcs. Arch. Soc.*, 3rd ser., ii (1968–9), pp. 21–5

E. A. Wrigley, 'Family Limitation in Pre-Industrial England', *Econ. Hist. Rev.*, 2nd ser., xix (1966), pp. 82–109

Index

Abitot, Urse d', 18, 45–6, 48, 50, 76
Abyndon, Richard, 279
administration, *see* estate administration; officials
Ælfred, prince of the Hwicce, 14
Æthelbald, king of Mercia, 13
Æthelburg, abbess of Withington and Twyning, 14
Æthelred, king of Mercia, 14
Æthelweard, ealdorman, 50
Æthilheard, prince of the Hwicce, 14
Ailworth, Anthony, 384
Agmondesham, Thomas de, 110–11
agriculture, *see* arable farming; pastoral farming
Alcock, John, bishop of Worcester 1476–86, 154, 180, 185, 206, 207, 230
Aldeswell, Jordan de, 377
ale, 29, 73, 76, 201, 346–9, 361–2
Alvechurch, Worcs., borough of, 61, 86, 107
Alvechurch, Worcs., manor of, 11, 22, 23, 36, 56–7, 59, 71, 75, 79, 92, 107, 179n, 336, 338; assarts, 56–7, 63, 79, 91; demesne, 62, 68n, 122, 134–5, 152; demesne leased, 82, 209; manor-house, 81; park, 57, 71, 202; rents, 101, 108, 119, 292; settlements, 37, 94–5, 246–7, 256, 258, 356; tenants, 82, 85–7, 100, 102, 107, 109n, 111, 160, 222, 238, 314
Alveston, Warks., 19n, 27, 36, 45, 49
appropriation of churches, 59, 81, 193
arable farming: crops, 69, 124, 320–1; by lords, 69, 72, 122–34; by peasants, 248, 250, 320–3, 326–7, 329–30, 333–8; productivity of, 29, 79, 83, 84, 128–9, 234, 322–3
Arche, Robert, 214
arkelands, *see* tenants, *avercmen*
Arnold, Thomas, 157, 158, 159, 160, 161, 167, 189, 211, 214–15, 383, 385
arrears, 117–18, 162, 179–90, 250, 276–7, 389
assarting, 56–7, 63, 79, 84, 89, 90–7, 105, 107, 256–7, 374
Aston Magna (in Blockley), Glos., 17, 250

Aston, White Ladies', Worcs. (formerly Aston Episcopi), manor of, 57, 58, 61, 64, 103, 178, 387; demesne, 62, 68n, 122; demesne leased, 82, 118, 168; rents, 101, 107–8; settlements, 257; tenants, 85, 103, 238
Aust, Glos., 48

Bache, William, 359
Baldwin, bishop of Worcester 1180–4, 4n
Baldyng, Mr Thomas, 385
Ballard, William, 322
Barbourne (in Claines), Worcs., 27
Barford, Warks., 205
Barnsley, John, 157
Bate, Thomas, 307
Bate, Walter, 307, 309
Bath, Som., 15
Bath and Wells, bishopric of, 190, 199n
Batsford, Glos., 11
Battenhall (in St Peters without Worcester), 45
Battle Abbey, Sussex, 125n
Baty, John, 350
Bayly, Richard, 180, 184, 214
Beauchamp, family of, 48, 50, 76, 155n, 156
Beauchamp, Richard, 174, 205
Beauchamp, William (d. 1170), 53
Beauchamp, William (d. 1197), 48, 50
Beauchamp, William (d. 1269), 76–7
Beauchamp, William, earl of Warwick (d. 1298), 77
Bede, 14
Beke, John, 308
Belbroughton, Worcs., 368
Bell, John, bishop of Worcester 1539–43, 177, 376
Benet, William, 370
Bentley (in Holt), Worcs., 45
Berhtwulf, king of Mercia, 12
Berkeley, family of, 116
Berkeley, Elizabeth, countess of Warwick, 201
Bernard, Alice, 333
Berough, Walter atte, 379
Berton, Walter de, 378